# INDIGENOUS PEOPLES' INNOVATION

## Intellectual Property Pathways to Development

# INDIGENOUS PEOPLES' INNOVATION

## INTELLECTUAL PROPERTY PATHWAYS TO DEVELOPMENT

### Edited by Peter Drahos and Susy Frankel

Australian
National
University

E PRESS

**ANU**
**E PRESS**

Published by ANU E Press
The Australian National University
Canberra ACT 0200, Australia
Email: anuepress@anu.edu.au
This title is also available online at http://epress.anu.edu.au

National Library of Australia Cataloguing-in-Publication entry

Title:           Indigenous people's innovation : intellectual property pathways to
                 development / edited by Peter Drahos and Susy Frankel.

ISBN:            9781921862779 (pbk.) 9781921862786 (ebook)

Notes:           Includes bibliographical references.

Subjects:        Ethnoscience.
                 Traditional ecological knowledge.
                 Intellectual property.
                 Indigenous peoples--Legal status, laws, etc.

Other Authors/Contributors:
                 Drahos, Peter, 1955-
                 Frankel, Susy.

Dewey Number: 346.048

Cover design and layout by ANU E Press

# Contents

# Acknowledgements

The chapters in this volume were first presented at the conference 'Intellectual Property, Trade and the Knowledge Assets of Indigenous Peoples: The Developmental Frontier' in December 2010. That conference was hosted by the New Zealand Centre of International Economic Law (NZCIEL), at Victoria University of Wellington, New Zealand. The conference was organised in association with the Regulatory Institutions Network at The Australian National University. Susy Frankel is the Director of NZCIEL. NZCIEL acknowledges the support of the conference sponsors Henry Hughes, Patent and Trade Mark Attorneys, and the New Zealand Ministry of Economic Development. Peter Drahos and Luigi Palombi from the Regulatory Institutions Network acknowledge the support of The Australian Research Council (Discovery Grant: 'The Sustainable Use of Australia's Biodiversity: Transfer of Traditional Knowledge and Intellectual Property').

Peter Drahos and Susy Frankel would like to thank the two anonymous referees of the manuscript for their detailed and helpful comments on each of the chapters. Thanks also to Victoria University of Wellington students Lauren McManoman, Michelle Limenta and Anna Ker for editing assistance.

# List of Acronyms

| | |
|---|---|
| ABS | Access and benefit sharing |
| ACP | African, Caribbean and Pacific |
| AEK | Aboriginal ecological knowledge |
| AIPPI | International Association for the Protection of Intellectual Property |
| ALAI | Association Littéraire et Artistique Internationale |
| ARIPO | African Regional Intellectual Property Organization |
| CA | Cultural authority |
| CBD | Convention on Biological Diversity |
| CCD | Convention on the Protection and Promotion of the Diversity of Cultural Expressions |
| EC | European Community |
| EEC | European Economic Community |
| EPA | Economic Partnership Agreements |
| EPO | European Patent Office |
| ETC | Action Group on Erosion Technology and Concentration |
| EU | European Union |
| FAO | Food and Agriculture Organization |
| FLO | Fairtrade Labelling Organizations International |
| FTA | Free Trade Agreement |
| GATS | General Agreement on Trade in Services |
| GATT | General Agreement on Tariffs and Trade |
| GIs | Geographical indications |
| GRIN | Genetic Resources Information Network |
| I = P | Information = Power |
| ICH | Indigenous cultural heritage |
| IGC | Intergovernmental Committee on Intellectual Property and Genetic Resources, Traditional Knowledge and Folklore |
| INTA | International Trademark Association |
| IP | Intellectual property |
| IPA | Indigenous protected area |
| IPRs | Intellectual property rights |
| ITC | International Trade Centre |
| IWG | Intersessional Working Group |
| JPO | Japanese Patent Office |

| | |
|---|---|
| LDCs | Least developed countries |
| MFN | Most-favoured-nation treatment |
| MSG | Melanesian Spearhead Group |
| NCC | National Council of Chiefs |
| NGO | Non-governmental organization |
| NIAAA | National Indigenous Arts Advocacy Association |
| NPR | Non-product-related |
| OCTA | Office of the Chief Trade Adviser |
| OECD | Organisation for Economic Co-operation and Development |
| OHIM | Office for Harmonisation in the Internal Market |
| PAR | Participatory action research |
| PACER | Pacific Agreement on Closer Economic Relations |
| PBR | Plant breeding rights |
| PCT | Patent Cooperation Treaty |
| PI | Plant introduction |
| PICNIC | Prior informed consent or no informed consent |
| PIFS | Pacific Islands Forum Secretariat |
| PPMs | Processes and Production Methods |
| PVP | Plant Variety Protection |
| SCM | Agreement on Subsidies and Countervailing Measures |
| SPC | Secretariat of the Pacific Community |
| TBT | Agreement on Technical Barriers to Trade |
| TCEs | Traditional cultural expressions |
| TGKP | Traditional group knowledge and practice |
| TK | Traditional knowledge |
| TKDL | Traditional Knowledge Digital Library |
| TKECABS | Traditional Knowledge and Expressions of Culture |
| TPP | Trans Pacific Partnership Agreement |
| TRIPS | Agreement on Trade-Related Aspects of Intellectual Property Rights, 1994 |
| UN | United Nations |
| UNCTAD | United Nations Conference on Trade and Development |
| UNDP | United Nations Development Programme |
| UNDRIP | United Nations Declaration on the Rights of Indigenous Peoples |
| UNESCO | United Nations Educational, Scientific and Cultural Organization |
| USDA | United States Department of Agriculture |

| | |
|---|---|
| USPTO | United States Patent and Trade Mark Office |
| VCLT | Vienna Convention on the Law of Treaties |
| WIPO | World Intellectual Property Organization |
| WTO | World Trade Organization |

# List of Contributors

**Michael Blakeney** is a Professor in the Law School of the University of Western Australia.

**David Claudie** is the Chairman of the Chuulangun Aboriginal Corporation, PMB 30, Cairns Mail Centre, Cairns, QLD, 4871.

**Jen Cleary** is the Senior Research Development Manager in The Centre for Regional Engagement at the University of South Australia, and a doctoral student in the School of Agriculture and Food Science (Agribusiness) at the University of Queensland.

**Peter Drahos** is Professor in the Regulatory Institutions Network at The Australian National University and holds a Chair in Intellectual Property at Queen Mary, University of London.

**Susy Frankel** is Professor of Law at Victoria University of Wellington, Director of the New Zealand Centre of International Economic Law and Chair of the New Zealand Copyright Tribunal.

**Miranda Forsyth** is a Postdoctoral Fellow in the Regulatory Institutions Network at The Australian National University.

**Daniel Gervais** is Professor of Law and Co-Director, Vanderbilt Intellectual Property Program, Vanderbilt University Law School, Nashville, Tennessee.

**Christoph Graber** is Professor of Law and Head of i-call, the research centre for International Communications and Art Law Lucerne, and Director of lucernaiuris, the Institute for Research in the Fundaments of Law, School of Law, University of Lucerne, Switzerland.

**Jessica Lai** is a PhD candidate and researcher at i-call, the research centre for International Communications and Art Law Lucerne, School of Law, University of Lucerne, Switzerland.

**Daniel Robinson** is a Senior Lecturer in the Institute of Environmental Studies at the University of New South Wales.

**Susan Semple** is a Research Fellow at the Sansom Institute, School of Pharmacy and Medical Sciences, University of South Australia.

**Bradley Simpson** is a post-doctoral researcher at the Sansom Institute, School of Pharmacy and Medical Sciences, University of South Australia.

**Nicholas Smith** is an ethnobotanist and runs Nelumbo Botaniks, PO Box 1295, Aldinga Beach, SA, 5173.

**Antony Taubman** is Director, Intellectual Property Division, World Trade Organization.

**Daphne Zografos Johnsson** is a Consultant, Traditional Knowledge Division, World Intellectual Property Organization. At the time of writing she was a Lecturer at the School of Law at the University of Reading, United Kingdom.

# Preface

# Indigenous Innovation: New Dialogues, New Pathways

Antony Taubman[1]
Director, Intellectual Property Division
World Trade Organization

The subject of this timely and stimulating volume is potentially confronting, and certainly provokes new ways about thinking about old subjects. Trade, intellectual property and indigenous knowledge systems — the value systems, the cultural contexts, the very world views that these three simple terms can evoke are often assumed to be dramatically, fundamentally at odds with one another: worlds apart. Yet the past decade, especially, has seen the growth and maturing of a remarkable dialogue between these seemingly remote world views.

Perhaps the most heartening, and ultimately the most consequential, development has been the process of mutual learning fostered by an extensive international debate — above all, the greater acknowledgement of indigenous peoples in policy debates on intellectual property (IP) issues, and the deepening respect for their cultures and knowledge systems that has flowed, perhaps inevitably, from the opening up of new pathways for the exchange of ideas and the sharing of communities' experience. Respect for the distinctive character, and recognition of the inherent dignity and worth, of indigenous cultures and knowledge systems are surely at the heart of any endeavour — practical, legal, political, conceptual — to build stronger links, to reconcile differences, to create new means of advancing the rights and interests of the custodians and practitioners of traditional knowledge systems.

With this greater respect and acknowledgement comes a clearer, wider recognition that traditional knowledge systems are indeed innovative, dynamic and directly relevant to practical needs; that collective and cumulative forms of innovation and creativity have value and worth in themselves; that indigenous

---

1   This commentary is provided in a personal capacity only, and does not present any views or legal analyses that can be attributed to the WTO, its Members, or its Secretariat.

peoples do trade and do engage with the wider community, have done so for millennia, and today simply seek to do so on terms that are more equitable and culturally attuned.

Yet the same traditional knowledge debate can also lead the IP policy community to reflect deeply about the central tenets of the IP system, its core principles and cultural assumptions, indeed its very legitimacy and fundamental policy rationale. The traditional knowledge debate may in time be seen as a tonic for the policy domain of IP, helping to open up a more informed, more inclusive, more broadly based discourse on the role, the principles and the legitimacy of the IP system. Critics of IP from the indigenous perspective have helped open up a more pluralistic view about the nature of what the IP system can and should be, whom it should benefit and how. While some criticism has been intensive, and some formal positions expressed in debates can seem irreconcilable, this dialogue has required us to unearth some of the foundational principles of IP and go back to basics. Why is there such a system of law, what is it for, does its actual practice line up with its objectives, what are its policy roots and essential principles, what are the embedded values in the system; and, most challenging, perhaps, do we need to revisit those values and think about the evolution of a more pluralistic system or at least a system that is more representative of or practically responsive to the diverse needs, interests and values of peoples across the globe, in particular indigenous peoples and local communities?

Equally, however, dialogue and the sharing of experience have shown more positive and culturally appropriate forms of IP protection that transcend the constraints, limitations and embedded values that its critics attributed to the IP system. First is the assumption that 'IP' is inherently atomistic, is concerned about private rights for individuals and commercial firms, and lacks a collective or communal character. Secondly, there's the assumption that it is inherently time bound, alien to the intergenerational context of traditional knowledge systems, with a short-term focus linked to commercial cycles, at best a single generational perspective. Thirdly, there's the assumption that IP is a form of commodification, that in operation it takes a rich cultural intellectual tradition, captures its commercial value — isolates the easily exploited expressions of a tradition of ancient wisdom, culture and spirituality— and crudely turns them into a commodity to be traded on global markets. Each of these assumptions manifests a perception of the IP system and perhaps a predominant set of practices, rather than articulating its essence and its core principles.

For those working within traditional knowledge systems, or in other policy domains, it is very helpful and timely to revisit such assumptions about the IP system, assumptions that may be self-imposed limitations and unwitting impediments to new avenues for promoting and defending the interests of indigenous peoples and local communities. This is the essential challenge:

to explore fundamental ideas about IP that are not constrained by these limitations, but rather offer practical pathways to meeting, in part at least, the needs and expectations articulated by indigenous communities. The United Nations Declaration on the Rights of Indigenous Peoples has, in setting out the rights of peoples as such, articulated their entitlements concerning IP. And forms of IP that are communal or collective in character do currently exist, and have their place within the formal system; some even need to be implemented under the WTO's TRIPS Agreement — consider performer's rights, protection of confidential traditional knowledge, collective marks and geographical indications, and the suppression of acts of unfair competition such as false claims of indigenous authenticity. But the actual operation and further possibilities of these legal mechanisms are explored comparatively little in policy debate, and much practical learning is needed about how that collective characteristic can be mapped across to the collective legal personality or the cultural identity of indigenous peoples. Further, there are indeed mechanisms in the current IP system that can transcend a single generation or product cycle — it is not a concept inherently alien to the IP system for rights to endure beyond a limited tenure, even if most IP rights are deliberately time-bound. There are ways of ensuring an equitable and fair form of IP that does evolve with time and does take account of intergenerational factors. The third point of critique is perhaps the most challenging and confronting: yet IP need not be about commodification or, ironically 'propertisation' as such. What is the essence of the IP mechanisms? What is the essential legal character of an IP 'right'? Your IP right is not, at core, an entitlement for you to enter the market yourself; rather, its central characteristic is that it empowers you to object to my 'commodification' of what is yours — your knowledge, your cultural work or your distinctive sign. In principle, its basic legal function is not to promote illegitimate or unauthorized commodification of that which someone else has originated, but rather to provide a legal means to prevent such commodification. So, properly arranged, organised, understood and exercised, there is a notion of IP in the broadest sense that amounts to giving indigenous communities a say, a degree of leverage over their knowledge, over their distinctive signs and symbols, over their cultural works.

Thus IP mechanisms can — in principle at least — offer three general modes for giving practical effect to the expectations of indigenous peoples. One is the capacity to object to illicit commodification of their material: a right to object if someone misappropriates traditional knowledge and seeks to trivialise it as a commercial product. The second aspect is the notion of recognition, the moral rights aspect, essentially a right to object when use of material is derogatory or insulting, taking reference from this aspect of copyright in particular. The third aspect is the right to set the terms for how others make use of protected materials, such as traditional works and traditional knowledge — this last aspect has drawn most attention in the debate over the interplay — current, actual and desired — between traditional knowledge systems and the international trade system, notably in the calls for better defined linkages between the operation of the patent system and the circumstances and conditions of access to traditional knowledge and genetic resources. Much concern has been expressed about inappropriate choices, about the wishes and values and interests of indigenous peoples being set aside altogether; but there are also interesting positive opportunities for communities that do wish to make use of their distinctive cultural materials and traditional knowledge in an international context to develop economic, scientific and cultural partnerships beyond the community.

Reflecting on these options recalls an important practical imperative when considering the interactions between the IP system and traditional knowledge systems: the point is surely not for an external expert with a laptop and a set of fixed ideas to intrude into the domain of the traditional community, to tell them how to organise their interests, how to manage their own existing knowledge systems. Rather, ideally, at least, it is the other way round: the point is to learn from the community about what their interests, and aspirations are as a community, and construct mechanisms to enable those values, interests, aspirations to be carried beyond the community as it interacts with not only its immediate neighbours but also potentially with partners and the general public across the globe. Ultimately the most important aspect of the IP system is not, after all, the absorbing policy and legal debate that continues to unfold internationally, but rather the challenge of developing implementation strategies and the application of practical tools that deliver the expected benefits in a workable manner that is appropriate for the community itself — yielding in actual practice the implicit promise of the general principles and objectives of the IP system.

So, if the focus should be on the specific context of local communities, and on the practical use of IP tools at the grass roots level, what then to make of the international dimension? How to bridge between the intrinsically local and the fully global is surely the defining challenge of the debate about traditional knowledge, IP and trade. Once again, we have seen a broadening of perspective and a wider sense of the interests engaged by multilateral IP and trade systems. Surveying the array of recent international debates and negotiations dealing with these intersecting policy domains, one can discern a widespread push for the recalibration of what can be considered the 'terms of trade' for knowledge resources — redefining the distribution, on what is argued to be a more equitable basis, of the benefits that result from the use of knowledge resources as feedstocks for trade and commerce. Several international negotiations seek to rebalance the relationship between those who can provide access to traditional knowledge and genetic resources — the gatekeepers and custodians — and those who seek to benefit from access to those materials. Understanding and redefining the relationship between the providers of access, the custodians of traditional knowledge systems and genetic resources on the one hand, and the downstream users of this material on the other, is a more productive and enabling way of considering the IP issues. It offers an opportunity to move beyond the conventional structurings of IP policy, which divide the world into static binary caricatures separating right holders and content consumers — North and South, private and public, haves and have-nots — and instead to explore a more pluralist and fluid set of rights, interests and responsibilities in the light of the intellectual and cultural riches of indigenous peoples and traditional communities. This recalibration of the equitable terms of access to traditional knowledge resources has been evident in the work of the Convention on Biological Diversity (CBD). The Nagoya Protocol under the CBD is a significant milestone in this development, not least through its more extensive recognition of traditional knowledge as such and the obligation for foreign jurisdictions to respond to breaches of access rules in the country of origin. A pivotal instance, too, is the work currently under way in the World Intellectual Property Organization (WIPO) Intergovernmental Committee (IGC) to develop international legal instruments on traditional knowledge, traditional cultural expressions and genetic resources. This active process offers the prospect of a major advance in recognising the entitlement of custodians and holders to set the terms of access and use of their traditional knowledge, traditional cultural expressions and genetic resources. A similar recalibration of interests has been apparent in the work of the World Trade Organization (WTO). Driven in particular by a coalition of like-minded developing countries, one of the principal trade-related IP issues discussed as an implementation issue under the aegis of the Doha Declaration concerns whether, and if so how, the patent system should take account of or otherwise link to the obligations that a user of traditional knowledge and genetic resources assumes when accessing and exploiting these materials.

While the TRIPS Agreement is focused entirely on conventional forms of IP, its conclusion and implementation within the context of trade law and policy presaged a broadening of the array of interests and active players engaged with the international law and policy of IP. Its perceived reach and impact have also precipitated critical analysis about the role and limitations of the IP system in the form of a series of 'TRIPS and...' debates: TRIPS and food, biodiversity, development, human rights, health and so on.

While other vital questions such as patents and access to medicines have pressed forward in international IP policy debates since TRIPS came into force in 1995, it is the traditional knowledge debate that has been the most searching, the most far reaching, and ultimately the most insightful as to the essential character and rationale of the IP system. Its significance is apparent from the trajectory the debate has taken over the past decade. Concerns about possible tensions between traditional knowledge and IP have emerged, in turn:

- first, as a point of resistance to conventional IP norms — a critical and defensive position;

- secondly, as a point of pressure for reform and for resituating the system — a revisionist position; and

- thirdly, as embodying social and economic concerns that form part of the interests which are positively asserted in trade fora — a position asserting positive trade interests.

The initial tenor of the debate was essentially critical and sceptical of the relevance and appropriateness of the IP system for traditional knowledge systems. Critics assumed the IP system to be diametrically at odds with traditional knowledge systems, and argued that it was little more than a tool of misappropriation and illicit commodification: that IP is atomistic, concerns only private individual rights, takes a narrow, culturally specific approach, and lacks applicability to intergenerational and collective forms of innovation and creativity. This critical agenda saw traditional knowledge systems as in need of protection *from* IP, and ruled out the search for solutions within the IP system as inherently inappropriate. The second phase — building on a richer, broad-based dialogue about the essential principles of IP law and legal mechanisms — identified positive avenues for the fulfilment of the needs and expectations of indigenous peoples and other traditional communities. The 2007 recognition, in the UN Declaration on the Rights of Indigenous Peoples, of the right of indigenous peoples to 'maintain, control, protect and develop their intellectual property over … cultural heritage, traditional knowledge, and traditional cultural expressions' marked a significant insight into IP within the indigenous context. Partly this development entailed making practical use of IP mechanisms to provide immediate solutions, but at a policy level this shift in emphasis saw concerns about traditional knowledge acting as a point of pressure for reform, and for resituating the system — almost literally recentring the system on a wider geographical and social base to recognise the needs and context of knowledge-holders beyond the scope of those conventionally perceived as having an interest in the IP system. The traditional knowledge perspective provided a fresh perspective for the reconsideration, reform and refocusing of the IP system. The work of the WIPO IGC, drawing on the existing array of IP principles, adapting and applying them to traditional knowledge, and developing further cognate principles, is the epitome of this second stage.

The third phase, a kind of systemic consolidation of the second stage, is characterised by traditional knowledge forming part of the concrete interests that some countries bring to the table when they debate and negotiate on a fair and equitable IP system and seek to settle the conditions of international trade. For instance, the 2008 Economic Partnership Agreement between the CARIFORUM states and the European Union (EU) included a significant section on genetic resources, traditional knowledge and folklore. The later EU-Central America association agreement also recognised the significance of these issues, and the 2011 Multiparty Trade Agreement between the EU, Colombia and Peru included more detailed provisions. In 2008, a broad coalition of developing countries and European countries proposed that as part of the WTO's Doha Work Programme, WTO members should agree to amend the TRIPS Agreement 'to include a mandatory requirement for the disclosure of the country providing/ source of genetic resources, and/or associated traditional knowledge ... in patent applications'. While the scope and practical impact of these measures is currently uncertain (and ongoing work on the link between the TRIPS Agreement and the CBD has not yielded substantive results to date), the immediate point to observe is that developing countries are now identifying interests in this domain as one element what, to them, should comprise an overall comprehensive deal on a host of trade issues.

This recalibration of interests can be seen from at least four perspectives:

- empirical: the evidence of patent statistics and the development of new standards, metrics and classification tools recognising aspects of traditional knowledge;
- jurisprudential: the forms of innovation, 'skill in the art', that are recognised by the patent system, and the assumptions about innovation and creativity that lie within ostensibly 'technical' standards;
- the practice of trade negotiations: the emergence of traditional knowledge as a concrete strategic trade interest;
- development policy: traditional knowledge systems as a contribution to sustainable, culturally appropriate development strategies.

Empirically, patent statistics provide evidence of a sustained increase in the efforts of researchers in the developing world to capture the benefits of traditional knowledge systems that are rooted in their own countries. Without entering into analysis of the nature and impact of such research programmes and patenting activities, they do at least illustrate how some developing countries are exercising their interests in their heritage of genetic resources and traditional knowledge systems. Jurisprudentially, the concerns that drive the traditional knowledge debate have had some influence on the character of IP law. Often cited in this context are the Australian Federal Court cases in the field of copyright which gave recognition to the customary law background and cultural context of indigenous artistic creativity, and the interests of the community that stands behind a traditional artist. We see more recently a series of initiatives to build recognition of traditional knowledge and traditional creativity directly into IP law. Examples include the 2005 revision to the Patent Law of India, which explicitly excludes from patentability certain forms of traditional knowledge out of concern that they are inappropriate subject matter for patents; and the New Zealand Trade Marks Act of 2002 which gave explicit protection to Māori culture under the broader principle of avoiding offensive registration of trade marks, with the guidance of a Māori Trade Marks Advisory Committee which forms part of the registration process.

The trade and development dimension of this recalibration of interests is apparent in the negotiations and policy debates touched on earlier. It is striking that the two clusters of issues regarding the TRIPS Agreement that are being actively considered under the aegis of the Doha work programme — TRIPS and the CBD, and geographical indications — both have significance for traditional knowledge systems. The TRIPS-CBD debate specifically pivots on the question of what recognition, if any, the patent system might be required to give to the circumstances of access to, and use of, traditional knowledge and genetic resources. And geographical indications have been explored as one tool for ensuring recognition in international markets of the distinctive qualities of indigenous products when traded with the consent and involvement of communities. When local and indigenous communities do choose to develop wider commercial relationships, protection of distinctive signs and traditional names is often one of the important entry points into the international trading system. The two clusters of issues both have a bearing on the development interests of developing countries, and both concern the claims of indigenous peoples and local communities for their interests to be appropriately protected. Another example of this recalibration of interests is the recommendation under the WIPO development agenda that the WIPO IGC should indeed accelerate its work towards an international instrument on the protection of traditional knowledge. Accordingly, we have seen a major rebasing of the interests that countries bring to the table. Ideas, concepts and concerns that were perhaps considered tangential or barely relevant to the IP system a little more than a decade ago are now central to work being done by two of the main international institutions — WIPO itself and the WTO. And from the human rights perspective, it is striking that the one multilateral human rights instrument that explicitly recognises rights over IP as such is the Universal Declaration on the Rights of Indigenous Peoples. This recognition is surely a remarkable sign of a more pluralistic understanding of what IP is and whose interests should be recognised within an IP system — an indication of a broader and more inclusive framework than was conceived of some two decades ago when the main elements of the TRIPS Agreement were concluded.

One of the most challenging and fascinating questions that has arisen in this debate, raising deep jurisprudential issues, concerns the recognition of indigenous customary law in the framework of enhanced protection of traditional knowledge and cultural expressions. There has been a consistent call for this form of recognition by a number of indigenous representatives in international discussions. It is a question that raises policy, academic and theoretical issues, but also highlights the difficulties of establishing a fully international form of recognition and protection of traditional knowledge systems which is workable and effective, yet remains true to, and a legitimate expression of, the local, customary context of such systems. Some advocates contend that an overarching comprehensive system of recognition and protection of indigenous knowledge will always be incomplete, will always be subject to some unease or uncertainty, unless it is able to give some form of recognition to the customary law that defines custodianship rights, responsibilities or other obligations over traditional knowledge, that defines what amounts to appropriate use and inappropriate use of traditional knowledge. The challenge is to take what is a matter of law, practice and custom intrinsically embedded in the life of a community and have that recognised in an international or foreign context — 'foreign' in two senses: literally, in a jurisdiction potentially across the other side of the earth; and in the sense of not having an understanding of deeper values, spirituality, customs and traditions that are embedded in the traditional knowledge system. If an ignorant or malign external third party enters into an indigenous community, into the traditional customary context, and appropriates aspects of traditional knowledge in violation of customary law or practices, what would it mean for an effective legal system to apply in a foreign jurisdiction so as to recognise the breach of customary law or practices? If customary law is to provide any kind of guidance, its very diversity needs to be recognised.

An illuminating element of the international debate has been the willingness and the capacity of indigenous and local communities to step forward directly and explain to IP policy makers the practical role of customary law and practices within their communities' use and custodianship of traditional knowledge systems, and the rich diversity of custom, law and practice that are embedded within communities' lives. Yet this very diversity underscores the inevitable constraints that will be struck when seeking recognition of customary law beyond the original community. Some options may, however, merit exploration and speculation. The pivotal issue in the traditional knowledge debate has, after all, been how to recalibrate, and then to monitor and police, the conditions of access to traditional knowledge. When I enter a community, or deal with it, I may, as a direct undertaking on my part, agree to be bound by certain customary constraints as a condition of access to traditional knowledge, potentially constituting one element of the mutually agreed terms governing downstream use and application of traditional knowledge and genetic resources. This process would both educate and sensitise me as to what my liabilities and responsibilities are, and would also bind me in a direct legal sense to recognise what constraints I need to recognise in my downstream use of that material. This is not to advocate any particular approach, but to reflect on some pathways that might yet be explored. The customary law issue is emblematic of the wider challenges addressed in this volume — it raises fundamental legal and policy questions, alongside basic practical questions, about what tools and mechanisms will be of actual use and benefit to indigenous peoples and local communities as they seek to promote and defend their interests beyond the traditional circle. Sustainable, effective solutions will ultimately need to reconcile legal, policy and practical demands so as to yield an inclusive and sound legal and policy platform, the basis for the effective deployment of practical tools for the more immediate benefit and interests of communities. The wealth and diversity of insights in this volume — joining together indigenous, IP and trade policy perspectives — offer invaluable ideas for how this might be achieved. The volume exemplifies the kind of dialogue and mutual learning that must underpin true progress in this vitally important but still challenging domain of policy debate, normative development, and the application of law in practice.

# 1. Indigenous Peoples' Innovation and Intellectual Property: The Issues

Peter Drahos and Susy Frankel

## 1. Introduction

It is easy to find examples of international fora in which actors engage with the issues raised by the confluence of indigenous knowledge and intellectual property. A list would include the Convention on Biological Diversity (CBD), the Food and Agriculture Organization (FAO), the International Union for the Protection of New Varieties of Plants, the United Nations Educational Scientific and Cultural Organization (UNESCO), various UN human rights bodies, the World Intellectual Property Organization (WIPO) and the World Trade Organization (WTO).[1]

Intellectual property and indigenous knowledge are concepts that for a long time travelled separate historical pathways. Intellectual property (IP) is a generic term for systems of positive law, some of which, such as patent law, have medieval origins and some, such as integrated circuits law, that are of comparatively recent origin. A definition by extension would include copyright, database protection, designs, geographical indications, integrated circuits protection, plant variety protection, patents, trade marks, trade secrets, and actions in passing off or unfair competition (the nature and titles of which will vary between jurisdictions). These different systems are grouped together because they grant exclusive rights of ownership in abstract objects such as signs, algorithms and gene sequences.[2] Indigenous knowledge is a much older phenomenon than IP, but it has existed as a concept within Western scholarship for only a short time, previously being most closely linked to anthropology and emerging as a distinct concept in the 1980s.[3]

The intersection of indigenous knowledge and IP comes about because of a number of factors, including the creation by indigenous people of global

---

1   For a full discussion of the work of these organisations see C Antons, 'The International Debate about Traditional Knowledge, Traditional Cultural Expressions and Intellectual Property' in C Antons (ed), *Traditional Knowledge, Traditional Cultural Expressions and Intellectual Property Law in the Asia-Pacific Region* (Kluwer Law International, 2009) 39.
2   For the full theoretical account see P Drahos, *A Philosophy of Intellectual Property* (Dartmouth, 1996).
3   S B Brush, 'Indigenous Knowledge of Biological Resources and Intellectual Property Rights: The Role of Anthropology' (1993) 95 *American Anthropologist* 653, 659.

political networks in the second half of the twentieth century, the recognition of the economic value of indigenous knowledge and the increasing activism of developing countries around international IP rights. The next section of this chapter focuses on this history in a little bit more detail, bringing out the way in which the international discussions around indigenous knowledge and IP have conceptually partitioned the protection of indigenous knowledge from the core issue of land rights justice — the very issue that led indigenous people to globalise networks of resistance to colonisation. The report of the New Zealand Waitangi Tribunal, published in 2011, is perhaps unique in that it recognises that mātauranga Māori (Māori knowledge) and rights in its intangible values are intimately connected to Māori relationship with the land and the environment. The report states:

> Māori culture as we know it today is a creation of its environment... [T]he elements that make it distinctive in the world can be traced to the relationships kaitiaki [guardians] built up with the land, water, flora, and fauna of this place. In this way, the mauri, or inner well-being of land and water spaces, and the whakapapa [genealogy] of flora and fauna do not just serve to articulate the human relationships with these things; they are the building blocks of an entire world view and of Māori identity itself. They play a similar role to the core definers of Western culture such as the arts, democracy, the rule of law, and so forth. But while the more human-centred Western culture tends to define itself by reference to its own thought and labour, Māori culture relies on pre-existing, pre-human definers – mountains, rivers, plants, animals, and so on. Māori culture seeks to reflect rather than dominate its surroundings. That is why the relationship between humans and taonga species is a definer of Māori culture itself. It is a preoccupation of the body of distinctive Māori knowledge that today we call mātauranga Māori.[4]

The principal purpose of this chapter is to address the broad question of whether IP systems can serve indigenous innovation systems. To foreshadow our argument a little, indigenous innovation is often place-based innovation that is cosmologically linked to land and an indigenous group's relationship with that place, rather than to laboratories. Supporting indigenous innovation requires an integrated model of IP rights, real property, and traditional law and customs. That poses a challenge for Western legal traditions that have over a long period parsed property into finely grained taxonomies of real and personal property rights, the latter underpinning complex processes of securitisation in

---

4   Waitangi Tribunal Report, *Ko Aotearoa Tēnei: A Report into Claims Concerning New Zealand Law and Policy Affecting Māori Culture and Identity* (2011) vol 1, ch 2, 115-116 ('WAI 262'). <http://www.waitangi-tribunal.govt.nz/news/media/wai262.asp>

early, middle and late capitalism.[5] In Australia, the High Court has recognised the spiritual dimension of Aboriginal native title, but has also made it clear that native title rights and interests do not constitute a separate system of IP for the control of cultural knowledge.[6] Native title is not an institution of the common law, but its interpretive evolution does take place within the basic structure of Australia's statutory and common law property institutions.[7] This considerably diminishes the prospect of Australian courts recognising a system of native title rights for the control of intangible property.

Indigenous or traditional knowledge (on the use of these terms, see section 4 below) is often said to have a dynamic quality, but there has been little explicit analysis of the features of indigenous innovation systems that presumably must be responsible for this dynamism. Instead the tendency is to conceive of indigenous knowledge, either explicitly or implicitly, as useful knowledge in propositional form. Innovation is often conceptualised in terms of firms developing new products and processes.[8] The ethnobotanical records in Australia and New Zealand provide some examples of indigenous innovation that fit with this standard approach. For example, recorded interviews with Wagiman elders show that the Wagiman people developed products and processes. The leaves of the ironwood tree, for example, were used as a fish poison and the roots provided the basis for the production of a glue.[9] Similarly, the Wagiman discovered a method for producing a damper from the seeds of *cycas canalis* (bush palm) that is suitable for long-term storage and has high food energy.[10] Much is also known about the uses of New Zealand endemic plants and Māori uses of them.[11] Harakeke (commonly called flax) is central to mātauranga Māori (Māori knowledge) and to traditional Māori life. It 'provides shelter, garments, fine fibre for weaving (muka), and powerful medicines for a multitude of ailments'.[12] Another example is manuka, a tree that is valued for numerous properties, including its oil and honey that has exceptionally high antibacterial properties.[13] These properties have been investigated by Western scientists[14] and utilised in many business ventures.

---

5   On property and the securitisation process see J Braithwaite and P Drahos, *Global Business Regulation* (Cambridge University Press, 2000) 143.

6   On the spiritual dimension see *Yanner v Eaton* (1999) 201 CLR 351. On the limits of native title as the basis for creating rights in intangibles see *Western Australia v Ward* (2002) 213 CLR 1.

7   See *Fejo v Northern Territory of Australia* (1998) 195 CLR 96, 128.

8   C Greenhalgh and M Rogers, *Innovation, Intellectual Property, and Economic Growth* (Princeton University Press, 2010) 4. On how IP rules relate to the decision to innovate see W van Caenegem, *Intellectual Property Law and Innovation* (Cambridge University Press, 2007).

9   L G Liddy et al, *Wagiman Plants and Animals: Aboriginal Knowledge of Flora and Fauna from the Mid Daly River Area, Northern Australia* (Department of Natural Resources, Environment and the Arts, NT Government and the Diwurruwurru-jaru Aboriginal Corporation, 2006) 39.

10   Ibid, 35.

11   See e.g. M Riley, *Maori Healing and Herbal* (Viking Seven Seas NZ, 1994).

12   WAI 262, above n 4.

13   Ibid, 128-131.

14   Ibid, 130, see explanation of the isolation of the active ingredients by German scientist.

If we think of indigenous knowledge in terms of useful propositions, then it follows naturally — at least for lawyers — that one can ask and answer the question of whether a given item of propositional knowledge falls within the scope of protection of one or more IP systems. Detailed rule-based analyses of the various individual IP systems show that some systems, especially copyright, have some utility for the protection of traditional knowledge.[15] However, the limitations of those systems are precisely why much of the discussion about the protection of indigenous knowledge has primarily developed in fora, such as the CBD and the FAO, which are not primarily concerned with IP.[16]

However, the focus of this book is not the on protection of indigenous knowledge propositionally conceived, but rather on the system of indigenous innovation that is responsible for the Wagiman people, for example, producing new products and processes. The generation of useful knowledge and techniques implies a set of institutions working in convergent ways to produce innovation.[17] A systems perspective on innovation requires one to look more broadly at the institutions that contribute to innovative performance, as well as the distinctive linkages and interactions amongst institutional actors that characterise an innovation system.[18] In the context of modern economies, this usually involves an examination of the linkages amongst firms and their industrial research laboratories, universities and government laboratories, as well as an examination of the role of institutions such as tax and venture capital markets.[19] In the case of indigenous innovation systems, there will obviously be a different set of institutional linkages, including linkages amongst cosmological institutions, sacred sites and kinship systems. These linkages may extend to Western scientists working within a framework that is compatible with indigenous peoples' expectations (for an example, see Chapter two). The fifth section of this chapter suggests some institutional features of indigenous innovation, but this part of the analysis should be seen as preliminary. The analysis draws on the studies of Aboriginal people from Australia and Māori in New Zealand. Institutions of indigenous innovation are highly context dependent and less susceptible to the kind of harmonising influences of globalisation that have brought about

---

15    See e.g. T Janke and R Quiggin, 'Indigenous Cultural and Intellectual Property and Customary Law' (Background Paper 12, Law Reform Commission of Western Australia, 2005) <http://www.lrc.justice.wa.gov. au/> See also S Frankel, 'Trademarks and Traditional Knowledge and Cultural Intellectual Property Rights' in G B Dinwoodie and M D Janis (eds), *Trademark Law and Theory: A Handbook of Contemporary Research* (Edward Elgar, 2008) 433 for discussion of the utility of trade mark law in protecting indigenous knowledge that is sometimes manifest in trade marks.

16    One exception is perhaps the negotiation in the World Intellectual Property Organization discussed in several chapters in this book.

17    On institutions and a theory of useful knowledge see J Mokyr, *The Gifts of Athena: Historical Origins of the Knowledge Economy* (Princeton University Press, 2002).

18    R R Nelson, 'National Innovation Systems: A Retrospective on a Study' (1992) 1 *Industrial and Corporate Change* 347.

19    For examples of this approach see ibid; P A Hall and D Soskice (eds), *Varieties of Capitalism: The Institutional Foundations of Comparative Advantage* (Oxford University Press, 2001).

the institutional convergences that we see taking place in capitalist innovation systems. This sets limits on the extent to which one can generalise about them. A full institutional analysis of indigenous innovation is an interdisciplinary quest in which a number of disciplines, including ethnobotany, cognitive anthropology and human ecology, play a crucial role.[20]

The primary purpose of this chapter is to bring into focus a distinction between indigenous knowledge and indigenous innovation, and then to identify some of the institutional characteristics of the latter. Following on from this, the last section of the chapter discusses which systems of IP are likely to best support systems of indigenous innovation. Other chapters in this book also explore this issue. This is a different question from asking which items of propositional knowledge are most effectively protected by which IP rules. A patent may represent the best fit between an active ingredient derived from a plant and the indigenous group with traditional rights over the plant, but it does not follow that the patent system is the best system for the innovation system of people of which that group is a part.

# 2. The Search for Justice: From Individuals to Global Indigenous Networks

When European states colonised countries, the land ownership systems of the original inhabitants of those countries generally underwent a radical transformation[21] or, as in the case of Australia, were extinguished altogether.[22] Unable to find land rights justice within settler societies, some indigenous groups from countries such as Australia, Canada and New Zealand took their cause to seats of power in Europe. For example, delegations of Māori travelled to England in 1882, 1884, 1914 and 1924 in an attempt to meet with monarchs.[23] Among the petitions organised by the Aboriginal leader William Cooper was a petition of 1937 addressed to King George V. It contained 1,814 signatures of Aboriginal people, and asked for Aboriginal representation in the Australian

---

20   For a discussion of the contribution of these disciplines see Brush, above n 3; P Sillitoe, 'The Development of Indigenous Knowledge: A New Applied Anthropology' (1998) 39 *Current Anthropology* 223; F Berkes, *Sacred Ecology* (2nd ed, Routledge, 2008) 22.

21   For a study of Crown Māori land policy and practice in the period 1869–1929, see R Boast, *Buying the Land, Selling the Land: Governments and Maori Land in the North Island 1865–1921* (Victoria University Press, 2008).

22   More than 200 years later this was found to be the wrong view of the law. The Australian High Court in its famous *Mabo* decision found that the reception of British law into Australian colonies did not produce the chain of extinguishment supposed by colonial legal authorities. See *Mabo v Queensland [No 2]* (1992) 175 CLR 1 ('*Mabo*').

23   See D Sanders, 'The Formation of the World Council of Indigenous Peoples' (Fourth World Documentation Project, Center for World Indigenous Studies, 1980) <http://cwis.org>

Parliament.[24] In 1923 Deskaheh, a chief of the Cayuga, travelled to the League of Nations as a spokesman for the Six Nations of the Iroquois League.[25] In essence he wanted the League of Nations to help the Iroquois League gain the sovereign independence and territory that had been agreed to by King George III but was now opposed by the Canadian Government. Anthony Fernando, whose mother was Aboriginal, left Australia for Europe in the early 1900s. Deported from Italy to Britain in 1923 for distributing pamphlets declaring the extermination of indigenous people by the British in Australia, he spent his days in England in sole protest, at one stage regularly appearing outside Australia House in London in a coat covered with toy white skeletons.[26] The skeletons, he said, depicted the fate of his people.

These and other attempts like them generally ended in failure. The Australian authorities never forwarded Cooper's petition. Deskaheh left Geneva without success, and died alone in New York in 1926. Fernando died in a mental hospital in Essex in 1946.

Indigenous people nevertheless persisted with the strategy of globalising their fight for justice. The evolution of the UN system, which began with the United Nations Charter of 1945, created new opportunities for them. The language of human rights treaties seemed full of evocative promise: 'All peoples have the right of self-determination' (Article 1.1 of the International Covenant on Civil and Political Rights). The indigenous networks of political mobilisation and negotiation that evolved around indigenous peoples' issues concentrated on developing a broad rights-based agenda at the highest levels of international law-making.[27] However, IP remained a technically obscure subject and there was little understanding of its connections with indigenous knowledge systems. This, as the next section makes clear, began to change slowly in the 1980s.

# 3. Enter Developing States

After World War II many developing countries became sovereign states. One of the consequences of this particular wave of decolonisation was that developing states began to press for the reform of the international IP framework.

---

24    Cooper's story is told in B Attwood and A Markus, *Thinking Black: William Cooper and the Australian Aborigines' League* (Aborigines Studies Press, 2004).
25    J Rostkowski, 'The Redman's Appeal for Justice: Deskaheh and the League of Nations' in C F Feest (ed), *Indians and Europe: An Interdisciplinary Collection of Essays* (University of Nebraska Press, 1989) 435.
26    Fernando's story can be found in the Australian Dictionary of Biography. See <http://adbonline.anu. edu.au/biogs/AS10160b.htm> For a more detailed account see F Paisley, 'Australian Aboriginal Activism in Interwar Britain and Europe: Anthony Martin Fernando' (2009) 7 *History Compass* 701.
27    R Niezan, 'Recognizing Indigenism: Canadian Unity and the International Movement of Indigenous Peoples' (2000) 42 *Comparative Studies in Society and History* 119. See also C Charters, 'A Self-Determination Approach to Justifying Indigenous Peoples' Participation in International Law and Policy Making' (2010) 17 *International Journal on Minority and Group Rights* 215.

These reform attempts, which became part of a broader and deeper push during the 1970s for a New International Economic Order, ultimately failed.[28] Moreover, during the 1980s developing countries came under trade pressure from the US to comply with standards of IP protection that favoured US export interests.[29] Developing countries also found themselves having to defend against moves by the US and EU to bring IP standards into the Uruguay Round of multilateral trade negotiations that had begun in 1986. Developing country attempts to defeat this US and EU agenda also failed.

The issue of indigenous knowledge and IP remained in the shadows. It gained some limited recognition in the publication of the Tunisian Model Copyright Law in 1976.[30] This law recognises copyright in works of national folklore, a concept that has some overlap with indigenous knowledge.[31] Two events in the early 1990s helped to bring about the convergence of IP and indigenous knowledge as part of the formal work programmes of international organisations. The CBD, which came into force in 1993, expressly recognises the importance of indigenous and local knowledge to the conservation and sustainable use of biodiversity. The field of ethnobiology had grown during the 1980s, and more international organisations had established research programmes on indigenous knowledge.[32] Its value, both economic and non-economic, was slowly gaining recognition. The other event was the inclusion of the Agreement on Trade-Related Aspects of Intellectual Property Rights (TRIPS) in the package of Uruguay Round agreements that were signed by states in 1994.

The 1990s saw a complex negotiating agenda evolve amongst states within the WTO and the CBD around the issues of the patentability of biological materials and the protection of traditional knowledge (the term that came to be preferred to indigenous knowledge). International legal instruments have dissected traditional knowledge into that related to biological materials and that more directly connected to works of art and culture. The latter has acquired the terminology traditional cultural expressions.[33] The division of traditional knowledge into these categories reflects a categorisation analogous to that found in IP law. Copyright and expressive uses of trade marks are analogous to traditional cultural expressions, and biological materials are associated with patents and

---

28   For the history see S K Sell, *Power and Ideas: North-South Politics of Intellectual Property and Antitrust* (State University of New York, 1998).

29   P Drahos and J Braithwaite, *Information Feudalism: Who Owns the Knowledge Economy?* (Earthscan, 2002) 99.

30   D Zografos, *Intellectual Property and Traditional Cultural Expressions* (Edward Elgar, 2010) 14.

31   *Berne Convention for the Protection of Literary and Artistic Works* (Paris Act, 1971) 1161 UNTS 18388, art 15(4) recognises folklore as copyright works. The recognition is not dependent on identification of the exact author as other copyright protection under the Convention is. However, this is not the same as recognition of indigenous knowledge on its own terms; rather it is recognition that it might in some circumstances be protected as copyright.

32   Berkes, above n 20, 21-22.

33   The chapter by Daphne Zografos Johnsson in this book discusses that terminology.

plant variety rights. The concept of traditional knowledge transcends both. This sort of categorisation does not necessarily reflect the ways in which indigenous peoples see their knowledge. It is no coincidence that biological materials that are important to Māori, for example, are frequently found in works of art and in carvings on or within buildings. Representations of the distinctive blooms of the kōwhai ngutukākā plant are found in the wharewhakairo (carved house) at Te Pakirikiri marae. The same representations are also found on Ruatepupuke, a meeting house located in the Field Museum in Chicago.[34]

The CBD makes it clear that states have sovereignty over their biological resources.[35] It also requires access to genetic resources to be based on prior informed consent and the fair and equitable sharing of benefits from those resources.[36] Patents are, as TRIPS recognises, available for inventions, but not for discoveries. Naturally occurring biological resources are not patentable, but can be converted into inventions, often through a minimal technical step of isolation and purification.[37] The conversion of raw biological materials to be found in nature into an invention through some minimal intervention can be seen as the patent system allowing a form of selective free riding. Further, as we will see in section five of this chapter, the idea of raw biological materials existing in nature awaiting conversion into inventions by patentees is deeply problematic from the perspective of indigenous innovation. As we will see, indigenous people in Australia were managing the land with a view to improving the biological materials to be found in it. The biodiversity that confronted arriving colonists was not that of nature in raw form, but rather the many products of the land that had resulted from thousands of years of intervention and management of that land by indigenous people.

During the early 1990s non-state actors began to point to the unfairness of this selective free-riding effect, characterising it as 'biopiracy'.[38] Many developing states also began to argue that TRIPS undermines the CBD because it requires all WTO members to allow for the patentability of micro-organisms and microbiological processes and the protection of plant varieties (by means of patents or some other system, or some combination thereof).[39]

---

34   WAI 262, above n 4, 123-124.

35   See para 4 of the Preamble, arts 3 and 15.1 of the CBD.

36   See arts 15.5 and 15.7 of the CBD.

37   For a comprehensive history and analysis of the way in which the distinction between invention and discovery has been subverted in patent law see L Palombi, *Gene Cartels: Biotech Patents in the Age of Free Trade* (Edward Elgar, 2009).

38   D F Robinson, *Confronting Biopiracy: Challenges, Cases and International Debates* (Earthscan, 2010) 14.

39   The negotiations in the WTO over the relationship between the CBD and TRIPS date back to the late 1990s. There are a very large number of documents. For a summary of the many views of different coalitions of states, including the view that TRIPS undermines the CBD, see WTO Secretariat, *The Relationship between the TRIPS Agreement and the Convention on Biological Diversity: Summary of Issues Raised and Points Made*, WTO Doc IP/C/W/368/Rev.1 (2006).

A similar kind of selective free-riding argument can be developed around the use of indigenous knowledge. In those cases where indigenous groups have maintained their institutions they will, under their customary law systems, be able to identify who has ownership and use rights over knowledge. However, whether they have IP in that knowledge depends on the application of specific rules of protection to be found in the relevant IP system. Under these systems, an owner of the indigenous knowledge may not be found because, for example, IP systems do not recognise an ancestor as a legal person or because the knowledge is regarded as having entered the public domain. There is, however, considerable evidence that the willingness of indigenous peoples to share their knowledge is not, from their perspective, the equivalent of placing it in the public domain.[40] TRIPS does not set standards of protection that are specific to indigenous knowledge, but because it protects IP rights that utilise traditional knowledge, its impact on the holders of that traditional knowledge has been considerable. The CBD links the principle of equitable sharing of benefits to the use of traditional knowledge.[41]

TRIPS and the CBD catalysed the emergence of policy and activist networks around the issue of indigenous knowledge and IP. Definitional issues, as the next section shows, have loomed large for these networks.

# 4. The Quicksands of Definition

Law is obsessed with definition. Statutes, for example, frequently have a definitions section or an interpretation section. Without definitions, the discipline of law treats itself as undefined and uncertain. This has contributed to a plethora of definitions relating to traditional knowledge. Indigenous peoples do not usually attach the same value to abstract definition. If called upon to define their traditional knowledge, they will emphasise not the analytical facets of knowledge, but rather the relational boundaries and dynamics created by the possession of knowledge. This includes indigenous peoples' relationship with their knowledge, and their responsibility to maintain and develop the knowledge for the good of society and future generations. Māori, for example, are kaitiaki (guardians) of their knowledge. Additionally, being kaitiaki in part defines Māori culture and identity.[42]

---

40    S Frankel and M Richardson, 'Cultural Property and "the Public Domain": Case Studies from New Zealand and Australia' in C Antons (ed), *Traditional Knowledge, Traditional Cultural Expressions and Intellectual Property Law in the Asia-Pacific Region* (Kluwer Law International, 2009) 275.

41    See para 12 of the Preamble and art 8(j) of the CBD.

42    WAI 262, above n 4, 115-118.

The disciplines of cognitive anthropology and human ecology in particular have been important to recognising folk knowledge as systems of knowledge.[43] At first the terms 'indigenous' and 'folk' were used interchangeably, and in contrast to formalised systems of scientific knowledge. A similar interchangeability of the terms is to be found in the study of legal systems, the contrast here being with codified or positive systems of law.[44] As we noted in section 1 above, the concept of an indigenous knowledge system appears in anthropological literature in the early 1980s. Within anthropology, the term 'indigenous' comes to be linked to cases of distinct tribal groups involved in a rights struggle with a state not founded by those groups.[45] The meaning of the term is thereby narrowed.

Within international law, the term 'indigenous' is open ended. The United Nations Declaration on the Rights of Indigenous Peoples (DRIP) avoids proposing a definition, stating that indigenous peoples 'have the right to determine their own identity or membership'.[46] Self-identification appears to be the core principle within the UN system for determining the application of the term.[47] This devolutionary strategy may not always help. If being X depends upon a right of self-identification as X, and this right is open to all, then it follows that anyone may make use of the right to become X. A potential political problem arises for states, because being indigenous gives access to a rights-based discourse in which the principle of self-determination features prominently. Within South-East Asia and South Asia some states such as India, Indonesia and Malaysia have attempted to characterise their population at large as indigenous and to avoid the use of the term as a descriptor for minority groups such as hill tribes.[48] Moreover, in these regions, migration patterns, intermarriage and cultural cross-pollination make the ascription of indigenous to particular groups a matter of debate and complexity.

UN treaties tend to proliferate rather than restrict meanings in this field. The Indigenous and Tribal Peoples Convention of 1989 draws a distinction between tribal and indigenous people. Tribal people are linked to a group that self-regulates on the basis of custom, while indigenous people are those who existed as a group prior to an act of conquest or colonisation and have retained at least some of their pre-existing institutions. The CBD refers to 'indigenous and local

---

43   Brush, above n 3, 658-659.
44   See G C J J Van Den Bergh, 'The Concept of Folk Law in Historical Context: A Brief Outline' in A D Renteln and A Dundes (eds), *Folk Law: Essays in the Theory and Practice of Lex Non Scripta* (University of Wisconsin Press, 1994).
45   Brush, above n 3, 658.
46   For an indigenous peoples' discussion of the Convention see L Malezer, C Charters and V Tauli-Corpuz (eds), *Indigenous Voices: The UN Declaration on the Rights of Indigenous Peoples* (Hart Publishing, forthcoming).
47   United Nations Development Group, *Guidelines on Indigenous Peoples' Issues* (2009) 9.
48   G A Persoon, '"Being Indigenous" in Indonesia and the Philippines' in C Antons (ed), *Traditional Knowledge, Traditional Cultural Expressions and Intellectual Property Law in the Asia-Pacific Region* (Kluwer Law International, 2009) 195, 196.

communities'. Negotiations within WIPO are aimed at producing an international instrument of some kind to protect traditional knowledge. The current draft articles take the form of alternative options.[49] The term 'traditional knowledge' is preferred to 'indigenous knowledge'. The draft options use different terms such as 'indigenous people', 'local communities' and 'traditional communities'. It is anyone's guess what the final form of the international instrument will be.

Traditional knowledge is perhaps the most open-ended concept that one might choose in this field. Some knowledge, argues Polanyi, cannot be specified by means of rules and can be passed on only through relationships of close learning such as master and apprentice.[50] This form of personal knowledge depends on tradition. All societies, including capitalist societies, have traditional knowledge.

Not surprisingly, a range of definitions of traditional knowledge has emerged from the literature.[51] Traditional knowledge is sometimes linked to environmental or ecological knowledge, or to local knowledge held by groups such as farmers and fishermen (who may or may not be indigenous). Other definitional strategies include contrasting traditional knowledge with scientific knowledge, or specifying key properties for it such as oral transmission and its embeddedness in a non-materialist cosmology. All definitional strategies run into problems of one kind or another. For example, the contrast with science can be overplayed, as both traditional knowledge systems and science depend on the making of observation statements and testing. Returning to our earlier examples of the Wagiman people's knowledge of the calorific and storage properties of damper made from the bush palm, and of Māori knowledge of the properties of harakeke, it is clear that this kind of knowledge must have involved a process of observation and experimentation.

Trying to confine traditional knowledge to a class of knowledge (for example, ecological knowledge) or a class of people is very difficult. The reason that legal definitions place an emphasis on a determinate class of people is not necessarily related to the role that knowledge plays in a society, or even what constitutes knowledge, but rather it is to attribute rights, or ownership, to that class of persons. However, the value of indigenous knowledge sometimes arises because of the fact that it is attributable to an open-ended class, as in the case of the inter-generational development of plant knowledge: it has a proven pedigree.

Traditional knowledge is a potentially widespread phenomenon. For example, Mansfield's study of US companies and their foreign direct investment strategies

---

49 WIPO's work, as well as draft text aimed at protecting traditional knowledge, traditional cultural expressions/folklore and genetic resources, can be found at <http://www.wipo.int/tk/en/igc/index.html>
50 M Polanyi, *Personal Knowledge: Towards a Post-Critical Philosophy* (Routledge & Kegan Paul, 1958) 53.
51 For a survey see G Dutfield, 'Legal and Economic Aspects of Traditional Knowledge' in KE Maskus and JH Reichman (eds), *International Public Goods and Transfer of Technology Under a Globalized Intellectual Property Regime* (Cambridge University Press, 2005) 495.

revealed, amongst other things, that pharmaceutical company employees had personal knowledge about chemical processes that their employer companies held back as part of their licensing strategies.[52] Intimate knowledge about what makes a complex chemical process work optimally fits within Polyani's concept of personal knowledge, and is exactly the kind of knowledge that is passed on through personal training. It is a form of traditional knowledge. In the context of an international negotiation, the fact that the concept of traditional knowledge has an ever-expanding penumbra of meaning provides states which are minded to do so with numerous opportunities to exploit the uncertainty of the concept and thus slow down the negotiations of any treaty dealing with the concept.

Continuing on with our Wagiman example, both scientists and the Wagiman people can agree on the properties of the bush palm, and both will have made use of observational methods and testing in arriving at their knowledge of those properties. However, if we were to give a full specification of the pathway to discovery along which the Wagiman people travelled, we would find it is made up of different institutions from those on the pathway travelled by scientists. The institutions making up the Wagiman people's pathway might include a totemic system of classification in which the identity of some individuals is linked to the bush palm, as well as a cosmological system in which the bush palm features as a totemic ancestor. By shifting the focus onto an indigenous innovation system we can begin to ask about the institutions that form the discovery pathway in that system and that need to be supported for the pathway to remain open. IP systems may have a supportive function for an indigenous innovation system, but without a clear analysis of the institutions that make up this system we will not be able to work out which IP systems matter to this function. And once we embark on an institutional analysis of indigenous innovation we will also gain a better understanding of where IP sits in the lists of priorities for the support of indigenous innovation. In the case of Aboriginal people in Australia, the place-time nature of their system means that land rights justice is the primary necessary first step.[53]

Land rights justice, although not completely resolved, is considerably closer to having been achieved in New Zealand through the Waitangi Tribunal and Treaty settlement process. That may be one reason why Māori were able to bring the WAI 262 claim concerning the protection of their knowledge, culture and identity to the Waitangi Tribunal.[54] This claim shows how progress on land rights justice opens the way to progress on the protection of indigenous knowledge and culture more broadly.

---

52   E Mansfield, 'Intellectual Property Protection, Foreign Direct Investment, and Technology Transfer' (Discussion Paper 19, International Finance Corporation, The World Bank, 1994).

53   There is a broader question about whether IP can achieve much for the poor in developing countries in the absence of land reform. See D Rangnekar, 'The Challenge of Intellectual Property Rights and Social Justice' (2011) 54 *Development* 212.

54   WAI 262, above n 4.

An institutional approach also shows that support for indigenous innovation will require a multi-level governance approach. The global level of governance is the right level at which to be discussing the possibility of a treaty-based misappropriation norm for traditional knowledge, but at the state level of governance there are clearly many more issues — such as land rights and access to capital — that must be addressed if states genuinely want to support indigenous innovation.

# 5. Indigenous Innovation

Indigenous innovation is place-based innovation. In the case of Aboriginal people in Australia, it takes place on 'Country', a term we explain a little later. It is the place where the people observe and interact with the plants and animals to which they are cosmologically linked in some way. Their Country is their laboratory. The focal point of Māori innovation is also place. Rights over resources, and obligations such as that of being kaitiaki, are made concrete by being part of a group that is related to a place and is itself integrated into a network with human and non-human members (for example, the plants, animals, rivers of that place). It is this place-based network that maintains and advances knowledge. Individuals can, of course, leave the place of their spiritual affiliation and connection (their Country) but remain part of a network, communicating with its other members and contributing to its production of knowledge. Place anchors indigenous networks of innovation, but these networks can and usually do extend beyond place.

To expand the claim that indigenous innovation is place-based innovation, we need to outline the place-time cosmology that underpins this innovation system. Indigenous Australians have distinct and systematised beliefs about the true nature of the universe. These beliefs continue to exercise a profound influence on Aboriginal social organisation, including the organisation of indigenous knowledge and innovation systems. The term 'cosmology' does a better job of communicating the idea that these beliefs are thought to be true of the world than do the English words 'Dreamtime' or 'Dreaming'. The use of Dreamtime goes back to a mistranslation of a word from the Aranda language that is better translated as 'eternal, uncreated, springing out of itself'.[55]

In the broadest terms, these cosmologies deal with a class of eternal events involving ancestral beings that remain present in a place.[56] One of the features

---

55   T Swain, *A Place for Strangers: Towards a History of Australian Aboriginal Being* (Cambridge University Press, 1993) 21.
56   For more detailed discussions see H Morphy, *Ancestral Connections: Art and an Aboriginal System of Knowledge* (The University of Chicago Press, 1991); Swain, above n 55; F Dussart, *The Politics of Ritual in an Aboriginal Settlement* (Smithsonian Institution Press, 2000).

of Aboriginal cosmologies is their focus on explaining the origins of the physical features of particular areas of the country.[57] In these cosmologies ancestral beings in either animal or human form will often begin a journey in a specific place and end it in another known place. Along the way they will, through the exercise of their great powers, transform the landscape to give it the physical features by which it is known today. Through their geo-magical powers, the ancestors create the topography of an area that clan members come to know as their 'Country'. Ancestors also leave behind a landscape that is more propitious for the survival of its inhabitants. There are waterholes and freshwater springs, names to help classify animal and plant life, as well as useful tools such as fish traps and many other things. The features of the landscape are evidence of the ancestors' travels, with ancestors sometimes leaving behind personal signs such as footprints or bodyprints on cave walls.

Aboriginal cosmology is not one cosmology made up of an abstract set of truths in the canonical form of a text or set of equations. Rather it is many cosmologies that speak of great events, events that are made concrete because they are embodied in Country. There is no need for written records or archives because the land itself holds and displays to the trained knower all the knowledge that matters. The land is a living and signalling embodiment of knowledge. Prior to the arrival of mining and agricultural technologies, the land would have seemed to indigenous people to be the most permanent presence of knowledge imaginable. The details of this knowledge are poetically encrypted in stories, and transmitted through dance, singing, ritual and story-telling.

Country is an emotional centre of being. It is a place that one knows intimately at many levels, and in which one has countrymen and rights along with the safety and security that these things bring. It is where one can truly 'sit down'.[58] Cosmologies and Countries are indissolubly linked. Different groups of ancestors have shaped different areas of land in Australia. Exceptionally powerful totemic beings such as the Rainbow Serpent feature in more than one cosmology, but the stories in which they feature are not the same story. Ancestral beings are, as it were, local rather than universal forces. It follows, for example, that a Lardil person from Mornington Island who goes to central Australia where the Warlpiri live is not equipped, by virtue of Lardil cosmology, to understand the forces that shaped Warlpiri country.

---

57  I Keen, *Aboriginal Economy and Society: Australia at the Threshold of Colonisation* (Oxford University Press, 2004) 211.

58  D McKnight, *People, Countries, and the Rainbow Serpent* (Oxford University Press, 1999) 81.

Māori innovation is also in many ways place based. This is captured in many parts of the *Ko Aotearoa Tenei: A Report into Claims Concerning New Zealand Law and Policy Affecting Māori Culture and Identity* (WAI 262), and some of those passages are best quoted:

> In the 1,000 years or so in which Māori have lived on the islands of Aotearoa, they have developed — among countless other things — artistic and cultural traditions that are uniquely of this place. The underpinnings of these traditions are found in the environment itself — mountains, rivers, sea and sky, plants and animals — and their expression takes many forms, ranging from the architectural achievements of the great meeting-house and canoe builders, to the works of weavers, carvers, tohunga tā moko, musicians, and the like, as well as in te reo Māori, the language itself. These works, founded in and reflecting the body of knowledge and understanding known as mātauranga Māori, are what we call taonga works. Some of them are ancient, others not, but those who are responsible for safeguarding them, whether or not they are the original creators of the works, have a very particular relationship with them. We call this the kaitiaki relationship.[59]

> The people who arrived in Aotearoa from Hawaiki some 1,000 years ago embedded themselves in the new environment, changed it, and were in turn changed by it. Nowhere were these changes more evident than in technology and the arts. They reflected the incremental development of a new and unique culture. New technologies were required to cultivate, hunt, and gather food. New stories and traditions had to be built up to explain to succeeding generations why some methods worked and others didn't, and why some behaviours were good and others not. Methods had to be invented to cultivate and store canoe crops such as taro and kūmara in a climate that permitted only one planting cycle per year, and traditions were required around those methods to ensure adherence to conduct most likely to produce a successful harvest. Unfamiliar plants were tested for their utility as food, medicine, fibre, or building material, and then catalogued within an entirely newly constructed whakapapa (genealogy). As in Hawaiki, this whakapapa had then to be given texture and meaning through story and tradition that explained relationships. These relationships helped to ensure that the integrity of the catalogue could be maintained in memory, and they explained the value (and the dangers) of each species, as well as inter-species compatibility. Birds, fish, and shellfish were tested and ordered in the same way. This time whakapapa, supplemented by story and song, would explain habitat, growth cycle, sensitivity to environmental change, and edibility.[60]

---

59  WAI 262, above n 4, 31.
60  Ibid, 33.

If there is one thing that unites indigenous systems of knowledge it is the principle that most or all knowledge that is part of a group's system can be traced back to the acts of powerful ancestors. The acts of ancestors are the threads that connect different parts of an indigenous knowledge system. One can, for example, give independent descriptions of a group's botanical taxonomies, but the ultimate origins of these taxonomies lie in the names and classifications that ancestral spirits created along with the landscape and the animals and plants in it. Indigenous knowledge systems are said to be holistic, but we prefer the term 'connectionist', which better captures the densely networked way in which indigenous people in Australia and New Zealand perceive the world.

Indigenous people are born into social systems that, from the very beginning, multiply the number of connections that make up their world. Their kinship system links them to places for which they have duties as custodians and guardians, as well as to the places of other groups (primarily through inter-marriage), their ancestors and the events associated with those ancestors. Aboriginal societies are sometimes described as kinship societies because no individual of a given tribe is left out of a kinship calculation.[61] Kinship is foundational in Māori society. In the words of the *Ko Aotearoa Tenei*, kinship is 'a revolving door between the human, physical, and spiritual realms'.[62]

In this connectionist world plants, animals, rocks, rivers and other things have multidimensional natures. A tree may have utilitarian functions, such as providing shelter and being a source of medicine, but it may also be linked to a person by virtue of a kinship relation because, for example, it features in an ancestral story on that person's mother's side, leading that person to say that 'this tree is my mother'.[63] From this kinship connection there may flow a set of rights and obligations with respect to a tree species. A very large range of things can function as a totem, including plants, animals, wind, rain, thunder, fire, mist, tools and food, as well as parts of the human body.[64]

We can see even from this brief description that indigenous individuals are immersed in a social network that stretches well beyond the conventional understanding of a social network, because the units of the network include plants and animals and the land itself: 'The people of a place are related to its mountains, rivers and species of plant and animal, and regard them in personal terms.'[65] Connectionism refers to the fact that traditional knowledge systems are part of social networks that are characterised by variety in the types of

---

61  McKnight, above n 58, 33.

62  WAI 262, above n 4, 13.

63  I Keen, *Knowledge and Secrecy in an Aboriginal Religion* (Clarendon Press, 1994) 107.

64  W E H Stanner, *White Man Got No Dreaming 1938–1973* (Australian National University Press, 1979) 106, 127-129.

65  WAI 262, above n 4, 17.

units in the network, as well as density of connections amongst those units. The density of connection comes about because communication with the non-human members of the network is seen as possible. Indigenous cosmology, kinship systems and totems operate together to create a complex web of relations that for the most part remains opaque to outsiders.

Before we move on to discuss other features of indigenous innovation, it is important to note that states participating in international discussions of traditional knowledge and IP have conceptually partitioned IP issues from land rights issues. The WAI 262 claim explicitly recognises and articulates the importance of the connection to the land and the way in which the relationship with the land impacts Māori culture and identity.[66] International organisations like the WIPO and the WTO focus on IP issues raised by traditional knowledge, but stay silent about traditional land rights. Of course, this is exactly what the member states of these international organisations want, but it is a partition that makes no sense to indigenous people. Their knowledge systems are deeply rooted in the place-time relations of land. To protect the former, one must recognise rights to the latter.

As we have shown, placed-based innovation is integrated with a connectionist cosmological scheme in which knowledge is generated as part of a web of relations that include ancestors and totemic entities. As one might expect of ancient cultures that innovate under conditions of cosmological connectionism, many rules and restrictions concerning the use of knowledge have evolved.[67] Indigenous systems of governance for knowledge and innovation do not really accommodate the concept of unrestricted public domain rights that characterise some IP systems.[68] The expiry of patent and copyright terms sees information enter the public domain for use by competitors. Within indigenous knowledge systems, those with custodial rights over land, plants or animals and the knowledge related to those things do not hold those rights for a limited time. Potentially this sets up a problem of access to vital resources in indigenous societies, and so others are given use rights over resources held by primary custodians.[69] Kinship relations will be a determining factor in the kind of use rights a given individual can gain. In essence, IP systems and indigenous governance systems solve access problems to resources in different ways. IP systems, with some exceptions such as trade secrets and trade marks, make protection time-sensitive, while indigenous systems place the emphasis on use rights. In the former, exclusivity of use is offset by limiting the duration

---

66   Ibid.
67   For examples see Morphy, above n 56, 89.
68   K Bowery, 'Indigenous Culture, Knowledge and Intellectual Property: The Need for a New Category of Rights?' in K Bowery, M Handler and D Nicol (eds), *Emerging Challenges in Intellectual Property* (Oxford University Press, 2011) 46, 47.
69   For examples of use rights see Keen, above n 57, ch. 9.

of exclusivity, while in the latter case perpetual rights are offset by granting use rights to others. Interestingly, in the case of the perpetual rights allowed by systems of trade secret protection and trade marks one can see use-right solutions being employed to deal with access issues. For example, trade secret protection does not prevent a third party from using information that the party has discovered independently of the trade secret holder.

Another feature of indigenous innovation is the strong presence of uncodified knowledge. The information theoretic perspective on innovation draws a distinction between codified and uncodifed information, with the latter being best transferred by means of personal communication.[70] A subset of uncodified information may also be uncodifiable in that it cannot be captured by rules. As Polanyi argues, the transmission of such knowledge depends on personal teaching and tradition.

A good example of the role of personal knowledge in indigenous innovation is to be found in techniques of fire management. In Arnhem Land, Australia, there are areas of land that have been in the hands of traditional custodians for many decades, allowing those custodians to use a traditional system of fire management.[71] In outline, this system is based on a seasonally based method of burning. Burning begins in the early dry season, and is first targeted on the higher parts of Country where the moisture content of the grass — which acts as a natural control on the extent of the burn — has fallen. Burning continues throughout the dry season, moving into lower areas and reaching a peak in the coolest months of the dry season. As groups move about and carry out burning on their Countries, a mosaic pattern of burnt and unburnt patches develops. The essence of the method is to produce a large number of smaller, cooler fires that pose less risk for people and Country.

Achieving a 'cool burn' that causes minimal damage to trees and insect life, but at the same time stimulates grasses to the right level of re-growth, requires an intimate knowledge of how to manage the fire, as well as judgement about exactly the right time and conditions under which to burn. The mosaic method of burning requires supervision by masters of the method. It is not a matter of just strolling into the bush and randomly setting bits of it alight. Standing in the bush watching an indigenous man calmly and deliberately start a series of fires that culminate in a racing wall of flame makes one realise how much depends on accurate judgement about exactly when to start the fire so that it will run and stop in a predictable way.[72]

---

70   T Mandeville, *Understanding Novelty: Information, Technological Change, and the Patent System* (Ablex Publishing Corporation, 1996) 50.

71   D Yibarbuk et al, 'Fire Ecology and Aboriginal Land Management in Central Arnhem Land, Northern Australia: A Tradition of Ecosystem Management' (2001) 28 *Journal of Biogeography* 325.

72   Drahos was a participant in the Indigenous Fire Workshop Program, 12 July 2010 to Friday 16 July 2010. The workshop was hosted by the Chuulangun community which is based at Chuulangun on the upper Wenlock River, Northern Queensland.

The ecological value of this innovative technique has slowly been scientifically understood. The technique helps to avoid the highly destructive large-scale fires that are typical of late-season fires in Northern Australia.[73] One study of an indigenous estate in north-central Arnhem Land on which this traditional method of burning had been more or less continuously used to the present time showed that the method promoted ecological integrity as measured by a number of indicators such as biodiversity, and the presence of rare native fauna and threatened fire-sensitive vegetation types.[74]

The rights of Māori to some kind of control over waterways has been recognised in New Zealand as part of Māori rights under the Treaty of Waitangi. This has led to co-management structures to achieve, amongst other things, conservation and sustainable environment goals. In 2010 the Cabinet formed a new policy, 'Involving Iwi[75] in Natural Resource Management through Historical Treaty of Waitangi Settlements'.[76] As well as having the goal of settling grievances between Māori and the Crown, the aim of the policy is to enable iwi to have an effective role in natural resource management, and to create good 'environmental, economic, social and cultural outcomes for iwi and other New Zealanders'. Co-management can take many forms, ranging from consultation through to decision-making powers for Māori. One commentator has described co-management as 'knowledge sharing'.[77]

The level of Māori control in a co-management arrangement depends on the particular Treaty settlement that Māori have negotiated, or the arrangements they have made with the local council or that are required under the Resource Management Act.[78] Co-management arrangements are about far more than the settlement of grievances or the avoidance of future grievances. It is increasingly recognised that iwi have, both in the past and present, taken good care of New Zealand's great outdoors where they have been permitted to do so. The approach of Māori to the environment, and their techniques for managing resources, contribute to the conservation and sustainability goals of government. The Māori approach is a reflection of the relationship between the people and the environment, and the interconnectedness of people, the land, and the flora and fauna. What creates sustainable practices is the belief that if you harm one aspect

---

73    J Russell-Smith et al, 'Challenges and Opportunities for Fire Management in Fire-prone Northern Australia' in J Russell-Smith, P Whitehead and P Cooke (eds), *Culture, Ecology and Economy of Fire Management in North Australian Savannas: Rekindling The Wurrk Tradition* (CSIRO Publishing, 2009) 1.

74    Yibarbuk et al, above n 71.

75    Iwi is the Māori word for tribal group.

76    Office of Treaty Settlement, Involving Iwi in Natural Resource Management through Historical Treaty of Waitangi Settlements (2010) <http://www.lgnz.co.nz/library/files/store_024/Cabinet_decisions_treaty_ settlements_and_local_government_october_2010.pdf>

77    F Berkes, 'Evolution of Co-Management: Role of Knowledge Generation, Bridging Organizations and Social Learning' (2009) 90 *Journal of Environmental Management* 1692.

78    See WAI 262, above n 4, ch 3 for a full description of all legislation and council arrangements involved.

of the environment or those who live in it you harm them all. This approach is also found in other indigenous cultures and is reflected in modern discourse about sustainability.

The co-management of the Waikato River, a Māori taonga (treasure), is perhaps the best-known example of these arrangements. Co-management followed on from a settlement of the historical land claim of the Waikato-Tainui people in 2007, when the Crown signed the 'Waikato River Agreement in Principle' with Waikato-Tainui. A lengthy process of negotiation culminated in the Waikato River Settlement Act 2010. Situated in the North Island, the Waikato River is New Zealand's longest. Many towns depend on its water, and much industry, including electricity generation, is located near it. It once was a very important transportation route and the source of plentiful food. The aim of the co-management arrangement is to restore and protect the health and wellbeing of the river for future generations.[79] It allows Waikato-Tainui, who have economic and cultural relationships with the river, to be actively involved in restoring the health of the river. Māori techniques require the 'incorporation of Māori knowledge, cultural and social relationships, and social, cultural, and economic wellbeing in an integrated, holistic, and coordinated approach when managing the resources of the river'.[80] The arrangement is still young and its success, or otherwise, remains to be seen.

The WAI 262 report documents some of the impacts Māori have had on the environment, and acknowledges that some of these impacts have been damaging. But it also explains that Māori customs and practices reached an equilibrium with the environment that endured for several hundred years before Europeans arrived. The report also describes how Māori selected trees suitable for canoe paddles and carving, and how principles that protected the timber resources were observed. One witness in the claim gave evidence[81]

> ... about the system for managing native forests, based around strict selection and the minimisation of waste. For example, the wood from the pāhautea (New Zealand cedar) was both soft and longlasting, and was therefore reserved for specific limited uses. Except for making paddles and repairing boats, that type of tree would never be cut down. 'We would leave good trees to use for our next paddles.' The process for selecting the right tree to cut down for carving or other purposes was also careful and deliberate. A crucial part of this process was the karakia [prayer or incantation] to Tāne-mahuta. Mr Elkington

---

79    Raukawa and the Raukawa Settlement Trust and the Sovereign in right of New Zealand 'Deed in Relation to a Co-Management Framework for the Waikato River' (17 December 2009) 1.34.
80    Alex Steenstra, *The Waikato River Settlement and Natural Resource Management in New Zealand* <http://www.nzares.org.nz/pdf/The%20Waikato%20River%20Settlement.pdf>
81    WAI 262, above n 4, 245.

stated that this karakia was a means of 'asking for guidance' to ensure that only the correct tree would be cut down. 'We did not want to cut down the wrong tree, as that would be a waste'. This created a system for managing native forests based on the kaitiaki relationship. Similar systems were in place for the management of kaimoana [seafood]. Priscilla Paul and Jim Elkington both referred to the practice of managing and transplanting pipi, cockles, mussels, kina, pāua, oyster, and scallops for a variety of reasons, including sustainability. Transplantation was managed according to the spawning cycles of the various species, and traditional regulatory mechanisms such as rāhui [temporary ban, or ritual prohibition placed on an area or resource] were used to ensure sustainable quantities of kaimoana developed before any harvesting took place.

Another feature of indigenous innovation is the form of its expression. It is hard to avoid the pull of a technological artefact view of innovation in which new material technologies come to represent the innovative achievements of a society. If we look at the technological products of Aboriginal people prior to colonisation, they largely consist of the wooden and stone tools and hunting implements that are typical of hunter-gatherer societies.[82] But different theories of innovation illuminate different dimensions of a society's achievements in innovation. The information theoretic perspective locates innovation in collective processes of generating information to reduce uncertainty.[83] A society may choose to invest its resources into information that expresses itself more in services and processes than in technological artefacts. It may also emphasise the symbolic manipulation of information, meaning, amongst other things, that more time is devoted to the coding and transmission of information through story-telling, dance, ritual, art and other forms of symbolic manipulation. For Aboriginal people the sense of cosmologically derived duty to maintain a 'healthy Country' is overriding. A great many of their limited resources were devoted to generating knowledge and techniques to this end. Healthy Country would, at least in the eyes of indigenous people, represent their greatest innovative achievement. It would also have been an achievement largely lost on the colonists arriving in 1788. Indeed, evidence of Aboriginal peoples' innovation would have been seen but not recognised by the colonisers on a daily basis. Its most obvious presence was the fine-grained habitat produced by traditional methods of fire management.[84]

---

82   See Keen, above n 57, ch 3.
83   Mandeville, above n 70, 49.
84   J Russell-Smith et al, 'Contemporary Fire Regimes of Northern Australia, 1997-2001: Change Since Aboriginal Occupancy, Challenges for Sustainable Management' (2003) 12 *International Journal of Wildland Fire* 283.

The innovation output of indigenous societies is best understood at the level of systems maintenance, where the systems being maintained are interlocking ecological systems and sub-systems. Whether it is using systems of mosaic burning to maintain healthy Country or systems to maintain the health of waterways, the great contribution to innovation by the indigenous peoples of Australia and New Zealand has been in developing systems to maintain the healthy functioning of environmental systems. Innovation in terms of new technological artefacts has been less of a cultural priority for Aboriginal people.

One other aspect of indigenous innovation needs to be mentioned. Some areas of innovation such as biotechnology and information technology are said to have a high degree of cumulativeness.[85] In cumulative innovation, invention X depends on invention Y as an input. In a general sense, all innovation is cumulative, since no inventor invents every single input that contributes to his invention. Models of cumulative innovation operate with a narrow sense of the cumulative, looking at the sharing of rents between the first and second innovators and how IP rights affect the incentive setting.[86] This has limited relevance to innovation in the indigenous setting, where it is better to think in terms of cycles of innovation dependence. In a cycle of innovation dependence, the use of one technique at one point in time allows for the more efficient or innovative use of other techniques. For example, the use of fire regimes to improve the quality and quantity of plant life offers women, who are often involved in the gathering of plants for food and medicines, more opportunities to improve the use of those plants. Along similar lines, there is clear evidence that fire regimes also increase the efficiency of small-game hunting.[87] To maintain the health of a river is also to contribute to the maintenance of flora and fauna that depend on the river. In a cycle of innovation dependence, one technique or set of techniques acts as part of a set of complex conditions that help to promote other forms of innovation. The use of fire is not a direct input into the harvesting of a new plant, but it is part of a set of causal conditions that helped to promote its growth. Some sense of this complex conditionality, of which the apparently simple act (to outside observers) of setting fire to the bush is a part, can be glimpsed from the following statement:

> The secret of fire in our traditional knowledge is that it is a thing that brings the land alive again. When we do burning the whole land comes alive again — it is reborn. But it is not a thing for people to play with

---

85   S Scotchmer, *Innovation and Incentives* (MIT Press, 2004) 127.

86   S Scotchmer, 'Standing on the Shoulders of Giants: Cumulative Research and the Patent Law' (1991) 5 *Journal of Economic Perspectives* 29.

87   R B Bird et al, 'The "Fire Stick" Hypothesis: Australian Aboriginal Foraging Strategies, Biodiversity, and Anthropogenic Fire Mosaics' (2008) 105(39) *Proceedings of the National Academy of Science* 14796.

unless they understand the nature of fire. ... [T]he fire-drive is itself regarded as a sacred and very serious act, often first enacted by the major creative beings for that area.[88]

Summing up, we can see that indigenous innovation has at least the following features. It is a place-based form of innovation depending critically on land rights for the innovators. The innovative process is deeply integrated into a cosmological connectionist scheme in which all innovation has threads leading back to ancestors. The diffusion of innovation is dependent upon use rights rather than time-limited forms of protection. The innovation system depends on the transmission of non-codified personal knowledge. While many rules surround the use of knowledge, much of this knowledge has to be learnt through personal training rather than rules. Putting it starkly, robots could not be programmed through rules to run this place-based innovation system. The goals and expression of innovation have less to do with products and everything to do with services to Country. Resources are devoted to innovation in systems maintenance, rather than to the generation of technological artefacts. This systems maintenance means that indigenous innovators operate in cycles of innovation dependence. There is a time for burning Country so that the efficiency of other techniques and practices can be improved upon.

# 6. Indigenous Innovation and IP Pathways to Development

What role, then, for IP rights in systems of indigenous innovation? It should be clear from the preceding discussion that IP rights cannot be the prime mover of indigenous innovation systems. Rather, indigenous innovation is driven by that complex web of relations that we have argued lies in the cosmological connectionism of indigenous peoples. Cosmological connectionism anchors indigenous networks to places and creates relationships of caring about those places.

In Australia, it is on Country that Aboriginal people can maintain or rebuild the institutions that support their own distinctive path to discovery. It is on Country that elders have the best chance of passing on their personal knowledge in ways that will switch on young indigenous minds to distinctive ways of observing and understanding the land and its plants and animals. Without the on-Country experience, building a distinctive indigenous human capital with the capability

---

88   Yibarbuk cited in M Langton, '"The Fire at the Centre of Each Family": Aboriginal Traditional Fire Regimes and the Challenges for Reproducing Ancient Fire Management in the Protected Areas of Northern Australia' (National Academics Forum: Proceedings of the 1999 Seminar, *Fire! The Australian Experience* 2000) 3, 7-8.

to follow indigenous paths of discovery seems a slim prospect. The principle of co-management of resources, which we discussed earlier in the context of the management of New Zealand's rivers, is a regulatory principle that opens the door to indigenous innovation.

The systems of indigenous innovation that are being developed on Country are a mix of old and new ways of working. The cosmological framework and the duties to Country that it imposes remain invariable, but obviously there are new tools and new networks to help in the execution of those duties — helicopters to reach the remotest areas to do burning, software and data management technologies to help organise the detailed observational knowledge of Country, and networks with scientists and research institutions. Quietly some indigenous communities in Australia's north are building new capabilities with which to drive their innovation system. In chapter two of this book, David Claudie, Susan Semple, Nicholas Smith and Bradley Simpson show what is possible when indigenous innovators and scientists, each with their own path to discovery, build a common network and join their paths at the level of testing and observation. If indigenous people want to bring their innovations to markets beyond their customary ones, the networked cooperation between indigenous innovators and scientists described by Claudie, Semple, Smith and Simpson will be important.

But this also means that the locus of indigenous innovation will have to shift into a network where there are non-indigenous participants who do not see the world in terms of cosmological connectionism, at least not of the kind subscribed to by indigenous peoples. In chapter three, Jen Cleary shows that that is a frightening prospect for indigenous peoples. The participatory action research method she describes is a tool for forging these broader networks in ways that enhance indigenous peoples' chances of achieving respectful cooperation.

Much of the land controlled by Aboriginal people is characterised by ecological intactness and high biodiversity value.[89] The practical problem facing indigenous communities in many places is that their innovation takes the form of services to the land that have clear public good benefits in terms of biodiversity, and environmental and climate values that are difficult to turn into income streams. Biological diversity, for example, has an economic value. Importantly, it is the stock of biodiversity, rather than individual plants, that is the source of this value.[90] Maintaining that stock is precisely the area of innovation in which indigenous systems excel. However, patent and plant variety protections

---

89   J C Altman, G J Buchanan and L Larsen, 'The Environmental Significance of the Indigenous Estate: Natural Resource Management as Economic Development in Remote Australia' (Discussion Paper No 286, Centre for Aboriginal Economic Policy Research, 2007) 24 <http://caepr.anu.edu.au/>
90   T Swanson and S Johnston, *Global Environmental Problems and International Environmental Agreements: The Economics of International Institution Building* (Edward Elgar, 1999) 65.

allow only for the extraction of economic value from a particular product that meets the criteria of these systems (for example, the criteria of patentability for an invention). If market-based solutions to public good problems cannot be found, then the standard move is to argue that government must pay for the provision of these goods. This means government making income transfers to indigenous people for providing environmental services. This, of course, means that government must be willing to meet the fiscal and political cost of making those transfers.

So far we have been talking as if IP has no or little role in the support of indigenous innovation systems. However, this is not our position. As Tony Taubman has pointed out, the benefits of using conventional IP mechanisms to protect indigenous knowledge should not be overlooked.[91] What IP can or cannot do for a given indigenous community is always context dependent. All the chapters in this book suggest that IP pathways to development might be organically constructed to suit the circumstances of a given indigenous community. However, the experience of indigenous peoples in Australia and New Zealand suggests that for the benefits of IP to be fully realised, particular conditions need to be met. The most crucial condition is progress on land rights. Once indigenous groups recover control of place, the process of creating networks to take care of place can begin. Once indigenous groups have networks in place, they can begin to enrol other actors and networks into their own to assist innovation that respects their institutions of cosmological connectionism. Chapter two in essence describes the evolution of this model of innovation. In chapter four, Daniel Robinson also provides examples of how indigenous and non-indigenous researchers can join together as an innovation network.

It is also clear from the Australian and New Zealand experience that indigenous peoples will have to work with existing institutions of IP. As we saw at the beginning of this chapter, the Australian High Court has signalled that a native title system of IP is not likely to form part of the common law's recognition of native title rights and interests. Similarly in New Zealand, the recommendations of the Waitangi Tribunal on the 262 claim signal an integrative approach of reasonable reform of IP rights over traditional knowledge. Its summary of its recommendations concerning the controversial issue of IP regulation of biological resources is emblematic of its general approach: 'All the reforms we recommend in this chapter can operate within the existing frameworks around bioprospecting, GM, and IP.'[92]

---

91  A Taubman, 'Saving the Village: Conserving Jurisprudential Diversity in the International Protection of Traditional Knowledge' in K E Maskus and J H Reichman (eds), *International Public Goods and Transfer of Technology Under a Globalized Intellectual Property Regime* (Cambridge University Press, 2005) 521, 534.
92  WAI 262, above n 4, 210.

Modest incremental reform will not please everyone, but in chapter nine Miranda Forsyth suggests that new model laws may not solve very much and may open the door to destructive political contests amongst indigenous communities. Perhaps an implication of her argument is that more problems may be solved by bargaining in the shadow of imperfect IP laws than by attempting to radically rewrite them. The dissatisfied critic might reasonably reply that indigenous groups do not have enough bargaining power to secure the outcomes they want. But to some extent rules can be written that increase the negotiating power of indigenous groups when it comes to the use of their knowledge assets. The law, by creating veto rights over the use of such assets in certain circumstances, forces a negotiation that would otherwise not have occurred. The recommendations of the Waitangi Tribunal move in this general direction. For example, the Tribunal recommends the creation of a Māori Committee to work with the Commissioner of Patents on patent applications that affect Māori interests. The Tribunal also recommends the creation of a disclosure obligation for patent applicants where they have used Māori knowledge or species, with the possibility of patent invalidity for non-disclosure. Building these kinds of veto rights into IP law means that real risks attach to not entering into a process of negotiation with indigenous groups. States that are interested in fostering indigenous development networks should look to regulatory strategies that provide incentives for outsiders to negotiate with indigenous groups, and that give indigenous groups some bargaining power in those negotiations. A negotiation is an opportunity for trust to form between the parties, and it is deep trust, as Jen Cleary suggests, that will be needed in collaborations between indigenous and non-indigenous innovators.

Broadly speaking, IP rights can be divided into those that confer origination rights over a product (for example, patents and plant variety protection) and those which confer rights to distinguish a product in commerce (for example, trade marks, certification marks and geographical indications). Taken together, the chapters in this book suggest that indigenous peoples are most likely to build IP development pathways using systems that confer rights to distinguish their product in the marketplace. For reasons that Daphne Zografos Johnsson outlines in chapter seven, these systems do not offer indigenous groups comprehensive protection. They were, after all, not designed by them, but emerge out of capitalist economies. Still, the rise of ethical consumerism offers the possibility of linking products and services of indigenous innovation with consumers who are willing to pay a premium for those services and products. Every day millions of consumers around the world pay more for products that bear the fairtrade certification mark of the Fairtrade Labelling Organizations International because the mark represents a system made up of standards and fairtrade prices aimed at promoting the sustainable development of poor producers in developing countries. The evolution of this system in the context of protected agricultural markets and complex multinational supply networks is a remarkable story.[93] Along similar lines, one can imagine consumers being willing to pay for products produced on Country under indigenous fire management practices that helped to reduce Australia's carbon emissions.[94] In chapter five Christoph Graber and Jessica Lai draw together the lessons from the failure of Australia's national certification scheme for indigenous products, and present the case for why a globally recognised certification scheme might be the way forward.

The use of geographical indications (GIs) in the context of indigenous innovation is perhaps less obvious, given that they are less flexible than voluntary certification systems. But in chapter six Daniel Gervais builds an eloquent case for the possibilities. If GIs are to have a Foucaldian moment of creation in which they truly serve the indigenous collective, then it will have to be along the lines for which he argues.[95] In chapter eight Michael Blakeney reminds us of the hard geo-political trade reality of IP. He shows the connections between the EU agenda on GIs and its broader trade agenda on agriculture. His chapter is also a reminder that so much IP standard-setting now takes place in the crucible of trade agreements — a crucible that is hard for indigenous groups to penetrate and influence. One wonders, for example, whether Australia's trade negotiators consulted indigenous people in the context of the US–Australia Free Trade Agreement.

This opening chapter has suggested that a commodity regime like the patent system does not fit particularly well with innovation in systems that characterise much of indigenous innovation. For example, the techniques of indigenous fire management have a wide range of ecological benefits, including the reduction of carbon emissions through the reduced severity of late-season savannah fires in Northern Australia.[96] Capturing the value that these techniques generate depends more on government catalysing carbon markets in ways that allow for indigenous participation than it does on one indigenous group embarking on the fruitless task of trying to gain a monopoly over a method of burning

---

93 For an excellent account see A Hutchens, *Changing Big Business: The Globalisation of the Fair Trade Movement* (Edward Elgar, 2009).

94 For a study that examines the possibilities of fair trade in Australia see M Spencer and J Hardie, *Indigenous Fair Trade in Australia: Scoping Study* (Rural Industries Research and Development Corporation Publication No 10/172, 2011).

95 However, developing a GI requires the networked engagement of governmental actors. For a case study that shows the intensive networking demands of GIs see D Rangnekar, 'Geographical Indications and Localisation: A Case Study of Feni' (Research Report, Economic and Social Research Council, The University of Warwick, 2009). A GI system can have a lock-in effect when it comes to traditional methods of production, acting as an incentive against innovation. See W van Caenegem, 'Registered Geographical Indications: Between Intellectual Property and Rural Policy — Part I' (2003) 6 *Journal of World Intellectual Property* 699. See also S Frankel 'The Mismatch of Geographical Indications and Innovative Traditional Knowledge' (2011) 29(3) *Prometheus* 253.

96 For a full discussion of the benefits see Russell-Smith et al, above n 73.

that has been collectively practised by indigenous people in Australia for thousands of years. Moreover, in the unlikely event that a single group was able to persuade a busy patent examiner in the Australian patent office that this really was an invention and not part of the prior art, the grant of such a patent would be the worst possible outcome for both indigenous and non-indigenous Australians. Other indigenous groups would ask why one group should gain a monopoly over techniques that had been collectively developed and practised by indigenous people for such a long time. The patent system is a winner-take-all system that has huge potential to divide indigenous communities. Daniel Robinson's discussion of biopiracy in chapter four shows how the patent system struggles to maintain standards of novelty and inventiveness that meaningfully engage with innovation. Some indigenous people may, of course, want to take advantage of these low standards to obtain patents for themselves, but they are likely more often than not to be the victims rather than the beneficiaries of the patent system's low standards.

Perhaps the most important thing for indigenous innovation is to make 'indigenous innovation' rather than traditional knowledge the primary term of art in this field. Then policy-makers would have to start asking how they might support indigenous innovation, as opposed to dividing the spoils from traditional knowledge. Answering that question would lead to others. How might we encourage collaboration between cosmologically anchored indigenous networks and scientific networks? How might we intervene in the IP system to increase the bargaining power of indigenous innovators? What can we do to turn indigenous networks into development networks? One suspects this approach would lead to a more testing but ultimately richer world for science, and a better world for indigenous people in which they would gain the respect that comes from being seen as innovators.

# 2. Ancient but New: Developing Locally Driven Enterprises Based on Traditional Medicines in Kuuku I'yu Northern Kaanju Homelands, Cape York, Queensland, Australia

David J. Claudie, Susan J. Semple, Nicholas M. Smith and Bradley S. Simpson

## 1. Introduction

Since European arrival, indigenous peoples of Australia have suffered from the effects of chronic social, political and economic disadvantage. The statistics on health outcomes and life expectancy remain tragic and unacceptable. Data published in 2008 indicates that indigenous Australians have a life expectancy some 17 years lower than the national average, are hospitalised at twice the rate of non-indigenous Australians, and are twice as likely to report high or very high levels of psychological distress.[1] The social disadvantage of indigenous peoples is reflected in low rates of literacy and school completion, and high rates of unemployment, violence, suicide, drug abuse and imprisonment.[2]

Disruption of traditional law and governance systems, disempowerment, denial of land rights and forced removal of people from their traditional country or homelands are recognised as important factors contributing to poor health and welfare outcomes for indigenous peoples.[3] Some indigenous writers have highlighted the importance of relationships with land and its associated natural resources to indigenous health and wellbeing.[4]

Through sustainable indigenous natural resource management and development on their homelands, the Chuulangun Aboriginal Corporation, the organisation

---

1 B Pink and P Allbon, *The Health and Welfare of Australia's Aboriginal and Torres Strait Islander Peoples 2008* (Australian Bureau of Statistics, Australian Institute of Health and Welfare, 2008).
2 Ibid.
3 B Carson and T Dunbar et al (eds), *Social Determinants of Indigenous Health* (Allen & Unwin, 2007); N Watson, 'Implications of Land Rights Reform for Indigenous Health' (2007) 186 *Medical Journal of Australia* 534.
4 D Rose, *Nourishing Terrains. Australian Aboriginal Views of Landscape and Wilderness* (Australian Heritage Commission, 1996); G Phillips, *Addictions and Healing in Aboriginal Country* (Aboriginal Studies Press, 2003) <http://search.informit.com.au/documentSummary;dn=989261116787858;res=IELHSS>

driving the research described in this chapter, is working to improve social and economic outcomes for the Kuuku I'yu Northern Kaanju families it represents. It is also seeking to gain wider recognition by mainstream agencies of indigenous management and governance structures. Research on the medicinal and aromatic plants of the Kuuku I'yu[5] is one aspect of the corporation's overall natural resource management plan.

In this chapter we describe our approach to medicinal plant research (incorporating both indigenous and Western scientific perspectives) and some of the issues around this field of research. We include the perspectives of particular Kuuku I'yu families living on homelands through the traditional owner and chair of the Chuulangun Aboriginal Corporation (David Claudie) and scientists in ethnobotany (Nicholas Smith) and ethnopharmacology (Susan Semple and Bradley Simpson). We envisage that culturally appropriate development of medicinal plant products will contribute to improved opportunities for Kuuku I'yu people to live and work on homelands. This will also allow younger people to engage with and learn about natural resources on their homelands, and provide an alternative to life in centralised townships. For university-based researchers, this project has provided a unique opportunity to work closely with indigenous traditional owners in the study of their medicinal plants, and to learn about the uses and stories associated with these plants, and traditional understandings of the ways these plant medicines work. Furthermore, the project has allowed Western scientific investigation of the medicinal actions and components of a number of plant species for the first time.

## 2. Kuuku I'yu Homelands, Traditional Governance and the Chuulangun Aboriginal Corporation

The Kuuku I'yu Northern Kaanju homelands are centred on the upper Wenlock and Pascoe Rivers in Central Cape York Peninsula, Queensland, and encompass an area of approximately 840,000 hectares (Figure 1). Kuuku I'yu people living on these homelands recognise the traditional Aboriginal law and governance system for this 'Country'. In this system the Country is divided into different clan estates (named *Ngaachi*), each tied to a particular 'bloodline' or family[6] and to a particular traditional 'story'.[7] For the Northern Kaanju people living

---

5   The term 'Kuuku I'yu' is used throughout this paper as a shortened form for 'Kuuku I'yu Northern Kaanju'.
6   B Smith and D Claudie, 'Developing a Land and Resource Management Framework for Kaanju Homelands, Central Cape York Peninsula' (Discussion Paper 256, Centre for Aboriginal Economic Policy Research, The Australian National University, 2003).
7   D Claudie, '"We're tired from talking": The Native Title Process from the Perspective of Kaanju People Living on Homelands, Wenlock and Pascoe Rivers, Cape York Peninsula' in B Smith and F Morphy (eds), *The Social Effects of Native Title: Recognition, Translation, Coexistence. Research Monograph No. 27* (Centre for Aboriginal Economic Policy Research, The Australian National University, 2007) 91.

at Chuulangun on Kuuku I'yu Ngaachi, indigenous cosmology ties land, flora, fauna and people. The landscape was shaped by ancestral beings or 'stories' that left law (or governance) and language.

**Figure 1. Kuuku I'yu (Northern Kaanju) Ngaachi (homelands).**

Source: Chuulangun Aboriginal Corporation.

These Ngaachi or homelands have a huge diversity of flora and fauna, including several rare, threatened and endangered species.[8] As the traditional owners, the Kuuku I'yu people have a broad and in-depth knowledge of the ecology of these homelands and their associated natural resources. This knowledge includes information about the identification and description of species and habitats, and detailed knowledge of their uses for a variety of purposes including foods and medicines, species behaviour and distribution, seasonal variation, the effects of fire, and sacred information. Kuuku I'yu people also have their own system of natural resource management based on traditional governance systems.[9] 'Management', to Kuuku I'yu people, means the interwoven complex of ownership, use and nurturance inherent in Aboriginal peoples' relationship to the Country.[10]

In 2002, the descendants of a focal[11] Kuuku I'yu ancestor who were living on homelands at Chuulangun formed the Chuulangun Aboriginal Corporation under the Commonwealth Aboriginal Councils and Associations Act 1976 — an Act recently superseded by the Corporations (Aboriginal and Torres Strait Islander) Act 2006 (Cwealth). The corporation can be described as a contemporary extension of traditional governance structures.[12] The 'bloodlines' that tie people to different tracts of land are the foundation of indigenous governance, knowledge, land tenure and land management. This philosophy drives the Chuulangun Aboriginal Corporation in its efforts towards sustainable land management, ecological and socio-cultural restoration, and the reaffirmation of indigenous knowledge across the Kuuku I'yu Ngaachi.

To facilitate this development the corporation has developed a comprehensive land and natural resource management plan in keeping with traditional responsibilities to Country.[13] Key goals include:

- reaffirming Kuuku I'yu governance, land and resource management, and decision-making on Northern Kaanju homelands;

- protecting the indigenous and natural heritage values on Northern Kaanju homelands for the benefit of current and future generations of Kuuku I'yu people;

- supporting Kuuku I'yu people to re-occupy their homelands on a more permanent basis;

---

8   M Crisp, S Laffan et al, 'Endemism in the Australian Flora' (2001) 28(2) *Journal of Biogeography* 183; Smith and Claudie, above n 6.

9   Smith and Claudie, above n 6; B Smith, '"We got our own management": Local Knowledge, Government and Development in Cape York Peninsula' (2005) 2 *Australian Aboriginal Studies* 4.

10   Chuulangun Aboriginal Corporation, 'Kaanju Homelands Wenlock and Pascoe Rivers Indigenous Protected Area Management Plan' (Chuula, Cape York Peninsula, Queensland, 2005).

11   Focal ancestor here refers to an apical ancestor, that is, an ancestor who is at the apex of a lineage and from whom the members of a descent group trace their descent.

12   Claudie, above n 7.

13   Chuulangun Aboriginal Corporation, above n 10; Chuulangun, 'Kaanju Ngaachi Wenlock and Pascoe Rivers IPA Management Plan 2011-2017' (prepared by the Chuulangun Aboriginal Corporation with the assistance of funding from the Commonwealth IPA programme, Chuulangun, Cape York Peninsula, Queensland, Australia, 2011).

- facilitating the intergenerational transfer and maintenance of traditional knowledge and Northern Kaanju language;
- developing and operating homelands-based community enterprises that incorporate sustainable land management principles;
- developing homelands-based projects, education and training that will improve the capacity and self-esteem of Kuuku I'yu people and the wider community, and lead to meaningful employment which is culturally linked;
- incorporating, where appropriate, traditional knowledge with Western scientific processes to provide beneficial outcomes for natural and cultural resource management policy and practice.

Since 2008, part of the KuukuI'yu homelands has been recognised as an Indigenous Protected Area (IPA) under the National Reserve System.[14] This was the first IPA declared in Cape York. Under this programme, the Chuulangun Aboriginal Corporation is supported by government to manage a large part of the Kuuku I'yu Northern Kaanju Ngaachi for conservation.

The Kuuku I'yu Northern Kaanju medicinal plants project described in this chapter forms just one part of the overall programme of homeland activities developed by the Chuulangun Aboriginal Corporation.[15] However, this project seeks to contribute to a number of the key goals listed above. These include impacts on the development of homelands-based community enterprises, sustainable use of resources, training, improved self-determination and self-esteem for Kuuku I'yu people, the incorporation of Western scientific approaches, and the transfer and preservation of traditional knowledge. Furthermore, through this project the corporation seeks to add to discussions at the national and international level around the development of improved mechanisms to ensure the protection of the cultural and intellectual property of indigenous peoples.

To understand some of the innovation of the approach to this research, it is important to describe the context in which the majority of Western scientific research on medicinal plants used in traditional medicine is conducted.

---

14   Australian Government Department of Environment, Water, Heritage and the Arts, Kaanju Ngaachi Wenlock and Pascoe Rivers Indigenous Protected Area (2008) <http://www.environment.gov.au/indigenous/ipa/declared/kaanju.html>
15   Information on other activities can be found at the Chuulangun Aboriginal Corporation website, <http://www.kaanjungaachi.com.au>

# 3. 'Use' of Traditional Medicinal Plant Knowledge by Western Science

Traditional knowledge about medicinal plants has long been recognised as a useful guide for scientists working in the Western tradition concerned with the discovery of new medicines.[16] There are many examples of Western medicines that have their origins in plants used in traditional medicine: the painkillers morphine and aspirin, the anti-malarial medicine artemisinin, the anti-cancer agent teniposide, and the cardiac medicine digoxin. In recent years there has also been a growing trend amongst the general population in Western countries, including Australia,[17] towards using herbal and other 'natural' medicines (sometimes termed complementary medicines[18]). Many of the widely used herbal medicines have long histories of traditional use: echinacea (from Native American medicine), ginseng and ginkgo (from Asian medicine systems, including traditional Chinese medicine) and pygeum bark (used by traditional healers in Africa). Consequently, there has been, and continues to be, considerable interest in the Western scientific investigation of plants used in various systems of traditional medicine.

The fields of Western scientific research concerned with the study of traditional uses and pharmacological activities of plants include ethnobotany and ethnopharmacology. Ethnobotany involves the examination and documentation of the relationships between plants and traditional peoples,[19] including the uses of plants for purposes such as medicines. Ethnopharmacology is a multidisciplinary field that has been defined as the description of plants and other natural resources used in traditional medicine, and the scientific investigation of their medicinal activities and chemical constituents.[20] This research has primarily been undertaken with the goal of discovering new medicines or understanding the actions and efficacy of traditional medicine through the lens of Western scientific enquiry.

In the last decade, authors in the *Journal of Ethnopharmacology* (the major international journal for the field) and other publications have examined the

---

16   D Fabricant and N Farnsworth, 'The Value of Plants used in Traditional Medicine for Drug Discovery' (2001) 109 *Environmental Health Perspectives* 69.

17   A H MacLennan, S P Myers et al, 'The Continuing Use of Complementary and Alternative Medicine in South Australia: Costs and Beliefs in 2004' (2006) 184(1) *Medical Journal of Australia* 27.

18   Complementary medicines include a variety of medicinal substances including plant (herbal) medicines, homeopathic medicines, aromatherapy oils, dietary supplements, and vitamins and minerals. See Expert Committee on Complementary Medicines in the Health System 'Complementary Medicines in the Australian Health System' (Report to the Parliamentary Secretary to the Minister for Health and Ageing, Canberra, Commonwealth of Australia, 2003). The word 'complementary' is used to indicate that these are medicines and practices used outside of mainstream Western medical care, but that may complement it.

19   C Cotton, *Ethnobotany. Principles and Applications* (Wiley, 1996).

20   L Rivier and J Bruhn, 'Editorial' (1979) 1 *Journal of Ethnopharmacology* 1.

definitions, roles and future of ethnopharmacology.[21] In their critical review of the field, Etkin and Elisabetsky have highlighted that much of what is published as ethnopharmacological research focuses only on Western scientific understandings of traditional medicinal plants. They argue that research in this field often consists of published lists of traditional medicinal plants tested in a laboratory for a particular medicinal activity (such as anti-bacterial activity) and examination of the constituents of the plants with particular activities to identify the active components. While most of this is scientifically rigorous research, it fails to address the social and political implications of the findings. Very little of this research reflects an interest 'in the people whose knowledge and identity are embodied in these plants' or offers any insights into the experiences of these people 'in specific cultural and eco-political settings'.[22]

When one examines the drivers of ethnopharmacological and ethnobotanical research and the authors of published papers on this research, the overwhelming majority are scientists working in universities, other scientific research institutions or pharmaceutical companies. For the most part they, along with their institutions, are also the beneficiaries of this research (in terms of grants, publications, patents or new products).[23]

Over the past decade there has been increasing international recognition of the need for scientists and companies working in the field of medicinal plant research to ensure that indigenous communities benefit from the investigation and development of their traditional medicinal knowledge and to develop models for the equitable sharing of benefits of this research.[24]

While benefit-sharing agreements are certainly a step in the right direction, we argue that there is a need to further develop models of research on medicinal plants that is locally initiated and driven by indigenous peoples as part of their

---

21   M Heinrich and S Gibbons, 'Ethnopharmacology in Drug Discovery: An Analysis of its Role and Potential Contribution' (2001) 53 *Journal of Pharmacy and Pharmacology* 425; N Etkin and E Elisabetsky, 'Seeking a Transdisciplinary and Culturally Germane Science: The Future of Ethnopharmacology' (2005) 100 *Journal of Ethnopharmacology* 23; A Jäger, 'Is Traditional Medicine Better Off 25 years Later?' (2005) 100 *Journal of Ethnopharmacology* 3; International Society for Ethnopharmacology, 'Editorial' (2006) 6(1) ISE Newsletter 1.
22   Etkin and Elisabetsky, above n 21.
23   D A Posey, 'Commodification of the Sacred Through Intellectual Property Rights' (2002) 83 *Journal of Ethnopharmacology* 3; D Marinova and M Raven, 'Indigenous Knowledge and Intellectual Property: A Sustainability Agenda' (2006) 20 *Journal of Economic Surveys* 587; M Kartal, 'Intellectual Property Protection in the Natural Product Drug Discovery, Traditional Herbal Medicine and Herbal Medicinal Products' (2007) 21 *Phytotherapy Research* 113.
24   S King, T Carlson et al, 'Biological Diversity, Indigenous Knowledge, Drug Discovery and Intellectual Property Rights: Creating Reciprocity and Maintaining Relationships' (1996) 51 *Journal of Ethnopharmacology* 45; Carson and Dunbar, above n 3; M Guerin-McManus, K Nnadozie et al, 'Sharing Financial Benefits: Trust Funds for Biodiversity Prospecting' in S Laird (ed), *Biodiversity and Traditional Knowledge. Equitable Partnerships in Practice* (Earthscan, 2002); D D Soejarto, C Gyllenhaal et al, 'The UIC ICBG (University of Illinois at Chicago International Cooperative Biodiversity Group) Memorandum of Agreement: A Model of Benefit-Sharing Arrangement in Natural Products Drug Discovery and Development' (2004) 67 *Journal of Natural Products* 294.

own planning for sustainable natural resources management and economic development. Furthermore, indigenous peoples need to have the rights and legal mechanisms to protect their own cultural and intellectual property.

It is now widely recognised that projects in indigenous communities that are locally run, locally owned and culturally relevant will deliver more meaningful outcomes. However, most research on traditional Australian indigenous medicinal plants has been, and continues to be, driven and published by scientists working in the Western tradition.[25] They may have drawn on published information about indigenous peoples' knowledge, or have used information provided by indigenous people who are otherwise bystanders in the actual research processes. We argue that those engaged in research on medicinal plants need to move beyond using indigenous peoples as 'informants'. Indigenous peoples must become researchers, and share in the benefits of research.

# 4. The Kuuku I'yu Northern Kaanju Medicinal Plants Project

## (a) Traditional Owners 'Driving' Research

The remoteness and biodiversity and natural heritage significance of the Kuuku I'yu homelands have been the subject of considerable research interest over many years. Numerous papers, theses, books, reports and museum artefacts are devoted to aspects of the indigenous people and their homelands. More recently, however, many Kuuku I'yu traditional owners have been reluctant to participate in research. This is due largely to the past experience of Kuuku I'yu elders who took part in research activities initiated by 'outsiders', and shared their language and traditional ecological knowledge with them, but felt they received very little in return for their efforts. Today, traditional owners continue

---

25  M Pennacchio, Y Syah et al, 'Cardioactive Iridoid Glycosides from Eremophila Species' (1997) 4 *Phytomedicine* 325; SJ Semple, GD Reynolds et al, 'Screening of Australian Medicinal Plants for Antiviral Activity' (1998) 60(2) *Journal of Ethnopharmacology* 163; K Rogers, I Grice et al, 'Inhibition of Platelet Aggregation and 5-HT Release by Extracts of Australian Plants Used Traditionally as Headache Treatments' (2000) 9 *European Journal of Pharmaceutical Sciences* 355; E A Palombo and S J Semple 'Antibacterial Activity of Traditional Australian Medicinal Plants' (2001) 77(2-3) *Journal of Ethnopharmacology* 151; M Pennacchio, A Kemp et al, 'Interesting Biological Activities from Plants Traditionally Used by Native Australians' (2005) 96 *Journal of Ethnopharmacology* 597; J E Smith, D Tucker et al, 'Identification of Antibacterial Constituents from the Indigenous Australian Medicinal Plant Eremophila duttonii F. Muell. (Myoporaceae)' (2007) 112(2) *Journal of Ethnopharmacology* 386; A Tan and D Sze, 'Indigenous Herbs and Cancer' (2008) 7(1) *Journal of Complementary Medicine* 48. This includes some work undertaken previously by the current author, Susan J Semple, based on plants with published traditional uses.

to be concerned that some research activities (including the collection of plants and animals for study in universities and other institutions) are taking place on their homelands without their knowledge or consent.

The diverse natural resources of Kuuku I'yu homelands and the detailed traditional ecological knowledge held by its people represent a huge opportunity for the Chuulangun Aboriginal Corporation to address issues of social disadvantage, economic hardship and loss of connection amongst their people, and to sustain them into the future. To achieve this, the Corporation has taken actions to ensure that the people now initiate, manage and benefit from research on and about their homelands.

David Claudie, chair of the Chuulangun Aboriginal Corporation, has undertaken to 'research the researchers'. This has included a comprehensive literature search and review of published papers and other unpublished materials produced by 'outside' researchers about Kuuku I'yu homelands and associated resources. This has allowed traditional owners to better understand what research has already been undertaken on their land, and to direct development of further programmes of research.

The Corporation has also developed guidelines and protocols that must be observed by outsiders wanting to undertake research on Kuuku I'yu homelands and with Kuuku I'yu people. These guidelines emphasise the need for research projects to be collaborations underpinned by Memorandums of Understanding, and with the aim to protect Kuuku I'yu intellectual property (IP) rights and involve traditional owners as 'initiators and full collaborators in research'.[26]

As part of their land and natural resource management planning,[27] the Corporation has developed priority areas for research which will facilitate development of Kuuku I'yu homelands, while still allowing traditional obligations to the land to be met. Some of this research is being conducted by Kuuku I'yu people themselves, whilst other research has required strategic partnerships with outside agencies such as government, universities and non-government organisations.

## (b) Starting the Medicinal Plants Project

Development of a locally driven management plan for natural resources enabled relevant Kuuku I'yu traditional owners to invite Western scientific collaborators to work with them in areas they had prioritised in terms of their traditional

---

26   Chuulangun Aboriginal Corporation, above n 13.
27   Ibid.

medicines and aromatic plants. Moreover, traditional owners were able to work as collaborating researchers in the research process itself, rather than being 'stakeholders' or 'informants' and bystanders to the actual research process.

Nick Smith had been working with the corporation for two years, documenting and mapping plant species on Kuuku I'yu Northern Kaanju homelands with traditional owners. Other university-based researchers at the University of South Australia were invited to join the team, based on their experience in testing and analysing medicinal plants and medicinal product development.

## (c) Project Aims

Discussions between Kuuku I'yu and university-based researchers before starting the project examined the aspirations of Kuuku I'yu people in respect of the study and development of their traditional medicinal plants. University-based researchers provided advice on the types of laboratory investigations that would be feasible and the legislative requirements for plant-based medicines to be sold as medicinal plant products. Key objectives for the research were formulated. These included:

- investigation of extracts from medicinal plant species to assist community members to determine opportunities for developing economic enterprises based on sustainable use of plant products;
- investigation of the chemical composition and toxicology of the plant extracts demonstrating the most interesting pharmacological activities as determined by the research team;
- providing opportunities for Kuuku I'yu and university-based researchers and students to visit different research sites (homelands and university);
- supporting Kuuku I'yu elders to engage with younger people on homelands, and help transfer language and medicinal plant knowledge to younger generations through the harvesting of plant material and preparation of traditional plant extracts for the project;
- dissemination of information about research processes and findings through collaborative publications between Kuuku I'yu and university-based researchers.

## (d) Establishing Ways of Working — Kuuku I'yu Traditional Knowledge in the Project and How It May Be Used

Before starting the project, participants planned how they would work together. This included discussion of the key issues of how Kuuku I'yu traditional knowledge about plants should be used, and how this cultural and intellectual property should be protected.

For Kuuku I'yu people, knowledge of the ecology of their traditional homelands is based on many thousands of years of empirical observations and sustainable land and resource use and management. This knowledge has been passed down through particular Kuuku I'yu bloodlines to the current generation of traditional owners, managers and lawmakers living on homelands. Underlying this immense body of knowledge is a cosmological world view in which Kuuku I'yu people 'belong' to the land and are under the management of ancestral beings that formed the land and its associated resources. These ancestral beings are also the 'source' of particular knowledge.

There are rules for management and use of this traditional knowledge. For instance, some knowledge is freely available (public knowledge), some knowledge and information belongs to the realm of the restricted (sacred knowledge), and other knowledge and information falls into a category between public and sacred. Further, Kuuku I'yu governance and cosmology determine who can have access to knowledge. That is, only authorised persons can have access to sacred knowledge and can decide how it is used.

Only certain people have access to medicinal plant knowledge and are authorised to use such knowledge. This knowledge includes the uses of a particular plant, the location(s) where the plant should be collected, the maturity of the plant and the time of year at which it can be used, how the plant product is harvested, how the medicine is prepared, and how and to whom the medicine may be administered. Understanding who speaks for the land and who is authorised to use knowledge about the plants is critical to the working of the medicinal plants project. These authorised people decide what knowledge is appropriate to be shared in the project, how it is used, which medicines may be tested in the laboratory and what they may be tested for.

## (e) Collaborative Research Agreement

It was central to our research that a clearly negotiated collaborative research agreement must be in place before commencement of the project. This agreement had to ensure the protection of indigenous IP, confidentiality, and a mechanism for benefit sharing if any commercialisation results from the jointly generated project IP. The agreement had to allow Kuuku I'yu law and custom to dictate how traditional knowledge would be used in the course of the project, and for traditional owners to maintain control over any decisions to proceed with commercialisation of IP.

The Chuulangun Aboriginal Corporation and university-based researchers worked together to produce a research collaboration and IP agreement. The agreement incorporated relevant aspects of standard agreements between the University of South Australia and industry partners, but required special recognition and protection of the cultural and intellectual property of Kuuku I'yu participants and culturally appropriate ways of working. Drafts of the IP agreement were shared, with each party making comments and contributions to define their understanding of each of the following project areas:

- work and funding commitments;
- protection of indigenous cultural and IP rights;
- confidentiality;
- publication of research findings;
- ownership and utilisation of IP generated through the project.

The final agreement was reviewed and approved by the Human Research Ethics Committee of the University of South Australia.

Relevant documents such as the National Health and Medical Research Council (NHMRC) 'Values and Ethics: Guidelines for Ethical Conduct in Aboriginal and Torres Strait Islander Health Research'[28] and general guidelines for responsible research practice[29] were considered by the research team in the drafting of the agreement. However, the emphasis was on recognising members of the Chuulangun Aboriginal Corporation as drivers of the research process and as researchers in their own right. This meant that while it was necessary to comply with national research guidelines, local indigenous lore also dictated how the project would be conducted. The NHMRC Guidelines are based on six key values which the team agrees are crucial to the conduct of collaborative research between universities and Aboriginal peoples — namely 'Spirit and Integrity; Reciprocity; Respect; Equality; Survival and Protection; Responsibility'.[30] However, the guidelines talk about 'researchers' or the 'research community' on one hand and 'Aboriginal and Torres Strait peoples' on the other. For our team, the Aboriginal people represented by the Chuulangun Aboriginal Corporation are also the researchers.

A summary of the some key aspects of this negotiated collaborative agreement is given in Box 1.

---

28 National Health and Medical Research Council, 'Values and Ethics: Guidelines for Ethical Conduct in Aboriginal and Torres Strait Islander Health Research' (Commonwealth of Australia, Canberra, 2003).
29 National Health and Medical Research Council and Australian Vice Chancellors' Committee, 'Joint NHMRC/AVCC Statement and Guidelines on Research Practice' (Australian Government, Canberra, 1997).
30 Above n 28.

---

**Box 1. Key Aspects of the Collaborative Project Agreement**

- Recognition of the values of traditional knowledge is central to the research project.

- Kuuku I'yu people's participation will bring to the project valuable IP in the form of traditional knowledge about plants of cultural significance. This background IP remains in the ownership of traditional owners and is fully acknowledged in the allocation of any new IP generated through the project.

- Cultural and intellectual property of traditional owners is treated as confidential information that will not be disclosed to any third party.

- Indigenous law and custom govern how background IP will be used during the course of the project.

- Traditional owners will undertake plant collections for the project in accordance with the rights of certain people to prepare medicines under customary law.

- New IP developed through the project (such as findings of laboratory-based testing and chemical analysis) is jointly and equally owned by Chuulangun Aboriginal Corporation and the University of SA.

- Decisions to commercialise any aspects of project IP will require the consent of both parties. Both parties will work together in making decisions about the processes of any commercialisation.

- There will be an emphasis on joint publication of research findings by both university-based and Kuuku I'yu researchers contributing to relevant aspects of the work.

---

# (f) Approaches to Activities Undertaken in the Project

## (i) Collection of plant materials

Collection and preparation of plant materials to be laboratory tested in the project took place during collaborative field work involving both university-based researchers and Kuuku I'yu researchers. Only traditional owners with authorisation could prepare traditional medicines, lead the field work to collect the plant materials, or instruct other researchers on what and where to collect it. Inappropriate collection by the wrong person, collecting the wrong plant or entering the wrong part of the Country to collect it would be seen by traditional owners to make the medicine either not work or to do harm. Traditional owners say that the medicinal plant needs to 'pass through our hands' to work in the correct manner. In the past, this has been a source of concern for traditional owners when 'outsiders' have collected plants from homelands for testing in laboratories without their knowledge or consent.

Western scientific disciplines such as ethnobotany and ethnopharmacology require the use of voucher specimens of plants. Voucher specimens are reference specimens for a particular plant collection that are usually archived in a nationally recognised institution such as a state herbarium. This ensures the specimen is available to other members of the scientific community, and that the specimen is maintained and curated appropriately. Publication of the results of Western scientific research on medicinal plants in reputable peer-reviewed journals requires that a voucher specimen has been lodged and that the unique voucher number is published. In our project we have lodged voucher specimens for all the collections with herbaria. However, the public availability of these voucher specimens does present some issues for traditional custodians of the plants. When lodging the specimen for our study, some information about the plant was restricted and no information about traditional uses was recorded on the specimen. Specimens were linked to the particular clan estates on which they were collected, and the rightful traditional custodian of the plant was recorded as the plant collector. However, once specimens have been lodged in a herbarium, it is currently difficult for traditional owners to maintain control over what happens to them. Our research team is concerned that most herbaria can split up voucher specimens, make duplicates and then exchange or swap these with overseas institutions. While material transfer agreements may be signed, these do not seem to consider the issues of concern to indigenous people. Once the specimens have been sent overseas, they become the property of the overseas institution and it has control over them, and third parties may be able to access the genetic resources of these samples. It seems specimens lodged in most Australian herbaria can also be sampled (for example, for bar-coding of genetic information) as long as the process is not 'destructive' (that is, so long as the specimen is not destroyed or parts of the specimens such as flowers go missing).

## (ii) Preparation of plant materials

Kuuku I'yu people working in the project have emphasised that preparation of a traditional medicine is something that takes time and care to do properly. If one takes pride in the work and the appearance of the final medicine, this shows respect to the plant and to the ancestors who passed knowledge about it to the current generations. The way the plant material is harvested and prepared for extraction, and the actual water used to prepare the extract, are seen by Kuuku I'yu researchers as essential in ensuring the medicine has the desired effect when tested in the project (Figure 2).

**Figure 2. Preparation of a plant for the study according to traditional methods.**

Photo: S. Semple.

Where possible, traditional medicinal preparations have been prepared by traditional owners as part of the project for testing in the laboratory. In most cases these are prepared by boiling or soaking the plant material in water. This ensures that the components of the plant tested in the laboratory are those that would be present in the actual traditional medicine.

In some cases, the method of traditional use presents a challenge for laboratory testing. Some of the plants used in Kuuku I'yu traditional medicine are not prepared as water extracts; rather, the plant part is crushed and administered directly to the affected part of the body. For example, one plant researched in the study is used as a pain-relieving and anti-inflammatory medication for the mouth, with the plant material chewed and inserted directly onto an inflamed or infected tooth. Another small herb is used as a wound treatment by dabbing the juice from the stem or fleshy roots directly onto the affected area of the skin. In these cases, laboratory testing (which requires some kind of extract of the plant to put into the testing models) cannot directly mimic the traditional use. Discussions among the researchers concluded that the best approach to testing these types of plants was to transport the plant material to the laboratory, and to use laboratory solvents (such as alcohols) which will extract such a broad range of components from the plant that they should include those components released with the direct application.

Another aspect of the project has been an examination of essential oils from some of the aromatic plants that grow on Kuuku I'yu homelands. Essential oils are the volatile components of plants. These are often complex mixtures of components that contribute to a plant's characteristic smell and taste. In a Western scientific approach, essential oils are usually produced through steam distillation of plant material to produce a concentrated oil extract.

Obviously, distillation of essential oils is not among the traditional plant extraction methods. However, Kuuku I'yu people have traditionally recognised the value of the volatile components of some of their plants. For example, vapours inhaled from crushed leaves have been used for the relief of common cold symptoms, and particular scented plants have been used as 'love potions' to attract members of the opposite sex. Kuuku I'yu people also have knowledge of the content of the aromatic oils in different plants in different locations of their homelands, as well as the optimal time or season to harvest plant materials. The Chuulangun Aboriginal Corporation sees distillation of essential oils on homelands as a feasible means of generating income and local jobs. Essential oils and products made from them (such as soaps and skin lotions) may form the basis of small-scale businesses.

The distillation of essential oils has been undertaken on the homelands as part of the project. This has allowed Kuuku I'yu and university-based researchers to work together in examining yields of oils from different plant materials, the characteristics of the extracted oils, and the feasibility of the oil-distillation process on homelands (Figures 3a and 3b).

**Figure 3a. Plant collection for essential oils distillation on Northern Kaanju homelands.**

Photo: N. Smith.

**Figure 3b. Plant testing for essential oils distillation on Northern Kaanju homelands.**

Photo: N. Smith.

## (iii) Laboratory investigations of plant extracts

The focus of laboratory testing has been to examine activities suggested by the traditional uses of the plant. For example, plants that have uses for treating infected skin sores have been tested in the laboratory for activity against common bacteria that cause skin infections, and plants used to treat skin irritation or mouth afflictions have been tested for effects against inflammation. However, it is important to emphasise that Kuuku I'yu people involved in the project do not see indigenous knowledge as something that is static or 'stuck in the past'. Rather, they say that the 'old people' would have needed to adapt their knowledge to new challenges that confronted them, including new diseases. For this reason, relevant Kuuku I'yu traditional owners in the project feel it is appropriate for university-based researchers to test the traditional medicinal plants against a range of illnesses that confront indigenous and other Australians in modern society, such as diabetes, viral infections, cancer and antibiotic-resistant bacteria, as well as conditions that reflect the more traditional uses. They want broader recognition of the value of their medicines and the role they can play in maintaining health among both indigenous and non-indigenous people.

To date, the laboratory testing has been focused around three main areas. First, plant extracts including essential oils have been tested for activity against micro-organisms (including bacteria, yeasts and viruses) that cause human diseases such as skin, oral, respiratory and gastrointestinal infections. This testing has also included examination of activities against bacteria resistant to many of the modern antibiotics used in Western medicine. Some extracts have been tested in a model of skin inflammation. Discovery of extracts that can modulate inflammatory processes could play a role in management of a number of medical conditions for which inflammation is an important component, such as eczema, rheumatoid arthritis, cardiovascular disease, inflammatory bowel disease and some kinds of cancer. Anti-cancer testing, using cancer cells from a variety of cancer types such as skin, breast, lung and gastrointestinal cancers, has also been conducted on plant extracts. In the future it is planned to expand the testing to other areas of interest such as mental illness, diabetes, insect repellency and parasitic diseases.

Visits to the university-based laboratories by Chuulangun Aboriginal Corporation chair David Claudie were used to assist traditional custodians of the plants in understanding what was actually being done with the plant extracts in the laboratory (Figure 4). However, the distance between Adelaide in South Australia and central Cape York (and the expense of travel) has presented challenges in getting more Kuuku I'yu people to experience laboratory work first hand. In the future we hope to establish a small homelands-based laboratory and extraction facility that will allow some more of the Western scientific research and extraction processes to be conducted on the actual homelands, with university-based and Kuuku I'yu researchers working together.

**Figure 4. Chuulangun Aboriginal Corporation Chair David Claudie with Susan Semple at UniSA laboratories in Adelaide.**

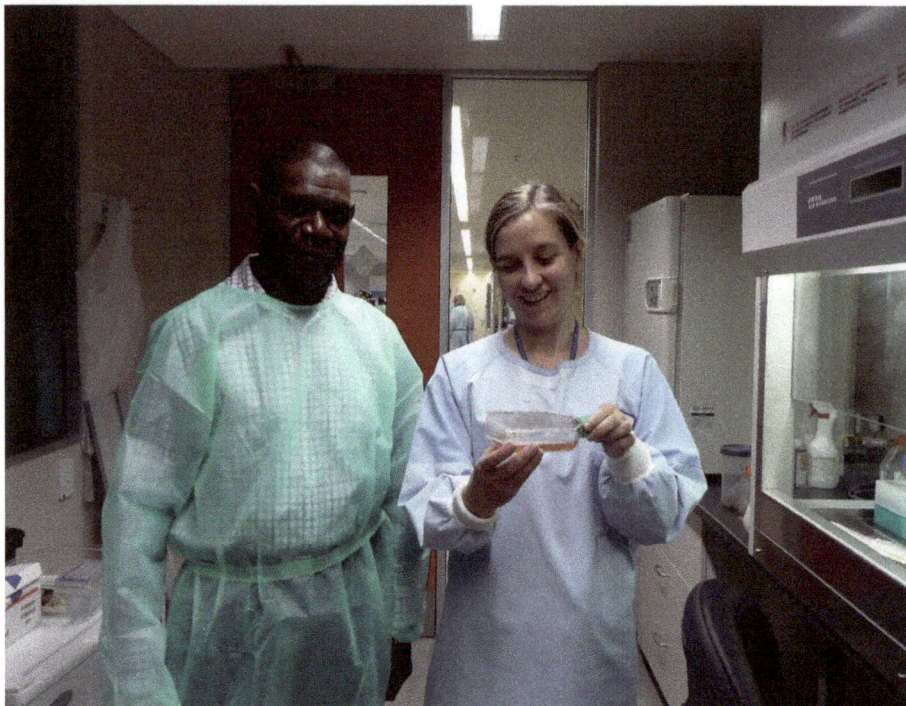

Photo: S. Semple.

Various extracts that have demonstrated the most promising activity in the laboratory-based testing have been subjected to chemical analysis techniques to work out what active components are present in them.

## (g) Project Findings and Moving Towards Plant-based Enterprises

This project has had the important aim of identifying plant species with potential for development as plant-based products that can support homelands-based development. A number of the plant species chosen for laboratory testing by the research team have demonstrated activities which reflect traditional understandings of these plants. These serve as examples of the way in which Western science and Australian indigenous science and culture may come to the same finding. Our experience so far with one of these plant species is described below.

# 5. Uncha (*Dodonaea polyandra*): An Example Case Heading Towards Commercialisation — And an Ongoing Learning Experience

## (a) Traditional Use and Western Scientific Investigation

Uncha (*Dodonaea polyandra*, Sapindaceae) is a plant species used for medicinal purposes by particular Kuuku I'yu traditional owners (Figure 5). Knowledge about the plant is passed through the patrilineal bloodline. The plant is used traditionally to decrease pain and discomfort in the mouth from toothache and infection.

**Figure 5. Uncha (*Dodonaea polyandra*).**

Photo: N. Smith.

The plant was first collected for our project as part of field work on Chuulangun homelands in 2006. Based on traditional uses, the team decided to undertake laboratory-based tests for anti-inflammatory, antibacterial and cell-toxicity effects. Traditionally the plant material (the join of leaf and stem) is applied directly to the mouth. For testing in laboratory models, the team made ethanolic (alcohol) extracts of leaf and stem to extract a range of the plant's chemical constituents that would otherwise be released directly if the plant was chewed or crushed. Both leaf and stem extracts showed significant activity in a model of skin inflammation (conducted by Dr Jiping Wang at the University of South

Australia). The comparable effects in this model were with the known anti-inflammatory medicine hydrocortisone (available in over-the-counter anti-inflammatory skin creams).

Further chemical analysis of the extracts has been undertaken as part of a PhD project by Bradley Simpson. This part of the study has led to the isolation of several compounds which are responsible for the anti-inflammatory effects of the extract in the laboratory model. Some of the purified compounds performed similarly to a potent (prescription) anti-inflammatory drug called betamethasone in the testing model. These components isolated from the plant are 'new' to Western science but related to other compounds known to exist in other species in the genus *Dodonaea*. The most active compounds are from a class called furano-clerodane diterpenoids. The actions of the components of *Dodonaea polyandra* are of course not 'new' to the particular Kuuku I'yu traditional owners who have used this plant medicinally for generations.

## (b) That's All Very Interesting — But Now What?

While compound isolation and identification from plants is no trivial task, in some ways the research to this point was the easy part, in that there were (and are) clear guidelines and methods for the conduct of such research. The next steps were (and continue to be) in some ways the most challenging. We now need to negotiate the pathway to getting a potential commercial outcome that can create enterprises on Kuuku I'yu homelands and bring benefits back to the Chuulangun Aboriginal Corporation.

### (i) Commercial partners and patenting

To develop medicinal plant products that can be sold widely (and that make therapeutic claims) it is necessary to meet the requirements of the Therapeutic Goods Act 1989 and regulations, and to seek approval from the Therapeutic Goods Administration in Australia (and similar agencies in other countries). The levels of evidence for the safety and efficacy of any new product entering the market require a great deal of research and hence financial support. Therefore, to progress to a commercial product it is almost inevitable that a commercial partner will have to be involved. University researchers are also under considerable pressure to publish the findings of the research to meet the needs of PhD candidature, to develop track records for further funding applications to support the work, and to demonstrate external review of the research which is important in satisfying the requirements of potential funders of commercialisation.

In 2009 the research partners decided to proceed with patenting the project IP related to their findings on the Uncha plant, and in November 2009 two provisional patent applications were filed. The first of these covered an extract and extraction process for the Uncha plant. The second covered the compounds themselves and likely derivatives for anti-inflammatory applications. These two applications were considered appropriate to allow different streams of product development, including herbal extract products or products containing the isolated components. The Chuulangun Aboriginal Corporation and the University of South Australia are joint applicants (owners) of the patent applications, and in November 2010 the applications moved to the Patent Cooperation Treaty (PCT) phase. All patent costs so far have been borne by the university's commercialisation company, ITEK (a wholly University of South Australia-owned company).

The team is also exploring the use of trade marks to identify extracts as belonging to the Chuulangun Aboriginal Corporation and sourced appropriately from the Kuuku I'yu Northern Kaanju homelands.

A number of common medical conditions involve inflammation. Anti-inflammatory applications therefore have potential in a variety of areas, including cosmetic uses, over-the-counter herbal complementary medicine products and conventional pharmaceuticals (isolated compounds or derivatives), and some potential commercial partners have already been identified. Cosmetic applications are likely to be the first commercial uses for the extracts.

Our wish is to maximise IP in the project by conducting as much research as possible in the university and on the homelands before linking with a commercial partner. The decision to file the patent applications was not taken lightly but was considered as our best option at the time. The patent process as it stands is far from ideal for this type of work. Filing of the applications allows the research to be published, but now sets a tight timeline (18 months) before the patents move to the 'national phase' of the application, where costs escalate rapidly. At the national stage we may need to have a third party on board to help pay for the upcoming patent costs, because the university commercialisation arm may not be able to support this specification in the absence of external funding and significant progression of the technology into a market-ready product. As a team we may need a long-term perspective on this. For our first products, we may need to take partners on earlier, with a view to eventually creating our own spin-out company with a pipeline of products. In the future we may be able to maintain more of the research in-house and maintain patents on other extracts to a later development stage.

## (ii) Issues around patenting and IP protection for the Chuulangun Aboriginal Corporation

This patenting process has raised other issues besides those of costs and timelines. Patents do not allow 'ancestors' or whole clan groups to be named — only 'inventors' according to a narrow definition. While the Chuulangun Aboriginal Corporation can be an owner on the patent, their ancestors or clan group as a whole cannot be named as the inventors. Traditional owner preference would also be to patent plants from the particular area. While it may be possible to genetically map plants to particular areas and patent extracts from them, a pharmaceutical commercial partner buying the right to use the IP covered by the patent may want to ensure it is covered for extracts from the species generally so no one else can produce what it perceives as the 'same' product. Additionally, patenting allows protection of IP only for a defined period of time.

Article 31 of the United Nations Declaration on the Rights of Indigenous Peoples (UNDRIP) states the right of indigenous peoples to 'maintain, control, develop and protect' their sciences, including medicines and botanical resources.[31] While still an aspirational document, rather than a treaty or law, the UNDRIP highlights the rights of indigenous peoples to maintain their own institutions, traditions and cultures, and the right to develop their economic and social needs and aspirations as a group. The Convention on Biological Diversity (CBD) is the major international convention that recognises the ownership of traditional knowledge by indigenous communities and therefore the right to protect this cultural and intellectual property. The CBD also highlights the need to preserve the knowledge of indigenous communities that can contribute to the conservation and sustainable use of biodiversity. However, a number of limitations of the CBD for indigenous peoples have been discussed, particularly the authority given to nation states to make agreements in relation to access to natural resources and benefit-sharing agreements. These may undermine the rights of indigenous peoples.[32]

In our experience, the current patent system places too much emphasis on the value of the novel and inventive steps from a Western scientific perspective. Indeed, inventors are defined from this perspective. The limited timeframe of protection is also problematic for traditional custodians who have held their knowledge over generations. If indigenous peoples are to protect their sciences, including medicines, as stated in the DRIP, new legal mechanisms need to be developed to allow them to do this 'from their side'. The Chuulangun Aboriginal Corporation is currently exploring options for legal changes in Australia that

---

31    United Nations Declaration on the Rights of Indigenous Peoples, (UNDRIP).

32    D Harry and L Kanehe, 'The BS in Access and Benefit Sharing (ABS): Critical Questions for Indigenous Peoples' in B Burrows (ed), *The Catch: Perspectives on Benefit Sharing* (Edmonds Institute, 2005) <http://www. ipcb.org/publications/other_art/bsinabs.html>

may be required to ensure that medicinal plant knowledge can be protected and to formalise their traditional knowledge of plant properties as the IP of the Kuuku I'yu Northern Kaanju people. While some aspects of 'cultural knowledge' are hard to define to outsiders, the knowledge of a plant species or population, the properties it affords and the preparation required are fairly concrete, and the Corporation believes such knowledge could and should be legally protected.

Australia's Native Title Act 1993[33] establishes a framework for the protection and recognition of native title over land and waters. In the native title case of *Western Australia v Ward*,[34] the High Court found that native title law did not extend to protecting cultural knowledge from misuse. To do so would extend it beyond the control of access to land to the control of access to cultural knowledge, in what the court considered to be a 'new species of intellectual property'. However, this is what the Chuulangun Aboriginal Corporation believes its people need if they are to ensure that their knowledge can be used for the benefit of the world of medicine and for their own economic benefit, and on their terms. From the Corporation's reading of it, the Act should afford these protections. The Corporation is currently seeking advice on whether reforms to Australia's Native Title Act may help in achieving protections, or whether legal reforms to IP laws are needed instead.

At a local level, the Chuulangun Aboriginal Corporation is planning to form a body representing the IP of the Kuuku I'yu people to arrange and distribute commercial benefits, decide on commercial use, investigate misuse and oversee research collaborations.

## (c) Supply and Sustainability Considerations in Product Development

Central to the vision of the medicinal plants project is the development of plant-based products to foster development on Kuuku I'yu Northern Kaanju homelands. This in turn would offer opportunities for employment, financial independence and increased self-esteem, particularly for younger Kuuku I'yu Northern Kaanju people. If sustainable plant-based products are to be developed, the sustainable harvest or production of plant materials on the homelands will be crucial.

In discussions with potential commercial partners, issues surrounding the supply of plant extracts and compounds have been raised as matters of high priority. A suggestion by some commercial operators that cultivation and harvesting of plant material in some kind of established horticultural facility

---

33   *Native Title Act 1993* (Cth).
34   *Western Australia v Ward* (2002) 191 ALR 1.

away from the homelands could overcome supply issues is not acceptable to our research team. The holder of the plant knowledge is attached to the plant by a 'story'. These holders of knowledge are individuals within clan groups. Under traditional law, growing the plant elsewhere for the natural resource that is known to Kuuku I'yu is not an option. It would cause problems for both the grower and the holder of the 'story'. We need to make sure that traditional governance systems are respected and that issues of plant supply can be met in a culturally appropriate manner. The timelines of the patenting process and need to have a commercial partner in place put considerable pressure on the team to ensure these issues are addressed quickly. As the research and commercial development moves into its next stage, there will be a need for on-ground research, led by relevant traditional owners on their homelands, to examine a range of sustainability issues. For each of the plant species that has commercial potential, including the Uncha plant, a variety of questions arise. These include questions such as:

- What quantities of plant materials can reasonably be harvested from plants growing naturally on Kuuku I'yu homelands?
- What impact would harvesting have on the number of these plants, and on other species (such as insects, birds, mammals) that depend on them?
- How quickly would the plants re-grow and when could they be re-harvested?
- Would it be feasible to cultivate the plant on homelands?
- Would plant materials obtained from cultivated plants have the same medicinal properties and components as those that are wild-harvested?
- What infrastructure and management structures need to be in place to allow a successful plant-harvesting and extraction enterprise to be developed on the homelands?
- How will issues of remoteness be overcome?

# 6. Conclusions

Our medicinal plants research project and journey towards development of locally driven enterprises based on traditional medicines in Kuuku I'yu homelands has raised, and continues to raise, a number of important issues. We believe that research of this type must be driven by indigenous traditional owners, and incorporate their own views of how their medicinal products should be researched and developed. Importantly, the project highlights inadequacies in current legal systems to support IP protection in work of this kind. There is a need for other mechanisms of indigenous cultural and IP protection which will be recognised and respected by potential commercial partners — not just an emphasis on the Western scientific aspects and their protection through patents.

A future in which Australian indigenous peoples' IP rights are recognised by the legal system is essential to traditional owners represented by the Chuulangun Aboriginal Corporation. With this in place, not only the Kuuku I'yu people but all Australians and people worldwide could benefit from 'new' medicines. Without it, Kuuku I'yu people's knowledge of medicines will be guarded closely to prevent IP 'theft' by unscrupulous companies.

## Acknowledgement

This project has been supported with funding from an Australian Research Council (ARC) Linkage Grant (LP0667713) and a National Health and Medical Research Council (NHMRC) Development Grant (APP1017556).

# 3. 'It would be good to know where our food goes': Information Equals Power?

Jen Cleary

## 1. Introduction

Wild or 'bush'[1] harvest of native desert species for consumption and customary trade has been actively pursued by Aboriginal peoples in central Australia for thousands of years.[2] Bush harvest for financial return has, by contrast, been occurring in central Australia for at least thirty to forty years[3] and is primarily undertaken by Aboriginal women in remote settlements.[4] However, to date, financial returns for these industry participants have been marginal. Harvesters have relied on the activities of non-Aboriginal traders (as they are known)[5] making buying trips to their communities, and this occurs in an ad hoc fashion, with little planning or advance notice.[6] This has created a situation where the women are entirely reliant on the traders in several ways: for market information, including the dynamics of product demand and in determining prices; and as sole buyers of their produce, which occurs via cash payments.[7] The women have stated that they are often unsure about what the traders will require from year to year, and have found that on some occasions they have harvested particular fruits and seeds only to find that there was no demand for them.[8] Added complexities include the harvesters' physical isolation from the market and a lack of transport and telecommunications — a common issue in remote Australia.[9]

---

1   Aboriginal harvesters in central Australia with whom the Desert Knowledge CRC has worked prefer the terms 'bush harvest' and 'bush food' when referring to native plants and their harvest, rather than 'wild harvest' or 'wild food', both of which infer that the plants are not cared for. M Ryder et al, 'Sustainable Bush Produce Systems: Progress Report 2004–2006' (DKCRC Working Paper No 31, Desert Knowledge CRC, Alice Springs, 2009).

2   K Akerman and J Stanton, *Riji and Jakoli: Kimberley Pearlshell in Aboriginal Australia Monograph Series 4* (Northern Territory Museum of Arts and Sciences, 1994).

3   G Miers, 'Cultivation and Sustainable Wild Harvest of Bushfoods by Aboriginal Communities in Central Australia' (Research Report, Rural Industries Research & Development Corporation, Canberra, 2004).

4   P Everard et al, *Punu: Yankunytjatjara Plant Use* (2nd ed, IAD Press, 2002).

5   See Ryder et al, above n 1.

6   J Cleary, 'Business Exchanges in the Australian Desert: It's About More than the Money' (2012) 7(1) *Journal of Rural and Community Development* 1.

7   Ibid.

8   J Cleary et al, 'Hands Across the Desert: Linking Desert Aboriginal Australians to Each Other and to the Bush Foods Industry' (Research Report, Desert Knowledge Cooperative Research Centre, Alice Springs, 2009).

9   Ibid.

Changing this situation of Aboriginal peoples' peripheral inclusion in the industry is one means of increasing broader Aboriginal participation in the Australian economy. Increased economic participation has been promoted as a means of decreasing disadvantage of Aboriginal peoples in Australia,[10] and there is thus considerable interest and activity directed at 'improving' the current situation. Attempts have been made in central Australia to increase the participation of remote Aboriginal peoples in the bush-foods industry through a variety of mechanisms, and with mixed results.[11] Most of these have been based on Western understandings of trade and commerce. To date, there has been little research undertaken on understanding the current ways in which Aboriginal peoples are already participating in the bush-foods industry, particularly those engaged in bush harvesting.[12]

The Desert Knowledge Cooperative Research Centre,[13] through its 'Bush Products from Desert Australia Core Research Project' situated within a programme of research entitled 'Thriving Desert Economies',[14] invested considerable resources in understanding and attempting to improve current participation rates by Aboriginal peoples. In part, this project helped researchers to understand the complex socio-cultural differences that exist between the Aboriginal harvesters and the rest of the bush-food supply chain in which they are situated. These differences relate to the 'two worlds' in which the women walk: the world of Western commerce, and their own cultural imperatives related to the harvesting of bush foods.

A critical factor in the 'two worlds' paradigm is the importance of the social and cultural context and dual knowledge systems within which industry participants are situated and operate.[15] For example, Aboriginal harvesters of fruit and seeds in the Northern Territory have articulated a range of reasons for harvesting: it is a customary activity associated with health and wellbeing; it helps to pass on traditional knowledge; and it is part of caring for Country — a cultural responsibility.[16] Since harvesting activities constitute only a small part of the individuals' income, all of these reasons are in addition to, and arguably

---

10   Families, Housing, Community Services and Indigenous Affairs, *Closing the Gap on Indigenous Disadvantage: The Challenge for Australia* (AGPS, 2009).

11   J Gorman et al, 'Assisting Australian Indigenous Resource Management and Sustainable Utilization of Species Through the Use of GIS and Environmental Modelling Techniques' (2008) 86 *Journal of Environmental Management* 104.

12   Ryder et al, above n 1.

13   The Desert Knowledge Cooperative Research Centre (DKCRC) was formed under the Australian Government Cooperative Research Centre Programme managed by the then Department of Innovation, Industry, Science and Research. DKCRC operated between July 2003 and June 2010.

14   DKCRC, *Legacy Website* <http://www.desertknowledgecrc.com.au>

15   Cleary, above n 6.

16   F Walsh and J Douglas (Alyawarr Speakers from Ampilatwatja), 'Angka Akatyerrakert: A Desert Raisin Report' (DKCRC, Alice Springs Australia 2009) <http://www.desertknowledgecrc.com.au/researchimpact/downloads/DKCRC_Angk-Akatyerr-akert_A-Desert-raisin-report.pdf>

override, the motive of financial return.[17] For these participants, harvesting is undertaken in the context of a world view which prioritises the importance of cultural traditions associated with kinship relationships and customary governance systems over economic participation. For non-Aboriginal and non-remote participants whose primary incomes are derived from the industry, participation is fundamentally for economic reasons and supported by a Westernised world view of what that means — a world in which negotiated relationships, rather than kinship relationships, are the norm. Understanding these differing perspectives is important, particularly at the nexus in bush-food supply chains where intercultural trade occurs. These perspectives impact upon the value attached to resource flows, financial return, relationships between chain participants, and, indeed, in considerations of the 'products' themselves as both cultural icons and commodities.

This chapter discusses a participatory action research (PAR) project undertaken with remote Aboriginal harvesters of katyerr[18] (*Solanum centrale*, bush tomato or desert raisin), entitled 'Information = Power: Walking the Bush Tomato Value Chain' (hereafter I = P project).[19] The chapter focuses on the participatory nature of the project and discusses the effectiveness of PAR as a methodological approach for negotiating the 'two worlds' paradigm. Further, it signals the importance of PAR as a methodological approach that can assist in navigating the complexities associated with intellectual property (IP) rights: for example, in understanding Aboriginal peoples' customary use rights around knowledge of bush plants and Western imperatives around efficiently defined IP rights. Developing governance systems for the commercial use of biological resources where there may be competing and/or complementary cultural and commercial imperatives around such resources is an urgent priority.

The chapter first grounds PAR in contemporary literature; provides background information on the I = P project; describes the activities undertaken within the project; and discusses the lessons from these in the context of the PAR literature. Following this, I reflect on my own learning as a participant in the project. Finally, the chapter provides recommendations on using PAR as a research approach in further bush-foods and bush-medicine research. This has relevance in the protection of Aboriginal ecological knowledge (AEK) in the context of the increasing commercialisation of native species. The chapter

17    Ryder et al, above n 1.
18    A number of different Aboriginal names in the central Australian desert region are also used for *Solanum centrale*, the fruit known commercially as 'bush tomato'. These include akatyerr, katyerr, akatyerre, katyerre, kampurarrpa, kampurarpa and jungkunypa. 'Bush tomato' is also known in non-commercial contexts as 'desert raisin.' The term 'katyerr' will be used here, except where otherwise explained, as a mark of cultural respect and as acknowledgement that it was the term consistently used by the Aboriginal participants during the course of the project being reported on in this chapter.
19    DKCRC, 'Information = Power: Walking the Bush Tomato Value Chain' (Project Proposal to NT NRM Board, Alice Springs, 2008).

highlights one example (plant breeder's rights) of some of the issues and challenges that could be associated with using this mechanism as a tool to protect AEK and IP rights.

# 2. Participatory Action Research

PAR is an approach to enquiry that attempts to incorporate the elements of both participation and action implied in the name. It is a process aimed at identifying a problematic social situation or existing phenomenon, understanding it, and then taking some action to rectify the problem, or changing the situation, with the active participation and intervention of the social actors who are the 'subjects' of the research. It attempts to integrate experience, action and reflection.[20] Reason describes two primary objectives in PAR: to produce both knowledge and action that is directly useful; and consciousness-raising (learning) that creates empowerment.

PAR as a research approach has its roots in research on social change in developing countries (particularly on colonised and oppressed peoples).[21] In the 1970s there emerged a growing and radical critique of social theory amongst those within the social science community (most particularly within the fields of sociology, anthropology, education and theology) engaged in research in the developing world. This critique related to academic insistence on value neutrality and its associated objectivity, plus academic rigour in the pursuit of science knowledge, when, simultaneously, social researchers were confronting situations of massive structural crises, oppression and social change related to increasing capitalism and modernisation in the developing countries with which they were engaged.[22] There resulted a move away from academic aloofness towards researchers taking personal positions that enabled them to take a new view of knowledge. Techniques were developed that allowed researchers to apply knowledge in social and political situations to effect transformation, and this led to the development of participatory methods of social inquiry.[23] Primary aims were to make knowledge more accessible to research 'subjects' and to help them to understand that knowledge could

---

20   P Reason, 'Human Inquiry as Discipline and Practice' in P Reason (ed), *Participation in Human Inquiry* (Sage Publications, 1994) 40.

21   P Freire, *Pedagogy of the Oppressed* (Herder & Herder, 1970); O Fals-Borda, 'Participatory (Action) Research in Social Theory: Origins and Challenges' in P Reason and H Bradbury (eds), *Handbook of Action Research* (Sage Publicatons, 2001) 27.

22   Fals-Borda, ibid.

23   Ibid.

be used as an instrument of power and control.[24] In recent times, PAR has been increasingly used in a number of fields of enquiry, including health, education, organisational change management and agriculture.[25]

PAR views social reality not as something pre-given or pre-defined but as something co-created.[26] Epistemologically speaking, PAR implies a methodological approach at the macro or 'stage-setting' level,[27] and that favours collaborative forms of enquiry as the means for gaining knowledge and applying it.[28] It is at once constructivist, dialogical and proactive, attempting to centralise participant and researcher values,[29] and falls most easily within the critical theory paradigm.[30] PAR can therefore be seen as a useful methodological approach to research questions of which differing knowledge systems and associated world views (for example, Western science and traditional ecological knowledge) are a feature, because it emphasises central participation in the research by people who are knowledgeable about the research topic from multiple perspectives, affected by it, and may wish to use the research to effect change.

There are numerous recent examples of PAR use in co-research between indigenous and non-indigenous peoples, both in Australia and internationally,[31] and it is an increasingly favoured approach with indigenous peoples in health research in particular.[32]

---

24 Freire, above n 21.

25 W F Whyte, *Participatory Action Research* (Sage Publications, 1991).

26 K Breu and C Hemingway, 'Researcher-Practitioner Partnering in Industry-Funded Participatory Action Research' (2005) 18(5) *Systemic Practice and Action Research* 437.

27 S Kidd and M Kral, 'Practicing Participatory Action Research' (2005) 52(2) *Journal of Counseling Psychology* 187.

28 P Reason, 'Sitting Between Appreciation and Disappointment: A Critique of the Special Edition of *Human Relations* on Action Research' (1993) 46(10) *Human Relations* 1253.

29 Kidd and Kral, above n 27.

30 Following J G Ponterotto, 'Qualitative Research in Counseling Psychology: A Primer on Research Paradigms and Philosophy of Science' (2005) 52(2) *Journal of Counseling Psychology* 126.

31 See, for example, E Tuck, 'Re-visioning Action: Participatory Action Research and Indigenous Theories of Change' (2009) 41 *Urban Review* 47; J Taylor et al, 'The Station Community Mental Health Centre Inc: Nurturing and Empowering' (2010) 10 *Rural and Remote Health* 1411; C de Crespigney et al, 'A Nursing Partnership for Better Outcomes in Aboriginal Mental Health, Including Substance Use' (2006) 22(2) *Contemporary Nurse* 275; J McIntyre, 'Yeperenye Dreaming in Conceptual, Geographical and Cyberspace: A Participatory Action Research Approach to Address Local Governance Within an Australian Indigenous Housing Association (2003) 16(5) *Systemic Practice and Action Research* 309; G A Getty, 'The Journey Between Western and Indigenous Research Paradigms' (2010) 2(1) *Journal of Transcultural Nursing* 5; G V Mohatt et al, 'Unheard Alaska: Culturally Anchored Participatory Action Research on Sobriety with Alaska Natives' (2004) 33(3-4) *American Journal of Community Psychology* 263; N B Wallerstein and B Duran, 'Using Community-based Participatory Research to Address Health Disparities' (2006) 7 *Health Promotion Practice* 312; and K Tsey et al, 'Indigenous Men Taking Their Rightful Place in Society? A Preliminary Analysis of a Participatory Action Research Process with Yarrabah Men's Health Group' (2002) 10(6) *Australian Journal of Rural Health* 278.

32 F Baum et al, 'Continuing Professional Education, Glossary: Participatory Action Research' (2006) 60 *Journal of Epidemiological Community Health* 854.

An important component of PAR is the positioning of the researchers as co-learners and facilitators, rather than as objective observers.[33] The emphasis is on collaboration and participation, rather than the detached perspective of objectivity associated with positivistic approaches. Carr and Kemmis describe three different aspects of the role of the researcher in PAR approaches—technical, practical or emancipatory — and that which is adopted is dependent on the nature and purpose of the research activity being undertaken.[34]

Under this schema, PAR differs significantly from other research approaches in that it is not extractive: that is, researchers are not 'experts' who study their subjects and then go away to write their papers. Rather they are co-participants, experiencing a problem situation or phenomenon in order to better understand it and to assist in changing it.[35] Participatory approaches have as an ideal the democratically negotiated processes between academics and other participants in the research.[36] One criticism of PAR relates to the balance of power in PAR and a legacy of colonialism in academic–indigenous research partnerships.[37] This colonial legacy (following Smith) privileges some knowledge types and the world view from within which such knowledge is formed, based on externally driven research and interventions. Power, and the challenge this presents to the democratic ideal of equal participation, is related to the level of influence different participants are able to wield in the research.[38] It is important to consider, therefore, the influence of externalities to the research, such as language (including whose language is used to discuss and formulate the research), research funding imperatives and the extent to which the proposed research sits within a broader institutional research framework or context.

## 3. Context to the I = P Project

I = P arose out of a Desert Knowledge Cooperative Research Centre (DKCRC) stakeholder consultation workshop held in Alice Springs in April 2007.[39] A number of bush-foods industry participants, both Aboriginal and non-Aboriginal, attended, including harvesters, growers, wholesalers, processors and retailers. The stated aim of the workshop was to seek guidance from

---

33  P Reason and H Bradbury, 'Inquiry and Participation in Search of a World Worthy of Human Aspiration' in P Reason and H Bradbury (eds), *Handbook of Action Research* (Sage Publications, 2001) 1.

34  W Carr and S Kemmis, *Becoming Critical: Knowing Through Action Research* (Deakin University Press, 1983).

35  Baum et al, above n 32.

36  L W Green et al, *Study of Participatory Research in Health Promotion: Review and Recommendations for the Development of Participatory Research in Health Promotion in Canada* (University of British Columbia: Royal Society of Canada, 1995).

37  L T Smith, *Decolonizing Methodologies: Research and Indigenous Peoples* (Zed Books, 1999).

38  M Cargo et al, 'Can the Democratic Ideal of Participatory Research Be Achieved? An Inside Look at an Academic-Indigenous Community Partnership' (2008) 23(5) *Health Education Research* 904.

39  DKCRC, above n 19.

participants about the direction of proposed research to be undertaken by DKCRC in its 'Bush Products from Desert Australia' core project.[40] Workshop participants endorsed the adoption of a value-chain approach,[41] but also determined that the research should be participatory, and focus primarily on katyerr as a high-demand desert product in the bush-foods industry. Katyerr is also highly significant for its spiritual importance, featuring in the Dreaming stories of many desert Aboriginal peoples.[42]

Participants believed that understanding the social context of the supply/value chain must precede any operational changes.[43]

The participants outlined a number of different personal values related to bush food during the course of the workshop. These values 'related to the importance of bush foods as an industry and an integral part of Indigenous livelihoods'.[44] Participants articulated values related to community and land and the recognition of cultural values: for example,

> future for kids; good healthy food; health food [for] colds; keep it strong for the young people; it's where we come from; land management; we need to live with the land; management of the land; integrity of the food related to Aboriginal values and the land; recognition of where it comes from.[45]

Other value statements related to the growth and development of the bush-foods industry and benefits for individuals, and included:

> It's my livelihood; exciting new and growing industry; economic — work hard; it's a catalyst for creating economies; self-sufficiency; independence; ownership.[46]

Participants clearly expressed values that demonstrated the importance of bush food both commercially and culturally. This can be summed up in the statement:

---

40   Ibid.

41   The value chain concept was first described by Michael Porter, see M Porter *Competitive Advantage* (The Free Press. New York, 1985) 11 and encompasses a chain of activities undertaken within firms or more broadly at the industry level where each activity in the chain adds value to a product as it moves from supplier to the market. Value chain analysis has become an accepted, useful, contemporary tool for determining where competitive advantage can be generated for the actors within value chains, particularly in the agri-industry sector, see K Bryceson and C Smith, 'Abstraction and Modelling of Agri-food Chains as Complex Decision Making Systems' (Proceedings of the EAAE Conference on 'System Dynamics and Innovation in Food Networks' Innsbruck-Igls, Austria, February 18-22, 2008). The bush-food industry can be classified as part of this sector.

42   P Latz, *Bushfires and Bushtucker: Aboriginal Plant Use in Central Australia* (IAD Press, 2005).

43   Hassall and Associates Pty Ltd, 'Value Chain Workshop Notes for Desert Knowledge CRC' (Report no. AU1-517, DKCRC, Alice Springs, May 2007).

44   Ibid, 3.

45   Ibid.

46   Ibid.

...[the] challenge lies in recognising that bush foods cross two cultures (economic and Indigenous) and needs [sic] to deliver values to both.[47]

Among the workshop participants was a group of remote Aboriginal women from a settlement approximately 270 kilometres north-east of Alice Springs, in the Northern Territory, who were invited to attend because of their involvement in the bush-foods industry as bush harvesters. These women made a number of comments[48] related to better understanding the movement of the katyerr they picked on their land after the fruit left their community. One woman said, '*It would be good to know where our food goes.*' This statement was pivotal to both the rationale for the subsequent development of I = P, and in formulating the activities undertaken within the project. As will be seen in the discussion section of this chapter, it was also pivotal in terms of the 'two worlds' paradigm of bush foods, and the various understandings and positions brought to the project by its participants.

Following the workshop, the DKCRC successfully sought funding from the Northern Territory Natural Resources Management Board to undertake the I = P project, which articulated its broadest aim as enabling the bush harvesters to 'see where their food goes'.

Along with the initial group from the stakeholder meeting, one other woman expressed her interest in being part of the I = P project. She was not involved in bush harvesting but, together with her partner, operated a small commercial katyerr plantation where fruit was harvested by hand. The project participants also included two representatives from a reference group[49] established to guide bush-harvest research in the broader Bush Products Core Project. In all, there were twelve project participants, including me and other research and supporting team members. The group determined that a physical journey, following katyerr to various (commercial) destinations beyond central Australia, would be a useful way of understanding where the fruit went, how it was used and who used it.

# 4. The Project

Ethical considerations were paramount in conducting this project. Researchers were mindful of the need to ensure it was conducted within Western regulatory

---

47 Ibid.

48 Comments were made through an interpreter, because English is not a primary language for this group of women.

49 Merne Altyerr-ipenhe (Food from the Creation time) Reference Group was established to guide bush-harvest research activities. It comprised respected Aboriginal women recognised as cultural custodians of bush-harvest knowledge, some of whom were also bush-food industry participants.

frameworks for human research, and also to ensure the project met Aboriginal participants' needs and expectations in this regard. While Western frameworks are aimed at protecting research participants, including Aboriginal peoples, the DKCRC also produced a set of specific research protocols[50] developed by remote Aboriginal desert peoples and used consistently across the life of the CRC. The project was conducted in accordance with these protocols, and also obtained ethics approval from the Central Australian Human Research Ethics Committee (CAHREC).[51] CAHREC is a committee of the Northern Territories Department of Health, and considers both health and non-health research involving Aboriginal peoples in the Northern Territory. It does this through its Aboriginal Committee, whose primary aim is to protect Aboriginal peoples in the Northern Territory in the conduct of research, and to ensure Aboriginal peoples benefit from such research.[52] The committee, which aims to span all major language groups in the Northern Territory, includes at least one male elder and one female elder among its all-Aboriginal members, as well as at least one person with research experience in non-health related research.

Following approval, the project team met at a workshop in Alice Springs in July 2008, during which the bush harvesters discussed the project and outlined what they currently knew about what happened to the katyerr they picked for sale. This session incorporated both talking and drawing, enabling participants (some of whom have English as a second or third language) to express their knowledge both verbally and pictorially. It provided the baseline observations of these participants about their knowledge prior to undertaking the journey. I noted that each of the women's drawings included clearly marked direction indicators, establishing where they were currently in relation to their home community. The activity also enabled the research team to fully explain their position as researchers and facilitators, and to talk about what they might do after the project: for example, writing about the project, and making a DVD and picture story boards so that other Aboriginal women engaged in harvesting activities might learn more about the market aspects of katyerr. In accordance with DKCRC research protocols, media release forms giving permission to film and take photographs of project activities were explained and completed by participants. Researchers undertook to ensure that any such materials would be available for review by all participants before being released more generally, and this was done at the completion of the project.

---

50 DKCRC, *Aboriginal Research Engagement Protocol Template* (DKCRC, Alice Springs, 2006).

51 Central Australian Human Research Ethics Committee, 'Walk the Value Chain: Information Equals Power' (Ethics approval letter, 14 July 2008).

52 Northern Territory Government, *Central Australian Human Research Ethics Committee, Policy and Procedures Manual* <http://www.health.nt.gov.au/library/scripts/objectifyMedia.aspx?file=pdf/12/26. pdf&siteID=1&str_title=CA HREC Policies and Procedures.pdf>

Immediately following the workshop, we travelled to the Sunshine Coast (via Brisbane) in Queensland. On arrival at the airport in Brisbane, the harvesters asked where they were in relation to their home communities, and spent some time establishing the direction in which those communities lay and the distance they had travelled. This was the first major journey many of the harvesters had made by air, and it seemed important for them to establish exactly where they were in relation to where they had come from.

We then travelled by road to the Sunshine Coast, where we met with an Aboriginal woman who operates a restaurant and catering business. We were officially 'welcomed to Country', as is customary between Australian Aboriginal peoples visiting locations beyond those with which they have immediate cultural ties. This business operator specialises in the use of bush foods, and participants experienced a commercially prepared bush-foods meal, the main course of which featured katyerr. For many of the harvesters, this was a new experience of bush food, prepared in quite a different way from the traditionally prepared bush food they were familiar with. Following the meal, the harvesters were able to share with the entire group their stories of bush food, using a series of photographs and story boards which had been prepared by members of the project team during earlier research with the bush harvesters. The harvesters appeared particularly animated and excited during this part of the visit, and were very keen to talk about who they were, where they came from and how they harvested bush food. In reviewing the subsequent video footage, I also noted that there was considerable discussion among the harvesters in their own language. They also pointed out the children and grandchildren in the story boards and talked about how important it was to 'keep the knowledge strong' with these young people. The harvesters also made a point of asking about the origin of the katyerr prepared in the meal they had eaten. The business operator explained that she bought it from her supplier, but that she wasn't sure from which part of central Australia it had started its journey.

After an overnight stay in Maroochydore, the group flew to Melbourne, Victoria. Again, on arrival the harvesters spent time establishing where they were in relation to their home communities. In Melbourne, the group visited a number of non-Aboriginal owned and operated commercial entities associated with bush food. These included a processing factory, a distribution business and a large supermarket.

At the processing factory, we were shown through the processes associated with preparing, cooking, bottling, labelling and packaging various bush foods for sale and distribution. The women were interested in learning about these various processes, but one incident in the factory stood out in my review of the video footage. When the harvesters viewed large bags of raw product that had been received at the factory from various suppliers around Australia, they were highly animated and keen to know from where the bags had originated. Comments included, '*Maybe this* [wattleseed, *Acacia* spp.] *came from [community name] near us? Those ladies have been picking lots of this.*' There was also much interest in unfamiliar (non-desert) products, and the women wanted to know who picked it, where it grew and how it got to the factory.

The group met with members of a distribution company which managed the movement of finished products from the factory to retail outlets. The company presented information about the importance of continuity of supply as a requirement for maintaining shelf-space of finished products at supermarkets. My review of the video footage indicated that there appeared to be lower levels of interest in this part of the activity. I noted that the presentation of information was quite abstract, and did not include any specific place-based references.

At a large supermarket, the group saw the finished products on the shelves. The harvesters expressed high interest in the variety of products available and, again, interest in where it had originated.

The group attended an up-market restaurant in the heart of Melbourne that features bush food as an integral part of its menu. This restaurant is owned and operated by an Aboriginal woman who described herself as the traditional owner of land in the Melbourne region. She welcomed us to her Country and provided some history and context about her family and about her business, and served a multi-course meal that featured bush foods. I noted (with some amusement) the various visual expressions of some of the harvesters as they tasted some items on the menu. Some of the dishes were clearly appealing, but some were perhaps removed from the women's expectations of what they would (or should) taste like.

The final activity undertaken by the harvesters was to redraw their understandings of 'where their food goes', based on the journey they had made. Again I noted the clearly marked direction indicators on the maps drawn by participants. The maps were not drawn in the usual abstract manner common in geography textbooks — that is, with 'north' at the top of the page, 'south' at the bottom, and 'west' and 'east' to the left and right respectively. Instead, the maps were drawn in relation to the direction the drawer was oriented. For example, one participant was facing south, and so drew her map with 'south' at the top of the map and 'north' at the bottom.

## 5. Project Outcomes

In all, the physical journey occupied one week. It provided many opportunities for learning, both on the part of the harvesters and for me. The harvesters were able to articulate a greater understanding of 'where their food goes', and this was evidenced in discussions and, particularly, in pictorial representations completed at the conclusion of the project. There is also evidence that, as a result of undertaking the journey and forming new relationships with others in the supply chain, the harvesters have subsequently made some changes in the way in which they sell their fruit. In some cases, they are selling more directly into the chain, and are initiating these transactions themselves, rather than relying on traders making buying trips to their communities. It is likewise evident that they have increased their returns via these transactions, and are receiving higher payments than previously.

## 6. Discussion

In an earlier section of this chapter, I highlighted a comment made by a participant in an early stakeholder workshop: '*It would be good to know where our food goes.*' In this section I want to reconsider that statement and the multiple meanings that have emerged in light of deeper understandings developed as a result of participating in the I = P Project.

From a Western perspective of participation in the bush-foods industry, there is a tendency to see the current participation of remote Aboriginal peoples as marginal, in that financial returns to this group are not high. The assumption is that increasing participation and knowledge of the Westernised view of commerce and what it entails, and the imperative to decrease costs and increase profit, is universally desirable. Using a supply or value-chain framework to examine participation and to work towards increasing economic participation is a logical extension of this thinking. In the context of the I = P project, both my interpretation and understanding of the comment '*It would be good to know where our food goes*' and the broader goals of the DKCRC 'Bush Products from Desert Australia' core project were framed by this thinking. From that position, the I = P project, and my role as co-researcher, could be seen to encompass the 'technical' aspects of participatory action research outlined by Carr and Kemmis.[53] Indeed, this is how I saw my role — as a facilitator in promoting learning that would increase the 'technical' capacity of the harvesters to participate in the bush-foods industry. I interpreted the harvesters' comment to mean that if they knew where 'their' food went, what happened to it (in relation to how others

---

53    Carr and Kemmis, above n 34.

value-added to it), who profited and why, they would then come to see that there could be opportunities for them to play a greater role in the value-adding process. Importantly, I also assumed that this was a shared interpretation. I also understood that increasing the harvesters' capacity to develop more direct relationships with others in the supply chain could help them secure buyers for their fruit, thus increasing competition and returns. Research in agrifood industries has shown that better connecting component parts of supply chains can improve efficiencies and increase multi-directional information flow, and to some extent this has occurred in this case. In the context of this chapter, however, my intent is to focus on the value of the participatory process as a learning mechanism, and in particular to highlight its value (in my case) for better understanding the 'two worlds' paradigm referred to in the introduction.

As a participant in the I = P project, and through the subsequent building of deeper relationships with the Aboriginal harvesters, I have come to develop different perceptions and understandings of bush food beyond the context of participation in an industry. These perceptions and understandings are increasingly shaping my thinking and research. To highlight the impact of these relationships in changing my perceptions, I will describe an incident that occurred subsequent to the I = P journey.

In another component of the 'Bush Products from Desert Australia' core project, horticultural development of 'bush tomatoes'[54] has been pursued. As part of that work, a trial planting of plants from various desert locations was developed. Plants were germinated from held seed stock. The aim of this research was to increase knowledge of the horticultural production requirements of 'bush tomatoes' as a means of developing a supply mechanism that was more reliable than bush harvest, with its inherent issues of climate variability that could sometimes limit supply. It would also provide information about horticultural production to enable the successful development of Aboriginal horticulturally based bush-food enterprises.

Very early in the development of this horticultural trial (and prior to the I = P project), bush harvesters were invited to visit the trial site to ensure that there was Aboriginal involvement and consultation around the project. There was no immediate indication from the bush harvesters that they had any issues with it, and they were politely attentive to the information that was shared with them. However, after developing greater mutual trust and much deeper relationships with the harvesters, I later learned that they were quite horrified by this project. At the time of their visit (which was during the growing season of katyerr), there had been very little bush harvest of katyerr in central Australia because of

---

54   The term 'bush tomatoes' is used here because in the context of the broader DKCRC project, this was the term consistently used, and is related to the commercial use of the fruit.

prevailing dry conditions that were not conducive to its growth in that season. The harvesters' interpretation of what they saw at the trial site (numerous rows of healthy katyerr plants) was later explained to me as a question: *'Why did you mob go out bush and dig up all the katyerr plants and put them in that place in Alice Springs? There was none left in the bush for us to pick.'* It had not occurred to me until that time that the harvesters could interpret what we were doing at the trial site in this way: that is, for them it explained why there was there was no bush katyerr for the women to harvest from the wild.

This anecdote highlights two important points. First, the thinking that underpins the assumptions we make is firmly rooted in the world view within which the thinking occurs, and the thinking itself is framed within the language in which the thoughts are formed. Secondly, it is only through the development of trust found in deeper relationships and engagement with others possessing different world views that one can approach new understandings based on those different world views. Taking a participatory approach to this project has, in that sense, provided the macro environment and indeed 'set the stage' for learning and its application to occur in the manner raised by Kidd and Kral.[55]

In applying this new understanding, how did I reinterpret the statement *'It would be good to know where our food goes'*? Did it mean something different from what I initially understood it to mean, and was the question itself framed from within a language that recognised different emphases and signifiers of what was important — different understandings of spatial and temporal concepts, for example? If one considers the actions of the harvesters at various stages along the physical journey — the desire to 'place' themselves in relation to their home communities on arrival in different locations, asking questions about where raw product inputs had originated and who had harvested them, the way in which directions were depicted on their pictorial representations of their journey, their animation in talking about their own harvesting activities, and the importance of passing on knowledge to their children and grandchildren — one can see a pattern emerging. This pattern, I would argue, relates primarily to the importance the harvesters attach to 'place' and 'belonging' both for themselves and the bush food they harvest. This importance relates to both the people themselves and the foods they harvest in the context of interrelationships between land and people. So, the statement *'It would be good to know where our food goes'* may be intrinsically and inextricably linked to place-based cultural identity, to language, and to customary systems of governance related to land, people and law. This may translate to a sense of 'belonging with' rather than 'ownership of' the fruit they harvested.

---

55   Kidd and Krall, above n 27.

Indeed, this relatedness is highlighted by Walsh and Douglas in their research on sustainable bush harvest, reported in Ryder et al.[56] In this research, remote Aboriginal harvesters articulated the cultural importance of some bush-food species with commercial value, including katyerr. Walsh and Douglas argued that katyerr and other bush-food plants continue to be 'key characters in Jukurrpa (dreaming) and ceremony'.[57] They also reported that certain Aboriginal peoples consider themselves to be custodians of these resources. This has important implications in developing governance systems that protect AEK, because it clearly implies an existing governance system for the control and use of these resources which predates any Western legal framework. It is also interesting to note the use of the term 'custodian' rather than 'owner' in relation to the plants. Again, this suggests belonging 'with', rather than belonging 'to', in the context of relationships between land, people and law.

On the question of language and its role in shaping thought, an important study by Lera Boroditsky and Alice Gaby was conducted with Pormpuraawan-language speakers in Pormpuraaw, a remote Aboriginal community on Cape York.[58] In this study, Boroditsky and Gaby demonstrated the differences between the way Pormpuraawan speakers and English speakers represented time spatially. They concluded that cross-cultural difference in thought is about more than style or preference, and is instead intrinsically related to the language used to shape the thoughts expressed. While this study was conducted on Cape York, Boroditsky and Gaby also pointed to similar differences in central desert Aboriginal-language speakers.

The extractive market process associated with bush food in central Australia has developed only in the past thirty to forty years,[59] but there is evidence that Aboriginal peoples have engaged in customary trade through kinship networks and as part of subsistence economies for at least 5,000 years.[60] It is highly likely that innovative practices associated with sustainable harvesting, such as the selection, manipulation and management of biological resources, would have arisen as a result.[61] In that sense, Western ideas of 'value adding' and the notion that this occurs post-extraction and only after the raw product has been sold by Aboriginal peoples to others in the value chain, may be incorrect. Cleary et al report, for example, on a customary post-harvest treatment of katyerr where the fruit is rubbed with clean sand to remove minute hairs reported by the harvesters to cause stomach irritation.[62] An important point here is that the AEK

---

56    Ryder et al, above n 1.
57    Walsh and Douglas, above n 16.
58    L Boroditsky and A Gaby, 'Remembrances of Times East: Absolute Representations of Time in an Australian Aboriginal Community' (2010) 21(11) *Psychological Science* 1635.
59    Miers, above n 3.
60    Akerman and Stanton, above n 2.
61    Walsh and Douglas, above n 16.
62    Cleary et al, above n 8.

that is being applied in selecting, manipulating and managing 'wild' species, and in applying any customary treatments to harvested fruit, is not currently recognised in the contemporary commercial trade of bush-harvested fruit, nor reflected in the prices paid for raw product.[63] I raise these issues here simply to highlight the value of PAR in developing 'two world' understandings, and its usefulness in revealing the many layers that might need to be peeled back to fully understand the intercultural complexity associated with both customary and commercial paradigms related to bush foods and their uses.

As a researcher, comprehension of the 'two worlds' paradigm (and thus the capacity to begin to consider complex questions outside my own world view) would not have been possible without first developing the relationships that have formed in sharing the I = P project experience. For that reason, it has been an *enabling* and perhaps emancipatory process,[64] which has allowed the formation of a new perspective outside the personal and institutional constraints within which my original thinking was formed. The notion of experience, action and reflection[65] inherent in PAR has been applied to my own approaches to better understanding bush foods and the various lenses through which the resources and activities associated with them might be viewed.

# 7. Conclusion

The purpose of this chapter has been to describe and discuss the effectiveness of PAR as an approach to research in the bush-foods area through the case-study exploration of the I = P project and its learning outcomes. The case study has provided useful insights into new ways of considering research approaches that emphasise participation, learning and application. I now conclude by drawing inferences from those insights and applying them to consideration of research issues related to the protection of AEK.

The protection of AEK is an urgent and high-priority area. Aboriginal peoples' legal control over this knowledge must be clear and unambiguous, and an appropriate regulatory system is an essential step in achieving that control. However, it is equally essential that such work is firmly grounded and tested within specific, 'real world' contexts where development around native biological resources is already occurring.

Participatory approaches which value and respect (and privilege equitably) AEK, customary law and Western legal systems will be essential in creating

---

63  Cleary, above n 6.
64  Carr and Kemmis, above n 34.
65  Reason, above n 20.

both a new regulatory administrative system and an environment in which it can flourish. The place where AEK, Aboriginal customary law and Western legal systems come together will undoubtedly require intercultural negotiation and translation to develop a new regulatory framework. The primary objectives of PAR as outlined by Reason[66] — that is, to produce both knowledge and action that is directly useful, and consciousness raising (learning) that creates empowerment — would seem a useful place from which to begin the process.

A specific and timely example of how PAR might be used in this context is in how AEK needs to be considered in any development of plant breeders' rights (PBRs) on bush-food and bush-medicine plants. The *Plant Breeder's Rights Act 1994* (Cth)[67] provides the mechanism for granting proprietory rights to breeders of certain new plant varieties and fungi in Australia. Currently, there is no existing legal requirement to recognise Aboriginal ownership of plant materials, nor any consideration of AEK in the development of varieties registered under the Plant Breeder's Rights Act. It is important to acknowledge that there are some concerns about the validity of some plant breeder's rights (PBRs) registrations under the Act, and a level of complexity exists with regard to the application of the Act.[68] My intent in this section is not to advocate or otherwise for the application of PBRs in relation to bush foods and bush medicine. However, work on developing PBRs for native species has already begun in Australia, so it is relevant to consider it in relation to AEK issues.

In the bush-foods context, the primary aim of PBRs is to develop and register new plant varieties which have desirable characteristics that decrease production costs and increase returns: for example, plants that have a higher fruit yield and that are adaptable to a range of growing and mechanical-harvesting conditions. For those bush-foods species that enter the market predominantly through harvest from the wild (like 'bush tomatoes'), PBRs are seen as a means of increasing and stabilising supply through horticultural production of 'improved' varieties.

There are multiple AEK protection issues to consider. These include but are probably not limited to:

• Who has cultural ties to the plants being considered for 'improvement'? Who are the plant's custodians? How will they be involved? 'Bush tomato', for example, is an extremely wide-ranging plant that grows across large areas of Western Australia, South Australia and the Northern Territory.[69] Many Aboriginal peoples will have cultural ties to the particular plants that

---

66   Reason, above n 20.
67   *Plant Breeder's Rights Act 1994* (Aus.).
68   J Sanderson, 'Intellectual Property and Plants: Constitutive, Contingent and Complex', in K Bowrey, M Handler and D Nicol (eds), *Emerging Challenges in Intellectual Property* (Oxford University Press, 2011).
69   Purdie et al 'Solanaceae' in *Flora of Australia Vol. 29* (Austalian Governement Printing Service, Canberra, 1982).

grow in their Country. These cultural ties include the Dreaming stories and AEK associated with those plants. What will be the cultural ramifications of creating 'improved' plants from hybridisations of plants from different Countries? What will the Stories for these 'improved' plants be, and who will be able to speak them, paint them and pass them on to children and grandchildren? Where will these 'improved' plants fit in the place-based relationships between people, land and customary law? Where will they belong?

- Will the new plants have a Dreaming? Or will they be like the cane toads that are infesting the ancestral lands of the Yanyuwa people in the Northern Territory and that have no 'law'?[70]

- Is the word 'improved' a culturally acceptable term, in that it implies that the plants themselves require something done to them to make them better?

- How will benefit-sharing arrangements and business models to commercialise such hybridisations be developed? Who will benefit financially, and who will decide on those who need to be consulted in the determining of who should benefit? How will this sit with existing subsistence economies[71] currently operating in remote Australia?

- The PBR itself, upon creation, becomes a commodity which can be traded. What protections will need to be considered to ensure the cultural rights to keystone species are not lost to Aboriginal peoples?

Finally, how will these and other important questions be asked? From whose understandings, world view and language will they be framed, developed and discussed? To ensure that 'improvements' such as those promoted through the development of PBRs align with both cultural imperatives and the effective protection of property rights in Western legal systems, engaging Aboriginal and non-Aboriginal peoples as co-researchers in partnerships where various knowledges, world views and languages can be considered and accorded respect will be critical. Finding solutions to PBR and other property rights issues in relation to bush foods and bush medicines will require more than just clever property rule design. Indeed, simply recognising that there *is* more to understand is where PAR can make a useful contribution to the process. This will require the establishment of deep relationships based on trust, and through which shared understandings can be developed. Such relationships are not

---

70   K A Seton and J J Bradley '"When you have no law you are nothing": Cane Toads, Social Consequences and Management Issues' (2004) 5(3) *Asia Pacific Journal of Anthropology* 205.

71   For an in-depth discussion of the value and importance of subsistence and hybrid economies in remote Australia see J C Altman 'Economic development and Indigenous Australia: Contestations over property, institutions and ideology' (2004) 48(3) *The Australian Journal of Agricultural and Resource Economics* 513; J C Altman 'Generating Finance for Indigenous Development: Economic Realities and Innovative options' (Centre for Aboriginal Economic Policy Research Working Paper No. 15/2002, The Australian National University, Canberra, 2002).

about superficial consultation with select, disparate and loud voices, but rather require the meaningful, shared dialogues that occur over time, and that are based on respect for the value of different ways of knowing and doing, and which enable quiet voices to be heard.

Following Fals-Borda,[72] understanding that value neutrality in social research is not always an ideal stance is especially meaningful and relevant in the bush-foods context. Deep involvement as participant rather than aloof academic observer[73] or external interventionist can help to build a rich picture of social situations that might otherwise be unattainable from more positivistic approaches. Thus, the trade-off between objectivity and collaborative learning in this intercultural space is extremely worthwhile. Indeed, I would argue that colonial understandings and manifestations of power and influence[74] which currently privilege Western ways of knowing and doing can only be broken down through engaging in the kind of deep relationships inherent in participatory approaches. Otherwise, as the case study reported on here has highlighted, so much may simply be lost in translation.

## Acknowledgements

This chapter has benefited significantly from critical comment provided by Susan Robinson, and I sincerely thank her.

The work reported here has been supported by funding from both the Northern Territory Natural Resources Management Board and the Australian Government Cooperative Research Centres Programme through the Desert Knowledge CRC. The views expressed herein do not necessarily represent the views of Desert Knowledge CRC or its participants.

---

72   Fals-Borda, above n 21.
73   Freire, above n 21.
74   Smith, above n 37.

# 4. Biopiracy and the Innovations of Indigenous Peoples and Local Communities

Daniel F. Robinson

## 1. Introduction

Biopiracy is a divisive term, and deliberately so. The original proponent of the term, Pat Roy Mooney of the NGO Action Group on Erosion Technology and Concentration (ETC), has previously stated that '[w]hatever the will and wishes of those involved, there is no "bioprospecting". There is only biopiracy.'[1] He explains that without adequate international laws, standards, norms and monitoring mechanisms, the theft of indigenous and local knowledge will accelerate in the years to come.

Although exaggerated for emphasis, Mooney's statement reflects a strong discontentment that was particularly prevalent in the 1990s and early 2000s amongst sections of the NGO community, many farmer's groups and indigenous communities. In the absence of adequate international standards, many bioprospecting activities in recent years have been heavily criticised, and relatively few have been widely considered to be 'fair and equitable'. However, it is very difficult to quantify the regularity and impacts of incidents that might be described as 'biopiracy'. The lack of clear definitions from any authoritative source has also given rise to confused understandings of bioprospecting, biopiracy and '[access and] the fair and equitable sharing of benefits'. The highly significant international agreement on the 2010 Nagoya Protocol on Access to Genetic Resources and the Fair and Equitable Sharing of Benefits Arising from their Utilization (Nagoya Protocol) to the Convention on Biological Diversity (CBD) may help resolve some of these ambiguities, but it has fallen short on at least one front — the section on monitoring, which is sandwiched within the compliance articles. Negotiators had the opportunity to include patent offices as checkpoints for the monitoring of access and benefit sharing (ABS) — a potentially critical inclusion for the prevention of patent-based biopiracy — yet it was dropped late in the negotiations as part of the compromise that has been achieved in the Nagoya Protocol. Given that the exploitation of traditional knowledge by innovations registered through the patent system has been one of the main perceived injustices, leading to the creation and use of the term biopiracy, this is a considerable gap in the Protocol.

---

1   P R Mooney, 'Why We Call It Biopiracy' in H Svarstad and S Dhillion (eds), *Bioprospecting: From Biodiversity in the South to Medicines in the North* (Spartacus Forlag, 2000) 37.

This chapter takes the polemical issue of biopiracy as a starting point, and explores the concepts of innovation and traditional knowledge within specific cases of bioprospecting and/or biopiracy (depending upon how or from where you view them). Specifically, the chapter demonstrates the flawed tendency by academics and policy-makers to perpetuate the 'traditional knowledge' and 'modern/scientific knowledge' dualism. A more useful focus of analysis is indigenous peoples' innovations, or at least their contributions to innovation (as described in Article 8(j) of the CBD), which may have helped to short-cut the research and development (R&D) process. Last, the chapter examines how 'traditional knowledge', used in a number of case-study 'inventions'/discoveries that are protected by intellectual property (IP) rights (typically patents and plant breeder's rights), might be treated differently if it was described and recognised as 'indigenous innovation'.

# 2. Biopiracy Typology

Biopiracy is a discursive tool that both describes an injustice and is used for political leverage. Although the colonial enterprise of plant and animal collection has been going on for centuries, the biopiracy discourse has emerged as a powerful counter to the perception of new hegemonies imposed by IP rules with global reach, such as the World Trade Organization (WTO) Agreement on Trade-Related Aspects of Intellectual Property Rights (TRIPS Agreement). Along with the biopiracy discourse has come lobbying for additional rights, particularly for indigenous peoples, including ideas for *sui generis* IP rights which must compete with an already competitive suite of private commercial rights that have come to be described as 'intellectual property'.[2] Lobbying for additional third-generation rights which we might call 'bio-cultural' rights of indigenous and local peoples has been comparatively more successful in forums such as the CBD, where we now see the United Nations Declaration on the Rights of Indigenous Peoples (UNDRIP) influencing the text of the Nagoya Protocol towards recognition of indigenous customary laws (Article 12).[3]

These developments and associated lobbying are deliberately targeted towards the issue of biopiracy, even if international forums are unable to address that issue directly. For example, in the absence of a definition of biopiracy, international organisations are left without an appropriate term to describe the specific or perceived injustices. In this void, delegates to the various agreements such as the CBD, or organisations such as the WTO, commonly use the term. For example:

---

2    P J Heald, 'Rhetoric of Biopiracy' (2003) 11 *Cardozo Journal of International and Comparative Law* 519.
3    K Bavikatte and D F Robinson, 'Towards a People's History of the Law: Biocultural Jurisprudence and the Nagoya Protocol on Access and Benefit Sharing' (2011) 7(1) *Law, Environment and Development Journal* 35.

One of the measures adopted [in Peru] was the creation of the National Anti-Biopiracy Commission, whose basic task is to develop actions to identify, prevent and avoid acts of biopiracy which involve biological resources of Peruvian origin and traditional knowledge of the indigenous peoples of Peru.[4]

More politely, the delegates also use the term misappropriation, yet this usually has a more limited connotation regarding failure to comply with ABS laws or principles. The Secretariat of the World Intellectual Property Organization (WIPO) has utilised the work of the Intergovernmental Committee on Intellectual Property and Genetic Resources, Traditional Knowledge and Folklore (IGC) for development of Draft Policy Objectives and Core Principles for the Protection of Traditional Knowledge[5] which provides principles against misappropriation:

Any acquisition or appropriation of traditional knowledge by unfair or illicit means constitutes an act of misappropriation. Misappropriation may also include deriving commercial benefit from the acquisition or appropriation of traditional knowledge when the person using that knowledge knows, or is grossly negligent in failing to know, that it was acquired or appropriated by unfair means; and other commercial activities contrary to honest practices that gain inequitable benefit from traditional knowledge.[6]

This gives us a very broad understanding of misappropriation. One of the greatest difficulties is an appropriate definition of terms such as 'unfair' or 'illicit' and, perhaps most difficult, 'traditional knowledge', which would presumably come at the national level if or when these principles are utilised.[7] The Draft Policy Objectives attempt to clarify in the next point that legal means should be available to suppress, amongst other things:

false claims or assertions of ownership or control over traditional knowledge, including acquiring, claiming or asserting intellectual property rights over traditional knowledge-related subject matter by a person who knew that the intellectual property rights were not validly held in the light of that traditional knowledge and any conditions relating to its access...[8]

---

4   TRIPS Council 'Communication from Peru to the WTO' (7 November 2005).

5   WIPO IGC Secretariat, *Protection of Traditional Knowledge: Overview of Policy Objectives and Core Principles*, WIPO Doc WIPO/TKGRF/IC/7/5 (2004).

6   Ibid, annex II, 21.

7   G Dutfield, 'A Critical Analysis of the Debate on Traditional Knowledge, Drug Discovery and Patent-based Biopiracy' (2011) 33(4) *European Intellectual Property Review* 237. Dutfield makes the useful comment: 'What is traditional knowledge anyway? We only speak of traditional knowledge at all because there is knowledge in the world that we assume to be radically different from "our" knowledge. The latter we prefer to label as "modern" or "scientific" knowledge. Holding to a traditional-modern epistemological dualism as if all knowledge is either all of one or all of the other is in fact simplistic, misleading and unhelpful.'

8   WIPO IGC Secretariat, above n 5, annex I, 5.

In this case we might ask: 'What is a false claim?' Is it, say, a claim that does not validly meet the requirements for a patent: novelty, invention and usefulness? Surely this is too narrow. Is it not possible to hold a valid patent that utilises traditional knowledge? Of course the answer is: 'Yes, it is possible', but these guiding principles would assert that prior informed consent would need to be obtained and benefits shared with the traditional knowledge holders in order to validate the patent.

These principles have been heavily debated in the IGC because of exactly these sorts of questions. What is probably lacking in these discussions is comparison against a suite of different examples that help distinguish what has been called misappropriation, but I will more specifically and usefully categorise as different typologies of biopiracy and misappropriation (see Box 1). The typologies are based on a review of various descriptions of biopiracy by academics and NGOs, as well as an examination of several biopiracy or bioprospecting incidents in the book *Confronting Biopiracy*.[9] This chapter will then examine specific cases which align with this typology, and which highlight some of the key problems associated with the current suite of IP rules for the recognition of indigenous contributions to innovation.

---

**Box 1: Biopiracy and Misappropriation***

**Patent-based Biopiracy**

The patenting of (often spurious) inventions based on biological resources and/ or traditional knowledge that are extracted without adequate authorisation and benefit sharing from other (usually developing) countries, indigenous or local communities.

**Non-patent Biopiracy**

Other IP control (through plant variety protection or deceptive trade marks) based on biological resources and/or traditional knowledge that have been extracted without adequate authorisation and benefit sharing from other (usually developing) countries, indigenous or local communities.

**Misappropriations**

The unauthorised extraction of biological resources and/or traditional knowledge for research and development purposes from other (usually developing) countries, indigenous or local communities, without adequate benefit sharing.

Note: 'Authorisation' involves obtaining (free) prior informed consent of the appropriate government authorities and, where relevant, local communities or other providers.

---

* Ibid, 21 [adapted].

In relation to patent-based biopiracy, it is worth noting that the patent claims are often spurious — what some might simply call 'bad patents'. However, this

---

9 D F Robinson, *Confronting Biopiracy: Challenges, Cases and International Debates* (Earthscan, 2010).

is not the limit of this form of biopiracy. Patents can legally be granted where the innovation is new and inventive, but can still be interpreted as biopiracy because they have not fulfilled the other legal and/or ethical conditions of prior informed consent and benefit sharing. Biopiracy is typically applied to cases from developing countries, but it is worth noting that biopiracy may also occur through the misappropriation and patenting (or other protection) of indigenous knowledge from communities residing in countries such as Australia, New Zealand, the US and Canada.

In addition to this typology, it is helpful to read the newly agreed scope of 'utilization of genetic resources' in the Nagoya Protocol to help decide what will be legal (which is a separate question from what is ethical). I have used the term 'biological resources' in my typology (written prior to the Nagoya Protocol) for two reasons. First, there is no traditional knowledge of 'genetic resources', but rather traditional knowledge exists in association with plants, animals and biological resources in the broader sense. I doubt that many would expect local communities to have been 'traditionally' examining genes through microarray. The term 'genetic resources' has been a red herring which developing countries and indigenous peoples have sought to enlarge, first with the Bonn Guidelines, and now more successfully with the Nagoya Protocol. Secondly, I use the broader term because many of the cases in which perceived injustices claimed as biopiracy or misappropriation have occurred relate to the utilisation of derivatives, extracts or biological materials in an R&D context. Usefully, the Nagoya Protocol now assists in this understanding by expanding the definition of 'Utilization of genetic resources' in Article 2:

- 'Utilization of genetic resources' means to conduct research and development on the genetic and/or biochemical composition of genetic resources, including through the application of biotechnology ...
- 'Biotechnology' ... means any technological application that uses biological systems, living organisms, or derivatives thereof, to make or modify products or processes for specific use.
- 'Derivative' means a naturally occurring biochemical compound resulting from the genetic expression or metabolism of biological or genetic resources, even if it does not contain functional units of heredity.

This can be summarised to say that R&D utilising biological resources and their biochemical derivatives for any technological application to make or modify products for specific (commercial) use must comply with the ABS provisions that the Nagoya Protocol will require of Parties. The key inclusions for the broadening of the scope of 'genetic resources', as previously narrowly defined in the CBD, are the broader definition of biotechnology and inclusion of references to the biochemical composition of genetic resources and derivatives (even if it does not contain functional units of heredity — DNA or RNA). Article 7 of the Protocol also clearly requires that domestic laws must have requirements for prior informed consent of traditional knowledge holders (indigenous and local communities) on mutually agreed terms (implying benefit sharing, which is discussed in Article 12) — an important addition to the Protocol.

In summary, this typology of biopiracy and misappropriation accords with the Nagoya Protocol. But the Protocol is silent on IP — a considerable problem for policy-makers and those confronting IP-related biopiracy cases.

The next step in this chapter is to challenge some misunderstandings about bioprospecting, biopiracy and misappropriation through specific case studies — real-world applications that often get forgotten in legal scholarship on these issues. In the following section, a specific focus on the idea of 'innovation', and a critique of IP rules for their inherent inability to adequately protect traditional knowledge, will be made through these case studies.

# 3. Case Studies of Bioprospecting, Biopiracy and Misappropriation

This section examines a number of cases that have been characterised as biopiracy or misappropriation, or questioned along these lines. They provide a useful point of examination regarding the way traditional knowledge may be used in the innovation process in different sectors (plant breeding, agriculture, medicines and cosmetics).

## (a) The Basmati Case — Plant Breeding and Innovation

South Asia has a long history of domestication and breeding of rice. For example, archaeological evidence indicates that rice has been cultivated in India from between 1500 and 1000 BC.[10] More specifically, basmati rice cultivars have been grown in South Asia, across India, Pakistan and also Bangladesh, probably for centuries, during which time they have been improved by local farmers through seed selection and conventional breeding practices. One of the earliest mentions of basmati is in the epic *Heer and Ranjha* composed in 1766. The most widely used rice variety — basmati 370 — was selected from local collections and released for commercial cultivation in 1933 at the Rice Research Station Kalashah Kaku (now Pakistan).[11]

---

10  M Rai, 'Genetic Diversity in Rice Production: Past Contribution and the Potential of Utilization for Sustainable Rice Production' in D Van Tran (ed), *Sustainable Rice Production for Food Security: Proceedings of the 20th Session of the International Rice Commission. Bangkok, Thailand, 23–26 July 2002* (FAO, 2003).

11  V P Singh, 'The Basmati Rice of India' in R K Singh, U S Singh and G S Khush (eds), *Aromatic Rices* (Oxford and IBH Publishing, 2000) 135.

The basmati rice 'biopiracy' controversy emerged in the late 1990s in response to a US patent. Specifically, the US Patent and Trademark Office (USPTO) granted patent number 5,663,484 on 'Basmati rice lines and grains' to the Texas-based company RiceTec Inc. on 2 September 1997. Originally the patent had twenty claims on the protected subject matter, covering the 'novel' basmati varieties that the researchers claimed to have developed. Unsurprisingly, this caused significant alarm and outrage amongst Indian farmers and NGOs. At the time, many interpreted the patent to mean an outright monopoly on basmati and thus restrictions on export to the US where the patent had been approved. As Ghosh notes, RiceTec's claims were for a specific rice plant (Claims 1–11, 14), for seeds that germinate the patented rice plant (Claim 12), for the grain that is produced by the rice plant (Claims 13, 15–17), and for the method of selecting plants for breeding and propagating particular grains of rice (Claims 18–20).[12] The overly broad wording and scope of the patent can be blamed for much of the public outrage.[13]

Shortly after the patent was granted, Indian NGOs began a campaign against it, garnering support from the Indian government and drawing international attention to the patent. A re-examination application was filed by an organisation named the Agricultural and Processed Food Products Export Development Authority in India, with government support.[14] Subsequently, RiceTec agreed to withdraw some claims, and under a re-examination certificate (4525, 29 January 2002) these were formally retracted. Claims 1–7, 10 and 14–20 were cancelled, and descriptions of the rice were altered in the certificate. However, Claims 8, 9 and 11 for specific novel rice lines were maintained.

Analysis of the description in the patent document indicates that Claims 8, 9 and 11 refer to crossed rice lines (varieties) to develop plant varieties that exhibit some similar characteristics to basmati rice grains. Most countries in the world do not allow plant patents, but under US patent law novel plant varieties are eligible for protection. South Asian activists are particularly frustrated by this, because it appears that the germplasm used to cross the varieties was originally obtained from the region. The patent description for the breeding of BAS-867 and RT1117 rice lines indicates that:

> Twenty-two basmati lines from the USDA World Germplasm Collection, Beltsville, Md. and thirteen semi-dwarf, long-grain lines were selected for the initial crosses … The basmati seed from the USDA were identified as having come from Pakistan.[15]

---

12   S Ghosh, 'Globalization, Patents, and Traditional Knowledge' (2003-2004) 17(1) *Columbia Journal of Asian Law* 101.
13   Robinson, above n 9.
14   Ghosh, above n 12.
15   USPTO Patent Number 5,663,484.

Activists such as Vandana Shiva have continued to argue that a simple cross-breed such as this is obvious to someone trained in plant breeding (and so it fails to achieve an inventive step), and that it is also not novel (new) because it free-rides on the existing prior art in the basmati rice's qualities.[16] However, the US standards of novelty and obviousness failed to recognise the contributions of Indian farmers as applied by the USPTO.[17] This brings us to our question about innovation: how is the plant breeding by the US researchers any more inventive than the breeding done by the South Asian farmers? The main difference is that one is a *new* cross-breed and the other is presumably a traditionally bred strain (improved slowly over generations through selection and more recent empirical breeding practices). But this does not negate the obviousness requirement, and we might well ask: 'Is the crossing of these specific cultivar lines for desirable traits an inherently obvious activity to someone trained in plant breeding?' Shiva thinks yes, and the innovation and IP policy-makers of many governments probably also agree.[18] The answer comes down to jurisdiction: an 'inventive' crossed hybrid will be allowed under the US plant patent rules but not under many other patent systems. For many, the 'traditional' empirical breeding of a cultivar might be seen as just as inventive as modern crosses, albeit through a slower (but nevertheless systematic) process.

## (b) The Bolivian Habanero Pepper and Plant Variety Protection

The previous example suggests a basic structural problem with the idea of 'plant patents' and the obviousness/inventiveness of plant varieties derived from different types of breeding practices. Here we examine the role of plant variety protection (PVP) as providing a similarly problematic structural incentive to free-ride on the breeding practices of others. In this case, a pepper (*Capsicum chinense*) cultivar was bred from a cross between an orange habanero pepper from the Yukatan Peninsula and a pepper from a US Department of Agriculture (USDA) gene bank with Plant Introduction (PI) number 543188 collected from Bolivia. This was then filed with the US Plant Variety Protection Office database with PVP number 200400329 for the 'TAM Mild Habanero Pepper' and issued in 2007.

---

16   V Shiva, *Protect or Plunder: Understanding Intellectual Property Rights* (Zed Books, 2001).

17   As some authors have noted, see S Kadidal 'United States Patent Prior Art Rules and the Neem Controversy: A Case of Subject-Matter Imperialism' (1998) 7(1) *Biodiversity and Conservation* 29. United States patent law does not recognise *foreign* prior art unless it is clearly documented and accessible. The geographical limitation on novelty is problematic in many biopiracy cases involving United States patents, particularly with regard to public knowledge or use of inventions in foreign countries which, in many cases, is orally transmitted rather than published or patented.

18   Shiva, above n 17.

The Texas A&M University System Agriculture Program put out an 'AgNews' press release on the pepper on 12 August 2004, describing it as a successfully bred mild version of the infamously hot and piquant habanero pepper. From a five-year breeding programme, the progeny of a cross 'between a hot Yukatan habanero and a heatless habanero from Bolivia began to show promise'.[19] Breeders from the Texas Agricultural Experiment Station have indicated their excitement at the possibility of selling the habaneros to salsa companies and as a fresh product at between $3 and $4 per pound, while the comparable jalapenos peppers fetch around 50 cents per pound.[20]

Here it is worth questioning whether the uniqueness of this mild habanero can be put down to the variety collected in Bolivia. The Texan breeders have obtained the germplasm from a USDA gene bank, and this is documented in the PVP certificate and admitted in their press release. The US Genetic Resources Information Network (GRIN) database record indicates that the original variety (GRIN PI 543188) is 'not piquant' and that it is 'said to be grown locally' in Bolivia. The records indicate that the original variety was purchased by a USDA official from a Brazilian vendor in the Cobija market of Nicolas Suarez Province (Pando Department) which borders Brazil on 13 November 1988. The plant material was then transferred to the USDA Plant Genetic Resources Conservation Unit in Georgia, and later accessed by the Texan breeders.

In this case a PVP certificate was obtained. It has different requirements from a plant patent. If this were a patent, an obviousness requirement might well have seen it rejected on the grounds that one of the parent plants contained substantially similar traits. Instead, there are requirements for the registered plant variety to be new, distinct, uniform and stable[21] in order to receive twenty years of protection. This means that there is little to prove in terms of 'innovation' except for the distinctness of the plant:

> The distinctness of one variety from another may be based on one or more identifiable morphological, physiological, or other characteristics (including any characteristics evidenced by processing or product characteristics, such as milling and baking characteristics in the case of wheat) with respect to which a difference in genealogy may contribute evidence.[22]

Conceivably, the cross-breeding may have changed the colour and look of the new variety from the original habanero. But in this case it appears that the most

---

19  R Santa Ana III, 'Texas Plant Breeder Develops Mild Habanero Pepper' *AgNews — News and Public Affairs. Texas A&M University System Agriculture Program* (Texas), 12 August 2004.
20  Ibid.
21  *Plant Variety Protection Act (PVPA)* 7 USC §§ 2321-2582 (1970), s 24(a).
22  Ibid, s 41(b)(5).

interesting or novel trait is that this habanero is non-piquant, a feature already present in the Bolivian parent — in all likelihood bred and 'grown locally' in Bolivia for exactly that trait.[23] In terms of innovation, we again have to question whether the law in place — this time a PVP law — is appropriate in rewarding something as being unique or 'distinct' when in fact it may have only minor differences with the original or parent variety. Is this not just a case of allowing and legitimising free-riding on the 'traditional' innovation and breeding of Bolivians?

## (c) *Artemisia judaica* — The Limits of Traditional Knowledge

It is worth pointing out that while traditional knowledge may make substantial contributions to the innovation process, it is also important not to over-romanticise traditional knowledge. While those decrying biopiracy incidents are often pointing out failures in the ethical practices of bioprospectors and 'innovators', or the failings of both biological resources and IP laws, there are plenty of examples where they may overstate the injustice.[24] US patent number 6,350,478 on an 'Artemisia judaica fractionation method', which is registered by the UK company Phytotech Ltd (a subsidiary of PhytopharmPlc), is worth examining for exactly this purpose.

This patent became a topic of controversy following a report produced by the Washington DC-based NGO, the Edmonds Institute and the African Centre for Biosafety, called 'Out of Africa: Mysteries of Access and Benefit-Sharing'.[25] This report portrays the US patent in respect of *Artemisia judaica* as one of the mysteries of ABS. Notably, the plant *Artemisia judaica* has been used in Libya and other neighbouring North African and Middle Eastern countries as a traditional medicine. There is considerable documented prior art regarding the traditional medicinal uses of the plant, including treatments for diabetes.[26]

---

23   There are a number of documents that indicate the extent of breeding and use of cultivars of the *Capsicum chinense* species, including the habanero pepper in South and Central America. B Pickersgill, 'Relationships Between Weedy and Cultivated Forms in Some Species of Chili Peppers (Genus Capsicum)' (1971) 25 *Evolution* 683, indicates that archaeological excavations have placed sedentary people practising agriculture east of the Andes, possibly as early as 2000 BC, indicating that it was probably these people who first domesticated cultivars of the *Capsicum chinense* species. Articles such as those by M J McLeod et al, 'Early Evolution of Chili Peppers (Capsicum)' (1982) 36 *Economic Botany* 361; P W Bosland, 'Capsicums: Innovative Uses of an Ancient Crop' in J Janick (ed), *Progress in New Crops* (ASHS Press, 1996) also indicate that the likely place of origin of the domesticated *Capsicum chinense* cultivars are the lowland Amazon Basin, with a potential range across Central America, South America and the Caribbean, see Robinson, above n 9.

24   See, for example, Dutfield, above n 7.

25   J McGown, *Out of Africa: Mysteries of Access and Benefit Sharing* (Edmonds Institute, Washington, and African Centre for Biosafety, 2006).

26   See C Z Liu et al, 'Regeneration of the Egyptian Medicinal Plant Artemisia judaica L.' (2003) 21(6) *Plant Cell Reports* 525; T Dob and C Chelghoum, 'Chemical Composition of the Essential Oil of *Artemisia judaica* L. from Algeria' (2006) 21(2) *Flavour and Fragrance Journal* 343; H Azaizeh et al, 'Ethnobotanical Knowledge of Local Arab Practitioners in the Middle Eastern Region' (2003) 74(1-2) *Fitoterapia* 99.

McGown cites part of the patent description: 'Artemis judaica is used in Libyan traditional medicine as an infusion for the treatment of "wasting disease", almost certain[ly] dia[b]etes mellitus.'[27] But what he does not explain is that the patent in question covers only a series of methods for extraction of fractions from the *Artemisia judaica* plant — it is a process patent.

This raises an important question: can process patents really be called biopiracy? If we take the biopiracy typology above, a process patent does not qualify as patent-based biopiracy (but potentially fits the misappropriation depiction). However, in terms of a broader question of justice, process patents can still potentially be used to restrain a very wide array of research activity, especially if the invention claims are broadly described. The existence of the patent or the threat of lawsuits can stifle the interests of others, given that it is really beyond the costs of indigenous communities to challenge these patents in court. There are several examples where the threat of a lawsuit has deterred indigenous or local producers, including a kwao krua process patent in Thailand[28] and the yellow enola bean example affecting Mexican producers.[29]

If we look to the Nagoya Protocol, the process patent does not raise any explicit conflict on its own. But presumably the researchers obtained the biological materials from Libya or a neighbouring country to conduct the research, and the way they extracted those materials is unknown. Surprisingly, the broader terms of the WIPO Draft Provisions description of misappropriation might depict this patent as such for 'deriving commercial benefit from the acquisition or appropriation of traditional knowledge'. However, we do not know if it was acquired through 'unfair' means.

In any case, there are important details in the patent itself that need further examination. The chromatographic fractions derived from this patented process are claimed to have 'non-mutagenic properties'. Other patent documents which cite the anti-diabetic properties of the *Artemisia judaica* plant[30] note the presence of a 'deleterious mutagen' in crude extracts of the plant, which would make it unsuitable for the treatment of mammals and humans. It seems that traditional healers may have been using it without clear knowledge of the potential for mutagenic effects.[31] While traditional knowledge has probably led scientists to this plant as a treatment for diabetes, the severe side-effects could be identified and removed only through modern scientific techniques — chromatographic

---

27    McGown, above n 26, 2.

28    Robinson, above n 9, 55.

29    Ibid, 51.

30    PCT Doc WO 97/35598; USPTO Patent Number 6,893,627.

31    Robinson, above n 9.

analysis in this case. In this sense, both 'traditional medicine' and modern science needed each other to provide a useful and safe innovation (which in any case does not yet appear to have come to market).

According to patent rules, this innovation would appear to satisfy the novelty and non-obviousness requirements. What is less clear is the consent and benefit-sharing process. As McGown points out, Phytopharm says that it maintains good agricultural practices to minimise environmental impacts by 'working with local agronomists and horticulturalists in each of the countries where we are growing crops'.[32] Yet the company does not specify further than this vague assurance. If the company does derive commercial benefit from this valid patent, then there is still a considerable argument for some sort of return benefit sharing to 'provider' groups for the *partial* contribution towards a useful end product.

## (d) White Kwao Krua — Yet Another Bad Patent?

There have been a number of claimed patents over the Thai vine 'White Kwao Krua' (*Pueraria mirifica*) that have received considerable criticism in the Thai media.[33] Some quite broad patents have been granted in the US and Japan on extracts of the plant used in compositions for treating the skin. For example, US patents with numbers 6,673,377 and 6,352,685 both claim an extract derived from *Pueraria mirifica* — a solvent and dry solid respectively — for use as a cosmetic ingredient that may help reduce wrinkles. These have received criticism with regards to novelty, obviousness, and use of biological resources and traditional knowledge without clear ABS procedures.

Yet another patent was granted in the US on 9 February 2010, with patent number 7,658,955 for 'Pueraria candollei var. mirifica A Shaw. & Suvat. Extract'. The claims are on a process for obtaining a dry extract, and the extract itself, for use in a cosmetic application. The authors of the patent attempt to differentiate this from the other patents and from the traditional application by claiming a dry extract that does not cause eye irritation. The claims do not appear to be particularly inventive in light of the prior art in the field — the descriptions of traditional medicinal use and the other patents. The patent even recognises the traditional medicinal use of kwao krua:

> For more than 500 years, people in South East Asia have been using the root of 'White Kwao Krua' for its profound anti-aging properties. This root has been identified as Puerariacandollei var. mirifica Airy Shaw et Suvat, which belongs to the family Papilionaceae (Leguminosae).

---

32  McGown, above n 26, 2.
33  D Robinson and J Kuanpoth, 'The Traditional Medicines Predicament: A Case Study of Thailand' (2009) 11(5-6) *Journal of World Intellectual Property* 375.

However, they do not indicate whether they are the ones who identified the specific variant of the species — it seems highly unlikely that they are, and the variant is widely known in Northern Thailand. Figure 6 is a photo taken of 'White Kwao Krua' in Northern Thailand as identified by a Karen elder.

**Figure 6. 'White Kwao Krua' as identified by Patthi Ta Yae, Baan Soplan, Samoeng, Chiang Mai, Thailand.**

Source: D. Robinson 14 February 2006.

Their claim hinges on the extract of the specific variant of the *Pueraria* genus. They indicate: 'The only species with distinct estrogenic activity was found to be Pueraria candollei var. mirifica A. Shaw. & Suvat (hereinafter **Pueraria mirifica** or P. mirifica).' They then contradictorily indicate that: 'The required species of the present invention is not *"**Pueraria mirifica**"* but Pueraria candollei var. mirifica A Shaw. & Suvat.' One has to wonder if a patent examiner actually read this document before granting the patent.

If we do a simple search for existing literature about 'White Kwao Krua', many prior art documents appear, going back to 1931. In English, an article by Kashemsanta et al. from 1952 describes the identification of the species sent from Thailand to Kew Gardens: 'Pueraria mirifica Airy Shaw et Suvatabandhu, sp. Nov., *P. Candollei* Grah.' This is likely to be the same plant — in fact, the variant 'Airy Shaw and Suvathabandhu' is apparently named after two of the authors. The plant is also described by Cherdshewasart (one of the US patent holders of other kwao krua patents) and colleagues in two recent articles as '*Pueraria mirifica* Airy Shaw et Suvatabandhu (synonymn: *Pueraria candollei* Wall. Ex Benth var *mirifica* (Airy Shaw & Suvat)', which is likely to be a description of the same plant.[34] These authors also note the identification of miroestrol, one of the phytoestrogens that is a key active of the plant, also listed as one of the key actives in the claims in the new US patent 7,658,955.

A few conclusions can be drawn from this case. First, there appear to be serious issues relating to prior art and obviousness in the case of this new patent. Secondly, all of these 'White Kwao Krua' patents are utilising traditional medicinal knowledge towards commercial gain — and they even acknowledge this. In these patents, the inventors have isolated the active ingredients — certain phytoestrogens — and have altered dosage levels to improve safety for human usage. Yet none of this identification would have been possible without the contributions made by traditional Thai healers who have experimented with the plant and transmitted knowledge of it going back about a century (if not further). Certainly there is scope to make scientific improvements for the safe application of this herbal product as a cream. But are these patentable? Aren't the links between 'traditional medicine' and 'modern cosmetic' blindingly obvious and in need of adequate recognition? The Thai government has established ABS requirements (under their PVP Act) as well as a Thai Traditional and Alternative Medicines Act with the aim of ensuring that traditional medicines are appropriately promoted and protected. To date it does not appear that there are any ABS arrangement between the researchers and the Thai government in relation to this plant. In the meantime, the white kwao krua plant has been heavily poached from forest areas as a result of recent public demand, highlighting the importance of ABS contributions to the conservation of useful species.

---

34   W Cherdshewasart et al, 'The Differential Anti-proliferation Effect of the White (Pueraria mirifica), Red (Butea superba) and Black (Mucuna collettii) Kwao Krua Plants on the Growth of MCF-7 Cells' (2004) 93 *Journal of Ethnopharmacology* 255; W Cherdshewasart and W Sutjit, 'Correlation of Antioxidant Activity and Major Isoflavonoid Contents of the Phytoestrogen-rich Pueraria mirifica and Pueraria lobata tubers' (2008) 15(1-2) *Phytomedicine* 38.

# 4. Conclusions

In three of the four cases discussed, the United States IP system, whether through patents or plant variety protection, has provided monopoly protection for 'innovations' that are incremental at best. The Artemisia case, although making an apparently more substantial inventive contribution, still has shortened its R&D process through the use of traditional knowledge (relating to diabetes treatment, although also potentially severe in its side-effects). The Artemisia case does, however, indicate that scientific and traditional innovation systems can interact in mutually beneficial ways. What is important is that the terms of the exchange between different parties is 'fair and equitable'. Indeed, there are more cases emerging wherein researchers or companies have successfully established mutually beneficial arrangements with indigenous communities (for example, the commercial use of Argan oil for cosmetics by Cognis and L'Oreal).[35]

However, what is frustrating about the cases described in this chapter (and in many other biopiracy cases) is that the 'traditional' contribution to the innovation is poorly recognised at best (as in the kwao krua case) and completely ignored in others. If we stopped thinking of the indigenous peoples' contributions as 'traditional knowledge' and formally recognised 'indigenous innovation', we may well find some patents and plant variety certificates are never actually granted because of their lack of novelty. We may find that inventiveness and obviousness are perceived differently if patent examiners are able to peer through the guise of 'technical' language to see that the wheel is being continually re-invented. For example:

- The remaining patented basmati rice lines could not be produced without the long-term breeding innovations of South Asia farmers.
- The protected cross-breed of habanero pepper almost certainly would not have such unique traits without the breeding contributions of Bolivian farmers.
- The Artemisia researchers would not have identified the plant as a diabetes treatment without the use of traditional medicinal knowledge (albeit apparently unaware of mutagenic effects).
- The white kwao krua plant would not continually be re-processed in different forms to serve the same purpose — as a cosmetic that reduces wrinkles — without the experimentation of Thai healers.

This highlights the importance of initiatives such as the Traditional Knowledge Digital Library (TKDL) which is clearly starting to make an impression on the

---

35    D F Robinson and E Defrenne, *Argan: A Case Study on ABS?* (2011) <http://www.ethicalbiotrade.org/dl/UEBT_D_ROBINSON_AND_E_DEFRENNE_final.pdf>

minds of examiners in the European Patent Office and Canadian Intellectual Property Office, with several patents withdrawn or set aside due to the influence of the TKDL. While this is an important achievement on its own, this initiative is likely to stop only patent-based biopiracy or 'bad patents', and will not prevent misappropriations or non-patent biopiracy, or provide mechanisms for the active promotion of the innovations of indigenous and local communities.

Drahos has made useful suggestions towards a treaty on Traditional Group Knowledge and Practice (TGKP).[36] He suggests in his conclusions that a treaty should focus on the enforcement dimension of TGKP, being modest in setting substantive standards but strong on coordinating national enforcement activities for the prevention of misappropriation of traditional knowledge through a Global Bio-Collecting Society. Given that there have been some considerable successes at the national level in Peru with the establishment of an 'Anti-Biopiracy Commission' which has investigated and lobbied for the successful withdrawal of several foreign patents that utilised biological resources and associated traditional knowledge or innovation, such a concept might prove useful if expanded internationally (at least for preventing patent-based biopiracy). Irrespective of whether an international system is in place, the development of national biopiracy and/or misappropriation ombudsmen would be a useful step for countries in which it has been a persistent problem. In fact, this idea was raised in the ABS negotiations prior to Nagoya, but was unfortunately dropped late in the negotiations in order to reach a compromise.

Despite some flaws, the Nagoya Protocol is an obvious step towards positive outcomes of ABS, and will hopefully result in some benefits for 'traditional knowledge holders' and for conservation, as well as adequate respect for their contributions through prior informed consent procedures. What might also be useful are *sui generis* systems for the protection and promotion of the innovations of indigenous peoples and local communities that are less prescriptive than IP laws and which reflect customary mechanisms of protection. However, the promise of custom-based *sui generis* systems is likely to be also hamstrung by the jurisprudential diversity of the many indigenous groups around the world.[37]

Lastly, while it might seem biased to square this criticism directly at the US (which is certainly not the only country guilty of allowing or legitimising biopiracy), the USPTO has consistently proven itself to be an open door for anything remotely resembling an invention. As Quillen and Webster note,

36    P Drahos, 'Towards an International Framework for the Protection of Traditional Group Knowledge' (Report from UNCTAD-Commonwealth Secretariat Workshop on Elements of National *Sui Generis* Systems for the Preservation, Protection and Promotion of Traditional Knowledge, Innovations and Practices and Options for an International Framework, Geneva, 4-6 February 2004).

37    A Taubman, 'Saving the Village: Conserving Jurisprudential Diversity in the International Protection of Traditional Knowledge' in K E Maskus and J H Reichman (eds), *International Public Goods and Transfer of Technology Under a Globalised Intellectual Property Regime* (Cambridge University Press, 2005) 521.

average grant rates were around 67 per cent at the European Patent Office (EPO) and 64 per cent at the Japanese Patent Office (JPO) for the period 1995–99, while at the USPTO the grant rate was found to be between 87 and 97 per cent during 1993–98, including continuation applications — essentially re-filings of existing applications.[38] The United States is also one of the only remaining countries in the world yet to ratify the CBD. With the agreement of the Nagoya Protocol, the rest of the world is now preparing to implement a comprehensive international regime on ABS, which will have one glaring absentee. We must let the US Government know that this is unacceptable.

---

38   C D Quillen and O H Webster, 'Continuing Patent Applications and Performance of the United States Patent Office' (2001) 11(1) *Federal Circuit Bar Journal* 1; C Martinez and D Guellec, 'Overview of Recent Changes and Comparison of Patent Regimes in the United States, Japan and Europe' in OECD, *Patents, Innovation and Economic Performance: OECD Conference Proceedings* (OECD, 2004) 144.

# 5. Indigenous Cultural Heritage and Fair Trade: Voluntary Certification Standards in the Light of WIPO and WTO Law and Policy-making

Christoph B. Graber and Jessica C. Lai

## 1. Introduction

For a long time, the issue of trading indigenous cultural heritage (ICH)[1] was discussed with a defensive attitude. The question was generally how indigenous peoples could be protected against third parties misappropriating their knowledge assets in national or international trade. Academic writings adopting this approach seconded indigenous peoples fighting against old injustices stemming from unresolved problems of colonisation and a subjugation of their culture under Western law. Only very recently has a new wave of scholarship started to challenge this type of defensive thinking and tackle the issue of trading ICH from the development perspective.[2] The question now is how trade in ICH can contribute to the economic and social development of indigenous peoples. The idea behind this approach is that an active participation in the trade of traditional cultural expressions (TCEs) and other traditional knowledge (TK) would offer indigenous peoples not only a source of income — allowing for a reduction of government aid dependency — but also a means for becoming architects of their proper future and, thus, increasing their sense of identity and dignity. Because ICH is a multidimensional asset, an important precondition for such indigenous empowerment would certainly be that the decision about which TCE can be traded and which TCE — because of its sacred or otherwise important meaning for a community — must not enter the market is a prerogative of the respective TCE- and TK-owning indigenous community.

---

1   Whereas indigenous cultural and intellectual property (ICIP) is a term also used to describe the subject matter, indigenous peoples often prefer to speak of indigenous cultural heritage (ICH). Accordingly, the latter term is used in this chapter.

2   An important step in this development was the launch of the Swiss National Science Foundation funded 'International Trade in Indigenous Cultural Heritage' research project in December 2009 at the University of Lucerne. This multi-year, international and trans-disciplinary project investigates how international law could be adjusted to allow indigenous peoples to actively participate in international trade with their cultural heritage without being constrained to renounce important traditional values. For more information see <http://www.unilu.ch/deu/research_projects_135765.html>

Recent developments at the level of international law and policy-making support efforts to view trade in ICH from a development perspective to some extent. The agenda of the World Trade Organization (WTO) Agreement on Trade-Related Aspects of Intellectual Property Rights (TRIPS Agreement) — as far as it deals with TK (including the relationship with the Convention on Biological Diversity (CBD))— and the United Nations Educational, Scientific and Cultural Organization (UNESCO) are both sensitive to development considerations.[3] Neither organisation, however, is much concerned with indigenous issues in particular.[4] The World Intellectual Property Organization (WIPO) has recently included the development dimension into its agenda, and the documents produced by its Intergovernmental Committee on Intellectual Property and Genetic Resources, Traditional Knowledge and Folklore (IGC) since 2001 show that development is taken seriously.[5] However, the IGC has been reluctant to clarify whether interests of indigenous peoples should be treated in a privileged manner.

An important shortcoming of all current initiatives at the international level is that they increase rather than reduce the existing fragmentation of the relevant law on ICH. There is also a risk that these top-down initiatives will be difficult to implement, since indigenous and non-indigenous stakeholders may have diverging views even on central matters of regulation. This chapter endeavours to take up an idea that has little been studied so far: that is, exploring the potential of bottom-up approaches, including private initiatives of voluntary certification standards, as alternatives to top-down approaches in the field of ICH and development. An interesting question to be addressed is whether the very successful Fairtrade labelling system could be extended to trade in ICH in a way likely to be accepted by indigenous peoples. A further question will be how such voluntary certification standards would relate to WIPO's draft provisions on TK/TCEs, and whether they would be in conformity with WTO/TRIPS law and policy-making.

---

3 Strengthening the contribution of culture to sustainable development has been a goal of UNESCO policy-making since the launch of World Decade for Cultural Development (1988–1998). For most recent developments see below n 10.

4 Although UNESCO stresses that its 'activities with indigenous peoples are framed by its missions to protect and promote cultural diversity, encourage intercultural dialogue and enhance linkages between culture and development', see <http://portal.unesco.org/culture/en/ev.php-URL_ID=35393&URL_DO=DO_TOPIC&URL_SECTION=201.html>, its Convention on the Protection and Promotion of the Diversity of Cultural Expressions (CCD) (UNESCO, 2005), does not respond sufficiently to the interests of indigenous peoples. This is because the CCD was designed by its drafters to protect national entertainment industries rather than creative expressions of indigenous peoples. Indeed, a reference to TCE and indigenous peoples was introduced only at a late stage of the negotiations. Although the adopted text does mention TCE and indigenous peoples a few times, the relevant provisions do not address the rights of the indigenous peoples themselves, but those of the states whose territory is affected. See C B Graber, 'Institutionalization of Creativity in Traditional Societies and in International Trade Law' in S Ghosh and R P Malloy (eds), *Creativity, Law and Entrepreneurship* (Edward Elgar, 2011) 234, 247-248.

5 See below n 13.

## 2. ICH International Policy-making and the Problem of Top-down Approaches

As most indigenous peoples appear in the lower end of socioeconomic statistics, the potential to generate an income from the trade of their cultural heritage — such as their designs, dances, songs, stories and sacred artwork — is not insignificant to their wellbeing. As recent research (including the Harvard Project on American Indian Economic Development)[6] shows, there is evidence 'that economic development in Indian Country has finally gained traction across many reservations only after policies of self-determination took effect'.[7] Similarly, we take the view that trade in indigenous knowledge assets may promote social and economic development of indigenous communities,[8] provided that such trade is controlled by them.[9] The requirement that indigenous communities decide beforehand whether a certain part of their cultural heritage may be traded must be a *conditio sine qua non*. The new scholarly approach to look at trade in ICH from a development perspective fits well with the growing international awareness of policy-makers that intellectual property (IP) and cultural expressions may be an important driver of social and economic development, including for indigenous peoples. As a follow-up to the 2010 UN Millennium Summit, the United Nations General Assembly adopted a resolution on culture and development on 20 December 2010.[10] The resolution emphasises the important contribution of culture for sustainable development, and for the achievement of national and international development objectives, including the Millennium Development Goals.[11] The 2008 UN Creative Economy Report

---

6    The Harvard Project on American Indian Economic Development has undertaken a comprehensive, systematic and comparative study of social, economic and political conditions of American Indian reservations over the last 20 years. See E C Henson et al (eds), *The State of the Native Nations: Conditions under U.S. Policies of Self-determination* (Oxford University Press, 2008).

7    Ibid 9.

8    For a more sceptical view on the question whether such commercialisation would be desirable as a consequence for indigenous peoples, see R K Paterson and D S Karjala, 'Looking Beyond Intellectual Property in Resolving Protection of the Intangible Cultural Heritage of Indigenous Peoples' (2003) 11 *Cardozo Journal of International and Comparative Law* 633, 634.

9    The requirement that trade in ICH must be controlled by indigenous communities is reflected at the level of international law by the United Nations Declaration on the Rights of Indigenous Peoples (UNDRIP). The UNDRIP emphasises collective rights of indigenous self-determination and self-government, including in cultural matters. Although the UNDRIP is not a binding instrument of international law and does not create new rights, it provides for a detailing and interpretation of the human rights enshrined in other international human rights instruments with universal resonance. See C B Graber, 'Aboriginal Self-Determination vs. the Propertisation of Traditional Culture: The Case of Sacred Wanjina Sites' (2009) 13(2) *Australian Indigenous Law Review* 18, 27.

10   See UNESCO Executive Office Sector for Culture, *The United Nations Recognizes the Role of Culture for Development* (2010) <http://portal.unesco.org/culture/en/ev.php-URL_ID=41466&URL_DO=DO_TOPIC&URL_SECTION=201.html>

11   This resolution is noteworthy insofar as the eight Millennium Development Goals do not mention culture explicitly. See UN, *Development Programme — What are the Millenium Development Goals?* (2011) <http://www.undp.org/mdg/basics.shtml>

emphasised the link between the economy and culture as a 'new development paradigm',[12] and WIPO started to look at IP from a development perspective in the framework of the WIPO Development Agenda.[13] The scope of the latter includes knowledge assets of indigenous peoples in developing and developed countries. Development is also an issue in ongoing WIPO negotiations within the IGC, eventually leading to binding or non-binding international instruments on TK, genetic resources and TCEs.[14]

Although the discussions in the WIPO IGC on TCEs and TK have been ongoing for over ten years, little progress has been made. After twenty sessions of the IGC,[15] no agreement is in view even with regard to the key objectives and principles of the new TCE (and TK) instrument, and views diverge between indigenous and non-indigenous stakeholders and often even between indigenous communities. For indigenous peoples, one central question is whether the new instruments should also extend to TCEs and TK of a non-indigenous origin. A further issue is that creating new WIPO instruments on TCEs and TK risks increasing rather than reducing the existing fragmentation of the relevant law on ICH. These difficulties have provoked critical comments questioning the feasibility of any top-down solution to the problem.[16] Taking such criticism seriously, in this

---

12   According to the UN Creative Economy Report, *The Challenge of Assessing the Creative Economy: Towards Informed Policy-making,* UN Doc UNCTAD/DITC/2008/2 (2008), 3 'a new development paradigm is emerging that links the economy and culture, embracing economic, cultural, technological and social aspects of development at both the macro and micro levels. Central to the new paradigm is the fact that creativity, knowledge and access to information are increasingly recognized as powerful engines driving economic growth and promoting development in a globalizing world.' Chapter 6.4 of the report explicitly deals with TCEs. The report was drafted jointly by United Nations Conference on Trade and Development (UNCTAD) and United Nations Development Programme (UNDP) in cooperation with UNESCO, WIPO and International Trade Centre (ITC).

13   The WIPO Development Agenda was established by the WIPO General Assembly in October 2007. It includes a set of 45 recommendations designed to enhance the development dimension of the organisation's activities. Recommendation 18 (related to norm-setting, flexibilities, public policy and public domain) urges the IGC 'to accelerate the process on the protection of genetic resources, traditional knowledge and folklore, without prejudice to any outcome, including the possible development of an international instrument or instruments'. In addition to the adoption of the Development Agenda, WIPO member states also approved a recommendation to establish a Committee on Development and Intellectual Property. See generally the chapters in N W Netanel (ed), *The Development Agenda: Global Intellectual Property and Developing Countries* (Oxford University Press, 2009).

14   The idea of 'development' underlies the whole WIPO Draft on the protection of TCE. To this end, two objectives of the draft are relevant: objective (iii), which aims to 'contribute to the welfare and sustainable economic, cultural, environmental and social development of such peoples and communities'; and objective (xi), which aims to promote the development of indigenous peoples and communities and 'legitimate trading activities'. Objective (xi) promotes the use of TCE for the development of indigenous peoples and communities, where desired by them. Moreover, the objective recognises the TCE as 'an asset of the communities that identify with them, such as through the development and expansion of marketing opportunities for tradition-based creations and innovations'. See WIPO IGC Secretariat, *The Protection of Traditional Cultural Expression/ Expression of Folklore: Revised Objectives and Principles,* WIPO Doc WIPO/GRTKF/IC/17/4 (2010).

15   The 20th session of the IGC took place on 14-22 February 2012.

16   See P Drahos, 'A Networked Responsive Regulatory Approach to Protecting Traditional Knowledge' in D J Gervais (ed), *Intellectual Property, Trade and Development: Strategies to Optimize Economic Development in a TRIPS-plus Era* (Oxford University Press, 2007) 385.

chapter we take up Peter Drahos's suggestion to think also about alternative bottom-up approaches to commercialising ICH.[17] Since the prevention of fakes and reducing the market share of imitations would be crucial to enhance trade in ICH, international law could assist indigenous peoples through the establishment of a system of origin certification that would work at the international level.

Such a strategy may also find support from indigenous brokers, since the United Nations Permanent Forum on Indigenous Issues recommended, in a 2003 report, that states should promote 'the knowledge, application and dissemination of appropriate technologies and indigenous peoples' local products with certificates of origin to activate product activities, as well as the use, management and conservation of natural resources'.[18] A prominent forum for discussing issues of origin of traditional knowledge assets is the CBD. Although the CBD focuses on TK that is associated with genetic resources, discussions on disclosure or certification of origin held therein may be relevant also for other forms of TK relating to the subject matter of IP applications. A report delivered by the United Nations Conference on Trade and Development (UNCTAD) on the invitation of the Seventh Conference of the Parties of the CBD[19] shows that certificates of origin are important in the realm of the CBD 'to certify that the source of genetic resources and associated traditional knowledge has the authority to provide access on specified conditions, and also to certify the existence of *ex ante* benefit-sharing requirements that are compliant with the CBD and with relevant laws and equitable principles of the country providing such resources or knowledge'.[20] Beyond enabling access to TK associated with genetic resources and demonstrating prior informed consent and equitable benefit sharing (as a precondition for obtaining IP rights);[21] certificates of origin may facilitate further commercial uses. If certificates of origin are linked with labelling systems or origin marks, they may be useful 'in promoting commercial recognition of the subject matter of intellectual property and in obtaining benefits for countries

---

17   Ibid.
18   UN Permanent Forum on Indigenous Issues, *Recommendations Specifically Pertaining to Indigenous Women and the Girl Child, adopted by the Permanent Forum on Indigenous Issues, Report of the Second Session*, UN Doc E/C.19/2003/22 (2003), 9; Drahos, above n 16, 402.
19   See UNCTAD, *Analysis of Options for Implementing Disclosure of Origin Requirements in Intellectual Property Applications. A contribution to UNCTAD's response to the invitation of the Seventh Conference of the Parties of the Convention on Biological Diversity*, UNCTAD Doc UNCTAD/DITC/TED/2004/14 (2006). In 2004, at its Seventh Meeting, the CBD Conference of Parties, in Decision VII/19, invited WIPO and UNCTAD to analyse issues relating to implementation of disclosure of origin requirements in the IP law system. Part VI of the report delivered by UNCTAD provides for an analysis of IP issues raised by international certificates of origin.
20   Ibid 69.
21   Prior informed consent and equitable benefit sharing are required under the *Nagoya Protocol on Access to Genetic Resources and the Fair and Equitable Sharing of Benefits Arising from their Utilization to the Convention on Biological Diversity* (2010), arts 4.1*bis*, 5.1*bis*, 5*bis*, 9.

and indigenous or local communities that exercise rights over genetic resources and associated traditional knowledge'.[22] The report cautions, however, that this may raise difficult questions regarding the 'authenticity' standard to be applied.

In fact, experiences with the Australian Authenticity Labels, certifying as 'authentic' goods and services deriving from a work of art created by an indigenous person or people, were negative. What were the reasons for this failure? Fairtrade, another example of voluntary certification standards, is by contrast a big success. Why is this? Fairtrade certification and its system of minimum pricing were designed for commodity products. Could one nonetheless learn from this model to avoid flaws, such as those identified in the Australian Authenticity scheme, and develop a model that would meet the interests of both indigenous peoples and consumers in a global market? These questions will be addressed in the next section.

# 3. Voluntary Certification Standards and ICH

## (a) Typical Features of a Voluntary Certification Standard

In its most general description, a voluntary certification standard consists of three key elements, including: (1) voluntary standard-setting; (2) certification; and (3) labelling and marketing.[23] When applied to ICH, an essential requirement would be that all three elements are controlled by indigenous communities. Accordingly, voluntary standard-setting would typically consist of a process whereby indigenous peoples agree on minimal requirements that select cultural goods or services should meet. These standard requirements could relate to the origin of a good or service, its physical properties, or the process through which it is produced or commercialised. Certification then would involve an independent body examining whether the good or service at issue would actually conform to the set standard. Finally, labelling would make the conformity of a good or service with the standard visible to suppliers, intermediate buyers or end consumers and would, thus, allow for a specifically designed marketing campaign. To protect the label against misuse, it could be registered as a regular trade mark or certification mark according to the national law that is applicable.

---

22  UNCTAD, above n 19, 73.
23  M Chon, 'Marks of Rectitude' (2009) 77 *Fordham Law Review* 101, 105.

## (b) Why Did the Australian Authenticity Label Fail?

Voluntary certification standards have been used in several countries as a means to promote trade in ICH.[24] These had had varying success. For example, whereas the Alaskan 'Silver Hand' certification mark has been around since 1961,[25] the New Zealand 'Māori Made' *Toi Iho* certification mark system was disinvested by the Government in 2009, as it had not achieved increased sales of Māori art by licensed artists or retailers.[26] Since the Australian Authenticity Label has been widely commented upon, we will have a closer look at this scheme and ask why it failed only two years after its introduction.

The Australian Authenticity Label was launched in 1999 along with a 'Label of Collaboration'.[27] The Label of Authenticity was for 'authentic' goods or services which were 'derived from a work of art created by an Aboriginal or Torres Strait Islander person or people, [and] reproduced or produced and manufactured by Aboriginal or Torres Strait Islander people'.[28] The Label of Collaboration was for works that were a result of collaboration involving 'authentic' creation by an Aboriginal or Torres Strait Islander, and reproduction or production and manufacture by non-indigenous persons, under a licence (for the copyright of the work) from a fair and legitimate agreement.[29] The purpose of the Australian Authenticity Labels was to maximise consumers' certainty 'that they were getting the genuine product',[30] to promote Aboriginal and Torres Strait Islander authorship,[31] and to help ensure a fair, equitable and improved return to indigenous authors.[32]

---

24 Australia, Canada, New Zealand and Portugal are examples of countries where certification marks have been used to ensure the authenticity and quality of indigenous artefacts, see WIPO, *Intellectual Property Handbook: Policy, Law and Use* (WIPO Publication 489, 2004) <http://www.wipo.int/about-ip/en/iprm/> para 2.306; D Zografos, *Intellectual Property and Traditional Cultural Expressions* (Edward Elgar, 2010) 103-42.

25 Zografos, above n 24, 114-119.

26 Creative New Zealand, 'Statement on toi iho™' (21 October 2001) <http://www.creativenz.govt.nz/en/news/creative-new-zealand-statement-on-toi-iho> The toi iho trade marks have been transferred to the Transition Toi Iho Foundation (made up of Māori) to continue the system.

27 M Rimmer, 'Australian Icons: Authenticity and Identity Politics' (2004) 3 *Indigenous Law Journal* 139, 141. The authenticity mark was officially registered in March 2000. Interestingly, the collaboration mark was not approved until August 2003, well after the marks had become defunct. See T Janke, *Minding Culture: Case Studies on Intellectual Property and Traditional Cultural Expressions* (WIPO, 2003) 140.

28 Board of Studies NSW, *Protecting Aboriginal Indigenous Art: Ownership, Copyright and Marketing Issues for NSW Schools* (Board of Studies NSW, 2006) 16.

29 Ibid 16; Janke, above n 27, 143.

30 See Drahos, above n 16, 402; see also Arts Law Centre of Australia, *Certificates of Authenticity* (2004) <http://www.artslaw.com.au/images/uploads/AITB_CertificatesOfAuthenticity.pdf>

31 J Anderson, 'The Politics of Indigenous Knowledge: Australia's Proposed Communal Moral Rights Bill' (2004) 27(3) *University of New South Wales Law Journal* 585, fn 76; see also M Annas, 'The Label of Authenticity: A Certification Trade Mark for Goods and Services of Indigenous Origin' (1997) 3(90) *Aboriginal Law Bulletin* 4.

32 Drahos, above n 16, 402; see also Annas, above n 31; Janke, above n 27, 145.

Both labels were registered as 'certification marks' under the Australian Trade Marks Act.[33] Whereas normal trade marks distinguish certain goods or services as those produced by a specific (natural or legal) person, certification marks indicate that the certified goods or services comply with a set of standards and have been certified by a certification authority.[34] The marks were owned by the National Indigenous Arts Advocacy Association (NIAAA).[35] The NIAAA was also the certification authority. In this function, the NIAAA certified that the protected goods or services complied with the required standard: that is, that they were or involved an 'authentic' creation by an Australian indigenous person.[36]

The first step required for use of the marks was registration to the NIAAA. To register an artwork or similar product, an artist had to show that he or she *identified* as Aboriginal or Torres Strait Islander. Artists also had to show that they indeed were indigenous *by descent* through providing two signed forms certified by an Aboriginal corporation and passed at a meeting.[37] They also had to show that they were accepted as indigenous by a community, and had permission from the relevant community to make the artwork or product.[38] For the Collaboration Label, the indigenous artist and the producer or manufacturer had to apply jointly.[39] Once registered, the artist had permission to use the label on his or her artwork or product.[40] Use had to comply with a set of rules, including that the works were created within indigenous customary law.[41]

---

33 See *Trade Marks Act 1995* s 169 (Cth) stating that:
A certification trade mark is a sign used, or intended to be used, to distinguish goods or services:
(a) dealt with or provided in the course of trade; and
(b) certified by a person (owner of the certification trade mark), or by another person approved by that person, in relation to quality, accuracy or some other characteristic, including (in the case of goods) origin, material or mode of manufacture; from other goods or services dealt with or provided in the course of trade but not so certified.

34 A Taubman and M Leistner, 'Analysis of Different Areas of Indigenous Resources, Traditional Knowledge' in S von Lewinski (ed), *Indigenous Heritage and Intellectual Property: Genetic Resources, Traditional Knowledge and Folklore* (2nd ed, Kluwer Law International, 2008) 59, 127-129; WIPO, above n 24, paras 2.330–2.332.

35 NIAAA, *Policy and Objectives* (2011) <http://www.culture.com.au/exhibition/niaaa/about.htm> The NIAAA had indigenous leadership. However, this leadership was unstable and fluctuated constantly. Moreover, there was much debate as to whether the organisation was representative of all Aborigines, as it was perceived as a Sydney-based entity, rather than an association enjoying wider support. Email from Matthew Rimmer, 25 February 2011 [on file with the authors].

36 L Wiseman, 'Regulating Authenticity' (2000) 9(2) *Griffith Law Review* 248, 252.

37 Janke, above n 27, 142.

38 Wiseman, above n 36, 261. Interestingly, many indigenous artists did not like having to prove their indigeneity and called it another 'Dog Tag' system.

39 Janke, above n 27, 143. Determining whether the contract between the indigenous artist and producer or manufacturer had 'fair trading terms' included assessing: (1) 'whether the Indigenous person who contributed to the work had the opportunity to obtain independent advice from NIAAA, an Arts Law Center or a legal adviser before signing the agreement'; and (2) 'whether the Indigenous person is required to assign their intellectual property rights in the work without additional payment of consideration'.

40 Arts Law Centre of Australia, above n 30, 1.

41 Janke, above n 27, 142.

On the retail level, the two marks allowed an indigenous arts and crafts retailer to inform customers that he or she supported the Authenticity Labels and that his or her business operated under a NIAAA licence. Practically, this licensing arrangement was exhibited by a sticker to be affixed on shop windows or doors.[42]

The two Authenticity Labels existed only for two years. According to commentators, there were a number of reasons for this failure, including difficulties in defining 'authenticity' and insufficient funding of the system's administration.[43] Difficulties in defining and monitoring what fell into the term 'authentic' were certainly the main factors in the system's failure.[44] Definition involved value judgements about Aboriginal art and — as had been feared by members of the indigenous arts and crafts community — the distinction of two categories of authentic and non-authentic indigenous art.[45] The NIAAA was criticised for introducing an 'authenticity' standard in a top-down way, without sufficient involvement of indigenous stakeholders.[46] As a matter of fact, the NIAAA did not reflect that certain indigenous communities already had their own identification marks prior to the inception of the NIAAA marks.[47] Moreover, artists who were part of local or regional art centres or organisations did not feel that they needed the NIAAA labels to denote the 'authenticity' of their products.[48] Thus, the labelling system was never widely accepted or used by the indigenous peoples of Australia.

Commentators emphasised the impossibility of developing a common authenticity standard in an environment where there is little agreement among various indigenous groups regarding the concept of Aboriginal identity. In particular, rural and peripheral indigenous communities did not like the idea of a 'homogenising' national labelling system.[49] And many urban indigenous artists were concerned that 'authentic' would denote indigenous art 'that employs traditional techniques, materials and imagery'.[50]

There were flaws not only in the definition of 'authenticity' but also in the implementation of the standard. According to commentators, the NIAAA's lack

---

42    Ibid 144.
43    L Wiseman, 'The Protection of Indigenous Art and Culture in Australia: The Labels of Authenticity' (2001) 23(1) *European Intellectual Property Review* 14; Rimmer, above n 27; Drahos, above n 16, 402; Janke, above n 27, 145.
44    Rimmer, above n 27, 157.
45    Wiseman, above n 43, 14. According to Matthew Rimmer, the labels served to 'typecast Indigenous artists in a narrow and rigid fashion'; Rimmer, above n 27, 158.
46    J Anderson, *The Production of Indigenous Knowledge in Intellectual Property* (PhD Thesis, University of New South Wales, 2003) 240; Rimmer, above n 27, 158-159.
47    Anderson, above n 46, 240-241; Wiseman, above n 36, 266-267.
48    Janke, above n 27, 147.
49    Rimmer, above n 27, 160.
50    Anderson, above n 46, 240. Wiseman noted that '[f]or urban and non-traditional artists, the way authenticity is defined raises the problem that they may be stigmatized for not being "real" or "authentic" Aboriginal artists' Wiseman, above n 43, 20. See also Wiseman, above n 36, 262.

of independence made it too easy to show indigeneity and to get the marks.[51] It seems obvious that independence cannot be assured in an organisational structure where — as in the case of the NIAAA — the owner of the mark also sets the standards and acts as the certification body.

Poor funding was considered to be a second main structural shortcoming of the Australian Authenticity scheme. Although the NIAAA received some funding from the Australia Council and the Aboriginal and Torres Strait Islander Commission, these funds were not sufficient to establish the scheme at a national and international level.[52] To make the labels work effectively, the NIAAA would have required more money for marketing campaigns to raise awareness of the labels among consumers and tourists.[53] Commentators reckon that the lack of funding was also the reason all the responsibilities were given to the NIAAA rather than to a separate body established to undertake the certification role, as was recommended by Terri Janke prior to the launch of the labelling system.[54]

Besides these structural flaws, there were also shortcomings in the implementation and administration of the Australian scheme through the NIAAA. As a result of allegations of misappropriated funds and failures of accountability, the federal government's funding to the NIAAA was discontinued.[55] The Aboriginal and Torres Strait Islander Arts Board of the Australia Council commissioned a review of the NIAAA in 2002.[56] The review concluded that the NIAAA had poor governance and management, tended to focus on Sydney[57] and under-represented other indigenous communities, set a problematic definition of 'authenticity', had problems implementing the system and failed to be financially accountable. The review also placed some blame on the funding agencies for not supervising the NIAAA and for creating a culture of non-accountability.[58]

---

51  D Jopson, 'Aboriginal Seal of Approval Loses its Seal of Approval' *Sydney Morning Herald* (online), 14 December 2002, <http://www.smh.com.au/articles/2002/12/13/1039656221205.html> Rimmer, above n 27, 159.

52  Drahos, above n 16, 403. The scheme was meant to be additionally financed through charging fees for applications and labels. However, the A$30 registration for the Label of Authenticity and A$50 for the Collaboration Label were considered to be prohibitive by many Aboriginal artists. This was because much of the artist community was made up of hobby artists whose income was insufficient to warrant the registration fee. See Wiseman, above n 36, 265; Janke, above n 27, 145.

53  Janke, above n 27, 146.

54  T Janke, *Our Culture: Our Future: Report on Australian Indigenous Cultural and Intellectual Property Rights* (Michael Frankel and Company Solicitors, 1998) 204, 207; Rimmer, above n 27, 164.

55  Anderson, above n 31.

56  This report was not made public, but is discussed by Rimmer, above n 27, 161-164.

57  Where the NIAAA was based.

58  Rimmer, above n 27, 164.

## (c) Could One Learn from the Fairtrade Label?

In comparison with the failure of the Australian Authenticity mark, the success of the Fairtrade label is striking. The history of the Fairtrade system goes back to 1988, when *Max Havelaar* was founded as the first Fairtrade label under the initiative of the Dutch development agency Solidaridad.[59] In the late 1980s to early 1990s, this initiative was replicated in several other markets in Europe and North America, each with its own mark.[60] To unite all the existing labelling initiatives under one umbrella, and harmonise standards and certification worldwide, in 1997 the Fairtrade Labelling Organization International (FLO) was established in Bonn, Germany.[61] The different labels remained until 2002, when the FLO launched the international FAIRTRADE Certification Mark and the former labels were gradually replaced.[62] Canada and the US still use their own labels.[63]

An overall concern of the fair trade movement is to fight for global justice and to equalise the north–south divide of producers in the world market for commodity products.[64] Accordingly, the purpose of the Fairtrade labelling system is to help small-scale farmers and workers in developing countries.[65] In addition to ensuring that suppliers are not unfairly exploited by the mechanisms of the global market, the Fairtrade system aims at contributing to social and environmental development in marginalised regions of the world.[66] From its beginning, a characteristic of the Fairtrade scheme was its grassroots collaborative approach.[67] Producers jointly own and manage the FLO, and producers are members on the Board of Directors.[68] Accordingly, producers determine the direction that Fairtrade will head towards, and decisions are taken

---

59   The history of Fairtrade is outlined by the FLO, *History of Fairtrade* (2011) <http://www.fairtrade.net> and A Hutchens, *Changing Big Business: The Globalisation of the Fair Trade Movement* (Edward Elgar, 2009) 55-77.

60   Max Havelaar (in Belgium, Switzerland, Denmark, Norway and France), Transfair (in Germany, Austria, Luxemburg, Italy, the US, Canada and Japan), Fairtrade Mark in the UK and Ireland, Rättvisemärkt in Sweden, and Reilu Kauppa in Finland.

61   FLO, above n 59. On the crucial role of FLO International, see Chon, above n 23, 134-135.

62   FLO, *About the Mark* (2011) <http://www.fairtrade.net>

63   Ibid, the 'Fair Trade Certified' label.

64   For a history of the fair trade movement, see Zografos, above n 24, 143-149.

65   Producers must come from countries with low to medium development status in Africa, Asia, Oceania, Latin America and the Caribbean. The products must come from small farmer organisations (small producers, small-scale farmers) who do not depend on hired workers all the time, but run their farm mainly by using their own and their family's labour. Companies with hired labour may apply for certain products. See FLO, *Geographical Scope of Producer Certification for Fairtrade Labelling* (2009) <http://www.fairtrade.net/uploads/media/Aug09_Geographical_scope.pdf>

66   FLO, *Aims of Fairtrade Standards* (2011) <http://www.fairtrade.net>

67   Chon, above n 23, 115.

68   FLO, *Fairtrade is Unique* (2009) <http://www.fairtrade.net/fileadmin/user_upload/content/2009/resources/Fairtrade_is_Unique.pdf> 2.

in an open and inclusive fashion.[69] In our view, the bottom-up, collaborative and open approach of the Fairtrade system makes an important contrast to the NIAAA and the Australian Authenticity Labels. As we have highlighted above, the NIAAA operated in a top-down manner, many indigenous communities were never consulted about the development of the marks, and most artists never felt that the mark was theirs.

Stakeholder involvement is an important element of Fairtrade standards. Whereas the Australian scheme was based on a NIAAA-imposed standard of 'authenticity', Fairtrade standards are set in accordance with the ISEAL Code of Good Practice for Setting Social and Environmental Standards.[70] According to ISEAL requirements, Fairtrade standard-setting processes are open, and involve the major stakeholders in the system, including producers and the FLO.[71] There are two sets of Fairtrade standards, for two different types of disadvantaged producers.[72] One applies to smallholders who are working together in cooperatives or other organisations with a democratic and participative structure. For these, a generic producer standard is that profits should be equally distributed among the producers. Furthermore, all members need to have a voice and vote in the organisation's decision-making process.[73] The other set of standards applies to workers, whose employers pay decent wages, guarantee the right to join trade unions (freedom of association), ensure health and safety standards, and provide adequate housing where relevant. Fairtrade standards also cover terms of trade.[74] Most products have a Fairtrade price, meaning that companies trading Fairtrade products must pay a minimum amount to the producers (to cover the costs of sustainable production).[75] This price is periodically reviewed by the FLO.[76] Producers also get an additional Fairtrade premium, which goes into a communal fund for workers and famers to invest in their communities: for example, for education or healthcare. The decision on how to do this is made democratically: for example, within a farmers' organisation or by workers on a plantation.[77] The standards also allow producers to request partial pre-payment of the contract.[78] This is important for small-scale farmers' organisations to

---

69   For example, when it was deciding on the future of the FAIRTRADE Mark, the FLO invited Fairtrade members, producers, traders and consumers to join them in developing a new strategy, see FLO, *Making the Difference: The Global Strategy for Fairtrade* (2009) <http://www.fairtrade.se/obj/docpart/c/c6ad566a479f109 86c87188d237057d1.pdf> 4. However, Hutchens concluded that the FLO is now so big and market orientated that it has 'effectively invalidated producer and FTO [Fair Trade Organization] voices/knowledge'; Hutchens, above n 59, 130.

70   FLO, above n 66.

71   Chon, above n 23, 115.

72   FLO, *What is Fairtrade* (2011) <http://www.fairtrade.net>

73   FLO, *Standards for Small-scale Producer* (2011) < http://www.fairtrade.net>

74   FLO, above n 72.

75   Ibid.

76   FLO, *Frequently Asked Questions* (2011) <http://www.fairtrade.net>

77   FLO, *Why Fairtrade is Unique* (2011) <http://www.fairtrade.net>

78   Ibid.

ensure they have cash flow to pay farmers. Buyers are required to enter into trading relationships so that producers can predict their income and plan for the future.

A second major difference between Fairtrade and the Australian scheme relates to the certification process. Whereas in the Australian scheme all functions were centralised in the NIAAA, in the Fairtrade system the process for certification is separate from the system's operational management and performed by FLO-CERT.[79] FLO-CERT is ISO 65 certified. ISO 65 is the leading, internationally recognised quality norm for bodies operating a product certification system.[80] ISO 65 certification guarantees: (1) the existence of a quality management system; (2) transparency in all processes; and (3) independence in the certification decision-making. To ensure compliance with ISO 65 rules, FLO-CERT is checked by an independent third party. As part of the certification process, FLO-CERT inspects and certifies producer organisations, and audits traders to check whether they comply with the standards.[81] The cost of audits — which also include on-site inspections of producers — is charged to the producer wanting to become part of the system. One important reason for the impressive dissemination of Fairtrade among marginalised producers is the financial and administrative assistance offered by FLO for initial applicants.[82]

The marketing aspect is a third major difference between Fairtrade and the Australian scheme. Whereas poor national and international marketing was one of the reasons for the failure of the Australian Authenticity marks, the Fairtrade system's marketing concept is considered crucial for the success of the Fairtrade movement.[83] The goodwill of Fairtrade is represented internationally by the FAIRTRADE Certification Mark, which is an internationally registered trade mark. The mark is a product label, mainly intended for use on the packaging of products that satisfy the Fairtrade standards.[84] It allows consumers to buy products in line with their value judgements regarding justice in the north–south divide.[85] Consumers' confidence in the FAIRTRADE mark and what it

---

79  Chon, above n 23, 135. Although FLO-CERT is owned by FLO, it is independent, FLO, *Certifying Fairtrade* (2011) <http://www.fairtrade.net>

80  FLO, above n 79.

81  This includes a review of the organisation's documents (e.g. financial, labour-related, statutes and internal policies) and interviews of organisation members (e.g. members of the Executive Committee and workers). See FLO-CERT, *Certification for Development* (2010) <http://www. flo-cert.net>

82  The FLO's Producer and Service Relations Unit can support producers to secure and retain certification. Grants amount to 500 euros for initial applications. See FLO, *Selling Fairtrade* (2011) <http://www.fairtrade.net>

83  FLO, above n 69, 11. See also Hutchens, above n 59, 78-101.

84  FLO, *Using the FAIRTRADE MARK* (2011) <http://www.fairtrade.net>

85  FLO, *Benefits of Fairtrade* (2011) <http://www.fairtrade.net>

represents is assured by the high quality of the standardisation and certification processes, and the continued checking of compliance. The mark is now the most widely recognised social and development label in the world.[86]

The FAIRTRADE mark is owned by FLO, but Fairtrade products are marketed by national labelling initiatives or marketing organisations working in twenty-five countries.[87] The national labelling initiatives may also license out the mark in their countries. The FLO is striving to streamline marketing operations of the national marketing initiatives while taking account of the cultural diversity of all its members and stakeholders.[88]

Finally, the Fairtrade label system is financially sustainable.[89] Comparatively, one of the reasons why the Australian system was deemed a failure was the lack of financial accountability.[90]

## (d) Preliminary Conclusion

Fairtrade aims to help farmers in developing countries exclusively. The system, moreover, is designed for commodity products.[91] Accordingly, it would not be possible to extend the current system to creative artefacts produced by indigenous peoples in developed countries such as Australia, New Zealand, the United States and Canada. First, such artefacts include tangible and intangible creations that in many ways are different from commodity products; and, secondly, indigenous peoples in these countries would be excluded from the system because of the development criterion.

Nonetheless, there are lessons that can be learned from the Fairtrade system. One important factor is certainly that Fairtrade did not begin from government or other top-down initiatives, but rather from the people in a grassroots manner. A second aspect is the institutional separation of the certification process from the other two functions of the system. Thirdly, in an environment of globalised markets, including markets for tangible and intangible artefacts of indigenous peoples, marketing strategies for an indigenous origin label must be developed at an international level. Finally, the success of such schemes depends largely on

---

86    At the end of 2008, there were 872 Fairtrade-certified producer organisations in 58 countries, representing over 1.5 million farmers and workers. FLO estimates that 7.5 million people directly benefit from Fairtrade. Over the last five years, sales of Fairtrade-certified products have grown almost 40% per year (on average) and, in 2008, Fairtrade-certified sales amounted to approximately € 2.9 billion worldwide, FLO, *Facts and Figures* (2011) <http://www.fairtrade.net>

87    FLO, *Fair Trade at a Glance* (2010) <http://www.fairtrade.com.au/files/FTF10/Glance.pdf> 1.

88    FLO, above n 69 , 11 and 13.

89    FLO, *Growing Stronger Together. Annual Report 2009-10* (2010) <http://www.fairtrade.net/fileadmin/user_upload/content/2009/resources/FLO_Annual-Report-2009_komplett_double_web.pdf> 24-25.

90    Rimmer, above n 27, 163.

91    FLO, *Products* (2011) <http://www.fairtrade.net/products.html> The products are: coffee, bananas, tea, cocoa, cotton, sugar, full range of herbs and spices, sweet potatoes, melons, olives and olive oil.

sufficient funding for proper marketing and consumer education. In the context of such a system for indigenous peoples, this may mean that strong state support may be required, at least initially.

# 4. Compatibility with International Law

In this section we will investigate how a voluntary standard certifying indigenous origin would relate to the in-progress WIPO legal instruments on TK/TCEs, and whether it would be in conformity with the TRIPS Agreement law and policy-making.

## (a) WIPO

In February 2012, WIPO's IGC met for its 20th session of debates regarding the development of new instruments of international law for the protection of TCE, TK and genetic resources. For the previous six years, divisive discussions in IGC meetings focused on the controversial 2005 draft provisions, prepared by the WIPO IGC Secretariat, for a *sui generis* protection of TK, TCEs and genetic resources.[92] In 2007, the WIPO General Assembly renewed the IGC's mandate for two years, during which time there were three sessions but no consensus.[93] Despite this, in October 2009 the General Assembly of the WIPO decided to renew the IGC's mandate for a further two years.[94] At the same time it was decided to start formal negotiations based on the draft proposals contained in the document on 'Revised Objectives and Principles' for TCE: that is, the 2005 draft provisions that had originally been prepared by the Secretariat.[95] In October 2011, the mandate was again renewed for the 2012-2013 biennium.[96]

---

92   WIPO IGC Secretariat, *The Protection of Traditional Cultural Expressions/Expressions of Folklore: Revised Objectives and Principles*, WIPO Doc WIPO/GRTKF/IC/8/4 (2005).

93   WIPO General Assembly, *Report of the Thirty-Fourth (18th Ordinary) Session*, Geneva, 24 September to 3 October 2007, WIPO Doc WO/GA/34/16 (2007), para 293(c).

94   WIPO General Assembly, *Report of the Thirty-Eighth (19th Ordinary) Session*, Geneva, 22 September to 1 October 2009, WIPO Doc WO/GA/38/20 (2009), para 217.

95   Ibid, para 217(c), specifically referring to WIPO IGC Secretariat, *The Protection of Traditional Cultural Expressions/Expressions of Folklore: Revised Objectives and Principles*, WIPO Doc WIPO/GRTKF/IC/9/4 (2006); WIPO IGC Secretariat, *The Protection of Traditional Knowledge: Revised Objectives and Principles*, WIPO Doc WIPO/GRTKF/IC/9/5 (2006); and WIPO IGC Secretariat, *Genetic Resources: List of Options*, WIPO Doc WIPO/GRTKF/IC/11/8 (a) (2007). No decision was taken on whether these negotiations should lead to a binding or a non-binding instrument.

96   Assemblies of Member States of WIPO, *Matters Concerning the Intergovernmental Committee on Intellectual Property and Genetic Resources, Traditional Knowledge and Folklore* (Agenda Item 31, Decision, Fortieth, 20th Ordinary Session, 26 September to 5 October 2011).

In its 17th session, the IGC decided to use the results of the Intersessional Working Group on TCE (IWG 1) as the new textual basis for further negotiations.[97] The IGC also established open-ended drafting groups to streamline the articles on TCEs and to identify any outstanding policy issues. The work of these groups resulted in the document 'The Protection of Traditional Cultural Expressions: Draft Articles',[98] which was discussed in the IGC's 18th session, the outcome of which was deliberated over in the 19th session in July 2011.[99]

Since the start of the text-based negotiations in the 16th session of the IGC, drafting proposals made by member states have been continuously inserted into the working document, and updated versions have been produced after every session.[100] The lack of certainty about the general acceptance of these suggested changes makes a substantive analysis of the draft treaty difficult. Furthermore, no decision has yet been taken on whether these negotiations should lead to a binding or non-binding instrument and, even if binding and adopted by the WIPO General Assembly, states can still decide on whether they wish to be signatories or not. Thus, the following discourse is made tentatively.

The current document on TCE provides text that is relevant for certification trade marks. Article 3 of the draft provisions generally distinguishes the scope of and conditions for protection with regard to 'secret' TCEs and 'other' TCEs. Secret TCEs are protected against disclosure and any kind of use. With regard to other TCEs, there are three options. All three alternatives require that indigenous peoples be acknowledged as the source of the TCE, unless this is not possible because of the manner of use of the product. Under Alternative 1, it would be required that, with respect to TCEs which are words, signs, names and symbols, there be a collective right to authorise or prohibit the 'offering for sale or sale of articles that are falsely represented' as TCEs of the beneficiaries, and any use that 'falsely suggests a connection with the beneficiaries'.[101] There is also

---

97  The IWG is an IGC-established expert group, within which every WIPO member state is represented by one person. It was decided by the IGC that three IWG meetings would take place. IWG 1 on TCE took place in July 2010, and IWG 2 and 3 on TK and Genetic Resources, respectively, took place in February and March 2011. Although IWG is primarily an expert group, it can also draft text proposals for the amendment of the existing draft proposals for revised objectives and principles. The results of IWG 1 are contained in document WIPO IGC, *Draft Articles on the Protection of Traditional Cultural Expressions/Expression of Folklore,* Prepared at IWG 1, WIPO Doc WIPO/GRTKF/IC/17/9 (2010); IWG 2 in WIPO IGC, *Draft Articles on the Protection of Traditional Knowledge,* Prepared at IWG 2, WIPO Doc WIPO/GRTKF/IWG/2/3 (2011); and IWG 3 in WIPO IGC, *Draft Objectives and Principles Relating to Intellectual Property and Genetic Resources,* Prepared at IWG 3, WIPO Doc WIPO/GRTKF/IWG/3/17 (2011).
98  WIPO IGC Secretariat, *The Protection of Traditional Cultural Expressions: Draft Articles,* WIPO Doc WIPO/GRTKF/IC/18/4 (2011).
99  WIPO IGC Secretariat, *The Protection of Traditional Cultural Expressions: Draft Articles,* WIPO Doc WIPO/GRTKF/IC/19/4 (2011).
100  Each drafting proposal is accompanied by a footnote indicating the delegation which made the proposal. The first significant alteration to the 2005 draft can be found annexed to WIPO IGC Secretariat, *The Protection of Traditional Cultural Expressions/Expressions of Folklore: Revised Objectives and Principles,* above n 95.
101  WIPO IGC Secretariat, above n 14, fn 106.

a provision which allows indigenous peoples to object to any 'false, confusing or misleading indications' on goods or services that suggest an endorsement by or linkage with them.[102] Alternative 2 is the weakest option and does not mention protection from false misrepresentation. Finally, Alternative 3 states that adequate measures need to protect against the use of 'non-authentic' TCEs in trade 'that suggests a connection that does not exist'.

The working document that was the basis for the negotiations until the 17th session of the IGC provided requirements to prevent misleading indications and false endorsement by, or linkage with, a traditional community that were very similar to Alternative 1 and consistent with Alternative 3 outlined above. In the IGC Secretariat's commentary on Article 3 of the earlier draft, it mentioned a 'handicraft sold as "authentic" or "Indian" when it is not' as a practical example to illustrate the possible implementation of the provisions protecting against 'false or misleading indications in trade'.[103] According to the comment, the suggested principle could be put into practice at the national level through a number of measures, including 'the registration and use of certification trademarks'.[104] Although these comments are not part of the current working document, which is free of comments, they show that a system of voluntary certification for standards on ICH would, in principle, be in conformity with the current IGC draft provisions on TCE.

# (b) WTO Law: TRIPS, GATT, GATS, Subsidies and the TBT Agreement

Together with the prohibition of discrimination, the elimination of tariff barriers and non-tariff barriers to market access of goods and services is a key instrument of trade liberalisation provided by the law of the WTO. In addition, the TRIPS Agreement specifically deals with the implications of IP systems on the conditions of competition in international trade.[105]

## (i) TRIPS Agreement

For certification-mark types of protection for ICH, the TRIPS Agreement is relevant insofar as it incorporates in its section on 'Trademarks' the relevant

---

102  WIPO IGC Secretariat, above n 99, arts 3C alternative 1.
103  WIPO IGC Secretariat, above n 14, annex 30.
104  Ibid, annex 31.
105  It is the rationale of the TRIPS Agreement to balance the competing private interests of holders of IPRs and the public interest to assure the free flow of goods and services across borders. See T Cottier, 'The Agreement on Trade-Related Aspects of Intellectual Property Rights' in PFJ Macrory et al (eds), *The World Trade Organization: Legal, Economic and Political Analysis* vol 1 (Springer, 2005) 1041, 1054.

provisions of the Paris Convention.[106] Article 15.1 TRIPS Agreement provides for a very broad definition of trade marks which covers all types of signs, so long as they are distinctive.[107] Although certification marks are not specifically mentioned, the TRIPS Agreement does not prevent this type of protection, since Article 1.1 explicitly authorises WTO members to 'implement in their law more extensive protection than is required by this Agreement'. Article 16.1 gives an exclusive right to a trade mark owner for the use of the trade mark 'in the course of trade'. Non-commercial use is not protected. However, this is not a problem when the proposed certification system is intended for traded goods and services. Article 16.2 TRIPS Agreement provides protection of well-known trade marks that goes beyond the Paris Convention. Whereas the Paris Convention limits the protection of well-known trade marks to trade marks used in respect of identical or similar goods, Article 16.2 TRIPS Agreement extends this protection *mutatis mutandis* to services, and Article 16.3 extends the protection of well-known marks to non-identical and non-similar goods and services.[108] These provisions may be relevant if one would consider extending the FAIRTRADE label, which is certainly a famous mark, to services. Finally, Article 18 TRIPS Agreement provides that the registration of a trade mark shall be renewable indefinitely.

## (ii) GATT and GATS

Since the General Agreement on Tariffs and Trade (GATT) and General Agreement of Trade in Services (GATS) obligations for market access and non-discrimination apply between states, it is difficult to see how non-government voluntary certification standards would be affected by these rules. With regard to Fairtrade and similar schemes, government involvement has recently been discouraged in the European Union. In a 2009 communication, the European Commission concluded that government regulation in this field would hamper the dynamic element of private initiatives and 'could stand in the way of the further development of Fair Trade and other private schemes and their standards'.[109] If a government were to consider regulatory mechanisms relating to private labelling schemes, it would need to comply with existing WTO obligations, in particular

---

106   Provisions on trade marks are enshrined in Articles 15 to 21 under the heading 'Trademarks' in Part II of the Agreement. Article 2.1 of the TRIPS Agreement provides that in respect of (*inter alia*) Part II of the agreement 'Members shall comply with Articles 1 through 12, and Article 19, of the Paris Convention (1967)'.
107   According to Article 15.1 of the TRIPS Agreement, '[a]ny sign, or any combination of signs, capable of distinguishing the goods or services of one undertaking from those of other undertakings, shall be capable of constituting a trademark'. See D Gervais, *The TRIPS Agreement. Drafting History and Analysis* (2nd ed, Sweet & Maxwell, 2003) para 2.160.
108   This is considered to be an important contribution to raised standards of international trade mark protection. See C Correa, *Trade Related Aspects of Intellectual Property Rights: A Commentary on the TRIPS Agreement* (Oxford University Press, 2007) 188.
109   EU Commission, Communication from the Commission to the Council, the European Parliament and the European Economic and Social Committee, *Contributing to Sustainable Development: The Role of Fair Trade and Non-governmental Trade-Related Sustainability Assurance Schemes*, EU Com Doc COM (2009) 215 final, 6.

with the principles of non-discrimination, market access and transparency. There exists significant support for the view that a government-led voluntary labelling system would nevertheless be consistent with both the Most-Favoured-Nation Treatment (MFN)[110] and National Treatment[111] obligations. There are also strong arguments that compliance with social standards, such as 'authenticity', could alone be sufficient to make products non-'like' and, thus, allowably differentiated.[112]

## (iii) Subsidies

Government support for a labelling system could be considered a subsidy. The law of the WTO provides rules on subsidies for goods but not for services.[113] Under the Agreement on Subsidies and Countervailing Measures (SCM Agreement), some subsidies are strictly forbidden if they are contingent on export performance or on the use of domestic over imported goods (Article 3.1), and others are actionable if they cause 'adverse effects' on another member (Article 5). According to Articles 1 and 2 of the SCM Agreement, a subsidy is defined

---

110   According to the 1991 GATT Panel Report, *United States — Restrictions on Imports of Tuna I (Mexico)* GATT Doc BISD 39S/155 (1991, unadopted) paras 5.42-5.43, this is so even if an 'authentic' good and a 'non-authentic' good are considered 'like products'. In that case, the panel decided that the US Dolphin Protection Consumer Information Act, according the right to use the label 'Dolphin Safe' for tuna harvested in the Eastern Tropical Pacific Ocean only if such tuna was accompanied by documentary evidence showing that it was not harvested with purse-seine nets intentionally deployed to encircle dolphins, was consistent with the MFN obligation (Article I GATT). In assessing MFN compliancy, the panel found that voluntary labelling for production or processing methods (PPMs), which do not affect the characteristics of the end product, are MFN compliant, as they do not restrict trade. Even though there was government involvement, a voluntary labelling system that ultimately affected the market only through the free choice of the consumer was stated not to be an 'advantage' granted by the state. Although the report was not adopted, the panel's decision concerning voluntary single-issue labelling remains largely unchallenged. See C Dankers, *Environmental and Social Standards, Certification and Labelling for Cash Crops, Food and Agriculture Organization of the United Nations* (UN FAO, 2003) 74, citing A E Appleton, *Environmental Labelling Programmes: International Trade Law Implications* (Kluwer Law International, 1997) 145.

111   The application of the National Treatment obligation to such voluntary labelling systems has never been assessed by a WTO Panel or the Appellate Body, whether state-supported or not. Even where there is state support for a voluntary labelling system, such a measure would not be a tax (Article III:2), a regulation or requirement (Article III:4) or any other measure mentioned in Article III:1 GATT. Furthermore, it is unlikely that the system would be perceived as 'affecting the internal sale offering for sale, purchase, transportation, distribution or use of products' (Article III:4), due to the voluntary nature. See Dankers, ibid 74-75, citing Appleton, ibid 153.

112   In GATT Panel Report, *United States – Restrictions on Imports of Tuna I (Mexico)*, above n 110, para 5.15, it was found that non-product-related (NPR) PPMs could not affect the 'likeness' of end products. However, this has been questioned by P Van den Bossche, *The Law and Policy of the World Trade Organization* (2nd ed, Cambridge University Press, 2008) 381, stating that a more 'nuanced' approach is now required, as NPR-PPMs can affect consumer tastes and preferences. Since this, in turn, affects the NPR-PPMs' competitive and substitutive nature, the use of such measures would affect the likeness of an end product. However, Van den Bossche cautions that this would rarely occur, as most markets are driven by price rather than concern over conformity with social standards.

113   Although Article XV GATS calls upon members to develop disciplines to avoid trade-distortive effects of subsidies, this is still a leftover. See P Sauvé, 'Completing the GATS Framework: Addressing Uruguay Round Leftovers' (2002) 57(3) *Aussenwirtschaft* 301, 324–333; P Poretti, 'Waiting for Godot: Subsidy Disciplines in Services Trade' in M Panizzon et al (eds), *GATS and the Regulation of International Trade in Services* (Cambridge University Press, 2008) 466-488.

as: (1) a financial contribution by a public body; (2) that confers a benefit; (3) to a specific enterprise or industry. The concept of 'financial contribution' is not limited to a direct transfer of funds, but includes reduction of costs, tax breaks[114] or other fiscal incentives to an industry.[115] On the other hand, the requirement of a 'financial contribution' means that not all government measures that confer a benefit are subsidies.[116]

Even if state funded, a support scheme, such as the Australian Authenticity Label, would not constitute a 'subsidy', as it would not be a financial contribution, as required by Article 1.1 SCM Agreement, or take the form of income or price support in the sense of Article XVI GATT. The funding of a trade mark would neither reduce the costs of producers (for example, in production or in the export process) nor directly affect production. It would be neither contingent on export performance nor trade distorting (directly artificially increasing exports), and would not affect comparative advantage.[117] Moreover, Article 14(d) of the SCM Agreement states that the provision of governmental services is not to be considered as conferring a benefit, if the service is provided for adequate remuneration. Thus, a financially self-sustaining certification system (such as the Fairtrade system, through membership fees and other income)[118] would be compliant with the SCM Agreement. Even if fulfilling the other requirements of a 'subsidy', the funding of a trade mark for authentic indigenous cultural products would be considered general and not specific, as it would apply to more than one enterprise, industry or region,[119] and would not be dependent thereon.

## (iv) TBT Agreement

With regard to technical regulations and standards for the trade in goods, the Agreement on Technical Barriers to Trade (TBT) must be respected to ensure that they do not create unnecessary obstacles to international trade.[120]

---

114  Whereas tax breaks discriminating between foreign and domestic goods would violate Article III(2) GATT, it seems likely that WTO Panels or the AB would consider a non-discriminatory tax cut a financial contribution within the meaning of Article 1.1 SCM. See C B Graber, 'State Aid for Digital Games and Cultural Diversity: A Critical Reflection in the Light of EU and WTO Law' in C B Graber and M Burri-Nenova (eds), *Governance of Digital Game Environments and Cultural Diversity: Transdisciplinary Perspectives* (Edward Elgar, 2010) 170, 199.

115  Van den Bossche, above n 112, 562; SCM Agreement, Article 1.1(1)(a).

116  WTO Panel Report, *United States – Measures Treating Exports Restraints as Subsidies*, WTO Doc WT/DS194/R (2001), paras 8.65 and 8.73.

117  WTO Panel Report, *Australia — Subsidies Provided to Producers and Exporters of Automotive Leather*, WTO Doc WT/DS126/R (1999). The concept of trade distortion is also used and clarified by the Appellate Body, in WTO Appellate Body Report, *Canada — Measures Affecting the Export of Civilian Aircraft*, WTO Doc WT/DS70/AB/R (1999), para 157.

118  FLO, above n 89, 24-25.

119  Van den Bossche, above n 112, 568; SCM Agreement Articles 1.2 and 2.

120  Preamble of the TBT Agreement. For a comprehensive analysis of the TBT Agreement, see R Wolfrum et al (eds), *WTO — Technical Barriers and SPS Measures* (Martinus Nijhoff Publishers, 2007).

The TBT Agreement covers packaging, marking and labelling requirements, and procedures for assessing conformity with the technical regulations and standards.[121] Since 'regulations' are mandatory for the purposes of the Agreement, a voluntary labelling system would be a 'standard' rather than a 'regulation'. Under the TBT Agreement, the requirements for voluntary systems are less stringent than those for mandatory systems.[122] 'Standard' is defined as:

> Document approved by a *recognized body*, that provides, for common and repeated use, rules, guidelines or characteristics for products or related processes and production methods, *with which compliance is not mandatory*. It may also include or deal exclusively with terminology, symbols, packaging, *marking or labelling requirements as they apply to a product, process or production method.*[123]

Although 'recognized body' is not defined in the TBT Agreement, it is not limited to governments or public authorities, but may also include non-governmental standardising bodies.[124] A 'non-governmental body' is a body other than a central government or local government body,[125] and includes 'a non-governmental body which has legal power to enforce a technical regulation'.[126] Private organisations managing the proposed label would fall into this definition.

It is evident that the TBT Agreement applies to processes and production methods (PPMs). However, there remain several open questions with regard to whether an authenticity standard for product differentiation would be covered by the TBT Agreement. To begin with, it is not clear whether such a standard would be product related.[127] Assuming that such a standard is non-product related (NPR),

---

121  Preamble of the TBT Agreement.

122  Interestingly, countries often argue against the differentiation between mandatory and voluntary standards, saying that, because the standard creates market segregation, compliance with the standard becomes de facto mandatory. See Dankers, above n 110, 76, citing a submission made in 2001 by Switzerland to the WTO Committee on Trade and Environment, 'Marking and Labelling Requirements', WTO Docs WT/CTE/W/192 and G/TBT/W/162 (2001). See also Kommerskollegium National Board of Trade, Global Trade Division, Sweden, 'Eco-Labelling and the WTO: Issues for Further Analysis and Clarification', (Report No. 119-007-2002, 2002) 5. However, this would not be the case with the proposed standard and labelling system, as it would not be possible for everyone to apply for the certification, thus it is not possible for it to be de facto mandatory.

123  TBT Agreement, annex 1, para. 2 [emphasis added].

124  Van den Bossche, above n 112, 813-814.

125  'Central government body' and 'local government body' are defined in TBT Agreement annex 1, paras 6 and 7 respectively.

126  Ibid, annex 1, para 8.

127  It is also not clear whether authentic and non-authentic products would be like. In addition, the concept of 'likeness' has not yet been clarified under the TBT Agreement (but is relevant for the assessment of conformity with the MFN and National treatment principles within the TBT Agreement and the annexed Code of Good Practice). Whereas 'likeness' has been expounded upon by Panels and the Appellate Body in the realm of Articles I and III GATT, it must be recalled that the concept of 'like products' may have a different meaning in the different contexts it is used. According to Van den Bossche, above n 112, 818, structural differences between the GATT and the TBT Agreement stand in the way of applying this GATT-related case law to the TBT Agreement. Whereas the assessment of 'likeness' in general depends greatly on the consumer perception of the goods at issue, 'likeness' and 'product-relatedness', under the TBT Agreement, are much more technical

it is furthermore uncertain whether the TBT Agreement would be applicable at all,[128] since there has been a lot debate regarding the interpretation of the concept of 'standard' as defined in Annex 1 to the TBT Agreement. The first sentence of the definition of 'standard' (as outlined above) specifically mentions product-related PPMs, but the second sentence (which deals with marking or labelling requirements) leaves the word 'related' out.[129] Apparently, the negotiators failed to agree on whether NPR-PPMs for terminology, symbols, packaging, marking or labelling requirements would be covered by this definition. Whereas Van den Bossche[130] favours a text-based interpretation that would include NPR-PPMs, other authors have argued for a contrary view.[131]

To be sure, even if the standard of authenticity were covered by the TBT Agreement, its reach would be limited, because — like in all other WTO law — only government actions are regulated. Article 4.1 of the TBT Agreement requires full compliance only from central governmental bodies, and members need only to take 'reasonable measures' as may be available to them to ensure non-governmental bodies' and local governmental bodies'[132] compliance with the 'Code of Good Practice for the Preparation, Adoption and Application of Standards'.[133] There is no WTO case law explaining what 'reasonable measures'

---

in nature. It has also been argued that the fact that the TBT Agreement offers no explicit exceptions to MFN and National Treatment (unlike in GATT), 'like' may be read more narrowly, otherwise members would be left little room to distinguish products for environmental, health or social reasons, as allowed by Article XX GATT. N Bernasconi-Osterwalder et al, *Environment and Trade: A Guide to WTO Jurisprudence* (Earthscan, 2006) 16, 215.

128    No WTO Panel or Appellate Body has yet looked at the applicability of the TBT Agreement to voluntary standards that are NPR-PPMs. Bernasconi-Osterwalder, above n 127, 207. The TBT Committee discusses the applicability of the TBT Agreement to NPR-PPMs (J. Stein, 'The Legal Status of Eco-Labels and Product and Process Methods in the World Trade Organization' (2009) 1(4) *American Journal of Economics and Business Administration* 285, 287). The Committee on Trade and Environment has also been tasked with considering the relationship between WTO provisions and environmental standards, due to the recent trend of eco-labelling: WTO *Environment: Issues Labelling* (2011) <http://www.wto.org/english/tratop_e/envir_e/labelling_e.htm>

129    Dankers, above n 110, 76; Bernasconi-Osterwalder et al, above n 127, 214; M Koebele, 'Agreement on Technical Barriers to Trade. Article 1 and Annex 1 TBT' (2007) in R Wolfrum et al (eds), above n 120, 178, 196.

130    Van den Bossche, above n 112, 808-809.

131    See Dankers, above n 110, 77, citing Appleton, above n 110, 93-94, 124; Bernasconi-Osterwalder et al, above n 127, 214; Koebele, above n 129, 196-197. They argue that the second sentence must be read in light of the first, as the second sentence was never meant to be a stand-alone provision, and that NPR-PPMs arguably were not intended to be covered by the TBT Agreement, which is indicated by the negotiation history. These arguments appear to give much weight to the negotiation history. However, according to the *Vienna Convention on the Law of Treaties (VCLT)*, 'preparatory work' should only be a supplementary means of interpretation in the sense of Article 32 VCLT.

132    This is contrary to general international law, which holds states responsible for all governmental actions, regardless of whether central or local. See M Koebele and G LaFortune, 'Agreement on Technical Barriers to Trade. Article 4 and Annex 3 TBT' (2007) in R Wolfrum et al (eds), above n 120, 243, 255-256.

133    The Code can be found at TBT Agreement, annex 3.

means in the TBT context.[134] In any case, these are only 'best effort' or 'second-level' obligations of members.[135] Moreover, there is nothing to suggest that the proposed system would be contrary to the Code.[136]

In conclusion, whereas the TRIPS Agreement provides for positive protection for certification trade marks, there is no evidence suggesting that voluntary certification standards — even if government supported — would not be consistent with the GATT, the GATS, or the TBT and the SCM Agreements.

# 5. Conclusion

The burgeoning market for indigenous goods and services has resulted in a parallel increase in the production of non-authentic products of this nature. In recognition of this, many label schemes have been initiated in an attempt to validate authenticity, and educate and sway consumers away from non-authentic products. However, none of these has achieved success comparable with the Fairtrade label. Indeed the Australian certification label system was shut down after only two years of operations, and the New Zealand Māori-made (toi iho) system was disinvested by the government in late 2009.

The four main structural reasons for the failure of the Australian system were: (1) the 'top-down' nature of the system and the poor consultation with the relevant stakeholders prior to its inception; (2) difficulties in defining the standard of 'authenticity' and then controlling what fell into this; (3) non-independence of the certifier, which was the same body that set the standards and owned the trade marks; and (4) poor funding of the system, which meant an inability to market the initiative adequately in Australia, let alone internationally. Conversely, the FLO Fairtrade scheme started as a 'bottom-up' initiative and continues to integrate stakeholder involvement into every aspect of its decision-making processes, including the setting of standards. Moreover, certification is not performed by the FLO, but by FLO-CERT. Though owned by FLO, FLO-

---

134 Bernasconi-Osterwalder et al, above n 127, 207. The term 'reasonable measures' was derived from Article XXIV:12 GATT, which requires that a member 'shall take such reasonable measures as may be available to it to ensure observance of the provisions of this Agreement by the regional and local governments and authorities within its territories.' It is limited in scope to situations where the central government body is in the position to direct or influence compliance, e.g. if there are legal means available for this. Political resistance or sensitivity would not be sufficient to deter the obligation, but requiring a change in law (particularly constitutional law) would likely not be reasonable. See ibid, 225-257.

135 Koebele and LaFortune, above n 132, 255; R Muñoz, 'Agreement on Technical Barriers to Trade: Article 8 TBT' (2007) in R Wolfrum et al, above n 120, 298, 300.

136 The Code of Good Practice includes requirements of MFN and National Treatment and promotes international harmonisation and the avoidance of duplication of the work of other standardising bodies. Standards should not restrict trade unnecessarily and should be published 60 days before adoption to allow interested parties to submit comments. These are outlined and discussed in Koebele and LaFortune, above n 132, 247-253.

CERT is a completely autonomous and independent organisation. FLO-CERT is also ISO 65 certified, which ensures (a) a quality management system; (b) transparency; and (c) independence in decision-making. Finally, Fairtrade is financially self-sufficient and well marketed around the world.

In Australia, there is some movement towards using a fair trade scheme and a voluntary labelling system for indigenous TK/TCEs.[137]

It is not perceived that a voluntary certification system for TK/TCEs would be contrary to either WIPO or WTO law or policy. Such a system is in conformity with the current line of thought in the WIPO forum. Regarding WTO law, a voluntary certification system appears to be consistent with the GATT and the SCM Agreement. The most relevant agreement is likely to be the TBT Agreement. TBT compliance of a voluntary scheme has never been assessed by any WTO dispute body and it is thus not clear whether it would fall into the Agreement's scope. Much of this would depend on whether the standard of authenticity was deemed to be 'product related' and capable of making authentic and non-authentic products non-'like'. Compliance would also depend on whether the system is supported by central government or not. In any case, the voluntary system would not be contrary to any of the principles of the TBT Agreement (including MFN and National Treatment) or the Code of Good Practice.

The extension of the FLO Fairtrade system to TK/TCEs would be problematic. One of the options that Australia is looking at is co-branding through a joint Fairtrade label.[138] Currently, not all producers qualify to apply for the Fairtrade label.[139] Moreover, the products for which the mark can be used are also limited and include only commodity products.[140] The FLO has indicated its plan to widen the range of people able to benefit from the system, including adding more countries and more products.[141] Indeed, the FLO recently added the first service to its mandate, now certifying travel tours.[142] However, the FLO has admitted that introducing new products is slow and costly because of the great deal of research that is involved in assessing whether the introduction will really benefit the producers.[143] It is difficult to create standards (particularly those that can be consistently certified) for handicrafts and other products (and services) made by small-scale producers, each of which may be unique

---

137  M Spencer and J Hardie, *Indigenous Fair Trade in Australia: Scoping Study* (Australian Government Rural Industries Research and Development Corporation, 2010).

138  Ibid.

139  See above n 65.

140  See FLO, above n 91.

141  FLO, above n 87, 2.

142  'Fair Trade hält auch in der Reisebranche Einzug' Neue Zürcher Zeitung (2010) <http://epaper.nzz.ch/nzz/forms/page.html>

143  FLO, above n 76.

and involve varying production processes and costs.[144] Consequently, it could be argued that the Fairtrade system is more suited for TK- rather than TCE-related products. However, given the large variety of agricultural goods among indigenous communities, the creation of standards could prove complicated even for these goods. Moreover, considering the difficulties in getting different Australian Aborigines to identify with an Australian labelling system, it may be equally (if not more) problematic to convince many different indigenous peoples from around the world to stand behind a pan-global label which is to some extent meant to reflect identity.[145] The vast differences between indigenous communities would make the creation of the standards logistically difficult. Finally, it is worth noting that the democratic structure required under the FLO general standards could contradict the customs of certain indigenous communities.

Although the idea of employing the FLO scheme for indigenous purposes is tempting, a great deal of research would be needed to make this work. An avenue to explore could be the formulation of only one set of FLO standards for all indigenous products or services, aside from those otherwise certified by the FLO. These standards would have to be quite broad and general, and capable of covering a wide range of products or services. A difficult question to resolve would be what exactly it is they should address. Moreover, we suggest studying the possibilities of interfacing 'Fairtrade philosophy' with existing marketing structures successfully operated by indigenous people at the local level, such as the Aboriginal cultural centres that exist in Australia. These centres could be of help in the most difficult task of developing a standard of 'Aboriginal origin' or 'Aboriginal authenticity' that would be accepted by indigenous people (locally) while, at the same time, complying with broader FLO standards (globally).

# Acknowledgements

The authors would like to thank Maggie Chon, Benny Müller and Matthias Oesch. The support from the Swiss National Science Foundation and the Ecoscientia Foundation is gratefully appreciated. This chapter is an updated version of an article published in (2011) 39(3) *Prometheus* 287, which was based on a paper presented at a conference hosted by NZCIEL in December 2010. The authors would like to express thanks to Susy Frankel and Peter Drahos for hosting the conference and for their comments on earlier versions of the text.

---

144 Ibid. For a discussion on the use and problems of non-FLO fair trade labels on craft products, see Zografos, above n 24, 155-159.
145 This could be a particular issue given the problem outlined by Hutchens, above n 69.

# 6. Traditional Innovation and the Ongoing Debate on the Protection of Geographical Indications

Daniel Gervais

## 1. Introduction

Michel Foucault commented that the modern concept of author 'constitutes a privileged moment of individualism in the history of ideas'.[1] Indeed, the authors who pushed for the adoption of international copyright rules were basking in the sun of the Enlightenment, stroked by the rays of individualism.[2] The underlying Hegelian framework — a transfer of the author's personality in literary (or artistic) expression — led to an insistence on the right of attribution, a component of the moral right enshrined in the Berne Convention.[3]

For inventions, a similar insistence on individual self-actualisation and responsibility for scientific advances is evident. Isn't the history of science taught in schools around the world centred on individual inventors? Foucault again:

> The history of knowledge has tried for a long time to obey [...] the claim of attribution: each discovery should not only be situated and dated, but should also be attributed to someone; it should have an inventor and someone responsible for it. General or collective phenomena on the other hand, those which cannot be 'attributed', are normally devalued: they

---

1   M Foucault, 'What is an Author?' in J Harari (ed), *Textual Strategies: Perspectives in Post-Structuralist Criticism* (Cornell University Press, 1979) 141.
2   The first Diplomatic Conference to negotiate the Berne Convention was held in 1884. Association Litteraire et Artistique Internationale (ALAI), an international organisation of authors, had submitted a draft which the Swiss government modified and submitted as a draft treaty. ALAI continued to take part (as what in modern parlance would be called a non-governmental organisation) in the discussions, however. ALAI was founded in 1878 by French playwright and public intellectual Victor Hugo, its first President. ALAI Congresses were held (during the relevant period) in 1879 (London); 1880 (Lisbon); 1881 (Vienna); 1882 (Rome); 1883 (Amsterdam) and 1884 (Brussels). See *Actes Du Congres De Dresde* (1895) 11.
3   *Berne Convention for the Protection of Literary and Artistic Works* (Paris Act, 1971) 1161 UNTS 18388 (1971), art 6*bis*.

are still traditionally described through words like tradition, mentality, modes; and one lets them play the negative role of a brake in relation to 'originality' of the inventor.[4]

While *plagium* has been frowned upon for centuries, and invention has been around for at least as long (the Babylonians, Aristotle, and so on), *individual* invention and authorship of *well-identified* works and inventions — and certainly monetary rewards — emerge as normative precursors and bulwarks of 'Western' intellectual property rights.[5] The Berne Convention refers several times to the author (for example, to the 'life of the author', which serves as a basis to calculate the term of protection). Similarly, the Paris Convention — though, unlike its Berne cousin, it was written not by authors or inventors but by patent and trade mark office administrators — is infused with the personality of the inventor and steeped in the nineteenth-century Western European zeitgeist.[6] By contrast, many indigenous artists were seen as creating only as part of a collective. As Dan Monroe, Executive Director of the Peabody Essex Museum in Salem, Massachusetts, noted, 'recognizing that Native American art was made by individuals, not tribes, and labelling it accordingly, is a practice that is long overdue'.[7]

There are a few possible exceptions that come to mind, of course, but are they real exceptions in the sense of an abandonment of the premise of individuality? Not really. Most countries recognise collective works in copyright, for example, but then create the fiction that the 'arranger' is the author because of the originality she transferred to the collective work.[8]

---

4   M Foucault, quoted in Noam Chomsky and Michel Foucault, *The Chomsky-Foucault Debate on Human Nature* (New Press, 2006) 15.

5   See W Van Caenegem, 'Pervasive Incentives, Disparate Innovation and Intellectual Property Law', in C Arup and W Van Caenegem (eds), *Intellectual Property Policy Reform: Fostering Innovation and Development* (Edward Elgar, 2009) 250, 253-254. On plagiarism, see George Long, 'Plagium', in William Smith, *A Dictionary of Greek and Roman Antiquities* (John Murray, 1875) 921. Admittedly, this is a bit of an oversimplification. China had a complex individual v collective view of creativity during much of its imperial period. See William P Alford, *To Steal a Book is an Elegant Offense: Intellectual Property Law in Chinese Civilization* (Stanford University Press, 1995).

6   See *Paris Convention for the Protection of Industrial Property*, (Stockholm Revision Conference, 1967) 828 UNTS 305, art 4*ter* which states that: 'The inventor shall have the right to be mentioned as such in the patent.' If one looks at the revisions of the Paris Convention and Berne Conventions (until 1967 and 1971 respectively), one sees that all revision conferences took place in Western Europe except for a conference held in Washington in 1925. This may seem at odds with the development of innovation clusters and online innovation using 'network effects', both focusing on teamwork and on clusters on a university-government-industry triple helix. However, the teamwork need not annihilate individual effort and reward. See C Arup, 'Split Entitlements? Intellectual Property Policy for Clusters and Networks', in C Arup and W Caenegem (eds), above n 5, 285; and on clusters as innovation engines, see D Gervais, 'Of Clusters and Assumptions: Innovation as Part of a Full TRIPS Implementation' (2009) 77(5) *Fordham Law Review* 2353.

7   Quoted in J H Dobrzynski, 'Honoring Art, Honoring Artists', *New York Times* (online), 6 February 2011 <http://query.nytimes.com/gst/fullpage.html?res=9C06E4DF1E39F935A35751C0A9679D8B63&pagewanted=all> She traces the beginning of the attribution movement in 'Indian art' to the 1960s.

8   See *Berne Convention*, above n 3, art 2(5).

Yet there *is* one area of intellectual property which bucks this philosophic-cultural trend: the protection of geographical indications (GIs). In fact, it is not entirely clear whether this area is 'intellectual property'.[9] Its underlying premise is different: it holds that a combination of natural and human (but not individual) factors anchored in (usually longstanding) tradition can give certain products special characteristics. These unique admixtures — sometimes referred to as *terroir* — are both commercial instruments and symbols of national or regional identity.[10]

A system of protection for denominations of origin uses that combination as a marketing tool to extract additional rent in various commercial offerings, but also to affirm the special nature of the place it designates as the origin of a GI product. Put differently, the consumer is asked to pay more (or less) because the GI validates not just the factual claim that a white wine made with Sauvignon grapes will not be the same — even if made by the same person using the same technique — in the Loire valley of France and the Marlborough region of New Zealand, but that its origin reflects both a know-how and natural conditions that make that wine 'special'.[11] Wine experts agree that the acidity of the soil, and the amount of rain and sun exposure will affect the outcome, but the GI does even more: it recognises a collective right of producers in a given region to claim and capture the (real or perceived) special quality or characteristic of the product.

A legal mechanism, namely the 1958 Lisbon Agreement for the Protection of Appellations of Origin and their International Registration, was designed to capture that special value and protect it against usurpation or imitation.[12] As such, it could mesh well with forms of traditional innovation and both old and new forms of economic exploitation of traditional knowledge related to crafts or food. It could conceivably extend to other forms of innovation (for example,

---

9   *Convention Establishing the World Intellectual Property Organization*, (1967) 848 UNTS 3, art 2 defines intellectual property as follows: '"intellectual property" shall include the rights relating to: literary, artistic and scientific works, performances of performing artists, phonograms, and broadcasts, inventions in all fields of human endeavor, scientific discoveries, industrial designs, trademarks, service marks, and commercial names and designations, protection against unfair competition, and all other rights resulting from intellectual activity in the industrial, scientific, literary or artistic fields'. The only possible pigeonhole for GIs would be as commercial designations or perhaps a general form of unfair competition regulation.
10   'The notion that food is both sacred and site-specific is the root of the emotionally charged French concept of "terroir." First applied to describe the association of grape variety and soil in winemaking, it has come to evoke the wholesome, earthy qualities of regional foods and cooking.', D Downie, 'Let Them Eat Big Macs', *Salon* (online), 7 July 2000, <http://www.salon.com/business/feature/2000/07/06/frenchfood/index. htm> D Menival, 'The Greatest French AOCs: A Signal of Quality for the Best Wines' (Working Paper 1, 2007) <http://www.vdqs.net/Working_Papers/Text/WP_2007/Menival_249.pdf>
11   Among the soil-related factors that are most important are the drainage capacity, salinity, and the ability of the soil to retain heat, thus encouraging ripening and the development of stronger roots. See D Bird, *Understanding Wine Technology: The Science of Wine Explained* (Wine Appreciation Guild, 2005) 1.
12   *Lisbon Agreement for the Protection of Appellations of Origin and their International Registration* (Stockholm Revision, 1967 and amended 1979) 923 UNTS 205.

traditional medicinal products) if one of the perceived characteristics of the product was anchored in a specific region because the land has a special quality, because the inhabitants have a special way of exploiting it, or both.

In this chapter, I proceed as follows. I discuss, first, the Lisbon Agreement and then the more recent Agreement on Trade-Related Aspects of Intellectual Property Rights (TRIPS Agreement) in the WTO context. This rather technical analysis is then broadened to consider how GIs mesh normatively with the protection of traditional innovation.[13] Finally, I suggest possible changes to the Lisbon Agreement, some of which are under consideration at the World Intellectual Property Organization (WIPO), as of the time of writing, that would allow some forms of traditional innovation to benefit from a reform of the international protection of GIs.

# 2. The Lisbon Agreement

To understand the Lisbon Agreement, let us consider briefly its current membership and current use; whether what it protects — namely 'appellations of origin' — are different from the 'geographical indications' protected under the TRIPS Agreement; and then the way in which it operates both substantively (scope of protection) and administratively (as a register of geographical denominations).

## (a) Membership and Current Use

There were only twenty-seven countries party to the Lisbon Agreement as of June 2012.[14] As such, it cannot be said to have established a *worldwide* system of protection for geographical denominations used in association with specific products. That said, there has been progress in recent years: approximately one-third of the Lisbon member states joined after the conclusion of the TRIPS Agreement in 1994.[15] In spite of those additions, however, the Agreement's membership is still largely concentrated in the Mediterranean world. An

---

13  See also M Blakeney, 'The Pacific Solution: The EU's IPR Activism in Australia's and New Zealand's Sphere of Influence', ch 8 in this volume.

14  Algeria, Bulgaria, Burkina Faso, Congo, Costa Rica, Cuba, Czech Republic, Democratic People's Republic of Korea, France, Gabon, Georgia, Haiti, Hungary, Iran (Islamic Republic of), Israel, Italy, the former Yugoslav Republic of Macedonia (FYROM), Mexico, Montenegro, Nicaragua, Peru, Portugal, Republic of Moldova, Serbia, Slovakia, Togo and Tunisia. Greece, Morocco, Romania, Spain and Turkey signed the 1958 Agreement but never ratified it.

15  Democratic People's Republic of Korea (2005), FYROM (2010), Georgia (2004), Iran (2006), Montenegro (2006), Nicaragua (2006), Peru (2005) and Moldova (2001). It is worth noting that *sui generis* systems (as separate from trade mark law) exist in approximately 75 countries. See I Kireeva and B O'Connor, 'Geographical Indications and the TRIPS Agreement: What Protection Is Provided to Geographical Indications in WTO Members?' (2010) 13(2) *Journal of World Intellectual Property* 12.

examination of all current appellations on the register shows that almost all emanate from fewer than ten countries. Indeed, eleven countries hold 97.5 per cent of all entries, and in fact the top three hold over 78 per cent, with one country, France, holding 62.5 per cent of the total (almost 90 per cent of which are for wines and spirits).[16] In terms of product areas, of the 813 accessible entries on the register,[17] 588 (72.3 per cent) were for wines and spirits (519 for wines, and thus potentially of interest for the Article 23.4 register) and an additional 11 for beer.[18]

## (b) Appellations of Origin v Geographical Indications

One feature of the Lisbon system is that it applies to 'appellations of origin'. By contrast, the TRIPS Agreement uses the expression 'geographical indications'. Is there a difference? This will matter when deciding where to house a new GIs system. The Lisbon Agreement defines 'appellations of origin' as follows:

> [...] the geographical name of a country, region, or locality, which serves to designate a product originating therein, the *quality or characteristics* of which are due *exclusively or essentially to the geographical environment, including natural and human factors.*[19]

Appellations of origin are denominations that designate a geographical location to distinguish products produced in that location, and produced either according to regulations or 'local, constant and trusted usage'[20] in such location, which results in a certain quality or characteristics of the product and in the acquisition of a reputation.

The notion of 'geographical indication' used in TRIPS also focuses on the quality or characteristics of goods that derive from a geographical origin.[21] However, TRIPS adds a measure of semiotic flexibility by encompassing any *indication* (denomination or otherwise) that would point to a particular geographic origin as long as a certain quality or characteristic (and/or reputation) is attributable to that origin. That difference seems theoretical today, because the current practice under the Lisbon Agreement is to register denominations that may not be 'denominations' *stricto sensu.*[22]

---

16   Data extracted from the Lisbon Express Database <http://www.wipo.int/ipdl/en/lisbon/>
17   As of 10 December 2009. See WIPO, *Search Appellations of Origin (Lisbon Express)* <http://www.wipo.int/ipdl/en/search/lisbon/search-struct.jsp>
18   I separated wines and spirits from other products, including beer, following in the footsteps of the TRIPS Agreement, art 3.
19   *Lisbon Agreement*, above n 12, art 2(1), emphasis added. Quality or characteristics should include natural factors because human factors are moveable and thus hard to pinpoint geographically.
20   *Actes De La Conférence Réunie À Lisbonne Du 6 Au 31 Octobre 1958 (Actes)* (BIRPI, 1963) 813. The Acts of the Lisbon Conference were published in French. All translations are the author's own.
21   TRIPS Agreement, art 22.1.
22   M Ficsor, *Challenges to the Lisbon System*, WIPO Doc WIPO/GEO/LIS/08/4 (2008).

Another difference is in the treatment of reputation. The Lisbon Agreement defines 'country of origin' as 'the country whose name, or the country in which is situated the region or locality whose name, constitutes the appellation of origin which has given the product its *reputation*.'[23] Lisbon focuses on quality and characteristics that provide a reputational advantage (the land, its particular use or, more typically, both), while TRIPS lists the three notions as separate phenomena that may emerge from the link to a specific geographic origin. It is essential to bear in mind that reputation is only a mental link between that product and a perceived quality or characteristic tied to a geographical origin. Put differently, if potential buyers of a product want it because a quality or characteristic associated with it stems from its geographical origin (whether the cause is human or natural factors, or a combination of both), then that product may be said to have a given reputation.[24]

## (c) Scope of Protection

If TRIPS and Lisbon apply to essentially the same subject matter, is the scope of protection in the two instruments comparable? Article 3 of the Lisbon Agreement provides that protection must be conferred against *usurpation or imitation*, even if the true origin of the product is indicated or the appellation is accompanied by terms such as 'kind', 'type', 'make', 'imitation' or the like.[25] The *Actes* define usurpation as the 'illicit adoption' of an appellation (and provide counterfeiting as a possible synonym) and, as to the latter, refer to 'fraudulent imitation'.[26] This seems reasonably limited in scope. The *Actes* also make it clear that it is up to each country to decide what remedies should be available.[27] There is thus sufficient implementation flexibility to accommodate different legal systems. I will suggest below that a protocol to the Agreement should be added to the current framework. One of its key purposes would be to align the Lisbon terminology and prohibitions with the TRIPS language to avoid the inherent risks associated with a dual standard of protection.

Determining the scope of protection also means determining how conflicts with prior trade marks might be handled. The Lisbon Agreement *allows,* but does not obligate, its members to adopt or continue to use: (1) the 'first in time, first in right' approach, as promoted, *inter alia*, by the International Trademark Association (INTA)[28] and the International Association for the Protection of

---

23  Article 2(2) provides that the 'country of origin is the country whose name, or the country in which is situated the region or locality whose name, constitutes the appellation of origin *which has given the product its reputation*' [emphasis added].

24  See WIPO IGC Secretariat, *Geographical Indications*, WIPO doc SCT/10/4 (2003), para 25.

25  *Lisbon Agreement*, above n 12, art 3 [emphasis added].

26  *Actes*, above n 20.

27  *Actes*, above n 20, 818.

28  INTA, *Resolution on Protection of GIs and Trademarks* (1997) <http://www.inta.org> See also the General Assembly of the International Vine and Wine Office Resolution O.I.V./ECO 3/94 <http://www.oiv.int>

Intellectual Property (AIPPI);[29] (2) a co-existence approach (that is, a GI and trade mark with similar legal effect);[30] or (3) a GI superiority approach. Members may do so with or without a good faith requirement concerning the prior trade mark.[31] Some members actually use more than one approach. GIs have superior rights over prior trade marks in EC Regulation 1493/1999,[32] which provides for discontinuation of the use of a prior trade mark if a confusingly similar designation is later on protected as a GI for wine; but EC Regulation 2081/92[33] and amended Council Regulation (EEC) No. 2392/89 provide for co-existence under certain conditions between a prior trade mark and a later GI (but not vice versa); and Article 3(4) of Regulation 510/2006[34] provides that a 'designation of origin or geographical indication shall not be registered where, in the light of a trademark's reputation and renown and the length of time it has been used, registration is liable to mislead the consumer as to the true identity of the product'. The United States and most if not all countries that protect GIs under trade mark law prefer, and would likely insist on, the 'first in time, first in right' approach.[35] As noted below, a *refusal* under Lisbon can be partially withdrawn to allow co-existence with a prior trade mark for an indefinite period or to allow co-existence of homonymous denominations.

---

29  See AIPPI, 'Resolution on Q62' (Yearbook 1998/VIII) 389-392. The acronym comes from the original (French) version of the Association's name, the Association internationale pour la protection de la propriété intellectuelle.

30  This can also be the case between two appellations. By using a declaration of partial refusal, a country may allow an appellation but preserve the right of another country to use that same appellation, as was done for Pisco. Mexico, for instance, refused Pisco but only to the extent that the registration by Peru 'constitutes an obstacle to products from Chile bearing the denomination of origin Pisco'. Mexico's withdrawal of refusal is dated 24 October 2006 [author's translation].

31  In WTO Panel Report, *European Communities — Protection of Trademarks and Geographical Indications for Agricultural Products and Foodstuffs*, (Australian Report), WTO Doc WT/DS290/R (2005), the panel seemed to conclude that the first two options are TRIPS compatible, though there are some constraints on the second. There is a doubt as to the TRIPS compatibility of the third option.

32  *Council Regulation (EC) No 1493/1999 of 17 May 1999 on the Common Organisation of the Market in Wine* [1999] OJ L 179, annex VII at point F.

33  *Council Regulation (EEC) No 2081/92 of 14 July 1992 on the Protection of Geographical Indications and Designations of Origin for Agricultural Products and Foodstuffs* [1992] OJ L 208.

34  *Council Regulation (EC) No 510/2006 of 20 March 2006 on the Protection of Geographical Indications and Designations of Origin for Agricultural Products and Foodstuffs* [2006] OJ L 93 (which replaced Council Regulation 2081/92, ibid, following the WTO panel case dealing with GI protection in the European Union, see European Communities, above n 31).

35  'For marks that are geographically descriptive of the origin of particular goods, the first person that establishes acquired distinctiveness may be able to prevail against a person attempting to use a similar mark where the latter cannot show acquired distinctiveness', see A Simpson et al, 'The Relationship between Trademarks and Geographical Indications' (United States Group Report Q191/AIPPI Report 11, 2006) <http://www.aippi-us.org/images/AIPPI-Q191(2006)(2).DOC> 11. According to Irena Kireeva and Bernard O'Connor, the United States, Canada, Australia, Japan, and many African and Arab countries protect geographical denominations of origins associated with certain products under trade mark law. See I Kireeva and B O'Connor, above n 15, 12.

## (d) Registration

Applications for registration on the Lisbon register may be made only by or through the appointed authority of a member state.[36] The national authority applies in the 'name of any natural persons or legal entities, public or private, having, according to their national legislation, a right to use such appellations'.[37] Two conclusions can already be drawn: (a) a national authority must be appointed to interface with the Lisbon register; and (b) it is up to each country of origin to decide who has the right to register a Lisbon appellation.[38]

Are Lisbon members obligated to accept any appellation registered by another member? The dispute resolution component of the system is simple: any national office may declare that it 'cannot ensure the protection of an appellation of origin whose registration has been notified to it ... together with an indication of the grounds therefore'.[39] This declaration of refusal must be made within one year of the receipt of WIPO's notification and may not be made later.[40] If a declaration of refusal is made within the appropriate timeframe and with justification, WIPO then notifies the country of origin which, in turn, notifies the applicant. The *only* remedy available at that juncture for the applicant/right holder is to resort, in the refusing country, to the judicial and administrative remedies open to the nationals of that country.

Moreover, there are no limits imposed on the grounds that may be invoked in support of a declaration of refusal under Article 5(3). The negotiating history provides one example: when a member considers that an appellation has become generic in its territory.[41] There are several other grounds for a refusal, however.[42] The *Actes* show

---

36   *Lisbon Agreement*, above n 12, art 5. The official French text speaks of *'administration compétente'*. See M Geuze, *Let's Have Another Look at the Lisbon Agreement: – Its Terms in Their Context and in the Light of Its Object and Purpose* WIPO Doc WIPO/GEO/BEI/07/10 (2007).

37   *Lisbon Agreement*, above n 12, art 5(1). The obligation to apply through a national authority is similar under the Madrid system (trade marks). See *Madrid Agreement Concerning the International Registration of Trademarks*, 828 UNTS 389 (1891) and the *Protocol Relating to the Madrid Agreement Concerning the International Registration of Marks* (1989) 28 *Industrial Property Law and Treaties* 3-007, 001. One potential difference is whether the national authority is required to pass on an application to the international level (WIPO) or whether it could refuse to do so if it considered the application unfounded. The latter is certainly permissible under Lisbon.

38   Regulations under the *Lisbon Agreement for the Protection of Appellations of Origin and Their International Registration*, above n 12, art 4 provides that each country must inform WIPO of the name and address of the authority competent to effect each of the notifications possible under the Agreement.

39   Ibid, art 5(3).

40   Ibid, art 5(4).

41   In a document prepared for the recently established Working Group on the Development of the Lisbon System, the WIPO Secretariat notes: '[A] contracting country may refuse to protect an appellation of origin because *it considers* that the appellation has already acquired a generic character in its territory in relation to the product to which it refers or because it considers that the geographical designation does not conform to the definition of an appellation of origin in the Lisbon Agreement or because the appellation would conflict with a trademark or other right already protected in the country concerned.' WIPO Doc, *Possible Improvements Of The Procedures Under The Lisbon Agreement*, WIPO Doc LI/WG/DEV/1/2 (2009), annex II, 4 [emphasis added] <http://www.wipo.int/edocs/mdocs/mdocs/en/li_wg_dev_1/li_wg_dev_1_2_rev.pdf> The Working Group was established at the twenty-third (6th extraordinary) session of the Assembly of the Lisbon Union (22–30 September 2008) and is responsible for exploring possible improvements to the procedures under the Lisbon Agreement. The Working Group met in Geneva from 17–20 March 2009. See the Summary by the Chair, WIPO doc LI/WG/DEV/1/3 (2009).

42   See *Actes*, above n 20, 817.

that Italy suggested an amendment to limit refusals *only* to cases where an appellation has become generic in the declaring country, and this amendment was refused by a vote of 7–1.[43] Other possible grounds for refusal include cases where an appellation is used for a product that violates *ordre public*,[44] and cases where what was registered is not considered a proper appellation.[45] The *Actes* make that clear: 'The proposed procedure gives countries which receive the notification of an appellation of origin from the International Bureau the possibility of using any legal or factual situation to oppose the grant of protection for all or part of the territory of the Special Union.'[46]

As a possible alternative to a refusal, Article 5(6) of Lisbon provides that if an appellation which has been granted protection in a given country pursuant to notification of its international registration was already in use by third parties in that country — and assuming that no refusal is notified under Article 5(3) — such third parties may be given a delay of up to two years to cease using the appellation.[47] A notification to WIPO is required.

The twelve-month period to notify a refusal is not quite the last word. Under Lisbon Rule 16, a Lisbon member may *invalidate* a registered appellation. Once the invalidation is final (usually after all rights to appeal have been used or expired), it must be notified to the International Bureau.[48] A court or other competent authority in the country where protection is claimed can invalidate an appellation *for any reason*.

The fundamental underpinning of the Article 5 registration system is thus that the system, and especially the decision to file a declaration of refusal, is administered by each member state. The negotiating history makes plain that the negotiators did *not* want an international supervisory or oversight authority.[49] A Lisbon member can refuse any appellation notified to it. If and when approached by the country of origin, it may negotiate the withdrawal of such refusals[50] in the same way that bilateral agreements are now negotiated to protect certain GIs.[51] The *Actes* are similarly clear in that respect: 'The refusal

---

43   *Actes*, above n 20, 835-837.

44   As Iran did in refusing 'PILS'. See IRAN – Declaration of Refusal of Protection, Appellation 001 and 002 (10 December 2007). Iran joined Lisbon in 2006.

45   The appellation 'Bud' (Appellation 598) was similarly refused by many Lisbon members as not referring to a geographical location. The case also highlights the differences between appellations and trade marks.

46   *Actes*, above n 20, 817 [author's translation].

47   See also Regulations made under the Lisbon Agreement, above n 12, rule 12.

48   For example, the appellation 'Bud', which was refused by several Lisbon members, was invalidated in Hungary, Italy and Portugal, see Lisbon Registration 598. The Italian invalidation refers to a final decision by the Italian Supreme Court no. 13168/02 of 18 June 18 2002, confirming a decision by the Court of Appeal of Milan. See *Lisbon Bulletin* No. 37 <http://www.wipo.int/lisbon/en/bulletin/archive.html>

49   *Actes*, above n 20, 836.

50   A mechanism to withdraw declarations of refusal is provided in the Lisbon Regulations, above n 12, art 11.

51   For example, in 2005 a bilateral agreement was reached between Europe and the United States on products of the vine. See B Rose, 'No More Whining about Geographical Indications: Assessing the 2005 Agreement between the United States and the European Community on the Trade in Wine' (2007) 29 *Houston*

must be accompanied by the grounds for which the country has decided not to grant protection. Those grounds constitute a basis for possible discussion with a view to arriving at an agreement.'[52]

There is, however, one substantive limit to refusals: Article 6 of the Lisbon Agreement provides that a registered appellation cannot be *deemed to have become* generic as long as it remains protected in the country of origin.[53] The expression 'deemed to have become' plainly refers to an evolution in time. Put differently, genericness is not an event; it is a process. As noted in a WIPO document, Article 6 is not as harsh as it sounds: 'Exceptions to this general rule may apply, in particular in cases of *acquiescence, i.e.* if the exclusive right to use the appellation of origin has not been enforced vis-à-vis certain persons, who are using the appellation of origin in respect of products that do not meet the specific geographically-determined qualifications linked to the appellation of origin.'[54] This seems to imply that a Lisbon member may, in bilateral discussions, recognise the generic nature of one of its appellations in another member's territory.

# 3. The TRIPS Agreement

There are two main areas where differences between TRIPS and Lisbon appear — apart from the difference between the notions of geographical indication and of appellation of origin, discussed in the previous section. The first is the dual level of protection in TRIPS, and its special treatment of wines and spirits. The other is the presence of a number of conflict rules that go well beyond the possibility of a refusal in Lisbon. I will consider each one in turn.

## (a) Two Levels of Protection

The TRIPS Agreement provides for two types of protection of GIs. Article 22.2 obliges WTO members to provide Paris-type protection for GIs. That level of protection is described here as 'legal means' for interested parties to prevent (a) the use of any means (not limited to a name)[55] in the designation or presentation of a good that could mislead the public into believing that the good in question originated in a geographical area other than the true place of origin; or (b) any

---

*Journal of International Law* 731.

52 *Actes*, above n 20, 817 [author's translation]. A number of proposed amendments to the Rules would streamline the system. See WIPO Doc, *Report adopted by Assembly*, LI Doc LI/A/25/1 (2009), annex 1.

53 *Lisbon Agreement*, above n 12, art 6.

54 Geuze, above n 36, 8.

55 It would seem that the reference to 'any means in the designation or presentation', combined with the open-ended mention of 'indication which identify a good' (regardless of the means), covers also indirect indications.

use which constitutes an act of unfair competition within the meaning of Art.10 *bis* of the Paris Convention. This provision does not create a full exclusive right.[56] Significantly, under Article 22.2 (a), one must show that the *public might be misled* — a level of protection that resembles trade mark law.[57] In fact, protection of GIs may be provided as collective or certification marks.[58]

TRIPS provides a higher (Lisbon-type)[59] level of protection for *wines and spirits*.[60] Using a GI identifying wines or spirits for those not originating in the place indicated by the indication is prohibited, even where the true origin of the wines and spirits concerned is indicated and/or a translation is used and/ or the indication is accompanied by expressions such as 'kind', 'type', 'style', 'imitation' or the like. There is no need here to show that the public might be misled or that the use constitutes an act of unfair competition. Under Article 22.3, a WTO member must, either *ex officio* if its national law so permits, or at the request of an interested party, refuse or invalidate[61] the registration of a trade mark which contains or consists of a GI if (a) the goods do not originate in the territory indicated; and (b) use of the indication in the trade mark for such goods in the territory of the 'Member' concerned is *of such a nature as to mislead*[62] the public as to the true place of origin.[63] Article 23.2 more or less corresponds to Article 22.3, but applies specifically to indications identifying wines and spirits, except of course that deception (misleading the public as to the true place of origin) need not be present.

## (b) Conflicts with Prior Trade Marks

Important conflict rules between GIs and trade marks are contained in TRIPS Articles 24.5 and 24.6. Under the former, a GI conflicting with a trade mark does not supersede the mark, provided that an application for registration of the mark was filed or the mark registered, or the right acquired by use (and the trade mark was in fact used in good faith)[64] in the WTO member concerned either

---

56  Civil judicial procedures must be available to the right holder, TRIPS Agreement, art 42.

57  See J T McCarthy, *McCarthy on Trademarks and Unfair Competition* (4th ed, Clark Boardman Callaghan, 2002), para 2:35.

58  See J Hughes, 'Champagne, Feta, and Bourbon: The Spirited Debate about Geographical Indications' (2006) 58 *Hastings Law Journal* 299, 310.

59  McCarthy, above n 57, para 29.28.

60  TRIPS Agreement, art 23.1.

61  Compare with 'cancellation' in arts 15 and 19.

62  Article 22(2)(a) uses 'which misleads', Article 10bis(3) of the Paris Convention uses 'is liable to mislead' and Article 22(3) uses 'is of such a nature as to mislead'. The latter two tests seem very close indeed. The likelihood that the public will be misled may, as in the case of trade marks, be inferred in appropriate circumstances.

63  This element could exclude marks having acquired a secondary meaning.

64  This test is sometimes difficult to apply, as evidence of good (or bad) faith is not always easy to produce. Showing bad faith based entirely on circumstances is sometimes rendered more difficult in legal systems that presume good faith until the contrary is shown. In applying the test, the fact that an indication is particularly

before the TRIPS Agreement became applicable in the member concerned,[65] or before the indication in question was protected in its country of origin.[66] A WTO panel examining the *EC — Trademarks and Geographical Indications* dispute explained that the co-existence of a protected indication and a trade mark was a limited exception justified under TRIPS Article 17.[67] The purpose is to allow a trade mark to be registered (and registration applied for) and used, even if it is identical with or similar to a GI,[68] provided, however, that the trade mark is at least applied for (including if it was registered, naturally) or the rights acquired through use, either before the WTO member concerned must apply Article 23 or before the indication is protected in its country of origin.

Article 24.6 is also relevant in this context. It provides that WTO members may decide not to protect a GI used in connection with foreign goods or services for which the relevant indication *is identical with the term customary in common language as the common name for such goods or services in the territory of that member*.[69] It also states that members are not required to protect foreign GIs 'with respect to products of the vine for which the relevant indication *is identical with the customary name of a grape variety* existing in the territory of that member as of the date of entry into force of the WTO Agreement'.[70]

# 4. Traditional Innovation and GIs

## (a) Types of Traditional Knowledge in Traditional Innovation

In 2003, I suggested that one should distinguish four types of *traditional knowledge* (TK).[71] This type of knowledge is likely to be a major source of traditional innovation and development. In thinking about this matrix, the

---

well known and/or used (directly or indirectly) by undertakings located in or near the 'true' place of origin should be taken into account. See AIPPI, 'Working Guidelines Q191: Relationship Between Trademarks and Geographical Indications' (Yearbook 2006/II), 18.

65   For the most industrialised nations, 1 January 1996. See TRIPS Agreement, art 65.1. For developing countries other than least-developed ones, most substantive provisions of the Agreement applied as of 1 January 2000.

66   See WIPO Doc, *Possible Solutions for Conflicts Between Trademarks and Geographical Indications and for Conflicts Between Homonymous Geographical Indications*, WIPO Doc SCT/5/3 (2000), 11-12.

67   WTO Panel Report, *European Communities — Protection of Trademarks and Geographical Indications for Agricultural Products and Foodstuffs*, (US Report) WTO Doc WT/DS174/R (2005); *European Communities*, above n 31. The Panel concluded, 'with respect to the coexistence of GIs with prior trademarks, the Regulation is inconsistent with Article 16.1 of the TRIPS Agreement but, on the basis of the evidence presented to the Panel, this is justified by Article 17 of the TRIPS Agreement.' US Report, para 7.688 and *European Communities* (Australian Report), above n 31, para 7.686.

68   See *Lisbon Agreement*, above n 12, art 5(6); and F Gevers, 'Geographical Names and Signs Used as Trade Marks' (1990) 8 *European International Property Review* 285.

69   See TRIPS Agreement, art 24.6.

70   See ibid [emphasis added].

71   D Gervais, 'Spiritual but Not Intellectual? The Protection of Sacred Intangible Traditional Knowledge' (2003) 11 *Cardozo Journal of International and Comparative Law* 467.

question to be answered is whether GIs may be used to capture the special value attributed to products embodying TK and, more particularly, any special value associated with a geographic origin following from the land the product comes from and/or the way in which the people living on that land produce the product.

The TK matrix I suggested looked as follows:

| I sacred tangible | II secular tangible |
| --- | --- |
| III sacred intangible | IV secular intangible |

Q1 includes rights, including property rights in tangible objects used as part of or pertaining to something sacred. Examples include sacred sites.

Q2 includes rights in photographs, choreographies, music or audiovisual productions used in non-sacred events and ceremonies and often offered for sale to visitors and tourists;

Q3 includes intellectual property and other intangible rights applicable to, e.g., knowledge, costumes, artistic works, etc.

Q4 includes tangible arts and crafts (to which intangible rights may also apply); it may also be extended to apply to natural and genetic resources.

In its latest (2011) proposals on this issue, WIPO prefers to distinguish *secret* (as opposed to sacred) from non-secret TK.[72] Arguably this is more practicable: a sacred practice may be kept secret. However, if its custodians have no objection to its public use, then presumably they may not require any specific legal protection to keep it from others. According to the proposed WIPO text, in respect of secret TK, beneficiaries of the right 'should have the means, through adequate and effective [legal and practical] appropriate measures, to prevent any unauthorized fixation, disclosure, use, or other exploitation'.[73] Independently of this debate on secret versus sacred, it seems rather self-evident that GIs will not be of much use for TK on the left-hand side of the matrix. GIs could, however, apply to some forms of secular or commercially exploitable forms of expressions of TK — that is, the right-hand side of the matrix.

The protection of GIs to assist in the development of traditional innovation is admittedly a limited tool. The following diagram (Figure 7) may help explicate the issues:

---

72   WIPO IGC Secretariat, *The Protection of Traditional Cultural Expressions: Draft Articles*, WIPO Doc WIPO/GRTKF/IC/18/4 (2011).
73   Ibid, proposed art 3A.

**Figure 7. The intersections of commerce, technology and culture**

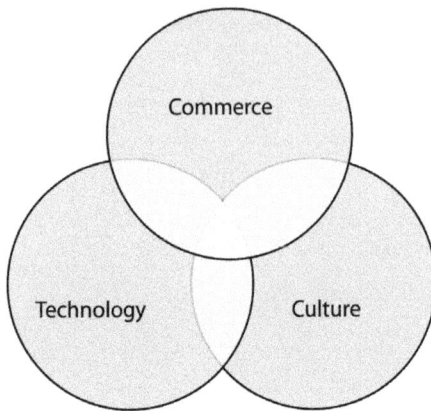

In this diagram, culture must be defined broadly as the relationship with the land that forms part of a culture, but also to the very preservation of that land, including its biodiversity. The intersections in our diagram are instructive. The intersection between culture and commerce, for instance, happens when a traditional product, one in which a traditional culture is embedded, is marketed and becomes (potentially) subject to market forces. This is not incompatible with Traditional Innovation, the dynamic nature of which one cannot deny. However, this may lead to the intensification of the exploitation, in particular for agricultural-based products.

Technology might be brought to bear to intensify exploitation and increase outputs, thus generating additional income but increasing risks of changes to the traditional product and overexploitation of the land. The question becomes one of stewardship, community empowerment and the role of the state in protecting traditional communities (or not) against those risks.[74]

Traditional innovation itself may often be situated at the intersection of 'culture' and technology. By contrast, GIs are generally situated at the intersection of culture and commerce though in many cases also at the triple intersection (with technology). The main focus of GIs is on commercialisation, not preservation of the underlying knowledge. The additional resources that exploitation might

---

74   The Preamble to the TRIPS Agreement refers to intellectual property rights as private rights, a statement mostly designed to limit obligations of state enforcement of those rights. In the case of GIs, the communal (or state) ownership of the right and the link with broader cultural and societal aspects make GIs a special category of intellectual property, at least where they are protected not as simple trademarks but under a *sui generis* regime. Here the question is basically who decides if changes to an existing traditional product is acceptable, and on what basis.

generate can help with preservation but they may also induce changes to increase efficiency that will in turn affect the product and underlying 'culture'. As such, commercialisation may in some cases make preservation more difficult.[75]

In New Zealand, for example, the way in which mātauranga Māori forms part of whakapapa; the custodianship (kaitiakitanga) of iwi, hapū (and perhaps individual whānau); and the forms of use (for example, the use of rongoā by tohunga) are all testimony to the fact that, while commercial exploitation of mātauranga Māori is not organically incapable — and certainly not unworthy — of commercial exploitation, that form of use has not been a primary driver for the preservation and development of mātauranga Māori.[76] Additionally, the sacred/ secular and secret/non-secret distinction is not always easy to superimpose on knowledge that is typically situated and contextual.[77] Yet resort to GIs might be appropriate for commercially exploited traditional innovation that outsiders might describe as secular or non-secret. As I discuss below, this requires some perhaps unpalatable 'packaging' of TK to fit the GI scheme.

In spite of those important shortcomings, the protection of GIs meshes well with several, perhaps most, of the normative concerns identified by WIPO in its efforts to design an international framework for non-secret TK protection. More specifically, it meshes with respect for traditional cultural expressions (TCEs), which WIPO defines as 'any form, tangible or intangible, or a combination thereof, in which traditional culture and knowledge are embodied and have been passed on [from generation to generation],tangible or intangible forms of creativity of the beneficiaries'.[78] This includes stories, epics, legends, poetry, riddles and other narratives; *words, signs, names and symbols*; musical or sound expressions, such as songs and instrumental music, and the sounds which are the expression of rituals; dances, plays, ceremonies, rituals, rituals in sacred places; games, puppet performances, and other performances, whether fixed or unfixed; expressions of art; and architecture and tangible spiritual forms, and sacred places.[79]

There would be much to say about this list and its juxtaposition with copyright, if the term 'expression' were replaced with 'work'. 'Expressions' might be seen here as *über-works*, rights in which would belong to a community and may

---

75    The resources generated by commercialisation may also create the resources/interest in maintaining some food/drink-making and other traditions.

76    I found the traditional approach to rongoā illustrative of the reductionist view of medicine and dominant Western memes in that respect. Few Western doctors — and fewer patients still — would argue that life-saving medicines have only a commercial value. They obviously have much broader social and spiritual implications.

77    See M Leiboff, 'Law's Empiricism of the Object: How Law Recreates Cultural Objects in its Own Image' (2007) 27 *The Australian Feminist Law Journal* 23, 23-24.

78    WIPO IGC Secretariat, *The Protection of Traditional Cultural Expressions: Draft Articles*, above n 72, annex at 4.

79    Ibid.

not expire. This difficult cohabitation has been discussed at length elsewhere. Moreover, most forms of intellectual property (designs, patents and so on) are vulnerable to the same critiques. By contrast, a permanent right (or non-expiring right after a certain date) belonging to a community is precisely what a GI is.

I suggest that there are many other forms of TK that may be commercially exploited and in which a 'TK rent' could be captured by a GI. Traditional knowledge more generally is defined in the latest draft WIPO document as:

> [I]ntellectual activity in a traditional context, and includes the know-how, skills, innovations, practices and learning that form part of traditional knowledge systems, and knowledge embodying traditional lifestyles of indigenous and local communities, or contained in codified knowledge systems passed between generations and continuously developed following any changes in the environment, geographical conditions and other factors. It is not limited to any specific technical field, and may include agricultural, environmental and medicinal knowledge, and any traditional knowledge associated with cultural expressions and genetic resources.[80]

## (b) Packaging TK as GIs to Promote Innovation

There are several forms of TK that might thus lead to traditional innovation. Indeed, the use of GIs to generate 'development from within' is not new, although it was mostly advocated for the 'global south'.[81] GIs have been linked to rural development in particular, and this may be compatible with many forms of indigenous innovation and production.[82]

Several indigenous communities have developed sustainable land use and conservation models that are viewed by some environmental advocates as possible 'organic' alternatives to pouring billions of tons of chemicals into the ground.[83] Certain forms of environmental TK could be 'packaged' as best-practice models using GIs, much in the way that Leadership in Energy and Environmental Design standards have evolved over the past decades for 'green

---

80  WIPO IGC Secretariat, *The Protection of Traditional Knowledge: Revised Objectives and Principles*, WIPO Doc WIPO/GRTKF/IC/18/5 (2011), annex at 18 [emphasis added].

81  See S Bowen, 'Development from Within? The Potential for Geographical Indications in the Global South' (2010) 13(2) *Journal of World Intellectual Property* 231, 233.

82  See P van de Kop et al (eds), *Origin-Based Products: Lessons for Pro-Poor Market Development* (Royal Tropical Institute and French Research Centre for International Development (CIRAD, 2006); and C Fink and B Smarzynska, 'Trademarks, Geographical Indications and Developing Countries' in B Hoekman et al (eds), *Development, Trade, and the WTO: A Handbook* (World Bank, 2002) 403.

83  See, for example, Small Grants Programme, 'Replacement of Chemical fertilizer and pesticide by organic farming for sustainable production of vegetable crops' (IND/SGP/OP4/Y2/RAF/2009/34/BHR 05) <http://sgp.undp.org/web/projects/14100/replacement_of_chemical_fertilizer_and_pesticide_by_organic_farming_for_sustainable_production_of_ve.html>

building' certification.[84] A possible example is the mosaic method of burning land used by indigenous peoples in Australia.[85] A GI might apply to methods certified by custodians of this knowledge even if transported to a different technological domain, such as mosaic burning using helicopters.[86]

Another form of traditional innovation might come from greater respect for the use of genetic resources. Those resources seem quintessentially linked to the land they originate from and thus natural candidates for GIs when exploited commercially or, indeed, to prevent their appropriation. One of the aspirational objectives suggested by WIPO in this context is to 'curtail the grant or exercise of improper intellectual property rights over traditional knowledge and associated genetic resources'.[87] In a separate set of proposals dealing specifically with genetic resources, one of the options identified by WIPO is to '[e]nsure those accessing/using genetic resources and associated traditional knowledge comply with requirements for prior informed consent and fair and equitable benefit-sharing, including customary laws and procedures of the communities'.[88] Some scholars point to the example of *Maytenus buchaniti*, a plant from the Shimba Hills of Kenya from which the US National Cancer Institute (NCI) developed a drug known as maytansine.[89] While over twenty-seven tons of the shrub were collected, no agreement was made to either share or acknowledge its origin. A similar situation arose over the collection of *Homalanthus nutans* in the Samoan rainforest. In both cases, the work of the NCI was reportedly based at least in part on traditional medicinal knowledge about the plants.[90]

The use of a GI could potentially play a slightly different role here — namely to acknowledge both origin as such and the fact that a benefit-sharing agreement is in place — if the use of the GI was authorised by its holder only after the successful conclusion of such an agreement. This type of GI protection seems consonant with efforts to get patent holders to disclose the origin of genetic resources used during the invention process.[91]

---

84    See See US Green Building Council, *What LEED Is* (2012) <http://www.usgbc.org/DisplayPage. aspx?CMSPageID=1988>

85    See Department of Sustainability and Environment, *Landscape Mosaic Burns: Land and Fire Management Information Sheet* (2010) <http://www.land.vic.gov.au/CA256F310024B628/0/58AF2C45BEF36828CA2577490 00BE0D2/$File/landscape+mosaic+burning_factsheet_JUN10.pdf>

86    See H Verran, 'A Postcolonial Moment in Science Studies: Alternative Firing Regimes of Environmental Scientists and Aboriginal Landowners' (2002) 32(5-6) *Social Studies of Science* 729, 745.

87    WIPO IGC Secretariat, above n 72, annex at 6.

88    WIPO IGC Secretariat, *Draft Objectives and Principles Relating to Intellectual Property and Genetic Resources at IWG 3*, WIPO Doc WIPO/GRTKF/IC/18/9 (2011), annex at 3.

89    See W Pretorius, 'TRIPS and Developing Countries: How Level Is the Playing Field?' in P Drahos and R Mayne (eds), *Global Intellectual Property Rights: Knowledge, Access and Development* (Palgrave Macmillan/ Oxfam, 2002) 183, 186.

90    See ibid and D Posey and G Dutfield, *Beyond Intellectual Property* (IDRC, 1996), 35.

91    See P Drahos, 'A Networked Responsive Regulatory Approach to Protecting Traditional Knowledge' in D Gervais (ed), *Intellectual Property, Trade and Development* (Oxford University Press, 2007) 385, 404.

This use of GIs on indigenous products might also coincide normatively with fair trade issues, although the two should not be confused.[92] GIs more generally feed into the 'quality turn' in consumer preferences and the emergence of 'values-based' labels.[93]

# (c) Meeting the WIPO TK/TCEs Protection Objectives

WIPO identifies several objectives that the protection of TK/TCEs should aim to achieve. These objectives seem consonant with GIs, perhaps more so than other intellectual property rights. Let us take a brief look at the most relevant aims in the WIPO proposal.

## (i) Recognise value

This first aim is described as the recognition that 'indigenous peoples and communities and traditional and other cultural communities consider their cultural heritage to have *intrinsic value*, including *social*, *cultural*, spiritual, *economic*, scientific, intellectual, *commercial* and educational values...' GIs capture and reflect the value that a community places on a product because of its origin. It embodies the 'land' in the product much as authors' rights embody the Hegelian 'author' in the work.

## (ii) Promote respect

The second aim is 'to promote *respect for traditional cultures* and folklore, and for the dignity, cultural integrity, and the philosophical, intellectual and spiritual values of the peoples and communities that *preserve and maintain expressions* of these cultures and folklore'.[94] The GI is a symbol of the origin of the product, and the fact that consumers both recognise this origin and are willing to pay for it is arguably a mark of respect, but at the very least it might afford economic tools to the custodians to help them preserve and maintain the knowledge embodied in the making of the product and perhaps others forms of TK.

## (iii) Meet the actual needs of communities

This aim, to be 'guided by the *aspirations and expectations expressed* directly by indigenous peoples and communities and by traditional and other cultural communities, *respect their rights* under national/domestic and international law,

---

92   A Taubman, 'Thinking Locally, Acting Globally: How Trade Negotiations over Geographical Indications Improvise "Fair Trade" Rules' (2008) *Intellectual Property Quarterly* 3.

93   See D Goodman, 'Rural Europe Redux? Reflections on Alternative Agro-Food Networks and Paradigm Change' (2004) 44(1) *Sociologica Ruralis* 3. See also P Drahos, above n 91, 402-403.

94   WIPO IGC Secretariat, above n 72, annex at 1. I will use quotes from this document but the objectives identified in respect of TCEs closely parallel those on TK more broadly. See the WIPO IGC Secretariat, above n 78, annex at 3-7.

and *contribute to the welfare* and sustainable economic, cultural, environmental and social development of such peoples and communities',[95] is likewise well served for some forms of TK. The GI registration process is itself an expression of the aspiration and expectation that the product, and specifically the natural and human factors at its point of origin, should be protected, and its exploitation might contribute to the welfare of the community of origin.

## (iv) Prevent the misappropriation and misuse of traditional cultural expressions

This aim is defined as providing 'indigenous peoples and communities and traditional and other cultural communities with the *legal and practical means, including effective enforcement* measures, to prevent the misappropriation of their cultural expressions [...] and [control] ways in which they are used *beyond the customary and traditional* context and promote the equitable sharing of benefits arising from their use'.[96] An internationally recognised GI would arguably prevent the use of tradition and know-how embodied in a product, with or without consumer confusion. It is clearly designed to tackle use outside the community, notably when the product enters (international) channels of commerce. Whether the use is a misappropriation without consumer confusion is a separate debate. Increasingly, however, the need for confusion is disappearing as the mooring of trade mark law as global brands get protection well beyond the traditional contours of passing off.[97] This is normatively questionable for pure commercial marks, in particular as it affects freedom of expression. However, the Lisbon system is a high form of protection that recognises the special nature of GIs (even where they might be protected under a trade mark regime).

## (v) Empower communities

The aim is to find a balanced and equitable yet effective manner to empower 'indigenous peoples and communities and traditional and other cultural communities to exercise in an effective manner their rights and authority over their own traditional cultural expressions'. GIs must be balanced against other concerns, including freedom of expression and consumer interests. I am certainly not suggesting a watertight right that would go beyond what is required to achieve the aim of protecting equitably the legitimate interests of the holder and custodians. In the Lisbon context, the debates have focused not on conflicts with, say, (other) human rights, but on conflicts with trade marks appropriating pre-existing GIs (often in good faith).[98]

---

95   WIPO IGC Secretariat, above n 72.
96   Ibid.
97   See M Lemley and M McKenna, 'Irrelevant Confusion' (2010) 62 *Stanford Law Review* 413.
98   The most famous is the conflict between Anheuser-Busch 'Budweiser' and Budweiser, the German-language term for bier from the Budějovický brewery in the Czech Republic. Parties split the two most

## (vi) Contribute to safeguarding traditional cultures

WIPO suggests that TK/TCE protection 'should contribute to the preservation and safeguarding of the environment in which traditional cultural expressions are generated and maintained, for the direct benefit of indigenous peoples and communities and traditional and other cultural communities, and for the benefit of humanity in general'. GIs may contribute to this aim by making the preservation and maintenance of the knowledge associated with the making of a GI product easier.

## (vii) Encourage community innovation and creativity

This aim is to 'reward and protect tradition-based creativity and innovation especially by indigenous peoples and communities and traditional and other cultural communities'. GIs function mostly as guarantors of tradition. Yet, as products enter channels of commerce, innovation might be more easily rewarded — for example, in the creation of versions of the products that combine GI-protected knowledge and new ideas.

## (viii) Contribute to cultural diversity

This aim is to 'contribute to the promotion and protection of the diversity of cultural expressions'. Having access to more products produced in local communities around the world might contribute to this objective by making consumers more aware of the cultural aspects at the point of origin which infuse

---

recent decisions. Anheuser-Busch Inbev essentially won a case before the European Court of Justice (Grand Chamber) decided on 8 September 2009 (Case C 478/07). The Court decided that EC law was exhaustive in respect of appellations for beer and that additional protection in a bilateral agreement between Austria and the Czech Republic was ineffective. Earlier, on 16 December 2008, the Court of First Instance of the European Communities (CFI) overturned four decisions by the Board of Appeal of the Office for Harmonisation in the Internal Market (OHIM). See *Budějovický Budvar v Office for Harmonisation in the Internal Market (Trade Marks and Designs)*, Joined Cases T 225/06, T 255/06, T 257/06 and T 309/06, 16 December 2008. For a discussion of the judicial saga, see N Resinek, 'Geographical Indications and Trade Marks: Coexistence or "First in Time, First in Right" Principle' (2007) 29 *European Intellectual Property Review* 446, 447. The crux of the debate in the Court of First Instance was whether the appellant had shown it was the proprietor of a sign 'of more than mere local significance. 'Use', as the Court rightly noted (and, on this point, agreeing with the OHIM Board), means 'genuine use of a trade mark where the mark is used in accordance with its essential function, which is to guarantee the identity of the origin of the goods or services for which it is registered, in order to create or preserve an outlet for those goods or services; genuine use does not include token use for the sole purpose of preserving the rights conferred by the registration.' (CFI Opinion, para 161.) In a somewhat unconvincing twist, the Court then found that this rule, which it says applies to earlier trade marks, did not apply to 'when, as in the present case, the sign is an appellation of origin registered under the Lisbon Agreement or an appellation protected under the bilateral convention', see ibid, para 163. If one were to accept this conclusion of law, (not necessarily) genuine use in one European Union member state whose law does not protect a given appellation may be combined with the legal protection available in a different member state where no facts establish use (whether genuine or not). Concerning the 'not merely local' requirement, the Court limited itself to a finding that protection under Lisbon in a country other than the country of origin is sufficient, even, it seems, without any factual evidence, see ibid, para 181.

the product with special value and, generally, by insisting on the importance of less uniform sources for food and other GI products. This feeds into the desire expressed by many consumers to know more about what they eat and drink.[99]

## (ix) Promote the [community] development of indigenous peoples and communities and traditional and other cultural communities and legitimate trading activities

For reasons that are discussed above, GIs would likely 'promote the use of traditional cultural expressions for the [community based] development of indigenous peoples and communities and traditional and other cultural communities'.

## (x) Preclude unauthorised intellectual property rights

This aim was mentioned above. It is more an effect than a normative claim. GIs would 'preclude the grant, exercise and enforcement of intellectual property rights acquired by unauthorized parties over traditional cultural expressions and [derivatives] [adaptations] thereof'. This does not avoid, however, the need to deal fairly with issues concerning pre-existing trade marks. In addition, if 'unauthorized' is extended to mean use of genetic resources without a benefit-sharing agreement in place, then use of a GI that would increase value and benefit all those involved in the distribution chain could be licensed only if such an agreement was in place. Conversely, one must prevent the use of GIs to misappropriate the GI rent that is associated with a specific origin.[100]

If a GIs system is implemented as a certification of collective mark, which the Lisbon Agreement allows, typically the state will not check the validity of the claimant's rights. This may increase the risk of misappropriation.

## (xi) Enhance certainty, transparency and mutual confidence

The final aim is to enhance 'certainty, transparency, mutual respect and understanding in relations between indigenous peoples and communities and traditional and cultural communities, on the one hand, and academic, commercial, governmental, educational and other users of traditional cultural expressions, on the other'. It might be served by providing proper recognition for the value of the origin of a product based on tradition. Respect is often the first and most important step to a fruitful dialogue.

---

99  See D Giovannucci et al, 'Defining and Marketing "Local" Foods: Geographical Indications for US Products' (2009) 12 *Journal of World Intellectual Property* 6.

100  This issue is distinct from the multiple claims of 'ownership' of the same GI, which is discussed in the next section below.

In sum, the protection of GIs, properly calibrated, could serve the aims identified by WIPO (after years of serious deliberation on the issue) that the protection of TK should strive to achieve.

## (d) Issues

The use of GIs will not go forward without significant issues, however. These will emerge in any scenario where a collective right is established or recognised. The major issue might be one of ownership, meant here as the authority to license the use of a GI. Because GIs are anchored in the land, forced displacements of indigenous peoples (due to colonisation, for example) or 'artificial' colonial borders that do not map well over actual land use might lead to conflicts of ownership. As with the Pisco issue between Chile and Peru, there are potential sharing arrangements that could be negotiated.[101] Admittedly, the optimal use of GIs also relies on the assumption that a collective ownership arrangement can in fact be established even without a conflict among two peoples, clans, and so on.

Another troubling prospect is the capture of a GI by 'powerful extralocal actors', as was apparently the case with an otherwise very successful GI, Tequila.[102] This and the ownership issue mentioned previously are examples of what might be referred to more generally as issues of governance. This supports the case for a strong but fair involvement by the state.[103]

A second set of problems is the possible emergence of micro-GIs. While micro-GIs, like (micro-)niche products are not necessarily a negative, the risk is that they might overcrowd the GI space for a specific product class if each clan, tribe, nation and so on has a version of what is perceived as essentially the same thing. As the product use moves further from its point of origin, this may become more acute. French consumers may be familiar with hundreds of wine appellations, for example, but that may not be true elsewhere. A single GI system, even if international by design, needs to be used globally for every GI, however. There are three 'circles' of *erga omnes* protection. A first circle would be to the territory of origin; another would be a regional circle — or perhaps a non-geographically delimited circle of like-minded countries taking similar or compatible approaches to the protection of TK. A third possible circle would be an extension to all WIPO and/or WTO members. Naturally, the first level can be established by a local law. The second circle requires a regional or sectoral

---

101　See above n 30.
102　Bowen, above n 81, 235. There have been conflicts for decades between growers of agave and Tequila bottlers on issues such as the minimum required proportion of agave for Tequila to bear the name, and the exportation of bulk Tequila (tequila mixto). That said, GIs cannot be either delocalised or outsourced.
103　Bowen, above n 81, 243-244.

agreement, providing for (for example) reciprocal protection. Yet all three can make use of an international system, even if not all micro-GIs are used globally. In my view, the real challenge is to successfully pick and use some GIs globally without overcrowding.

# 5. A Protocol to the Lisbon Agreement as TK Protection

## (a) Towards a Protocol

We have now seen the two existing international frameworks for GIs (Lisbon and TRIPS) and demonstrated that GIs might serve the needs of custodians of TK. In our look at Lisbon, we saw that the system is not widely subscribed to, especially in the 'New World', owing to real or perceived deficiencies. A second level of enquiry is to ask how TRIPS and Lisbon should interface. A protocol to the Lisbon Agreement could certainly ameliorate and revitalise the current system. I also suggest that it could and should tackle the interface issue in a way that reflects the concerns and interests of TK custodians and users.

The question to ask at this juncture is whether a protocol is realistic to begin with, and then how would it interface with TRIPS norms. In a recent paper, I argued that there were two ways to proceed. The first I termed *Lisbon Light*. Under this approach, WTO members would establish a new international register, possibly limited to wines and spirits, to be administered by WIPO, thus relying on the expertise of the Lisbon staff and, more generally, on WIPO's experience in administering international intellectual property registration systems. The protocol would mirror the current registration process but apply to GIs (copying the TRIPS definition) and contain no substantive protection norms. Essentially, under this approach a new multilateral system is established but most substantive rules set aside, thus allowing TRIPS and the WTO dispute settlement system to fill the gap. This would be of little help as TK protection, especially if limited to wines and spirits.

The second approach (which I favour) I called a *TRIPS Zero* protocol. Under this second approach, WIPO members would adopt a protocol that mirrors not just the administrative provisions of the current Lisbon system but also the TRIPS provisions concerning GIs, and conflicts between GIs and trade marks.[104] The register would be open to all products.

---

104   Naturally, 'TRIPS provisions' is potentially a dynamic notion, as TRIPS may be amended in the future. An amendment to the TRIPS Agreement was adopted by a decision of the WTO General Council of 6 December 2005, art 31bis. See *Amendment to the TRIPS Agreement*, WTO Doc WT/L/641 (2005).

## (b) Applicable Precedents

There are clear precedents. First, in 1989 a Protocol to the 1891 Madrid Agreement Concerning the International Registration of Marks was adopted.[105] More countries are party to this Protocol (83) than to the original Agreement (56).[106]

The core idea is simple: step out of the historical flange-ways and known road blocks, and thus avoid the related path dependency which has manifested itself in *sui generis* regimes with particular attributes, such as their variable precedence over prior marks, and establish a true multilateral register for denominations of origin to which products owe specific qualities, characteristics and indeed their reputation in the marketplace.

On the substantive side, a second relevant precedent is the addition of TRIPS-compatible norms in new WIPO instruments. A recent precedent is the adoption of two 'Internet' treaties in 1996.[107]

Clearly, no country should have to adhere to the Lisbon Agreement to adhere to the Protocol, and not just countries could join. A full revision would also make it possible for intergovernmental bodies, such as the European Union, to join.[108]

## (c) Application to Other Products

The question of the application of a new register to products other than wines and spirits must be tackled if the needs of TK holders and custodians are to be addressed.

Under TRIPS Article 23.4, the new multilateral register need only apply to wine, although political agreement exists to extend it to spirits.[109] If WTO members agreed to extend high (Article 23) protection to all products, then the register could be opened to reflect such an extension. Another possibility, which I consider a possible solution to the extension quagmire, is to establish a register with two distinct domains: one for wines and spirits (the traditional domain of appellations), for which Article 23 protection would apply; and one for all other products, for which Article 22 protection would apply (that is, more generally to all 'indications'). In my suggestion, existing Lisbon entries would *not* be

---

105   *Madrid Agreement and Protocol*, above n 37.

106   See WIPO, *Members of the Madrid Union* <http://www.wipo.int/madrid/en/members/>

107   *WIPO Copyright Treaty* (1996), 2186 UNTS 121; and *WIPO Performances and Phonograms Treaty* (1996), 36 ILM 76, 86.

108   See P Wilner, 'The Madrid Protocol: A Voluntary Model for the Internationalization of Trademark Law' (2003), 13 *De Paul University Journal of Art and Entertainment Law* 17, 20-21.

109   See D Gervais, *The TRIPS Agreement: Drafting History and Analysis* (3rd ed, Sweet & Maxwell, 2008) 86-97.

extended to protocol members, and the protocol would require a per-country notification (as most other international applications and registrations do), as opposed to applying to all Lisbon Protocol members by default.

## (d) Comparison with Most Recent WIPO Proposals

In March 2011, WIPO released proposed changes to the Lisbon system.[110] They are in large part consonant with the above analysis and recommendations. The main proposed changes are as follows:

- Allowing members to recognise appellations and/or indications, without having actually to use either term. This is useful mostly on a political level, by allowing members to keep current systems, and a spate system for wines and spirits, on the one hand, and for other products on the other. European legislation recognises both. The practical distinction is less clear.

- An 'entity' should be designated in each member to process international applications for registration, although the source of the right in a given member may be a legislative or administrative act, a judicial decision or national registration. However, under one proposal, federations, associations and other persons could apply directly 'provided that the application is accompanied by a document signed by the competent authority'.

- The protocol would allow intergovernmental organisations (for example, the European Union) to join.

- Finally, the proposals on substantive rights and the priority of prior marks more or less track TRIPS, though not specifically on the spate status of wines and spirits.

Those proposals are a great step in the right direction. They would allow the emergence of a multilateral GI system that could be used for commercially exploited GIs on traditional knowledge, without discrimination as to the type of product and without endangering prior marks used in good faith, subject to specific rules in each member state.

# 6. Conclusion

The aim of this chapter has been to demonstrate that the 1958 Lisbon Agreement on the Protection and Registration of Appellations of Origin could, if properly revised by way of a protocol, function as a multilateral register for GIs of products of all types. This type of collective right is unique in intellectual

---

110  WIPO IGC Secretariat, *Draft Provisions on Certain Matters Addressed by the Working Group in the Context of the Review of the Lisbon System* WIPO Doc LI/WG/DEV/3/2 (2011).

property law, a set of rules developed in Western Europe, with limited input from other industrialised nations, starting in the late nineteenth century and reflecting a belief in the individuality of the author and inventor and of the need to reward and/or protect individuals because of their intellectual contribution. By contrast, the Lisbon Agreement and the related provisions on GIs in the TRIPS Agreement focus on collective knowledge rooted in land and tradition, a notion that may appeal much more naturally to custodians of TK desiring to commercially exploit forms of TK to develop local innovation and improve economic development. This would apply to TCEs such as crafts, as well as to food and to more technical knowledge such as land use and conservation and traditional medicines.

I discussed the possible use of GIs to reflect the presence of an appropriate benefit-sharing and disclosure of origin agreement (as recognised by the right to use the GI). While an amendment to TRIPS on this point seems unlikely, a Doha Round result — if it ever materialises — could include a Ministerial Declaration on this issue.[111]

The chapter also argues that the revision of the Lisbon Agreement should bring it closer to the multilateral register foreseen in Article 23.4 of the TRIPS Agreement. To achieve this goal, I considered the substantive differences between the notions of GI used in TRIPS and of appellation of origin used in the Lisbon Agreement. I also considered the level of protection in Lisbon, and rules concerning conflicts between indications and trade marks, a major sticking point in the development of the international protection of GIs.

I also reviewed the compatibility of GIs with the main aims identified by WIPO (after years of deliberations) that a system to protect TK should achieve, and found a significant degree of consonance between the two. Finally, I applied the relevant findings to the protection of TK and concluded that a *TRIPS Zero* protocol, reflecting the substantive TRIPS rules in the possible protocol, would be better for TK protection, and noted the existence of credible precedents to show that the conclusion of a protocol is realistic.[112]

---

111   See D Gervais, 'Traditional Knowledge & Intellectual Property: A TRIPS-Compatible Approach' (2005) *Michigan State Law Review* 137, 160-164.

112   The author has previously published other articles on GIs and the Lisbon Agreement, which contain additional details and information. See 'Reinventing Lisbon: The Case for a Protocol to the Lisbon Agreement' (2010) 11(1) *Chicago Journal of International Law* 67; Christophe Geiger et al, 'L'Arrangement de Lisbonne, un véhicule pour l'internationalisation du droit des indications géographiques?' (2010) 35 *Propriétés Intellectuelles* 691; Christophe Geiger et al, 'Towards a Flexible International Framework for the Protection of Geographical Indications' (2010) 1(2) *WIPO Journal* 147 (English version of previous article); and Daniel Gervais,'The Misunderstood Potential of the Lisbon Agreement' (2010) 1(1) *WIPO Journal* 87.

# 7. The Branding of Traditional Cultural Expressions: To Whose Benefit?[1]

Daphne Zografos Johnsson

## 1. Introduction

This chapter is concerned with the legal issues surrounding the branding of traditional cultural expressions (TCEs). Over the past few decades, ethnicity trends combined with today's digital culture have prompted a significant increase in both the commercial and non-commercial branding of TCEs by indigenous communities as well as by third parties. Branding is a process that involves the creation of a unique name and image for a product in the consumers' mind through advertising campaigns or merchandising with a consistent theme. Branding aims to establish a significant and differentiated presence in the marketplace that attracts and retains loyal customers. It is not limited to goods and services, and can also apply to people, places and communities.

Traditional words, images, symbols, music, performances or objects are increasingly being used to brand products, people, communities, corporations and disciplines. Third-party branding practices that use indigenous names, signs and symbols raise issues of ownership, authorisation, attribution and exploitation. On the other hand, some indigenous communities would like themselves to benefit from the branding of their TCEs and to protect their economic interests in indigenous names, signs and symbols. In this perspective, the holders of TCEs are concerned about how best to use intellectual property rights (IPRs) as differentiation tools in the marketplace, prevent misappropriation and misuse, and contribute to the preservation and safeguarding of indigenous names, signs and symbols, and of TCEs generally.

1   The views expressed in this chapter are the author's own and do not necessarily reflect the views of the World Intellectual Property Organization or any of its Member States. A version of this paper was delivered at the Trade, Intellectual Property and the Knowledge Assets of Indigenous Peoples: The Development Frontier conference at Victoria University of Wellington, 8-10 December 2010. The trip to New Zealand was funded by the UK Arts & Humanities Research Council within the context of a project entitled 'Who Owns the Orphans? Traditional and Digital Property in Visual Art'.

This chapter examines how intellectual property (IP) tools can assist indigenous communities in addressing the above issues in relation to the branding of their TCEs.

# 2. Third-party Branding

## (a) Ownership and Authorisation

Some of the questions that may arise in relation to third-party branding of TCEs are: who owns TCEs, who can authorise their branding, and in which situations is such an authorisation required?[2] Very often, it may not be possible for those wishing to exploit TCEs to identify who to get consent from. This may be the case, for example, in situations where paternity is lost or contested, or where such expressions have been produced within a community, and where it is not possible to identify a specific author or authors, but where the paternity and ownership are vested in the community as a whole. Indeed, the very nature of TCEs is often that they do not have an author, but are attributable to a cultural group or traditional community who are seen as the 'guardians' of the work, and have responsibility for the work, but do not 'own' the work in the Western copyright sense. Having said that, the distinction between individual IPRs and communal traditional knowledge (TK) rights is often an oversimplification, and it should also be kept in mind that there is not one single model of a communal TK rights system.[3]

While it is accepted that many indigenous communities generate and share knowledge from generation to generation collectively, there are also situations in which individual members of these communities can be recognised as creators or inventors distinct from their community. In many cases, contemporary works inspired by traditional styles can and do have an author, and this author can benefit from IP protection such as copyright. Despite that, in some traditional communities the right to create contemporary TCEs and to use pre-existing styles or designs resides with the traditional owners or custodians, who together have the authority to determine whether these TCEs can be used in an artwork and by whom the artwork may be created or exploited.[4]

---

2   On these questions, see generally, M Torsen and J Anderson, *Intellectual Property and the Safeguarding of Traditional Cultures, Legal Issues and Practical Options for Museums, Libraries and Archives* (WIPO, Geneva, 2010) <http://www.wipo.int/tk/en/publications/1023.pdf>

3   See C Visser, 'Culture, Traditional Knowledge, and Trademarks: A View from the South', in G B Dinwoodie and M D Janis (eds), *Trademark Law and Theory, A Handbook of Contemporary Research* (Edward Elgar, 2008) 468; and WIPO, *Draft Paper on Customary Law & the Intellectual Property System in the Protection of Traditional Cultural Expressions and Traditional Knowledge* (2006) <http://www.wipo.int/tk/en/consultations/customary_law/issues.pdf>

4   See, for example, *Milpurrurru & Ors v Indofurn Pty & Ors* (1994–1995) 30 IPR 214: 'The right to create paintings and other artworks depicting creation and dreaming stories, and to use pre-existing designs and

## (b) Attribution

The holders of TCEs would like the right to be attributed for their TCEs, as well as to be able to object to any false attribution. The latter issue may arise where, for example, imitation products are presented as genuine TCEs in the marketplace. In some industries, it has become common practice to promote non-indigenous products and businesses by using indigenous or traditional names or signs as brand names, trade marks and business names, because consumer belief in authenticity lends tremendous weight and value to cultural objects and handicrafts.[5] Holders of TCEs are concerned that this practice misleads consumers by falsely suggesting a connection with the community, and leads consumers to believe that the business is owned and run by indigenous people, or that benefits flow back to indigenous or traditional communities.

## (c) Exploitation by Third Parties

Over the past decades, there has been an increasing use, in the course of trade, of indigenous names, signs and symbols by third parties. Well-publicised examples of unauthorised use of such signs can be found in various parts of the world.

In Canada, names of First Nations, such as Algonquin, Mohawk, Haida and Cherokee, as well as symbols such as Indian heads, tepees or tomahawks, are used as trade marks by many non-Aboriginal companies to market products ranging from firearms and axes to tobacco, gasoline and cars.[6] In the United States, there are many examples of exploitation of Indian names and imagery, notably in relation to college or professional sports teams' names. It is estimated that more than 2,600 high school, college or professional teams have used Native American names and images as mascots, logos and team names.[7]

In New Zealand, there are many examples of unauthorised use of Māori imagery and text by third parties. They include the use of Māori and Polynesian names

---

well recognised totems of the clan, resides in the traditional owners (or custodians) of the stories or images [...] [w]ho together have the authority to determine whether the story and images may be used in an artwork, by whom the artwork may be created, to whom it may be published, and the terms, if any, on which the artwork may be reproduced. [...] If unauthorised reproduction of a story or imagery occurs, under Aboriginal law it is the responsibility of the traditional owners to take action to preserve the dreaming, and to punish those considered responsible for the breach. [...] If permission has been given by the traditional owners to a particular artist to create a picture of the dreaming, and that artwork is later inappropriately used or reproduced by a third party, the artist is held responsible for the breach which has occurred, even if the artist had no control, or knowledge, of what occurred.'

5   See M Asplet and M Cooper, 'Cultural Designs in New Zealand Souvenir Clothing: The Question of Authenticity' (2000) 21(3) *Tourism Management* 307.

6   See M Cassidy and J Langford, 'Intellectual Property and Aboriginal People: A Working Paper' (Ministry of Indian Affairs and Northern Development, Ottawa, 1999) 22.

7   See K E Behrendt, 'Cancellation of the Washington Redskins' Federal Trademark Registrations: Should Sports Team Names, Mascots and Logos Contain Native American Symbolism?' (2000) 10 *Seton Hall Journal of Sport Law* 396.

for a range of toys by Lego;[8] the use of Māori imagery by Sony Playstation in a game called the Mark of Kri;[9] the reproduction of various New Zealand icons, such as a hei tiki (greenstone pendant personifying a human ancestor), on paper mats produced by McDonalds and used in their restaurants to cover food trays;[10] the use of tā moko (Māori facial tattoo)[11] on the boot of a Ford truck; the use of the words 'MAORI MIX', together with a quasi-Māori design and a map of New Zealand, by tobacco company Philip Morris to market cigarettes in Israel;[12] and the use of Māori imagery in the fashion industry:[13] for example, the use of interlocking curvilinear koru designs on women's swimsuits by New Zealand swimwear manufacturer Moontide in 1998, or Paco Rabanne's Spring 1998 collection featuring two models wearing metal outfits reproducing a stylised moko, to name only a few.

In addition to the commercial exploitation of Māori imagery and text, many personalities have demonstrated a growing fascination with Māori culture. Celebrities such as rock star Robbie Williams and boxer Mike Tyson have exhibited Māori-style tattoos, and soccer player Eric Cantona appeared on the cover of British style magazine *GQ* with a painted moko on his face. In 1997, the Spice Girls caused offence when they performed a spontaneous haka with fans in Bali.[14]

Finally, a growing number of imitation products, mass-produced outside New Zealand, or by non-Māori artists, can be found on the New Zealand market,

---

8   In 2001, Danish toy company Lego launched a game called Bionicle, which was challenged by Māori tribes for using Māori and Polynesian names, such as tohunga (a spiritual healer). The storyline of Bionicle is said to be based on stories told by the Rapa Nui people, who live on Easter Island. It features a range of action figures who inhabit an imaginary island called Mata Nui, which has fallen under the control of an evil spirit. The mission of the six heroes, called the Toa (meaning an especially brave Māori warrior), with names such as Whenua (land) or Pohatu (stone), is to liberate the inhabitants of the island. Māori groups approached Lego saying they considered the use of the Māori language by Lego to be inappropriate and offensive. After initially claiming that it hadn't done anything illegal, Lego later admitted it had drawn partly on Polynesian culture for inspiration and had borrowed names from the Māori culture to spice up its toys. The company said that 'future launches of Bionicle sets will not incorporate names from any original culture'. Furthermore, it added that it 'will seek to develop a code of conduct for cultural expressions of traditional knowledge'. See A Osborn, 'Māoris Win Lego Battle', *Guardian Unlimited* (online), 31 October 2001 <http://www.guardian. co.uk/world/2001/oct/31/andrewosborn>

9   In March 2003, Sony PlayStation released a game called the Mark of Kri, featuring Rau, a warrior wearing a facial tattoo and carrying a taiaha (an ancient Māori weapon). The game was criticised by Māori IP campaigners for its 'inappropriate and upsetting usage of New Zealand Māori imagery'. In addition, they thought that Rau was promoted as a violent barbarian, thus portraying Māori in a negative manner to the international audience and linking them with stereotyped violence.

10   See S Frankel, 'Third-Party Trade Marks as a Violation of Indigenous Cultural Property' (2005) 8 *The Journal of World Intellectual Property* 83.

11   Tā moko' is the Māori form of a tattoo tradition which extends throughout the islands of Polynesia.

12   See 'Māori Tobacco Branding Lights up Furore', *National Business Review* (online) 12 December 2005 <m.nbr.co.nz/article/maori-tobacco-branding-lights-furore-updated>

13   See P Shand, 'Scenes from the Colonial Catwalk: Cultural Appropriation, Intellectual Property Rights, and Fashion' (2002) 3 *Cultural Analysis* 74.

14   See 'Raids on Haka to Continue as Cultures Can't Copyright', *Dominion Post* (Wellington), 15 July 2006.

mainly for the tourism industry, to the detriment of local authentic works. It is argued that these products deprive Māori artists of a reliable source of income, and many are considered offensive. Examples of offensive products include tiki pendants made from modern materials such as plastic instead of the traditional pounamu (greenstone), and Matryoshka dolls (Russian-style nesting dolls) featuring a Māori whānau (extended family), that are being sold at tourist gift stores. The dolls were designed by a New Zealand artist and made to order in China. According to Aroha Mead, a senior lecturer in Māori business studies at Victoria University, the dolls are an insult to traditional artists: 'if you compare these to authentic Russian dolls, which are well-designed and beautiful with very intricate patterns, they are cheap and simplistic. They certainly don't have anything to do with Māori culture […] I don't think any Māori would make something like this.'[15]

The unauthorised exploitation of TCEs by third parties raises a series of questions and concerns. When is borrowing from a traditional culture legitimate, and when is it inappropriate, offensive adaptation or copying? While there is no single set of concerns in relation to third-party branding of TCEs, some common elements can be found. Indigenous communities would like to get protection against the misappropriation and misuse of indigenous names, signs and symbols. They would like to control the ways in which TCEs are used beyond the customary and traditional context, and get equitable sharing of benefits arising from that use. In addition, they would like to prevent the inappropriate and/or offensive use of indigenous names, signs and symbols, and the unauthorised use and commercial exploitation of culturally sensitive names, signs and symbols. Indigenous names, signs and symbols can have a sacred and cultural significance, and using sacred or culturally sensitive names, signs and symbols outside their traditional context, and in ways contrary to customary laws, may cause offence and undermine the social organisation of traditional communities. Also, they would like to preclude the grant, exercise and enforcement of IPRs acquired by unauthorised parties, such as the unauthorised use or the trade mark registration of identical, similar or suggestive signs on imitation products in the marketplace. Finally, they would like to prevent false or misleading indications in trade that suggest endorsement or linkage with a community or tradition-based creations.

Some IP tools can and have been used, with varying levels of success, to address some of these concerns. The next paragraphs focus on the use of trade mark law. The trade mark law system can provide protection against offensive and deceptive uses of indigenous names, signs and symbols, and has the ability to prevent third parties from using the signs.

---

15   See C Simcox, 'Māori Russian Dolls Made in China, Sold in NZ', *Dominion Post* (online), 11 April 2008 <http://www.stuff.co.nz/dominion-post/361204>

# 3. Trade Mark Protection Against Offensive and Deceptive Use

To be registered as a trade mark, a sign must satisfy the criteria of registrability which are laid down by the law. Some signs may be subject to absolute bars to registration and therefore be inherently unregistrable. These absolute bars exclude from registration signs that are contrary to public order or morality and may therefore be considered offensive to sections of the community, such as indigenous groups, and signs that are deceptive.

## (a) Offensive Marks

The concepts of 'contrary to morality' or 'contrary to public order' are very broad, and require a value judgement to be made by trade mark registries. Offence may relate to words and/or images, and to matters of race, sex, religious beliefs, general matters of taste and decency, or, in our case, cultural offence. There are examples in various jurisdictions of stakeholders attempting to use absolute grounds to prevent the registration of trade marks containing offensive imagery and text. In New Zealand, the Trade Marks Act was amended in 2002 to take into account cultural offensiveness during the trade mark registration process. Under the New Zealand Trade Marks Act 2002, a trade mark application can be denied on grounds of cultural offence to significant sections of the community, and in particular to Māori.[16] In addition, the Act provides for the creation of an advisory committee to help the Commissioner of Trade Marks assess the potential offensiveness of trade marks. In the United States, a trade mark may be refused registration if it consists of matter that may disparage, or falsely suggest a connection with, persons, living or dead, beliefs, or national symbols, or bring them into contempt or disrepute.[17]

## (b) Deceptive Marks

If the trade mark applied for seems to suggest that the good or service has an indigenous origin, where such origin would be a significant factor for the average consumer, and this is not actually the case, the trade mark must be objected. The prohibition will apply to marks which, though distinctive, contain some

---

16  *New Zealand Trade Marks Act 2002*, s 17(1)(c)(i). See Intellectual Property of New Zealand (IPONZ), *Practice Guidelines 16 – Maori Advisory Committee & Maori Trade Marks* (2012) <http://www.iponz.govt.nz/cms/trade-marks/practice-guidelines-index/practice-guidelines/16-maori-advisory-committee-maori-trade-marks>
17  *Lanham Act 1946*, 15 USC 1052, s 2(a).

kind of suggestion or allusion that is inaccurate. The risk of deception must, however, be a real one, and fanciful trade marks will be accepted even though they might be deceptive.

It should be noted that trade mark law will not prevent the offensive or deceptive use of indigenous names, signs and symbols where the user does not seek to register a trade mark,[18] nor will it prevent the registration of indigenous names, signs and symbols by third parties where the signs are not considered offensive or deceptive.

# 4. Trade Mark Registration to Prevent Others from Using the Sign

Holders of TCEs may also register indigenous names, signs or symbols to remove them from the field of trade and business, and prevent them from being used by third parties.

In Canada, the First Nations peoples have registered a series of petroglyphs (ancient rock painting images) as 'official marks'[19] to prevent their improper use by third parties. They wanted to protect the petroglyphs from unauthorised reproduction and commodification on commercial items such as T-shirts, jewellery and postcards. The petroglyphs have special religious significance to the members of the First Nation Snuneymuxw people, who considered such uses offensive. Once the petroglyphs were registered as official marks, the Snuneymuxw were able to ask local shops to cease selling items that reproduced the registered images without permission. Members of the Snuneymuxw First Nation subsequently indicated that local merchants and commercial artisans did stop using the petroglyph images, and that the trade mark registration, accompanied by an education campaign to make others aware of the significance of the petroglyphs to the Snuneymuxw First Nation, had been very successful.[20]

---

18   In situations where the a third party does not seek to register a trade mark, it may be possible to use unfair competition laws or passing off to prevent competitors from misrepresenting their goods as to the source or quality, i.e. to prevent them from suggesting that they originate from a community or are authentic/genuine goods.

19   'Official marks' are special types of marks under section 9 of the Canadian Trade-Marks Act which prohibit the adoption, in connection with a business, of any badge, crest, emblem or mark which has been adopted or used by a public authority. In turn, a 'public authority' is defined as any entity which operates under a significant degree of government control and whose activities benefit the public as opposed to profiting private interests. Aboriginal groups and native organisations which meet these criteria are eligible to qualify as public authorities.

20   See WIPO IGC Secretariat, *Report on the Review of Exisiting Intellectual Property Protection of Traditional Knowledge*, WIPO Doc WIPO/GRTKF/IC/4/7 (2002), annex II, 1.

It should be noted that the defensive use of trade marks may require an amendment to the trade mark legislation of countries in which the commercial use of trade marks is mandatory. Furthermore, in some countries, national legislation requires that only legitimate businesses may file for trade mark registration. Such a requirement would also impose an amendment.

The trade mark system does not offer a comprehensive system of protection, as it would be prohibitively expensive to register all names, signs and symbols associated with a community's TK and TCEs. It would also be unreasonable and unrealistic to consider, or to aim for, a blanket prohibition on the use of all words and imagery with an indigenous connotation.

# 5. Branding by the Holders of TCEs

Brands are multi-faceted tools that can also be used to the advantage of the holders of TCEs for the purpose of identification, authentication, protection and commercial exploitation of their own products. In particular, where issues of livelihood, reward and profitability are prominent motivators for the creation of cultural expressions, the use of marketing strategies and IPRs can be very valuable.

The recipe for a successful business is one that uses quality products, a distinctive brand and an effective marketing strategy. The essence of branding lies in its capacity to foster the sales of a product by creating an emotional link with its consumers. This should in turn be combined with an effective marketing strategy that will create demand for the product. These key elements are often coupled with other important factors, such as raw materials, financial capital, good distribution networks and special skills.[21]

From an IP perspective, successful branding can involve the use of legal tools such as trade marks, certification and collective marks, and geographical indications (GIs), each operating according to their own sets of rules and pursuing related yet distinct objectives of protection. The following paragraphs will examine each of these IPRs in turn.

## (a) Trade Marks

Trade marks are signs which distinguish goods or services of one undertaking from those of other undertakings,[22] and convey information about the source

---

21  See ITC and WIPO, 'Marketing Crafts and Visual Arts: The Role of Intellectual Property. A Practical Guide' (ITC and WIPO, Geneva, 2003) 13.
22  TRIPS Agreement, art 15(1).

or trade origin of the goods or services in respect of which they are used. In addition to their distinguishing function, trade marks have an advertising function. They play a pivotal role in a company's branding and marketing strategies, contributing to the definition of the image and reputation of the company's products in the eyes of consumers. The image and reputation of a company create trust, which is the basis for establishing a loyal clientele and enhancing a company's goodwill. Finally, they provide information about, amongst other things, the quality of the goods and services. Consumers need this information to make informed purchasing decisions. Trade marks provide an incentive for companies to invest in maintaining or improving the quality of their products to ensure that products bearing their trade mark have a positive reputation. Consumers who are satisfied with a product are likely to buy or use that product again.

The trade mark system can help indigenous communities benefit from the branding of their TCEs, and protect their economic interests in those TCEs by allowing the registration of distinctive indigenous names, signs or symbols. Trade mark registration, combined with an appropriate marketing strategy, can enable indigenous communities to differentiate their products, and build a brand image and reputation. This can increase consumer recognition of TCEs and the commercial benefits for holders of TCEs, as the addition of a trade mark on a good increases its value. However, it should be noted that there are costs associated with the registration of a trade mark: for example, in relation to the registration and renewal fees, the enforcement of rights and the implementation of a marketing strategy.

## (b) Geographical Indications

'Geographical indications' (GIs), as defined in Article 22(1) of the Agreement on Trade-Related Aspects of Intellectual Property Rights (TRIPS Agreement) are indications[23] which identify a good[24] as originating[25] in the territory of a

---

23   Under the TRIPS Agreement, a geographical indication is any 'indication' pointing to a given country, region or locality. This differs from the definition of appellations of origin under the Lisbon Agreement, which provides that appellations of origin are necessarily 'geographical names' of a country, region or locality. Although Article 22(1) does not provide what form indications can take, it is accepted that an indication is not expressly limited to the name of a place. A word or a phrase, for example, may serve as a GI without necessarily being the name of a territory and so may 'evoke' the territory. For example, 'Basmati' is known as an indication for rice coming from the Indian sub-continent, although it is not a place name as such. In addition, while a word may be an indication, other types of symbols, such as pictorial images, icons or emblems (for example, the symbol of the Eiffel Tower to designate French products) may also serve as identifiers. See UNCTAD–ICTSD, *Resource Book on TRIPS and Development* (Cambridge University Press, 2005) 289.

24   Whereas appellations of origin designate a product, the name of which is usually the same as the appellation of origin, it is well established that GIs, for the purpose of TRIPS, apply to any 'good', be it natural, agricultural, agri-industrial or manufactured, in respect of which an appropriate geographical link is made. See J Audier, *TRIPS Agreement Geographical Indications* (Office for Official Publications of the European Communities, 2000) 16.

25   GIs identify a good 'originating' in the territory of a member, or a region or locality in that territory. This should be understood as referring to goods that must be mined, grown or manufactured in that territory.

member, or a region or locality in that territory, where a given quality, reputation or other characteristic[26] of the good is essentially attributable to its geographical origin.[27] In other words, under the TRIPS definition, GIs communicate important information on: (a) the name of the product; (b) the area of geographical origin of the product; and (c) its given quality, reputation or other characteristics which are essentially attributable to that geographical origin.

Article 22(2) of the TRIPS Agreement establishes the general standard of protection that must be available for all GIs. It provides that 'legal means' must be provided to interested parties to prevent the use of GIs which mislead the public as to the geographical origin of the goods. It also requires that legal means be provided to prevent use which constitutes an 'act of unfair competition' within the meaning of Article 10 *bis* of the Paris Convention. However, while it is mandatory for member states to provide protection to GIs, they are free to determine the appropriate method of protection when implementing the provisions of the Agreement within their own legal system and practice.[28] Over the past decade, a variety of different legal concepts have been used to protect GIs at the national and regional levels. They include, in particular, laws of unfair competition and passing off, protected appellations of origin and registered GIs, collective and certification marks, and administrative schemes of protection.[29] The choice of a protection mechanism or a combination of systems of protection will usually depend on the legal tradition and historical and economic conditions of the jurisdiction concerned. However, the differences between these systems will have a bearing on important questions, such as conditions of protection, entitlement to use and scope of protection.

---

26   Under TRIPS, 'quality, reputation or other characteristics' of a good can each be a sufficient basis for eligibility as a GI, where they are 'essentially attributable' to the geographical origin of the good in question. The word 'attributable' seems to suggest an objective criterion. However, while this might be possible for a quality or characteristic, reputation suggests a subjective element. Indeed, the reference to quality refers to physical characteristics of the good. On the other hand, the reference to reputation makes clear that the identification of a particular objective attribute of the good is not a prerequisite to conferring protection. It is enough that the public associates a good with a territory because the public believes the good to have desirable characteristics. Indeed, GIs, like trade marks, may be built up through investment in advertising. The drawback is that the public may be deceived as to the quality of goods and their territorial link through false or misleading advertisement. See UNCTAD–ICTSD, above n 23, 290.

27   The words 'essentially attributable' to the geographical territory are intended to establish the link between the product and the relevant territory. While a literal reading of 'territory' would suggest that the link must be physical: that is, that the product must embody certain characteristics because of the soil conditions, weather or other physical elements in a place, the terms 'reputation' and 'essentially attributable' allow flexibility. Therefore, 'essentially attributable' can be understood also to refer to human labour in the place or to goodwill created by advertisement in respect to the place. See UNCTAD–ICTSD, above n 23, 290-291. This also seems to be confirmed by the drafting history of TRIPS. In the 1990 draft (Draft of 23 July 1990 (W/76), para 2), the quality, reputation or other characteristic of the product had to be attributable to its geographical origin, including natural and human factors. The qualification 'natural and human factors' did not, however, reappear in the final text of TRIPS, which uses the broader term of 'geographical origin'. See D Gervais, *The TRIPS Agreement, Drafting History and Analysis* (2nd ed, Sweet & Maxwell, 2003) 188-189.

28   TRIPS Agreement, art 1(1).

29   See UNCTAD–ICTSD, above n 23, 291.

GIs have traditionally been associated with agricultural products, foodstuffs, wines and spirits. However, in recent years GIs have been said to be potentially useful in protecting indigenous knowledge. At the fifth session of the World Intellectual Property Organization (WIPO) Intergovernmental Committee on Intellectual Property and Genetic Resources, Traditional Knowledge and Folklore (IGC), it was pointed out that some TCEs, such as handicrafts made using natural resources, may qualify as 'goods' which could be protected by GIs.[30]

TCEs can be tangible expressions in which culture is manifested or expressed, such as productions of art or handicrafts. They include, in particular, drawings, designs, paintings, carvings, sculptures, pottery, terracotta, mosaic, woodwork, metalware, jewellery, baskets, needlework, textiles, glassware, carpets, costumes and musical instruments.

These tangible expressions or 'handicrafts' may qualify as goods which could be protected by GIs if they present the necessary qualities for GI protection.[31] Such qualities would usually include a symbolic association between the handicraft or artisanal product and a particular culture which acknowledges the influence of tradition in its creation. Furthermore, these handicrafts would be produced either completely by hand or with the help of hand-tools or mechanical means, as long as the direct manual contribution of the craftsperson remains the most substantial component of the finished products. They would be produced using raw materials from sustainable resources, and their distinctive features could be utilitarian, aesthetic, artistic, creative, culturally attached, decorative, functional or traditional, or have a religious or social symbolism. Finally, the creative activity would occur within a small group or a community-based environment.[32]

A number of common features can be identified between, on the one hand, GIs and the goods they relate to and, on the other, TCEs. They are (a) the communal element: while GIs identify a good that is produced by a number of different producers, TCEs are usually produced within a community; (b) the element of tradition: while GIs are often based on traditional formulae and processes, TCEs are produced according to traditional methods; (c) the element of time: the

---

30   See WIPO IGC Secretariat, *Consolidated Analysis of the Legal Protection of Traditional Cultural Expressions*, WIPO Doc WIPO/GRTKF/IC/5/3 (2003) 52.

31   On GIs and TK/TCEs, see generally M Blakeney, 'Protection of Traditional Knowledge by Geographical Indications' in C Antons (ed), *Traditional Knowledge, Traditional Cultural Expressions and Intellectual Property Law in the Asia-Pacific Region* (Kluwer Law International, 2009) 87.

32   See UNESCO/ITC, 'International Symposium on Crafts and the International Market: Trade and Customs Codification' (Final Report, Manila, 1997) 6; K Basu, 'Marketing Developing Society Crafts: A Framework for Analysis and Change' in J A Costa and G J Bamossy (eds), *Marketing in a Multicultural World: Ethnicity, Nationalism and Cultural Identity* (Sage Publications, 1995) 261, D S Gangjee, *Geographical Indications Protection for Handicrafts under TRIPS* (MPhil Thesis, University of Oxford, 2002) 5 <http://users.ox.ac.uk/~edip/gangjee.pdf>

know-how attached to both GIs and TCEs is transmitted from one generation to the other; (d) the geographical link: while GIs are granted for products which have a relationship with the land, local resources or the environment, TCEs are generally linked to a specific place where a certain product is made, or to traditional methods or conditions used in a specific place for making a product, often using raw material from sustainable resources. In addition, while the value of a GI is linked to its origin, the value of TCEs is linked to the knowledge that a particular community from a particular region has produced it.

The GI system is therefore consistent with the nature of indigenous knowledge in that GIs work as a collective right and provide protection that is potentially unlimited in time, as long as the distinctive link between the goods and the place is maintained and the indication has not fallen into genericity.

There are many examples around the world of indigenous names, signs and symbols that have been registered as GIs. These include TALAVERA DE PUEBLA pottery and OLINALÁ handicrafts from Mexico; JABLONEC jewellery, glass and crystal from the Czech Republic; MADEIRA embroidery from Portugal; GORODETS paintings, ROSTOV enamel and KARGOPOL clay toys in the Russian Federation; and Mysore silk, Kashmir Pashmina and Pochampally Ikat in India.[33]

While GIs do not directly protect the actual knowledge associated with TCEs, which remains in the public domain and is open to misappropriation, they can indirectly contribute to their protection in several ways. First, GIs protect the reputation or goodwill accumulated over time, and can safeguard a niche market segment. They can provide protection to TCEs against misleading and deceptive trading practices, and prevent third parties from using a protected GI on goods that do not originate from a given region and/or do not possess the requisite quality or characteristics. Secondly, GIs enable product differentiation. Where a product is successfully differentiated through the use of a GI, the market is segmented, and access to a specific market segment can be restricted to producers of products possessing the necessary quality, reputation or other characteristics, and who are carrying on their activity in the relevant geographical area. Thirdly, the registration of a GI can create value for the holders of TCEs and enhance the development of rural communities.[34] For example, the registration of a GI has been shown to increase production output and land value, and the certainty afforded by legal protection can create opportunities for investment in a product and region. Fourthly, the registration of indigenous names, signs

---

33 On Indian GIs, see K Das, 'Prospects and Challenges of Geographical Indications in India' (2010) 13 *Journal of World Intellectual Property* 148.

34 See T W Dagne, 'Harnessing the Development Potential of Geographical Indications for Traditional Knowledge-Based Agricultural Products' (2010) 5 *Journal of Intellectual Property Law & Practice* 441; D Zografos, 'Geographical Indications & Socio-Economic Development' (I Qsensato Working Paper 3) <http://www.iqsensato.org/pdf/iqsensato-wp-3-zografos-dec-2008.pdf>

or symbols as GIs can help indigenous groups gain recognition for the cultural significance of their TCEs and preserve them for future generations. Finally, GIs provide information and educate consumers about the origin, quality and characteristics of the goods.

## (c) Certification and Collective Marks

Certification and collective marks are special types of marks. They inform the public about certain characteristics of the products or services marketed under the mark. Article 7 *bis* of the Paris Convention provides for the mutual obligation of registration and protection of collective marks in the countries of the Union.[35] However, it leaves each country be the judge of the particular conditions under which a collective mark shall be protected, and provides that it may refuse protection if the mark is contrary to the public interest. Even though the Paris Convention refers only to collective marks, it is generally understood that the term also includes certification marks.[36] Certification and collective marks can be indications of geographical origin. As such, they can be protected under the TRIPS Agreement. The TRIPS Agreement incorporates by reference a number of articles of the Paris Convention, including Article 7 *bis*. As a consequence, collective marks which belong to associations and are serving as GIs are protected under TRIPS.[37]

A certification mark is a mark which indicates that the goods or services in connection with which it is used are certified by the proprietor of the mark in respect of geographical origin, material, mode of manufacture of goods or performance of services, quality, accuracy, or other characteristics. In other words, it is an indication of the conformity of goods or services to particular standards, stipulated by the proprietor of the mark.

---

35    As originally established in Paris in 1883, the Paris Convention made no provision for the protection of collective marks. However, at the Washington Conference of 1911, Article 7bis was introduced in the Convention. It was later amended at the London Conference of 1934. Article 7bis of the Paris Convention provides that:

> The countries of the Union undertake to accept for filing and to protect collective marks belonging to associations the existence of which is not contrary to the law of the country of origin, even if such associations do not possess an industrial or commercial establishment.

> Each country shall be the judge of the particular conditions under which a collective mark shall be protected and may refuse protection if the mark is contrary to the public interest.

> Nevertheless, the protection of these marks shall not be refused to any association the existence of which is not contrary to the law of the country of origin, on the ground that such association is not established in the country where protection is sought or is not constituted according to the law of the latter country.

36    See N Dawson, *Certification Trade Marks, Law and Practice* (Intellectual Property Publishing Limited, 1988) 13.

37    See J Belson, *Certification Marks* (Sweet & Maxwell, 2002) 23. For a discussion of the protection of TCEs with geographical indications, see ch 6.

Any person or entity that authorises traders to use a certification in relation to certain products or services may apply for a certification mark. However, the applicant must be considered competent to certify the products concerned. The owner of the certification mark is ultimately responsible for controlling its use and for ensuring that the mark is not used on non-compliant goods. The applicant must also supply a copy of the regulations governing the use of the certification mark, which must indicate who is authorised to use the mark, the characteristics to be certified by the mark, how the certifying body is to test those characteristics and supervise the use of the mark, the fees to be paid in connection with the administration of the certification scheme, and the procedures for resolving disputes. Unlike collective marks, certification marks are not confined to any membership. They can be used by anybody who complies with the standards defined by the owner of the certification mark.

A collective mark is a mark which distinguishes the goods or services of members of an association which is the proprietor of the mark from those of other undertakings, without any requirement for certification of the goods or services. In most jurisdictions, applicants are required to supply a copy of the regulations governing the use of the collective mark. These generally indicate who is authorised to use the mark, the conditions of membership of the association, any conditions for use of the mark, as well as sanctions against misuse. The cost, duration and scope of protection applicable to collective marks are similar to those of ordinary trade marks. However, since the cost of registering a collective mark is divided among the members of the association, it becomes much cheaper for an individual member. This can be an attractive argument for indigenous and local communities for whom the cost of registering an ordinary trade mark to market their products or services could be dissuasive.

An association of indigenous producers or craftspeople can register a collective mark and authorise its members to use it in relation to their products or services. In that way, a collective mark can be used as a tool to help them obtain consumer recognition and customer loyalty, and develop a joint marketing campaign for their products. Collective marks are often used to show membership of a union, association or other organisation. Membership as such may be an incentive to some customers to buy a product bearing the collective mark. In addition, a collective mark can have the function of informing the public about certain features of a product associated with it. Unlike certification marks, the proprietor association of a collective mark does not have to set standards to be met before its members can use the mark. However, it may do so if it wishes. Consequently, collective marks may also perform a certification function.[38] This is particularly relevant in countries that do not provide for registration of certification marks.[39]

There are various examples, in a number of jurisdictions, of use of certification and collective marks to protect and promote TCEs. These have had varying levels of success. They include the toi iho[tm] certification mark in New Zealand,[40] the Alaska Silver Hand Program in Canada,[41] and the Marca Colectiva FIEB[42] and the Auténtico Pemon[43] certification marks in Venezuela, to name only a few.

Certification and collective marks can be valuable tools for the protection and promotion of TCEs. They allow for collective use and can denote common

---

38   Note that there is a certain level of confusion between certification and collective marks. As Jeffrey Belson pointed out, during the first century of the registration system there was confusion over the respective roles of certification and collective marks, and this situation has not improved due to a proliferation and growing divergence of policy and law on certification and collective marks. For example, a mark may become a Community Trade Mark collective mark and a national domestically registered certification mark. Also, because there can be varying degrees of conflation, the usefulness and specificity of the information conveyed by a collective mark may at times be close to that of a traditional certification mark and at other times less so. See Belson, above n 37, 42-43.

39   As regards certification and collective marks, national laws for the registration of trade marks can be classified into three categories: (a) those which permit registration of certification marks only, in which case use of the marks is open to all who meet the standards; (b) those which permit registration of collective marks only, in which case collective marks may also perform a certification function. However, because they are registered as collective marks, their use is permitted only to members of the proprietor association, and (c) those which permit registration of both certification and collective marks. In this category also, collective marks may perform a certification function. See Dawson, above n 36.

40   Toi ihoTM is a registered certification trade mark used to promote and sell authentic, quality Māori arts and crafts, and to authenticate exhibitions and performances of Māori arts and artists. It is intended to certify that the arts and crafts are made by a person of Māori descent and to provide a mark of quality. It was developed and implemented in response to calls from Māori to assist them retain ownership and control of their taonga (treasures) and maintain the integrity of their art culture. While, overall, the introduction of the toi ihoTM mark has been beneficial to artists and consumers alike, the certification mark was disinvested in 2010. Some of the reasons for the disinvestment were that: (a) toi ihoTM no longer fitted in the strategic priorities of Creative New Zealand; (b) there was insufficient funding and resources to run the scheme appropriately; (c) the breadth of the scheme's design was too wide. Despite the disinvestment, artists have not been deregistered and the toi ihoTM scheme is currently in a transition phase. One possible plan for its future would be for a group of Māori artists to create a trust to take over the toi ihoTM mark. See Creative New Zealand, *Statement on toi ihoTM* (2009) <http://www.creativenz.govt.nz/en/news/creative-new-zealand-statement-on-toi-iho>

41   The Alaska Silver Hand Program is a certification mark that certifies the authenticity of Alaska Native art and guarantees consumers that items bearing the Silver Hand identification seal were handcrafted in Alaska by an Alaska Eskimo, Aleut, or Indian craftsperson or artist, and made wholly or in significant part of natural materials. See Alaska State Council on the Arts, *Silver Hand Program and Permit Application* <http://www.eed.state.ak.us/aksca/Forms/individuals/SH.pdf>

42   The Marca Colectiva FIEB (Federation de Indigenas de Estado Bolivar) distinguishes goods and services manufactured or offered by indigenous people, associations or production centres affiliated to the Indigenous Federation of the Bolivar State. It demonstrates the material and spiritual bond between the goods and services manufactured or offered by the Bolivar State indigenous people, and the habitat and cultural background in which they have lived from ancestral times. See Grupo de Investigación sobre, 'Politicas Públicas de Propriedad Intelectual' (Universidad de Los Andes, Mérida, Venezuela) <http://www.cjp.ula.ve/gpi/documentos/fieb_content_def1.pdf>

43   The Auténtico Pemon certification mark certifies and promotes indigenous handicrafts, indigenous artisans and the Pemon culture more generally. It includes the Auténtico Pemon certification mark, collaboration mark and certified merchandiser mark. See ibid.

indigenous origin. They do not confer a monopoly right, but they limit the class of people who can use a certain name, sign or symbol. The cost of registering and renewing a collective mark is divided among the members of the association and is consequently much cheaper than registering an ordinary trade mark. Similarly, marketing costs can also be shared by the members of the association. Finally, they provide protection that is potentially unlimited in time, provided the necessary steps are taken for their renewal.

The registration of a certification or collective mark can help indigenous communities distinguish their TCEs, promote their art and artists nationally and internationally, and maintain the integrity of their culture. In addition, a certification or collective mark can be a valuable tool to help improve their economic position and ensure they get fair and equitable returns. Finally, these tools can be used by indigenous communities to raise public awareness and maximise consumer certainty as to the authenticity of the goods marketed under the mark.

Having said that, the effectiveness of a certification scheme depends on the way it is set up, implemented and policed. A successful certification scheme needs to gain the support of the stakeholders — that is, the indigenous communities — and the owner of the mark will need to engage in public education campaigns for the acceptance of the mark, so that the public, the relevant industry bodies and consumers become familiar with the characteristics that the certification scheme guarantees. Finally, where the certification or collective mark is also a quality mark, there needs to be an oversight of quality of the goods or services for which accreditation is sought.

# 6. Concluding Comments

The laws of trade marks, certification and collective marks, and GIs have not been designed, for the most part, with the protection of indigenous interests as an underlying policy goal. The utility of these laws as tools for holders of TCEs to protect their indigenous names, signs and symbols is therefore often coincidental.[44] Although these legal tools may help them achieve some of their objectives, they will usually not provide a comprehensive system of protection. For example, as was highlighted above, even if the registration of a trade mark may prevent the registration of offensive and deceptive marks, it will not prevent the offensive and deceptive use of indigenous names, signs and symbols where the user does not seek to register a trade mark, and nor will it prevent

---

44    See S Frankel, 'Trademarks and Traditional Knowledge and Cultural Intellectual Property' in Graeme B Dinwoodie and Mark D Janis (eds), *Trademark Law and Theory, A Handbook of Contemporary Research* (Edward Elgar, 2008) 437.

the registration of indigenous names, signs and symbols by third parties where the signs are not considered offensive or deceptive. In the same way, the use of a certification mark or authenticity label will not, in itself, prevent the sale of imitation products in the marketplace. Further, when dealing with the protection and branding of TCEs, a distinction must be drawn between the protection of the actual knowledge and the protection of the indigenous names, signs and symbols associated with the TCEs. The systems of protection discussed above may protect the indigenous names, signs and symbols associated with the knowledge, but the actual knowledge is not protected, remains in the public domain and is open to misappropriation by third parties.

Holders of TCEs should carefully plan how they will identify, protect and manage their IP assets. IP and marketing go hand in hand, so the use of IPRs to identify, authenticate, protect and exploit TCEs should form part of a planned and systematic marketing strategy. Similarly, IP assets are a basic requirement for a successful marketing strategy, as they can send messages about the product and help differentiate it from other products.

# 8. The Pacific Solution: The European Union's Intellectual Property Rights Activism in Australia's and New Zealand's Sphere of Influence

Michael Blakeney

## 1. Introduction

This chapter describes the activities of the European Union (EU) in providing technical assistance to Pacific Island countries in relation to traditional knowledge (TK), and the implications for Australian and New Zealand development cooperation activities in what was hitherto regarded as their 'lake'. Agriculture is the issue which has dominated Australia's and New Zealand's trade agenda, and intellectual property rights (IPRs), whether trade related or otherwise, are very much a subordinate issue. Both nations were foundation members of the Cairns Group of nineteen agricultural exporting countries which was formed in 1986, at the time of the Uruguay Round of the General Agreement on Tariffs and Trade (GATT), to agitate for global agricultural trade reform. The Cairns Group has been forthright in criticising the European Community (EC), the United States and Japan as protecting their agricultural markets through a combination of high tariffs on agricultural imports and subsidies to their farm sectors. This condemns agricultural exporters in developing countries in Latin America, South East Asia and Oceania to 'the role of residual suppliers to their traditional markets' and crowds them out of most other markets.[1]

The 35th Cairns Group Ministerial Meeting at Punta del Este, Uruguay, from 19 to 20 April 2010 conceded that the Doha Development Agenda must remain the top priority of World Trade Organization (WTO) members, but that the Cairns Group will continue to push for global trade reform in agriculture, which it perceived as critical to the development deliverables of the Uruguay Round.[2] In fact, the agriculture negotiations have been proceeding at a glacial pace and have not been assisted by the global financial crisis. An indication of Australia's

---

1   Cairns Group, *Agricultural Trade and the Cairns Group* <http://cairnsgroup.org>
2   35th Cairns Group Ministerial Meeting, *Punta del Este, Uruguay, Communiqué* (2010) <http://www.cairnsgroup.org/Pages/100420_communique.aspx?noredirect=1>

ranking of negotiating priorities can be seen in its negotiation in 2007 of the Free Trade Agreement (FTA) with the United States in which it was perceived as bargaining away IPRs for access to United States agricultural markets.[3]

For the EU, on the other hand, the maintenance of agricultural protectionism does not seem to have abated, but it maintains a substantial IPRs agenda to underpin both its pharmaceutical and digital-based industries. Also, member states of the EU, such as France, Spain and Italy, have pioneered the use of geographical indications (GIs) to underpin agricultural niche markets. The EU played a significant role in having GIs included within the TRIPS Agreement. This inclusion was incomplete, as the articles concerned with GIs had a number of 'built-in agendas' which envisaged further negotiations to finalise this subject. Thus, Article 24.2 required the TRIPS Council to conduct a review of the operation of the GIs provisions within the first two years of entry into force of the WTO Agreement. Article 23.4 provided that 'in order to facilitate the protection of geographical indications for wines, negotiations shall be undertaken in the Council for TRIPS concerning the establishment of a multilateral system of notification and registration of geographical indications for wines eligible for protection in those Members participating in the system', and under Article 24.1 members agreed 'to enter into negotiations aimed at increasing the protection of individual geographical indications under Article 23'. The EU, together with Switzerland, has played an active role in pressing for an expansion of the scope of the GIs provisions of TRIPS. Australia and New Zealand, on the other hand, have been active opponents of this expansion.

The EU has also pursued its GIs agenda outside the TRIPS Council. In February 2003, the EC proposed to the WTO's Committee on Agriculture that it 'claw back' certain GIs which were being 'used by producers other than the right-holders in the country of origin'.[4] The EC's approach to GIs in the context of the agriculture negotiations is complementary to the TRIPS negotiations. The EC explained that its objective was to negotiate 'specific commitments in order to guarantee fair market access opportunities for those wines, spirits and other agricultural and food-stuff products whose quality, reputation or other characteristics are essentially attributable to their geographical origin and traditional know-how'.[5] As a follow-up to this proposal, in September 2003 a preliminary list of products (wines, spirits, cheeses and ham) which fell into this category was notified to the Committee.[6] The claw-back proposal was strongly opposed by the same countries that were opposed to GIs extension in the TRIPS

---

3 See P Drahos et al, 'Pharmaceuticals, Intellectual Property and Free Trade: The Case of the US–Australia Free Trade Agreement' (2004) 22(3) *Prometheus* 243.
4 *A Proposal For Modalities in the WTO Agriculture Negotiations, Specific Drafting Input by the EC*, WTO Doc JOB(03)/12 (2003).
5 Ibid 3.
6 WTO Doc, above n 4.

Council. The EC sought to allay concerns by referring to the 'grand-fathering' clause of Article 24.4, which would allow the use of protected GIs by producers in third countries, providing that they have done so for more than ten years prior to the signing of an amendment.[7]

Within the Committee on Agriculture the view has been strongly pressed that GIs protection is a matter for the TRIPS Council because the agriculture negotiations focus on food products, whereas proposed negotiations under TRIPS would cover all products including agricultural products and handicrafts.[8] Certainly the WTO documents concerning the negotiations on agriculture over the past five years make no reference to GIs.

In urging their respective positions, both the EU and its antipodean opponents have sought to enlist third countries, particularly those in the large bloc of developing and least developed countries (LDCs), to their cause. However, as this chapter indicates, in the Pacific this rivalry has been played out in the field of traditional knowledge (TK) protection, which is perceived by Pacific Island countries as closer to their national interests.

## 2. The Pacific Islands Perspective

The Pacific Islands Forum[9] is the key regional political organisation in the Pacific. Its annual meetings have mainly focused on regional trade and economic issues. The foundation members were: Australia, the Cook Islands, Fiji, Nauru, New Zealand, Tonga and Western Samoa. They have since been joined by Niue, Papua New Guinea, Kiribati, Tuvalu, Vanuatu, Solomon Islands, the Republic of the Marshall Islands, the Federated States of Micronesia, and Palau. New Caledonia and French Polynesia were granted associate membership in 2006. Current Forum observers include: Tokelau, Wallis and Futuna, American Samoa, Guam and the Commonwealth of Northern Marianas; Timor Leste has special observer status.

The 40th Forum, held in Cairns in August 2011, issued the Cairns Communiqué, which included the Cairns Compact on Strengthening Development Coordination in the Pacific; a Call to Action on Climate Change, in advance of Copenhagen; agreement to commence negotiations on a new regional trade and economic agreement; and the hosting of meetings to strengthen protection and management

---

7   See *Geographical Indications — Communication from the European Communities,* WTO Doc TN/IP/W/11 (2005).

8   See WTO, *Agricultural Negotiations: Geographical Indications* <http://www.wto.org/english/tratop_e/agric_e/negs_bkgrnd21_ph2geog_e.htm>

9   Until 27 October 2000 it was known as the South Pacific Forum.

of regional fisheries resources, and to improve energy security.[10] The subsequent Forum, in Auckland, New Zealand, in September 2011 reaffirmed strong support for the Cairns Compact on Strengthening Development Coordination.

The Pacific Agreement on Closer Economic Relations (PACER) is an umbrella agreement between the Pacific Islands members of the Pacific Islands Forum and Australia and New Zealand. The agreement which was signed at Nauru on 18 August 2001, entering into force on 3 October 2002, established a framework for the future development of trade and economic relations across the Forum region as a whole. It envisaged a staged process of trade liberalisation, commencing with a free trade agreement in goods — the Pacific Island Countries Trade Agreement — among Pacific Island countries. Among other things, PACER provides for technical assistance to the Island country members in anticipation of future negotiations on a Forum-wide reciprocal free trade agreement (PACER-Plus). An underlying concern of the Forum Island countries is that the PACER-Plus agreement is being 'forced on them' by the currently dominant regional powers, Australia and New Zealand.[11] The Forum Island countries have fought to have established as an independent body the Office of the Chief Trade Adviser (OCTA) to provide advice and support for the negotiation of PACER-Plus. Australia and New Zealand have apparently sought to use their contribution to the funding of the OCTA to restrict the activities of that office.[12] The tension between Australia and New Zealand on the one hand and the Forum Island states on the other has created an opportunity of influence for the EU, which has announced its intention of negotiating Economic Partnership Agreements (EPAs) with the Pacific Island states.[13]

In July 2009, Papua New Guinea signed an interim EPA, followed by Fiji in December 2009. The situation of Fiji has also provided the EU with an opportunity to involve itself in Pacific affairs. On 2 May 2009, Fiji was suspended indefinitely from participation in the Pacific Forum because of the deteriorating human rights situation in the country. It remains outside the Pacific Forum. As one response, Fiji became the principal organiser of the Melanesian Spearhead Group (MSG), comprising Fiji, Papua New Guinea, the Solomon Islands and the Front de Libération Nationale Kanak et Socialiste of New Caledonia. The MSG had been founded as a political gathering in 1983, but became an

---

10   See Australian Government Dept. of Foreign Affairs and Trade, *Pacific Islands Forum* <http://www.dfat. gov.au/geo/spacific/regional_orgs/spf.html>

11   See J Kelsey, *Big Brothers Behaving Badly: The Implications for the Pacific Islands of the Pacific Agreement on Closer Economic Relations (PACER)* (2004) <http://www.bilaterals.org/IMG/pdf/pang_big_brother.pdf.>

12   See Senator L Rhiannon, *Adjournment Speech: 'Pacific Trade Negotiations* (2011) <http://lee-rhiannon. greensmps.org.au/content/parliament/speech/lees-speech-on-pacific-trade-negotiations> See also D Flitton, 'Pacific Islands Accuse Australia's Aid Agency of Coercion', *The Age* (online), 29 August 2011, <http://www. theage.com.au/national/pacific-islands-accuse-australias-aid-agency-of-coercion-20110828-1jgnv.html>

13   See European Commission, *Negotiations and Agreements* (2012) <http://ec.europa.eu/trade/wider-agenda/ development/economic-partnerships/negotiations-and-agreements/#pacific/>

international organisation on 23 March 2007. MSG members are the signatories of a preferential trade agreement between them. On the occasion of the 40th anniversary of the Pacific Islands Forum in September 2011, Fiji's military ruler, Frank Bainimarama, took the opportunity to organise a meeting with a number of Pacific Island states in Nadi. It was attended by the prime ministers of Papua New Guinea, Solomon Islands and Tuvalu, as well as the foreign ministers of Nauru and Timor Leste.[14]

The exclusion of Fiji from the Pacific Islands Forum has caused Fiji and MSG members to look to the People's Republic of China to fund the construction of a Secretariat building in Vanuatu. And, as is mentioned below, the EU provided technical assistance to the MSG to allow it to promulgate in 2011 a collaborative agreement providing for the protection of TK and expressions of culture.

Finally, it should be noted that an assumption of the Pacific development cooperation programmes of the EU and of Australia and New Zealand is that WTO membership is a desirable objective for Pacific Island states. However, some of those states have begun to question whether this is indeed in their best interests. Vanuatu, which completed its WTO accession process in 2001, has been reported to have 'put it on hold' because of the wide- ranging trade concessions it was required to make.[15] Similarly, Samoa and Tonga are reported to be deterred by the trade concessions which they have been obliged to offer.[16] The EU initiatives in relation to TK and GIs, underpinned by its EPAs, can be seen as an attempt to demonstrate the advantages of WTO engagement for the Pacific Island states.

# 3. An International TK Instrument

The Pacific region has been a global pioneer of initiatives for the protection of TK. The first regional instrument dealing with the protection of TK was the Suva Declaration which was issued by the Regional Consultation on Indigenous Peoples' Knowledge and Intellectual Property Rights, held in April 1995. The declarants committed themselves to raising public awareness of the dangers of expropriation of indigenous knowledge and resources; encouraging chiefs, elders and community leaders to play a leadership role in the protection of indigenous peoples' knowledge and resources; and to incorporating the concerns of indigenous peoples to protect their knowledge and resources in

---

14  R Callick, 'Fiji Casts Shadow on Pacific Forum', *The Australian* (online), 5 September 2011 <http://www.theaustralian.com.au/news/features/fiji-casts-shadow-on-pacific-forum/story-e6frg6z6-1226129262121>
15  J Kelsey, *Acceding Countries as Pawns in a Power Play: A Case Study of the Pacific Islands* (2007) <http://uriohau.blogspot.com/2007/08/acceding-countries-as-pawns-in-power.html>
16  Ibid.

legislation by including 'Prior Informed Consent or No Informed Consent' (PICNIC) procedures, and excluding the patenting of life forms.[17] The Suva Declaration called for the initiation of a treaty 'declaring the Pacific Region to be a life forms patent-free zone' and for a moratorium on bioprospecting in the Pacific until appropriate protection mechanisms were in place. The final article of the Declaration called on France 'to stop definitively its nuclear testing in the Pacific and repair the damaged biodiversity'.[18]

Responding to a number of indigenous persons' declarations calling for the protection of TK which had followed the Rio Earth Summit in 1992,[19] the World Forum on the Protection of Folklore was convened by the World Intellectual Property Organization (WIPO) and UNESCO in February 1996 in Phuket, Thailand, to explore issues concerning the preservation and protection of expressions of folklore. At that meeting the representatives of organisations of indigenous peoples called for the promulgation of an international convention to protect TK. In response, WIPO in its 1998–99 biennium instituted a schedule of regional fact-finding missions 'to identify and explore the intellectual property needs, rights and expectations of the holders of traditional knowledge and innovations, in order to promote the contribution of the intellectual property system to their social, cultural and economic development'.[20]

In a Note dated 14 September 2000, the Permanent Mission of the Dominican Republic to the United Nations in Geneva submitted two documents on behalf of the Group of Countries of Latin America and the Caribbean calling for the creation of a Standing Committee on access to the genetic resources and TK of local and indigenous communities. 'The work of that Standing Committee would have to be directed towards defining internationally recognized practical methods of securing adequate protection for the intellectual property rights in traditional knowledge.'[21] In 2000, WIPO established an Intergovernmental Committee on Intellectual Property and Genetic Resources, Traditional Knowledge and Folklore (IGC). At its first session, held in Geneva from 30 April to 3 May 2001, IGC member states determined the agenda of items on which work should proceed, and prioritised certain tasks. Principal among these was 'the development of "guide contractual practices," guidelines, and model intellectual property clauses for contractual agreements on access to genetic resources and benefit-sharing'.[22] This soft law approach to the protection of TK

---

17 Reproduced at UNDP *Consultation on Indigenous Peoples' Knowledge and Intellectual Property Rights* appendix 11 <http://www.idrc.ca/cp/ev-30152-201-1-DO_TOPIC.html>

18 Ibid, art 10.1.

19 For example Mataatua Declaration (1993), Kari-Oca Declaration (1992), Julayabinul Statement (1993).

20 See WIPO, *Report on Fact-finding Missions on Intellectual Property and Traditional Knowledge* (1998-1999) <http://www.wipo.int/tk/en/tk/ffm/report/final/> Cached, 9 March 2012.

21 See WIPO Doc, *Traditional Knowledge and the Need to Give It Adequate Intellectual Property Protection*, WIPO Doc WO/GA/26/9 (2000) annex I, 10.

22 See WIPO IGC Secretariat, *Operational Principles for Intellectual Property Clauses of Contractual Agreements Concerning Access to Genetic Resources and Benefit-Sharing*, WIPO Doc WIPO/GRTKF/IC/2/3 (2001), para 1.

continued for a number of years. In August 2004, the IGC began to consider the 'objectives' and 'principles' which should animate the protection of TK,[23] and this task has continued through all the subsequent sessions of the IGC.[24] A brief palpitation of enthusiasm on the international front was generated in October 2010, when the IGC identified its upcoming 17th session, to be held from 6 to10 December 2010, as the occasion for the first text-based discussion of the establishment of an international TK regime. The results of this session were not so exciting. An 'informal drafting group' was set up to provide a text on traditional cultural expressions (TCEs) for the next meeting of the IGC scheduled for 9 to13 May 2011.[25]

In relation to TK, matters were not as far advanced. An intersessional working group met from 21 to 25 February 2011 to discuss the latest draft of the Revised Objectives and Principles on TK. The report prepared by the working group for the May 2011 meeting of the IGC explained that 'the draft articles and comments, including specific texts suggested by experts, were noted ... and not adopted as such'.[26]

# 4. Pacific Regional TK Initiatives

Two early Pacific initiatives for the protection of TK were: the 2001 Model Law on Traditional Biological Resources, Innovations and Practices, developed by the Pacific Islands Forum;[27] and the Model Law on Traditional Knowledge and Expressions of Culture (TKEC), completed in 2002 and subsequently endorsed by the Pacific Community Ministers for Culture of the Secretariat of the Pacific Community (SPC) for adoption by member countries.[28] Despite their promulgation, neither of these instruments was implemented by national legislation. Apparently, the Pacific Island countries were urged by Australia and New Zealand to await international developments at WIPO.

The slow pace of these developments caused the Anglophone African countries at a diplomatic conference organised by the African Regional Intellectual

---

23   See WIPO IGC Secretariat, *Protection of Traditional Knowledge: Overview of Policy Objectives and Core Principles*, WIPO Doc WIPO/GRTKF/IC/7/5 (2004).

24   The most recent contribution in this regard is WIPO Doc, *Protection of Traditional Cultural Expressions/ Cultural Expressions of Folklore. Revised Objectives and Principles*, WIPO/GRTKF/IC/17/4Prov (2010).

25   See WIPO IGC Secretariat, *Decisions of the Seventeenth Session of the IGC* (2010) <http://www.wipo.int/ meetings/en/details.jsp?meeting_id=20207>

26   WIPO IGC Secretariat, *Draft Articles on the Protection of Traditional Knowledge prepared at IWG 2*, WIPO Doc WIPO/GRTKF/IC/18/7 (2011), para 2.

27   Founded in 1971 as the South Pacific Forum. In 2000, the name was changed to the Pacific Islands Forum 'to better reflect the geographic location of its members in the north and south Pacific'. Its members were: Australia, Cook Islands, Federated States of Micronesia, Fiji, Kiribati, Nauru, New Zealand, Niue, Palau, Papua New Guinea, Republic of Marshall Islands, Samoa, Solomon Islands, Tonga, Tuvalu and Vanuatu.

28   In addition to the Pacific Island states, SPC members included Australia, New Zealand and the USA.

Property Organization (ARIPO) on 9 and 10 August 2010 in Swakopmund, Namibia, to promulgate a Protocol on the Protection of Traditional Knowledge and Expressions of Folklore. The Protocol is meant to 'protect creations derived from the exploitation of traditional knowledge in ARIPO member states against misappropriation and illicit use through bio-piracy'.[29] The African group of countries at WIPO have been in the forefront of agitation there to accelerate international negotiations for a TK instrument. The Swakopmund Declaration can be regarded as either a reflection of their appreciation of the realistic likelihood of an international solution or a means of accelerating the pace of developments at WIPO.

In March 2007, at a high-level meeting of the executives of the Pacific Islands Forum Secretariat (PIFS) and the SPC, it was decided that lead agency responsibility relating to the Model Law would move from the SPC to the PIFS. As a first step, the PIFS convened a workshop in June 2007 to determine member countries' technical assistance needs with regard to progressing the Model Law's implementation at the national level. The conclusions and recommendations of that workshop were subsequently endorsed by Forum trade ministers in August 2007. A Traditional Knowledge Implementation Action Plan ('Action Plan') was, in part, a response to member countries' requests for technical assistance as conveyed to the PIFS at the workshop. Its overall objective was to assist the Forum Island countries in their efforts to establish a regional infrastructure for TK that would consist of a mutual recognition and enforcement regime founded on uniform national legal systems of protection. As a first step, the Action Plan would assist the Forum Island countries to develop policy and draft legislation based on the Model Law on TKEC and the Model Law on Traditional Biological Resources framework. Then, as a second step, a regional system of TK protection would be developed.

The Action Plan was developed with the technical assistance of the TradeCom Facility of the EU. Two EU projects were implemented as part of a broad programme of technical assistance. The first project provided technical assistance for the establishment of national systems of protection for TK in six of the member states of the Pacific Islands Forum, namely the Cook Islands, Fiji, Kiribati, Palau, Papua New Guinea and Vanuatu.[30] The terms of reference for the second project, concerning the formulation of a treaty for the reciprocal recognition of TK among the Melanesian Spearhead Group of countries (Fiji, Papua New Guinea, the Solomon Islands and Vanuatu), recognised that

---

29   See WIPO, *Swalopmund Protocol on the Protection of Traditional Knowledge and Expressions of Folklore within the Framework of the African Regional Intellectual Property Organization (ARIPO)* <http://www.wipo.int/wipolex/en/other_treaties/details.jsp?treaty_id=294>
30   Pacific Islands Forum Secretariat, *Traditional Knowledge Implementation Action Plan* (2009) <http://www.forumsec.org.fj/resources/uploads/attachments/documents/Traditional%20Knowledge%20Action%20Plan%202009.pdf>

... a global treaty for TK governance at international fora such as WIPO ...would present the best possible answer to the problem. However those processes are evolving slowly and are fraught with the political and diplomatic complexities of international negotiations. Running in parallel, a viable and faster alternative ... would be to consider reciprocal arrangements for recognition and enforcement between the MSG members ... While the focus for the MSG Secretariat at this time is clearly its own members, the MSG recognizes that ultimately the issue at hand is a global one and any future collective arrangement would not preclude other countries from the wider Pacific region to participate in the system. These developments would instruct and inform global treaty making processes currently taking place in institutions such as WIPO and possibly lead to engagement with other like-minded regions given the slow movements to conclude a global regime for TK at WIPO, WTO and CBD.[31]

# 5. Australian, New Zealand and EU Negotiating Positions on TK

The Pacific Island countries resort to EU assistance in relation to their TK protection agenda may derive from the respective negotiating positions of the EU, Australia and New Zealand in the various international fora considering this subject. Australia and New Zealand were two of only four countries (together with Canada and the United States) which originally voted against the United Nations Declaration on the Rights of Indigenous Peoples (UNDRIP) which was adopted by the General Assembly of the United Nations on 13 September 2007. Some 143 member states voted in favour of UNDRIP, a non-binding text which sets out the rights of indigenous peoples to 'maintain and strengthen their own institutions, cultures and traditions, and to pursue their development in keeping with their own needs and aspirations'. Article 31 of UNDRIP recognises the rights of indigenous peoples to maintain, control, protect and develop their intellectual property over their cultural heritage, traditional knowledge and traditional cultural expressions. The opposition of Australia and New Zealand, Canada and the United States attracted considerable opprobrium and could not have been very encouraging for the Pacific Island countries pursuing an international TK regime.

---

31 TradeCom Facility Program 'Technical Assistance to Study the Feasibility of a Reciprocal Recognition and Enforcement Mechanism for TK between Fiji, Papua New Guinea, Solomon Islands and Vanuatu', (AOR162-P177) [on file with author].

Senator Marise Payne explained in a speech in the Australian Senate on 10 September 2007 the various reasons for the Australian Government's opposition to UNDRIP. She explained that 'as our laws here currently stand, we protect our Indigenous cultural heritage, traditional knowledge and traditional cultural expression to an extent that is consistent with both Australian and international intellectual property law, and we are not prepared to go as far as the provisions in the text of the draft declaration currently do on that matter'.[32] In other words, Senator Payne seemed to indicate that the Australian Government was opposed to any *sui generis* protection of TK. She also indicated the Australian Government's opposition to 'the inclusion in the text of an unqualified right of free, prior and informed consent for indigenous peoples on matters affecting them' because the text did 'not acknowledge the rights of third parties — in particular, their rights to access indigenous land and heritage and cultural objects where appropriate under national law'.[33]

New Zealand's Māori Affairs minister, Parekura Horomia, was reported as criticising UNDRIP as little more than a wish list.[34] On the other hand, the country's Māori Party co-leader Tariana Turia was very critical of the New Zealand Government's position in opposing a Declaration which promotes 'merely a minimum standard of human rights for Māori'.[35]

With the change of government in Australia, Prime Minister Kevin Rudd announced on 3 April 2009 Australian support for the Declaration.[36] New Zealand followed suit on 19 April 2010, also after a change of government.[37]

Within WIPO, the 18th session of the IGC met from 9 to 13 May 2011 in Geneva to consider the latest draft of the Revised Objectives and Principles for the Protection of Traditional Knowledge.[38] Some perspective on the current negotiating positions of Australia and New Zealand can be gleaned from delegations' submissions on this document.

The Australian delegation considered that, without prejudice to any position on particular elements, the Objectives and Principles in Parts I and II should support and provide guidance to any suggested working text on the substantive

---

32  Commonwealth, *Parliamentary Debates*, Senate, 18 September 2007, 53-54 (Marise Payne).

33  Ibid.

34  New Zealand Government, 'Press Release: Māori Party's Head in the Clouds' (Press Release, 14 September 2007) <http://www.scoop.co.nz/stories/PA0709/S00272.htm>

35  'New Zealand Indigenous Rights Stance "Shameful" — Māori Party', *Stuff* (online), 14 September 2007 <http://www.stuff.co.nz/archived-stuff-sections/archived-national-sections/korero/45362>

36  United Nations News Centre, *Experts Hail Australia's Backing of UN Declaration of Indigenous People's Rights* (2009) <http://www.un.org/apps/news/story.asp?NewsID=30382>

37  T Watkins, 'New Zealand does U-turn on Rights Charter', *Stuff* (online), 20 April 2010 <http://www.stuff.co.nz/national/politics/3599153/NZ-does-U-turn-on-rights-charter>

38  WIPO IGC Secretariat, above n 26.

provisions contained in Part III.[39] It noted that 'the lack of agreement or consensus on elements of the Objectives and Principles made discussion of Part III very difficult'.[40] Specifically:

> With respect to part III, in general, it noted that references to 'Articles' resembled draft treaty text and pre-empt discussion about the form and status of any international legal instrument which would ensure the protection of TK. It noted the lack of consensus on the need for a legally binding instrument, and called for further general discussion at an appropriate time on the adoption of prescriptive principles that focused on conferring legally enforceable rights in light of the core General Guiding Principle (g) 'respect for and cooperation with other international and regional instruments and processes'.[41]

This negotiating position would seem to be out of sympathy with the aspirations of the Pacific Island countries for a legally enforceable international TK regime.

The New Zealand delegation, together with those of Japan and Switzerland, suggested that 'in-depth examination of policy objectives and principles was the prerequisite for the discussion on the substantive provisions'.[42]

The submission of the delegation of the EU and its member states indicates a more sympathetic position. It suggested that the Policy Objectives 'had become overly long, detailed and complicated', and expressed the view that 'the aim of the objectives should be to set out an overarching statement of what the Committee thought this instrument should do and not how it should be done'.[43] It agreed that there was a need to find a proper balance between the holders of TK and users in society at large, but that the proposed Objectives, Principles and substantive articles 'needed to respect the existing international regimes and in particular the IP regime'.[44] Finally, the delegation was of the opinion that the eventual protection of TK could not prevail in any way over the existing conventional IP regimes.[45] This final submission will raise problems for those who consider that TK has a human rights content.[46] Resolution 2000/7 of the United Nations Sub-Commission on Human Rights in Article 3 reminds all governments 'of the primacy of human rights obligations over economic policies and agreements'. Governments are requested in Article 6 to integrate into their

---

39  WIPO IGC Secretariat, *The Protection of Traditional Knowledge: Revised Objectives and Principles*, WIPO Doc WIPO/GRTKF/IC/18/5 (2011), annex at 15.
40  Ibid.
41  Ibid.
42  Ibid, 40.
43  Ibid, 9.
44  Ibid, 89.
45  Ibid.
46  For example see L Bernier, *Justice in Genetics: Intellectual Property and Human Rights from a Cosmopolitan Liberal Perspective* (Edward Elgar, 2010).

national and local legislations and policies 'provisions, in accordance with international human rights obligations and principles that protect the social function of intellectual property'.

Australia and New Zealand, together with Canada, Norway and the United States, have taken a lead at the IGC in proposing in May 2010 the objectives, principles and substantive provisions for international legislation which might be promulgated on the protection of genetic resources.[47] The IGC adopted this as a working draft and invited comments on it from other delegations. Chile's and Colombia's comments from the perspective of developing countries were that the proposals lacked both specificity and the crucial obligation of sharing benefits from the utilisation of others' genetic resources.[48]

In 2002, the EU had submitted to the TRIPS Council that the disclosure of origin of genetic resources involved in patent applications should be a mandatory obligation.[49] This was reiterated by the EU in May 2005 in its submission to the IGC on the 'Disclosure of Origin or Source of Genetic Resources and Associated Traditional Knowledge in Patent Applications'. It argued that 'there are good reasons for an obligation to disclose that an invention is directly based on traditional knowledge associated with the use of genetic resources'.[50] The African group of countries endorsed this EU proposal in its response to the Australia/New Zealand May 2010 submission to the IGC.[51] The African group also proposed the principle that IPRs and obligations be clarified 'with respect to the protection of traditional knowledge, genetic resources and traditional cultural expressions and certainty and clarity for prior informed consent and fair and equitable benefit sharing'.[52]

In general it would seem that the negotiating positions taken by the EU on TK and genetic resources are closer to the interests of the Pacific Island countries than those taken by Australia and New Zealand. The EU does not have the complication of significant indigenous populations, such as the Aboriginal and Torres Strait Islander peoples or Māori, who are calling for the protection of their TK.

---

47  WIPO IGC Secretariat, *Submission by Australia, Canada, New Zealand, Norway and the United States of America* , WIPO Doc WIPO/GRTKF/IC/16/7 (2010).

48  WIPO IGC Secretariat, *Compilation of Comments on WIPO/GRTKF/IC/16/7 'Submission by Australia, Canada, New Zealand, Norway and the United States of America'*, WIPO Doc WIPO/GRTKF/IC/17/INF/10 (2010), annexes 1 and 2.

49  *Communication by the EC and its Member States to the TRIPS Council on the review of Article 27.3 (b) of the TRIPS Agreement, and the relationship between the TRIPS Agreement and the Convention on Biological Diversity and the protection of traditional knowledge and folklore*, WTO Doc IP/C/W/383 (2002).

50  WIPO Doc, *Disclosure of Origin or Source of Genetic Resources and Associated Traditional Knowledge in Patent Applications*, WIPO Doc WIPO/GRTKF/IC/8/11 (2005).

51  WIPO IGC Secretariat, *Proposal of the African Group on Genetic Resources and Future Work*, WIPO Doc WIPO/GRTKF/IC/17/10 (2010).

52  Ibid, annex at 6.

# 6. EU Technical Assistance

The Pacific Island states are among the beneficiaries of the Partnership Agreement ('Cotonou Agreement') between the members of the African, Caribbean and Pacific (ACP) group of states and the EU, signed 23 June 2000 and concluded for a twenty-year period from March 2000 to February 2020. Article 46 of the Cotonou Agreement recognises the need for parties 'to ensure an adequate and effective level of protection of intellectual, industrial and commercial property rights, and other rights covered by TRIPS including protection of geographical indications'.

During 2010, the EU executed two IPR technical assistance projects in the Pacific. The first, entitled 'Technical Assistance to the Pacific Regional Action Plan for Traditional Knowledge Development', had as its specific objective the provision of technical assistance for the establishment of national systems of protection for TK and EC in six of the member states of the Pacific Islands Forum, namely the Cook Islands, Fiji, Kiribati, Palau, Papua New Guinea and Vanuatu.[53] A second project provided technical assistance to study the 'Feasibility of a Reciprocal Recognition and Enforcement Mechanism' for TK expressions of culture between Fiji, Papua New Guinea and the Solomon Islands: the so-called MSG countries.[54]

Under the first project, national mapping of TK and EC was conducted in the target states; draft IPR laws and policies have been formulated for Fiji, Papua New Guinea and the Solomon Islands; and a collaboration treaty was drafted for the MSG states.[55] The treaty was submitted to the 18th Melanesian Spearhead Group Leaders' Summit in Suva on 31 March 2011, which 'agreed in principle pending decisions by members on the signing of the Treaty'.[56] The treaty was signed by the Governments of Fiji and the Solomon Islands in September 2011.[57] The Governments of Papua New Guinea and Vanuatu are currently undertaking in-country consultations on the treaty before signing it.

The two EU projects concerned with TK were initiated as part of its assistance to be provided under the Cotonou Agreement, but interestingly TK is not a category of IPRs mentioned in the TRIPS Agreement. Another interesting feature of Article 46 of the Cotonou Agreement is that the only category of IPRs

---

53   *Action Plan*, above n 30.

54   TradeCom Facility Program, above n 31.

55   See M Blakeney, 'Protecting Traditional Knowledge and Expressions of Culture in the Pacific' (2011) 1(1) *Queen Mary Journal of Intellectual Property* 80.

56   18th Melanesian Spearhead Group Leaders' Summit, 'Communiqué' (2011) <http://www.msgsec.info/>

57   See Melanesian Spearhead Group, *MSG Framework Treaty on Traditional Knowledge and Expressions of Culture* (2012) <http://www.msgsec.info/index.php?option=com_content&view=article&id=103:msg-framework-treaty-on-traditional-knowledge-and-expressions-of-culture&catid=39:msg-culture&Itemid=162>

specifically mentioned is geographical indications (GIs). This is a category close to the heart of EU IPR interests, although it is something of a novelty for the Pacific Island countries. Given that the EU has not typically negotiated strongly for the protection of TK, its technical assistance to the Pacific Island countries in relation to TK might be regarded as the EU's price for garnering their support for its GIs agenda.

Resort to technical assistance from the EU in relation to TK is also explained in part by the slowness of developments in this area at WIPO, and by the perceived lack of enthusiasm for this subject on the part of Australia and New Zealand, countries which have traditionally provided technical legal assistance to Pacific Island countries.

# 7. International Negotiations on Geographical Indications and the EU's Agenda

Much closer to the interests of the EU are the WTO negotiations on GIs. Article 24.2 of the TRIPS Agreement requires the TRIPS Council to conduct a review of the operation of the GIs provisions within the first two years of entry into force of the WTO Agreement. The Council confined its initial review to the question of a multilateral register of geographical wine indications, as Article 23.4 provided that 'negotiations shall be undertaken in the Council for TRIPS concerning the establishment of a multilateral system of notification and registration of geographical indications for wines eligible for protection in those Members participating in the system'. Prior to the Ministerial Conference of the WTO held in Seattle in November 1999, a submission by Turkey proposed the extension of the multilateral register beyond wines and spirits.[58] This was endorsed by the African group of countries which requested that the protection of GIs be extended 'to other products recognizable by their geographical origins (handicrafts, agro-food products)'.[59] This proposal was also taken up by Cuba, the Czech Republic, the Dominican Republic, Honduras, India, Indonesia, Nicaragua, Pakistan, Sri Lanka, Uganda and Venezuela. A proposal from Bulgaria, the Czech Republic, Egypt, Iceland, India, Kenya, Liechtenstein, Pakistan, Slovenia, Sri Lanka, Switzerland and Turkey was that the special protection for GIs in Article 23 be extended to products other than wines and spirits.[60] Opposed to the proposals for an extension of the protection of GIs for wines

---

58   *Preparations for the 1999 Ministerial Conference Agreement on TRIPS Extension of the Additional Protection for Geographical Indications to Other Products*, WTO Doc WT/GC/W/249 (1999).

59   *Preparations for the 1999 Ministerial Conference the TRIPS Agreement Communication from Kenya on Behalf of the African Group* , WTO Doc WT/GC/W/302 (1999).

60   *Geographical Indications — Communication From Bulgaria, The Czech Republic, Egypt, Iceland, India, Kenya, Liechtenstein, Pakistan, Slovenia, Sri Lanka, Switzerland and Turkey*, WTO Doc IP/C/W/204/Rev.1 (2000).

and spirits under TRIPS to all products, Argentina, Australia, Canada, Chile, Guatemala, New Zealand, Paraguay and the United States sent a communication to the TRIPS Council on 29 June 2001.[61] It pointed out that proposals had insufficiently addressed the costs and administrative burdens of this extension. However, Clause 18 of the Doha Ministerial Declaration 2001 included within the negotiating subjects of the Round the establishment of a multilateral register for wines and spirits, as well as the extension of GI protection beyond wines and spirits as part of the Doha Development Agenda.[62] As will be seen below, both sets of negotiations have proceeded without any perceivable progress. It is in this context that the EU has looked to enlist the support of the Pacific Island states for its negotiating positions.

In June 2005, the EC submitted a proposal to amend the TRIPS Agreement to provide global protection for GIs in a multilateral system of registration.[63] This proposal sought to bring international protection for GIs into conformity with the EU, where a Community-wide system for their registration is considered an indispensable part of agricultural policy, serving both to preserve the incomes of small to medium-size producers and to guarantee the sustainability of the rural economy. Given that it possesses over 700 registered GIs,[64] a sophisticated institutional infrastructure and technical prowess, the EU is exceptionally well placed to leverage the benefits of an expanded international system of GI protection. On the other hand, the United States and its supporters largely endorse the status quo, favouring voluntary multilateral registration and the choice of the means of protection — whether by special system or the established trade mark system — left to national discretion.

---

61   *Geographical Indications — Communications from Argentina, Australia, Guatemala, Chile, Canada, New Zealand Paraguay and the United States,* WTO Doc IP/C/W/289 (2001).

62   WTO Ministerial, *Doha Declaration,* WTO Doc, WT/MIN(01)/DEC/1 (2001), para 18 provides: 'With a view to completing the work started in the Council for Trade-Related Aspects of Intellectual Property Rights (Council for TRIPS) on the implementation of Article 23.4, we agree to negotiate the establishment of a multilateral system of notification and registration of geographical indications for wines and spirits by the Fifth Session of the Ministerial Conference. We note that issues related to the extension of the protection of geographical indications provided for in Article 23 to products other than wines and spirits will be addressed in the Council for TRIPS pursuant to paragraph 12 of this Declaration.'

63   The EC proposed amending Section 3 of the TRIPS Agreement with a view to extending the regime of protection today available for GIs on wines and spirits to GIs on all products ('extension') and, in addition, a proposal for the inclusion of an annex to the TRIPS Agreement establishing a multilateral system of notification and registration of GIs. TRIPS Council, *Special Session on Geographical Indications— Communication from the European Communities* WTO Docs,WT/GC/W/547, TN/C/W/26, TN/IP/W/11 (2005). See earlier submissions of the EC, WTO Doc IP/C/W/107/Rev.1 (2000) with respect to the register, and submission in respect of the extension, *Communication from Bulgaria, Cuba, Cyprus, The Czech Republic, The European Communities and their Member States, Georgia, Hungary, Iceland, India, Kenya, Liechtenstein, Malta, Mauritius, Pakistan, Romania, The Slovak Republic, Slovenia, Sri Lanka, Switzerland, Thailand and Turkey,* WTO Doc IP/C/W/353 (2002).

64   'Since 1993, more than 700 names, designating *inter alia* over 150 cheeses, 160 meat and meat-based products, 150 fresh or processed fruits or vegetables and 80 types of olive oil, have been registered in this context. The Commission has also received over 300 further applications for the registration of names and/or amendments to specifications from Member States and third countries', see European Commission, *Proposal for a Council Regulation on the Protection of Geographical Indications and Designations of Origin for Agricultural Products and Foodstuffs* (Brussels, 2006), para.3.

The EC submission set out provisions for a centralised register that would be compulsory and have legal effect.[65] The EC proposal was aimed at preserving each WTO member's prerogative to determine whether a certain sign, indication or geographical name does indeed meet the TRIPS definition of a GI.[66]

Opponents of the EC proposal — Australia, Argentina, Australia, Canada, Chile, Ecuador, El Salvador, New Zealand and the US — took the position that the international protection of GIs is adequate as it stands, and that such a drastic development would serve only to undermine future gains in market access for non-European food and agricultural products.[67] Concern was also expressed about the additional costs and administrative burdens of implementing a distinct system of GI protection in addition to the TRIPS obligations. These countries advocated a system of voluntary notification and registration, with no obligation to protect registered GIs. A revised communication from Argentina, Australia, Canada, Chile, Costa Rica, the Dominican Republic, Ecuador, El Salvador, Guatemala, Honduras, Japan, Korea, Mexico, New Zealand, Nicaragua, Paraguay, Chinese Taipei, South Africa and the US proposed that the TRIPS Council should set up a voluntary system whereby notified GIs would be registered in a database. Those governments choosing to participate in the system would have to consult the database when taking decisions on protection in their own countries. Non-participating members would be 'encouraged' but 'not obliged' to consult the database.[68]

Hong Kong, China proposed a compromise under which a registered term would enjoy a more limited 'presumption' than under the EU proposal, and only in those countries choosing to participate in the system.[69]

In July 2008, a group of WTO members called for a 'procedural decision' to negotiate three intellectual property issues in parallel: these two GI issues and a proposal to require patent applicants to disclose the origin of genetic resources or TK used in their inventions.[70] WTO members remain divided over

---

65    Communication from the European Communities. The communication, dated, was circulated to the General Council, to the TNC and to the Special Session of the TRIPS Council at the request of the Delegation of the European Commission, *Geographical Indications*, above n 7. This proposal maintains the level of ambition of the EC as regards both 'extension' and the multilateral register of GIs, as contained in its earlier proposals in documents, above n 63.

66    European Commission, above n 64, para 3.2(a).

67    See *Communication from Argentina, Australia, Canada, Chile, Ecuador, El Salvador, New Zealand and the United States*, WTO Doc TN/IP/W/9 (2004).

68    Submission by *Argentina, Australia, Canada, Chile, Costa Rica, Dominican Republic, Ecuador, El Salvador, Guatemala, Honduras, Japan, Korea, Mexico, New Zealand, Nicaragua, Paraguay, the Separate Customs Territory of Taiwan, Penghu, Kinmen and Matsu, South Africa and the United States*, WTO Doc TN/IP/W/10/Rev.2 (2008).

69    *Multilateral System of Notification and Registration of Geographical Indications under article 23.4 of the TRIPS Agreement*, WTO Doc TN/IP/W/8 (2003).

70    *Communication from Albania, Brazil, China, Colombia, Ecuador, the European Communities, Iceland, India, Indonesia, the Kyrgyz Republic, Liechtenstein, the Former Yugoslav Republic of Macedonia, Pakistan, Peru, Sri Lanka, Switzerland, Thailand, Turkey, the ACP Group and the African Group*, WTO Doc TN/C/W/52 (2008).

the proposal to negotiate the three subjects in parallel, with opponents arguing that the only mandate for the TRIPS Council is to negotiate the multilateral register. Under the chairmanship of Ambassador Trevor C. Clarke (Barbados) during 2008 and 2009, the Special Session of the TRIPS Council considered the various proposals, and the chairman identified as 'crucial' the two issues of participation and consequences or legal effects of registration.[71]

With respect to the issue of whether participation in the system should be voluntary or mandatory, some WTO members interpreted the mandate's reference to 'a multilateral system' to mean that the system should apply to all members. Other members argued that the words 'those Members participating in the system' mean that not all members are expected to participate. Ambassador Clarke encouraged members 'to continue searching for an acceptable solution that would determine a participation of Members in the Register that renders it a useful and meaningful tool in line with its purpose to facilitate protection'.[72] With respect to the consequences or legal effects of registration, all members seem to accept an obligation to consult the information on the register and to take that information into account when making decisions regarding registration and protection of trade marks and GIs under their national procedures. However, views differ significantly as to how such information should be taken into account, what weight and significance should be given to it, and whether there should be a specific legal obligation to take the information into account.

Ambassador Clarke's successor as chairman of the Special Session of the Council for TRIPS, Ambassador Darlington Mwape (Zambia), announced upon assuming office that the specific negotiating mandate of the Special Session was limited to the negotiation of a register of GIs for wines and spirits.[73] Ambassador Mwape circulated a work programme suggesting a list of 'Possible Elements for Developing Texts' for the future register.[74] Applying this structure, a drafting group developed a single draft composite text on the register.[75] Ambassador Mwape reported that despite the fact that this text reflects both the current state of negotiations in the group and significant progress, views differed on whether it could be forwarded to the Trade Negotiations Committee by Easter 2011, the deadline set by the Director-General of the WTO for the conclusion of the Doha Round of negotiations.[76]

---

71  WTO Report of Chairman, *Multilateral System of Notification and Registration of Geographical Indications for Wines and Spirits*, TN/IP/19 (2009), para 10.
72  Ibid, para 11.
73  WTO Report of Chairman, *Multilateral System of Notification and Registration of Geographical Indications for Wines and Spirits*, WTO Doc TN/IP/20 (2010), para 4.
74  See *Multilateral System of Notification and Registration of Geographical Indications for Wines and Spirits*, WTO Doc TN/IP/21 (2011).
75  That was circulated as WTO Doc JOB/IP/3 on 11 April 2011.
76  Ibid, para 16.

Ambassador Mwape explained:

> I have made strenuous attempts to resolve this and have offered to use my prerogative as Chair to improve textual compliance with the Special Session of the Council for TRIPS mandate. However, Members have been unable to engage constructively on this question and have instead insisted that the purely bottom-up and Member-driven nature of the text be scrupulously respected at this time.[77]

His frustration would have been shared by the EU, given its desire to settle the issue of the multilateral register for its wines.

In view of the global markets at stake in the agricultural and food-processing sectors, the United States and Australia became so concerned at the systematic discrimination its trade mark owners faced in enforcing their rights against European-registered GIs that it invoked the WTO dispute settlement procedure. On 18 August 2003, the United States and Australia had requested the establishment of a WTO dispute settlement panel to review the consistency of the EU Regulation 2081/92 with the rules of the TRIPS and GATT Agreements.[78] The US and Australia argued that the EU scheme for the protection of GIs failed to comply with TRIPS, principally because it was discriminatory in imposing additional registration obligations on non-EU nationals, and thus was in violation of the national treatment obligation which requires countries to treat foreigners in the same way as locals are treated.

The Panel Report in the dispute decided in favour of the US and Australia in relation to the national treatment argument.[79] It recommended that the EU bring its regulation into conformity with the TRIPS Agreement by eliminating the additional registration requirements for foreigners. The EU Regulation was repealed and replaced by Council Regulation (CE) 510/2006 on the protection of GIs and designations of origin for agricultural products and foodstuffs.

The current position of New Zealand on GIs protection can be gleaned from the text of the Trans-Pacific Strategic Economic Partnership Partnership Agreement.[80] It provides in Article 10.5 for the recognition of GIs for wines and spirits, those terms listed in Annex 10.A 'within the meaning of paragraph 1 of Article 22 of the TRIPS Agreement'. The Agreement makes no reference to the

---

77   Ibid, para 16.

78   See WTO Panel Report, *European Communities – Protection of Trademarks and Geographical Indications for Agricultural Products and Foodstuffs*, WTO Doc WT/DS174/20 (2005).

79   WTO Panel Report, *European Communities – Protection of Trademarks and Geographical Indications for Agricultural Products and Foodstuffs*, WTO Doc WT/DS290/R (2005).

80   This agreement between New Zealand, Chile, Singapore and Brunei is in force and has open accesion. It is the predecessor to the now wider Trans Pacific Partnership negotiaitons. *Trans-Pacific Strategic Economic Partnership Agreement* <http://www.mfat.govt.nz/downloads/trade-agreement/transpacific/main-agreement.pdf>

extended protection for wines and spirits envisaged in Article 23 of TRIPS, and the terms contained in Annex 10A comprise only Chilean GIs, suggesting the reluctance of the other negotiating parties to embrace this form of protection.

The current position of the United States (and probably of Australia) on GIs protection can be gleaned from the leaked draft negotiating text of the Trans Pacific Partnership negotiations.[81]

Finally, it should be noted that despite the commitment of the EU to GIs, their utilisation seems to be limited to agricultural enterprises in France, Italy, Spain and Portugal. In 2006 the EC announced a review of its system for the protection of GIs, including an evaluation of trade marks as an alternative instrument for the protection of GIs.[82] The subsequent 'Green Paper on Agricultural Product Quality' of 2008 and 'Impact Assessment Report on Agricultural Product Quality Policy' of 2009 endorsed the complementary roles of trade marks and GIs in protecting agricultural products.[83]

# 8. The EU, GIs and the ACP Countries

As mentioned above, Article 46 of the Cotonou Agreement between the members of the African, Caribbean and Pacific (ACP) group of states recognises the need for parties to ensure an adequate and effective level of protection for IPRs 'including protection of geographical indications'. This obviously supports the EU's own negotiating priorities. In an endeavour to generate empirical evidence about the value of GIs for ACP countries, the EU has commissioned a project

> to generate empirical evidence, based on country/sub-regional and product case studies, regarding the benefits that African members of the ACP Group can obtain from enhanced multilateral Geographical Indication (GI) protection as a basis for the African Group to engage in the Doha negotiations on the establishment of the multilateral register for wines and spirits and the proposed extension of protection to products other than wines and spirits under Article 23 of TRIPS.[84]

---

81  See *The complete Feb 10, 2011 text of the US proposal for the TPP IPR chapter* <http://keionline.org/node/1091>

82  See G Evans, 'The Comparative Advantages of Geographical Indications and Community Trademarks for the Marketing of Agricultural Products in the European Union' (2010) 41 *IIC-International Review of Intellectual Property* 645.

83  European Commission, *Green Paper on Agricultural Product Quality: Product Standards, Farming Requirements and Quality Schemes* (Brussels, 2008) 13; European Commission, *Agricultural Product Quality Policy: Impact Assessment, Part B, Geographical Indications* (2009) 4-5.

84  *Action Plan*, above n 30.

The countries studied in January to March 2011 were: Cameroon, Gabon, Ghana, Nigeria and Senegal in West and Central Africa; and: Kenya, Mauritius, Rwanda and Tanzania in East and Southern Africa.[85]

The project was designed to produce 'a replicable methodology for analysing the dynamics of capturing economic value out of GIs; access to GI-protected products by local populations; the role of government in the GI framework; the costs of establishing and administering a GI regime in a country; and the costs of developing, registering and enforcing individual GIs'.[86] What the project established was that most of the countries surveyed had enacted GIs legislation but that it had not yet come into effect, with the result that industries were relying primarily on certification or collective trade marks to protect their geographical brands. However, a number of EU-funded projects are under way in Africa to build institutional competence to underpin GIs protection for Oku white honey and Penja white pepper from Cameroon; Dogon onions from Mali; and attiéké and Korhogo cloth from Côte d'Ivoire. The first country to protect GIs in Africa is Morocco, where argan oil and products of argan trees have been registered.

In February 2010, WTO Director-General Pascal Lamy, who was formerly head of the EC's Directorate General of Trade, explained that 'the Doha Round will help level the playing field for Africa, correcting historical injustices in the world trade rule-book'.[87] He also said that 'African agriculture needs to become more efficient, and in that efficiency it needs to discover "specialization"'. In other words, the WTO, in the same way as the EU, perceives that GIs are a useful adjunct to the promotion of agricultural trade.

# 9. Protecting TK through GIs

In the absence of an international regime to protect TK, existing categories of intellectual property have sought to be applied to its protection. As Panizzon and Cottier observed:

> Traditional Knowledge (TK) and Geographical Indications (GIs) share a common element insofar as they both protect accumulated knowledge typical to a specific locality. While TK expresses the local traditions of knowledge, GIs stand for specific geographical origin of a typical product

---

85  Industries studied were: Cameroon — Oku white honey; Gabon —Okoumé timber; Ghana — cocoa; Kenya — black tea; Mauritius — Demerara sugar; Nigeria — yams; Rwanda — coffee; Senegal — yêtt de Joal; Tanzania — cloves.

86  *Action Plan*, above n 30.

87  Opening the conference on *Harnessing Agriculture for Development through Trade in Geneva* (2011) <http://www.wto.org/english/news_e/sppl_e/sppl188_e.htm>

or production method. GIs and TK relate a product (GIs), respectively a piece of information (TK), to a geographically confined people or a particular region or locality.[88]

Similarly, in its *Review of Existing Intellectual Property Protection of Traditional Knowledge*,[89] the IGC Secretariat observed that:

> Geographical Indications as defined by Article 22.1 of the TRIPS Agreement and appellations of origin, as defined by Article 2 of the Lisbon Agreement … rely not only on their geographical connotation but also, essentially, on human and/or natural factors (which may have generated a given quality, reputation or other characteristic of the good). In practice, human and/ or natural factors are the result of traditional, standard techniques which local communities have developed and incorporated into production. Goods designated and differentiated by geographical indications, be they wines, spirits, cheese, handicrafts, watches, silverware and others, are as much expressions of local cultural and community identification as other elements of traditional knowledge can be.[90]

Three examples provided by the IGC Secretariat of traditional knowledge protected by geographical indications are: 'Cocuy the Pecaya' liquor from Venezuela, and 'Phu Quoc' fish sauce and 'Shan Tuyet Moc Chau' tea, both from Vietnam.

On the other hand, Kur and Knaak observe that:

> The indication for a product is the subject matter of this protection, not the product itself. For this reason tradition-based innovations and creations, as indicated in the WIPO Report on Fact-finding Missions on Intellectual Property and TK, cannot enjoy protection per se by means of geographical indications. The protection of GIs may apply only to signs indicating these innovations and creations.[91]

This is unquestionably the case, but it has been pointed out that all GIs whether 'Champagne' wine, 'Parma' ham or 'Roquefort' cheese, protect not only the use of the indication but also the innovations which stand behind the indication.[92] Indeed, one of the functions of trade marks is that they act as a warranty of quality as well as an indication of the source of a product.

---

88 S Biber-Klemm and T Cottier, Rights to Plant Genetic Resources and Traditional Knowledge: Basic Issues and Perspectives (CAB International Publishing, 2006) 82.

89 WIPO IGC Secretariat, *Review of Existing Intellectual Property Protection of Traditional Knowledge*, WIPO Doc WIPO/GRTKF/IC/3/7 (2002).

90 Ibid, para 40.

91 A Kur and P Knaak, 'Protection of Traditional Names and Designations' in SV Lewinski (ed) *Indigenous Heritage and Intellectual Property: Genetic Resources, Traditional Knowledge, and Folklore* (Kluwer Law International, 2004) 221, 227.

92 M Blakeney, 'Protection of Traditional Knowledge by Geographical Indications' (2009) 3(4) *International Journal of Intellectual Property Management* 357, 361.

Kur and Knaak also reject the possibility that 'kava' from the Pacific region and 'rooibos' from South Africa could be protected as 'they are not GIs per se as they have no direct geographical meaning'.[93] This interpretation appears to overlook the jurisprudence on indirect GIs. For example, the European Court of Justice held 'feta' to be a GI for cheese coming from Greece, even though there is no geographical place of that name,[94] and the UK Intellectual Property Rights Commission suggested that 'Basmati' might be registered as a GI to protect rice from India andPakistan.[95] Thus, on the same basis, 'kava' and 'rooibos' might be taken as indirect indications of the places from which they come.

Among the strengths of GI protection is that it might provide for protection of TK which is already in the public domain. For example, in relation to kava, the United States Patents and Trade Marks Office granted Natrol, Inc., a US-based company, a US patent for 'kavatrol', a dietary supplement composed of kava that serves as a general relaxant.[96] Two German companies, William Schwabe and Krewel-Werke, obtained a patent for kava as a prescription drug for treating strokes, insomnia and Alzheimer's disease.[97] In France, L'Oréal has patented the use of kava against hair loss.[98] As these products are promoted on the basis of their derivation from kava, GIs may prove to be the second best option for protecting kava by acting as a substitute for patent protection of the TK related to the plant itself.[99]

From 26 to 28 August 2010, the EU-ACP organised a regional workshops on the protection of GIs and TK in the Pacific. This meeting, held in Nadi, Fiji, replicated similar events organised by the ACP-EU in Douala, Cameroon; Cape Town, South Africa; and Port of Spain, Trinidad. A particular feature of the Nadi meeting was establishing the linkage between GIs and TK protection, including cultural products. Potential GI products in the Pacific region which were identified at the workshop included: fine mat weaving from Tonga, the Cook Islands and Tokelau; decorative weaving from Fiji; floor mats from Papua

---

93   Kur and Knaak, above n 91, 228.

94   *Federal Republic of Germany and Kingdom of Denmark v Commission of the European Communities* (2005) European Court of Justice, Joined Cases C-465/02 and C-466/02.

95   UKIPR Commission, *Integrating Intellectual Property Rights and Development Policy* (UKIPR, 2002) 89; see also G Giraud, 'Range and Limit of Geographical Indication Scheme: The Case of Basmati Rice from Punjab, Pakistan' (2008) 11 *International Food and Agribusiness Management Review* 1.

96   D R Downes and S A Laird, *Innovative Mechanisms for Sharing Benefits of Biodiversity and Related Knowledge Case Studies on Geographical Indications and Trademarks* (1999) <http://www.ciel.org/Publications/ InnovativeMechanisms.pdf>

97   M Panizzon, 'Traditional Knowledge and Geographical Indications: Foundations, Interests and Negotiating Positions' (Working Paper No. 2005/01 2006) <http://phase1.nccr-trade.org/images/stories/publications/IP8/ Traditional%20Knowledge.pdf 151>

98   Ibid.

99   It should be noted that the importation of kava to the EU had been prohibited on health grounds until 2009. See K Hoyumpa and L Schmiere, *Europe lifts kava ban and south Pacific hopeful for resumed kava trade* (2009) <http://www.nakamalathome.com/blog/europe-lifts-kava-ban-and-south-pacific-hopeful-for-resumed-kava-trade.html>

New Guinea; Solomon Islands baskets; carving from Papua New Guinea and the Cook Islands; bilum (string bag) products from Papua New Guinea; and kava from Fiji.

On the other hand, it has been forcibly pointed out by Susy Frankel that GIs are not co-terminous with TK, and it would be a mistake to assume that GIs protection could perform the same function as *sui generis* TK protection.[100] She observes that the French *appellations des origins controlées* system does not protect the TK of the producers of traditional products but protects only 'the name for use by those whom the associated bureaucracy deems merit worthy of its use'.[101] Also, it has been acknowledged that TK admits of dynamic development, whereas GIs are a static form of intellectual property fixed at the time of registration. Frankel asserts that GIs have been 'oversold as tools of development', since they are 'not in fact developmental in any innovative way, but are rather tools of maintaining the status quo' and 'the creation of a GI is not going to suddenly open greater markets for the knowledge held and products produced by indigenous peoples'.[102] However, as has been pointed out above, in the absence of TK protection — an absence which may persist for many years, given the glacial pace of progress at WIPO — GIs are only to be regarded very much as a second best solution. Frankel's strictures are a useful warning against acceptance of the current unsatisfactory state of affairs.

# 10. Conclusion

Although this chapter seeks to argue that the EU's Pacific agenda in relation to technical assistance concerning TK should be observed through the EU's GIs spectacles, there is, of course, a much broader economic perspective which has to be taken into account. EU development cooperation is provided to the Pacific Island countries in the context of the Cotonou Partnership Agreement between the EU and the African, Caribbean and Pacific states (ACP). The EU as an integrated regional entity prefers to deal with other regions wherever possible.[103] This is probably because of its comparative advantage in regionalism and the greater efficiency of dealing with, for example, six sub-groups within the ACP rather than negotiating seventy-eight bilateral partnership agreements.[104]

---

100  S Frankel, 'The Mismatch of Geographical Indications and Innovative Traditional Knowledge' (2011) 29(3) *Prometheus* 253.

101  Ibid, 262.

102  Ibid, 267.

103  See P Lamy, 'Stepping Stones or Stumbling Blocks? The EU's Approach Towards the Problem of Multilateralism vs Regionalism in Trade Policy' (2002) 25(10) *The World Economy* 1399.

104  See S Thomas, *EUphoria in the Pacific? Regional Economic Partnership Agreements — Implications for the Pacific* (Paper presented at the New Zealand Asia Pacific European Studies Association Conference 'Outside Looking In', Christchurch, 2004) <http://www.europe.canterbury.ac.nz/conferences/apeu2004/papers/thomas.pdf >

Any EU technical assistance must be viewed in the context of its regionalisation agenda. From 2008, a number of EPAs have been entered into between the EU and a number of groups of ACP countries. The EPAs will succeed the trade provisions of the Cotonou Agreement. By way of example, in the draft proposals with the Economic Community of West African States and Southern African Development Community, substantive obligations are proposed in the areas of copyright and related rights, trade marks, GIs, industrial designs, patents, plant varieties and IPR enforcement, in exchange for trade liberalisation and development assistance.

Matters are not as far advanced in the Pacific. In July 2009, Papua New Guinea signed an interim EPA with the EU, and Fiji signed an interim EPA with the EU in December 2009. The details of these EPAs are yet to be worked out, but following the African precedents, they will probably include provisions dealing with IPRs, including GIs.

Paralleling the EU's EPAs, Trans-Pacific Partnership Agreement (TPP) negotiations commenced in March 2010 in Melbourne, with the participation of Australia, Brunei, Chile, New Zealand, Singapore, Peru, the United States and Vietnam. Malaysia joined at the third round of negotiations in October 2010. The second sentence of Article 10.5.1, which deals with GIs, provides that '[s]ubject to domestic laws, in a manner that is consistent with the TRIPS Agreement, such terms will be protected as geographical indications in the territories of the other Parties.' The footnote to this provision states, for greater certainty, 'the Parties acknowledge that geographical indications will be recognised and protected in Brunei Darussalam, Chile, New Zealand and Singapore only to the extent permitted by and according to the terms and conditions set out in their respective domestic laws'. Presumably, Australia and the United States are not yet willing to acknowledge the existence of GIs, or they take comfort from the fact that their GIs are already protected by certification and collective marks.

Article 10.3.3 of the TPP provides that subject to each party's international obligations, the parties affirm that they may '(d) establish appropriate measures to protect traditional knowledge'.

# 9. Do You Want it Gift Wrapped?: Protecting Traditional Knowledge in the Pacific Island Countries

## Miranda Forsyth

The importance of customary law and customary institutions in the context of protecting the traditional knowledge (TK)[1] of indigenous people is gradually being more widely recognised.[2] However, translating this recognition into practice still seems a long way off, as very few countries have developed a protection framework that provides a role for customary institutions.[3] The Pacific Island countries are currently in the process of moving forward with such an initiative, and their experiences offer important insights into the challenges associated with it. This chapter begins by discussing the TK agenda as it has been pursued in the region for the past decade, and in particular the development of the Regional Framework for the Protection of Traditional Knowledge and Expressions of Culture (2002), which has been cited as a best practice approach.[4]

The Pacific Island countries have approached the protection of what may be called 'traditional cultural expressions' separately from the protection of biological knowledge, innovations and practices,[5] and as a result the scope of this

---

1   There are many definitions of TK in the academic and grey literature and draft legislation: see, for example, Antons' summary in C Antons (ed), *Traditional Knowledge, Traditional Cultural Expressions and Intellectual Property Law in the Asia-Pacific Region* (Kluwer Law International, 2009) 1-4. For the purposes of this chapter the definition provided in the Model Law is adopted, namely: 'traditional knowledge includes any knowledge that generally (a) is or has been created, acquired or inspired for traditional economic, spiritual, ritual, narrative, decorative or recreational purposes; and (b) is or has been transmitted from generation to generation; and (c) is regarded as pertaining to a particular traditional group, clan or community of people; and (d) is collectively originated and held'.

2   See Articles 18 and 31 of UNDRIP; Articles 8(j) and 10(c) of CBD; and the many references to customary law in the World Intellectual Property Organization's Intergovernmental Committee on Intellectual Property and Genetic Resources, Traditional Knowledge and Folklore, *The Protection of Traditional Cultural Expressions/ Expressions of Folklore: Revised Objectives and Principles* (2010) <http://www.wipo.int/edocs/mdocs/tk/en/ wipo_grtkf_ic_17/wipo_grtkf_ic_17_4.pdf>

3   Case studies of some countries that are attempting this are presented in International Institute for the Environment and Development, *Protecting Community Rights over Traditional Knowledge Project* (2005-2009) <http://www.iied.org/natural-resources/key-issues/biodiversity-and-conservation/protecting-community-rights-over-tradition>

4   See, for example, I Abeyesekere, 'The Protection of Expressions of Folklore in Sri Lanka' in Antons, above n 1, 341, 347; S von Lewinski, 'An Analysis of WIPO's Latest Proposal and the Model Law 2002 of the Pacific Community for the Protection of Traditional Cultural Expressions' in Antons, above n 1, 109, 119.

5   These are dealt with in the recent *Model Law on Traditional Biological Knowledge, Innovations and Practices* <http://www.sprep.org/legal/documents/MLv11.doc4Apr_000.pdf> The separation between these two types of TK could be argued to be unhelpful and as undermining an attempt to view TK as holistically as possible.

chapter is limited to the TK that is found in songs, stories, oral traditions, visual and performing arts, ritual and cultural practices, and architectural forms.[6] The chapter then builds the case that existing customary law and institutions are central to TK, and that this mandates the adoption of a pluralistic approach to the protection of TK. It then demonstrates that the current approach towards TK in the Pacific Island countries is not a truly (or deeply) pluralistic one, despite the many references to customary law and institutions in the legislation and policy documents. Moreover, it is based on a number of assumptions about the nature of customary law and the reach of state law and state institutions in the region that may not be valid. Following suggestions from academics such as Boyle[7] and Drahos[8] to look at the disadvantages as well as the advantages of extending the reach of any type of intellectual property protection, I then identify a number of problems that are likely to flow from an implementation of the current state-centric approach. In conclusion, the chapter outlines what a more pluralistic approach to the protection of TK in any jurisdiction would involve.

The main aim of the chapter is to urge caution with moves towards the protection of TK and to stress the necessity of properly respecting the existing customary regulatory structure that almost certainly exists in every country in which TK is present. The protection of TK by the state, which inevitably involves the creation of new rights and owners of those rights, is not self-evidently a step forward for indigenous people, and even risks endangering the TK it sets out to protect. Boyle's caution that 'when you set up property rule in some new space, you determine much about the history that follows'[9] is thus equally as apposite in the TK context as in that of genes and databases.

I acknowledge that I have already commented on the Model Law when it was first enacted in 2002.[10] Although the law itself has not changed since, my views of it have altered radically in the intervening period. This is largely a result of the intensive study of customary law in Vanuatu undertaken in 2002 to 2008, a field with which I was unfamiliar when I first encountered the Model Law. This study[11] and my understanding of the theory of legal pluralism inform the observations I make concerning customary law in this chapter.

---

6   For a complete description see section 4 of the Model Law.

7   J Boyle, *The Public Domain* (Yale University Press, 2008) 56.

8   P Drahos with J Braithwaite, *Information Feudalism* (The New Press, 2002) ix.

9   J Boyle, above n 7, 56.

10   M Forsyth, 'Cargo Cults and Intellectual Property in the South Pacific' (2003) 14 *Australian Intellectual Property Journal* 193.

11   M Forsyth, *A Bird that Flies with Two Wings: Kastom and State Justice Systems in Vanuatu* (2009) <http://epress.anu.edu.au/kastom_citation.html>

# 1. The Traditional Knowledge Agenda in the Pacific Island Countries

The move to protect TK in the region has been proceeding in fits and starts for over a decade. A Symposium on the Protection of Traditional Knowledge and Expressions of Indigenous Cultures in the Pacific Islands held by the United Nations Educational, Scientific and Cultural Organization (UNESCO) in 1999 concluded with a Declaration that recommended technical assistance and support for 'a homogeneous system of legal protection, identification, conservation and control of exploitation, of indigenous culture'.[12] This led to the production of the Model Law by the Secretariat of the Pacific Community in 2002.[13]

The movement for protection of TK thus began at a very high policy level, and at the initiative of international and regional, rather than local, institutions and actors. Right from the start it is possible to identify a number of different, and arguably competing, aims for TK legislation, all covered by the amorphous term 'protection'. Three main concepts associated with the term can be distilled: the conservation of TK in the face of pressures resulting from rapid social change; the misappropriation of TK; and the facilitation of commercialisation of TK by the TK holders themselves. All these different aims are present in the regional documents concerning TK, although to date there has been little acknowledgment of the fact that conservation of cultural heritage and traditions may well be incompatible with the establishment of a structure that facilitates their commercialisation.[14] A similar conflation of aims was identified in Papua New Guinea by Kalinoe, who argues that the difficulty in finding a suitable model for protection may in part be because people have been misled 'into thinking that these matters can be comfortably housed together'.[15]

The Model Law was adopted by the Forum Trade Ministers in 2003. In many ways it follows the general contours established by the UNESCO-World Intellectual Property Organization (WIPO) Model Provisions for National Laws on the Protection of Expressions of Folklore Against Illicit Exploitation and Other Prejudicial Actions (1985). It confers upon owners of TK the right to authorise others to exploit their TK, and to prevent others from exploiting it

---

12    UNESCO, *Symposium on the Protection of Traditional Knowledge and Expressions of Indigenous Cultures in the Pacific Islands* (1999) <http://portal.unesco.org/culture/en/files/14264/10645002355Noumea1999.pdf/Noumea1999.pdf>

13    Above n 5.

14    For an exception to this see K Serrano and M Stefanova, 'Between International Law, Kastom and Sustainable Development: Cultural Heritage in Vanuatu' in G Baldaccino and D Niles (eds), *Island Futures: Conservation and Development Across the Asia-Pacific Region* (Springer, 2011) 19.

15    L Kalinoe, 'Ascertaining the Nature of Indigenous Intellectual and Cultural Property and Traditional Knowledge & the Search for Legal Options in Regulating Access in Papua New Guinea' (2007) 27 *Melanesian Law Journal* 1, 8.

without their free, prior informed and full consent. It requires the authorisation to be in writing and to be approved by an expressly created national authority. Until 2009 there was little movement by individual countries in respect of implementing the law, but in that year the issue gained momentum with the creation of the Traditional Knowledge Implementation Action Plan (2009) (Action Plan).[16] The Action Plan is being implemented by the Forum Secretariat working with the Trade Commission, WIPO, the Secretariat of the Pacific Community (SPC) and Secretariat of the Pacific Regional Environmental Program, and is said to be based on a mandate of Forum Trade Ministers and the Forum Leaders' directives in the Pacific Plan (2005).[17] Perhaps not surprisingly, given the partners involved and the trade context in which it has developed, the Action Plan prioritises the commercialisation of TK over any other objective, stating 'Improved policy transparency, the creation of a supportive environment for private sector expansion and economic growth, and assuring accountability and good governance underpin the Action Plan.'[18] As of 2011, there were six countries drafting a national law based on the Model Law.[19] Of these, the only publicly available draft is that of Palau, which produced a Bill in 2005, but this has not yet been passed by its legislature.[20]

The Action Plan has a clear regionalisation agenda. A press statement refers to 'uniform national legal systems of protection'[21] and envisages a 'regional arrangement of mutual recognition and enforcement regime to protect and promote TK use'.[22] This regionalisation agenda is far more muted in the Model Law, which merely urges countries to adopt and adapt the Model as they see fit. It raises an important question about the expected reach of the legislation — or, to put it in another way, who is the intended target of the regulation?

To answer this it is necessary to examine the stated aims of the legislation. The Action Plan articulates the driving rationale as being that the 'continued exposure of Pacific TK to improper exploitation without due compensation demands that a regional approach be adopted as a matter of urgency while an international regime is being finalized'.[23] Leaving aside the fact that no empirical

---

16  Pacific Islands Forum Secretariat, *Traditional Knowledge Implementation Action Plan* (2009) <http://www.forumsec.org.fj/resources/uploads/attachments/documents/Traditional%20Knowledge%20Action%20Plan%202009.pdf>

17  Ibid, 2.

18  Ibid.

19  Ibid.

20  A Bill for an Act to establish a sui generis system for the protection and promotion of 'Traditional Knowledge and Expressions of Culture for the people of the Republic of Palau' (2005) <http://www.palauoek.net/senate/legislation/sb/sb_7-3.pdf>

21  Pacific Islands Forum Secretariat, 'TK Implementation Action Plan Progressing Well' (Press Release, 27 September 2010) <http://www.forumsec.org.fj/pages.cfm/newsroom/press-statements/2010/tk-implementation-action-plan-progressing-well.html>

22  Ibid.

23  Pacific Islands Forum Secretariat, above n 16, 3. It must be observed that the international protection regime is, unfortunately, very far from being finalised.

study is presented or cited to substantiate this belief, national or even regional legislation is unlikely to prevent this from occurring. With the exception of Fiji and possibly Samoa, the manufacturing capacity of most countries in the region is very limited, and therefore any mass production is likely to occur outside the jurisdictional limits of all the countries involved. The legislation must therefore primarily be considered in terms of its regulatory effects on the Pacific Islanders themselves, and their exceedingly small populations of non-indigenous citizens (except in Fiji). There is arguably thus little to be gained by working towards a uniform regional approach and, as discussed below, much to be lost from failing to take into account local differences across the region.

This brief discussion has argued that the movement to protect TK in the region is currently largely driven by economic considerations and is being pursued in a state-centred way. The next section argues that a different approach, one that supports, rather than cuts across, customary institutions in regulating TK, would be preferable for the region.

# 2. The Need for a Pluralistic Approach to Protection of TK

To understand the importance of a pluralistic approach to TK, the centrality of customary law and institutions to TK must be appreciated. This section briefly discusses the nature of customary laws and institutions in the region, and then goes on to demonstrate their inter-relatedness with TK and the social and economic underpinnings of the communities to which they belong. As Drahos argues, 'systems are nested phenomena',[24] and the customary law system in all countries is nested within particular economic and social systems. The third part of this section then argues that adopting a pluralistic approach to regulating TK would nurture the relationship between customary laws and institutions, even in the context of a nation state.

## (a) The Nature of Customary Laws and Institutions in the Pacific Island Countries

Whilst it is extremely difficult to make any generalisation about a region as diverse as the Pacific Islands, it is true to say that despite the forces of colonisation, decolonisation and the creation of independent liberal nation states, every one of the Pacific Island countries continues to have an indigenous

---

24   P Drahos, 'Six Minutes to Midnight: Can Intellectual Property Save the World?' in K Bowery, M Handler, and D Nichol (eds), *Emerging Challenges in Intellectual Property* (Oxford University Press, 2011) 30.

system of governance that exists largely independent of the state.[25] This system is generally administered at a community level by traditional leaders, known as chiefs in some places and 'old men' or 'big men' in others. These leaders were traditionally responsible for regulating all aspects of the social and economic relationships in their communities, and today continue to be responsible for a great many of them, especially in areas least affected by the cash economy and the institutions of the nation state.[26] This regulation is done through the use of established community norms (both explicit and implicit) and, perhaps more importantly, an autochthonous process of conflict management that varies across the region. This process is based on various principles, which vary from community to community and country to country, but are mostly restorative in nature and concerned with maintaining community peace. These principles are employed by the leaders, using various established procedures such as community meetings, to arrive at solutions that manage all community and inter-community disputes, including those over TK. For example, an anthropologist working with the Zia people in Papua New Guinea observes:

> From my work, it seems clear that there are set systems, patterns, procedures and rules involved in dispersing certain property. Also there are types of information available. Information that is general, specific, magical, ritual, sacred, secret, spiritual, etc, which is processed in accordance with the rules, how that information relates to a possessor (could be a group, individual, spirit, gender related etc)...cultural property exists within flows of transactions that are as intricate and precisely executed as those of an ecosystem.[27]

The system as a whole is dynamic and driven by the needs of a particular dispute or event, rather than by concerns to lay down a prescriptive normative framework. In other words, customary law, including that concerning TK, is continually evolving and is in many ways an ongoing dialogue about the way things should be done in the community, mediated by the customary leaders.

It is also true to say that in every country in the region these customary institutions are under a great deal of pressure as a result of both rapid social change in the region over the past several decades and the challenges of competing state governance structures.[28] Customary laws and institutions are

---

25 For example, the village *fono* system in Samoa, the *kastom* system in Vanuatu and the *maneaba* in Kiribati, to name a few.

26 See R Regenvanu, 'The Traditional Economy as the Source of Resilience in Melanesia' (Paper presented at the Lowy Institute Conference 'The Pacific Islands and the World: The Global Economic Crisis,' 2009).

27 S Kamene and K Sykes, 'The Work of the Zia Trust: A Holistic Extended Case Study from the Waria River Valley, Morobe' in K Sykes, J Simet and S Kamene (eds), *Culture and Cultural Property in the New Guinea Islands Region: Seven Case Studies* (UBSPD, 2001) 18.

28 In the context of Vanuatu, see for example Forsyth, above n 11.

thus just as vulnerable to extinction as other aspects of TK, and hence strategies for their reinforcement must be considered at the same time as protection of TK for the reasons discussed below.

## (b) The Centrality of Customary Laws and Institutions to TK

Customary law and institutions currently regulate entitlements to TK, but TK and customary law are linked in an even more fundamental way. Thus, while traditional leaders, institutions and laws are central to social and economic relations in the Pacific Island countries, TK is the very 'stuff' with which those social and economic relations are woven (and that dreams are made of — see below). For example, TK is crucial in determining leadership status, agricultural practices, navigation and trade routes, ceremonial practices, rights to land and land use, spiritual beliefs, healing practices, social organisation, concepts of belonging and exchange networks. Du Plessis and Fairbairn-Dunlop argue:

> The indigenous knowledge systems of the Pacific incorporate technical insights and detailed observations of natural, social and spiritual phenomena, which in turn are used to validate what is important in life — what sustains people and what connects them to particular places and spaces, and is crucial to their identity... In Pacific communities, knowledge is communally made, sanctioned, shared and used with the aim of achieving the good life for all members — however this is defined.[29]

Even the development of new knowledge is rooted in communal sources. Thus Lindstrom observes:

> Islanders do not explain their production of songs or other new knowledge in terms of a knower's individual talent, genius or creativity. Local epistemology seeks authorities and not individual authors...the Tannese intimate that they are repeating truths told by their fathers, whispered by spirits when intoxicated by kava, or revealed by ancestors in dreams.[30]

TK is often intimately bound up with social organisation in a particular community because access to it may be possessed only by certain members of that community. For example, knowledge about a particular ancestor-creator may be limited to people of certain status in a particular community. Thus, Whimp, in a study of Papua New Guinea, observes:

---

29  R Du Plessis and P Fairbairn-Dunlop, *The Ethics of Knowledge Production — Pacific Challenges* (UNESCO 2009) 100-111.
30  L Lindstrom, 'Big Men as Ancestors' (1990) 29 (4) *Ethnology* 313, 316.

> At least in some Papua New Guinea societies, the value of knowledge, for example, is inversely related to the number of people who possess it. The more people who know something, the less significant it is assumed to be. Restricting access to knowledge can reinforce cultural identity and strengthen social hierarchies and inequalities.[31]

The exchange of TK is also important to the maintenance and development of social networks. Busse and Whimp argue that 'the primary purpose and result of gift exchanges are to establish and maintain relations between persons making such exchanges'[32] and that 'the power of gift exchanges to create enduring social relationships lies precisely in the fact that the objects given are not completely alienated'.[33] The fruitful exchange of TK, which also stimulates the production of new TK, is facilitated in part by the decentralised nature of the customary laws and institutions that regulate it today.

Many anthropologists have commented upon the difficulty of divorcing the materiality of objects from their immateriality in this region. Jolly argues that 'the materiality of these objects [so-called primitive art] could not be so easily divorced from immateriality, the meanings, the ideas, the relations, the values, the agency with which they were endowed by their creators, users and original spectators'.[34] Bolton, for example, sees woven pandanus mats 'not as objects but as the materialisation of relations, as animated agents, like persons; their importance is "not what they mean, but what they do"'.[35]

This discussion of the nature of TK and of customary norms has at least two important ramifications for the protection of TK. The first is that neither TK nor customary norms can sensibly be separated from the social processes in which they have been developed, although this is often what Western reforms such as the Model Law attempt to do. A holistic approach is therefore necessary — one that sees TK in what Sillitoe calls 'a wider cultural context'.[36] The second is that it is difficult to boil down the multiple links and resonances that TK has within the community of which it is a part to a single 'right' that is 'owned' by a clearly defined group of people. Moreover, there can be all sorts of ramifications flowing from unauthorised access to TK that can only be dealt with by the

---

31   K Whimp and M Busse (eds), *Protection of Intellectual, Biological and Cultural Property in Papua New Guinea* (Oceania Publication, 2002) 19.

32   Ibid, 17.

33   Ibid, 18.

34   M Jolly, 'Material and Immaterial Relations: Gender, Rank and Christianity in Vanuatu' in L Dousset and S Tcherkezoff (eds), *The Scope of Anthropology* (Berghahn Books, 2012) 110.

35   Ibid.

36   P Sillitoe, 'Trust in Development: Some Implications of Knowing in Indigenous Knowledge' (2010) 16 *Journal of the Royal Anthropological Institute* 12, 15.

community leaders. These observations suggest that it is unwise to equate customary entitlements to access to TK with 'ownership'[37] and that the best people to regulate access to TK are the customary leaders themselves.

## (c) Weak and Deep Legal Pluralism

The aim of this section is to demonstrate that recognition of the centrality of customary law and customary institutions to TK dictates the adoption of a deep pluralist approach to TK. Such an approach involves the construction of a framework that supports the relevant customary institutions and allows them room to operate by themselves, rather than subsuming them within a state structure. This approach can be contrasted with so-called 'weak' legal pluralism, where customary norms are removed from their institutional context and applied by the state system.[38] In other words, deep legal pluralism involves the co-existence of legal orders with different sources of authority, whereas in weak legal pluralism there is only one legal order (the state) drawing upon two different bodies of norms.[39] As Griffiths observes, '[T]hese two perspectives give rise to different strategies for dealing with customary law namely whether to work for recognition of customary law within the state national legal system, or whether to claim recognition for it outside this system.'[40]

To date, these two different types of approaches have not been clearly differentiated in much of the literature concerning TK. The result is that weak legal pluralism is often being advocated as the appropriate way to recognise customary law and institutions. For example, Pigliasco argues: 'The question that arises is not whether or not the sanctions of customary law are applicable to outsiders, but rather the extent to which the rights relating to cultural expressions — as granted by custom to certain traditional custodians — are recognized by national legislations, and thus could be enforced.'[41] Kruk similarly states: 'Customary law would remain an effective method of protecting traditional knowledge only insofar as it is recognised and applied in national legal systems by the courts.'[42] He advocates attempts 'to recognize formally the legal status of customary law in the legal system and then to improve on the current methods of ascertaining and applying rules relating to traditional

---

37 This point is convincingly made in Kalinoe's excellent paper on TK in Papua New Guinea: L Kalinoe, above n 15, 1, 6-8.
38 See J Griffiths, 'What is Legal Pluralism?' (1986) 24 *Journal of Legal Pluralism* 1.
39 Forsyth, above n 11, 43.
40 A Griffiths, 'Customary Law in a Transnational World: Legal Pluralism Revisited' in R A Benton (ed), *Conversing with the Ancestors: Concepts and Institutions in Polynesian Customary Law* (Te Matahauariki Institute, University of Waikato, 2006) 9. See also M Davies, 'The Ethos of Pluralism' (2005) 27(1) *Sydney Law Review* 87.
41 G Pigliasco, 'Visual Anthropology and Jurisprudence: The Sawau Project' (2007) *Anthropology News*, 65.
42 P Kruk, 'The Role of Customary Law Under Sui Generis Frameworks of Intellectual Property Rights in Traditional and Indigenous Knowledge' (2007) 17 *Indiana International and Comparative Law Review* 67, 101-102.

knowledge'.[43] Antons also observes that 'stronger recognition of customary law principles could be very helpful in resolving some of the issues surrounding traditional knowledge', and then states: 'The big question is, however, how to integrate them into the state legal system.'[44] The error of this type of approach is in assuming it is possible to take customary norms out of their context and have them applied by a foreign system. As discussed above, norms, procedures and knowledge are interwoven in a complex and dynamic way, at least in the Pacific Island countries and probably in most indigenous legal systems, meaning that an exercise such as that which Pigliasco and Kruk advocate is not possible.

There are some who take a broader view, particularly indigenous scholars and anthropologists. For example, Solomon argues in a Māori context that there is a 'need to give priority to the strengthening and development of existing customary law systems, which reflect and nourish the underlying values of the relevant cultures and associated biodiversity'.[45] Whimp also argues: 'In considering laws to explicitly protect rights in intellectual property, it is critical that Papua New Guinean ideas about ownership, property, knowledge, and creativity are taken into account if those laws are to reflect the contemporary social and political contexts in which they will be applied.'[46] Most recently the International Institute for Environment and Development has recommended that customary law and customary authorities should be central to the development of protection systems.[47] However, to date no one has articulated how this can be done in practice. An attempt is made to do this in the last part of this chapter.

# 3. A Pluralistic Analysis of the Model Law and Action Plan

This section uses the theory of legal pluralism discussed in the preceding section to analyse the extent to which the Model Law and associated initiatives support customary law and institutions both procedurally and substantively. To date, academic commentary on the Model Law has been positive and has praised the Model Law's extensive references to customary law.[48] My analysis below is more critical.

---

43   Ibid, 116.
44   C Antons, 'The International Debate about Traditional Knowledge and Approaches in the Asia-Pacific Region' in Antons, above n 1, 39, 49.
45   M Solomon, 'Strengthening Traditional Knowledge Systems and Customary Laws' in S Twarog and P Kapoor (eds), *Protecting and Promoting Traditional Knowledge: Systems, National Experiences and International Dimensions* (United Nations, 2004) 155.
46   Whimp, above n 31, 21.
47   IIED, *Protecting Community Rights Over Traditional Knowledge: Implications of Customary Laws and Practices: Key Findings and Recommendations* (2005-2009) <http://www.iied.org/pubs/pdfs/G02583.pdf>
48   G Pigliasco, 'Intangible Cultural Property, Tangible Databases, Visible Debates: The Sawau Project' (2009) 16 *International Journal of Cultural Property* 255, 262-263; S von Lewinski, above n 4, 109, 119, 124.

On a procedural level, the TK initiative in the region has been almost entirely state focused. The top-down approach outlined in the Action Plan emphasises the drafting of legislation as an initial step, and envisages community consultation as occurring only significantly down the track. Even then, the community consultation is not seen primarily as a way of developing the framework along with the community leaders, but rather as an opportunity for TK owners to 'understand the implications of the Model Law and the effect of subsequent proposed legislation on their resources'.[49] The exploration of a possible role for customary laws and practices is regarded as only a 'medium-term period' activity.[50] This state-centred approach is also supported by various official statements. For example, the Director of the Institute of Fijian Language and Culture states that in Fiji 'We have a legal consultant who is finally working with this national law which will come into effect in 2010. So we hope that the law will also be taken down to the grassroots people, the owners and custodians of ICH in consultations, so their views will be heard and that the law will be amended accordingly.'[51] The problem with this approach is that it is significantly more difficult to alter a law once it has been drafted or even enacted than it is at the policy development stage: by then the general contours of the framework are fixed and there is relatively little room to negotiate. A far preferable approach would be to conduct research into the customary institutions and laws involved as a first step, and to consult widely amongst TK holders and customary leaders before drafting any laws. Ironically, the Action Plan refers to the importance of adopting a 'bottom-up'[52] and holistic approach[53] while outlining the opposite.

On a substantive level, at first and even second and third glances, the Model Law appears to create a central role for both customary law and customary institutions. The decisions concerning access are delegated to TK holders, and responsibilities given to customary institutions to, for example, decide ownership. However, a close analysis demonstrates that it is not a truly pluralistic law. It establishes a system and a value structure that are predicated upon certain views of TK, customary law and the type of protection that is important, and assumes that TK holders and customary institutions will just slot into them. The misfit between the aim of the legislation to be sensitive to customary law and the reality that it is not sensitive to it arises because the legislation is based upon a view of both TK and customary law as inert, so that clearly defined chunks of content can be removed from their context and still

49  *Action Plan*, above n 16, 5.
50  *Action Plan*, above n 16, 4.
51  M Qereqeretabua, 'The Safeguarding of Intangible Cultural Heritage in Fiji' (Paper presented at the International Seminar on the Safeguarding of Intangible Cultural Heritage: Current Situations and Challenges on the Safeguarding measures in the Asia-Pacific Region, 14 January 2010) 3 <http://www.tobunken.go.jp/~geino/e/ISSICH/IS2010.html>
52  *Action Plan*, above n 16, 3.
53  *Action Plan*, above n 16, 6.

make sense. However, as we have seen above, both are dynamic, amorphous and interactive. To demonstrate these points, this section now discusses four ways the Model Law refers to customary law and institutions.

## (a) The Distinction Between Customary and Non-customary Use

The Model Law draws a distinction between customary and non-customary use, and intends to regulate only the latter. However, it is no simple matter to determine what is meant by 'customary use', given the constantly changing nature of custom. The legislation defines customary use as 'use of traditional knowledge or expressions of culture in accordance with the customary laws and practices of the traditional owners'.[54] This does not, however, make it clear whether permission to use the TK following the custom of the relevant community is required, or if the use must be permitted by the custom of the relevant community. If it came to a dispute about this issue, it would be a matter for the courts rather than the customary institutions to decide, as they have *prima facie* jurisdiction over all disputes concerning state legislation. Lacking the flexible processes that underpin customary institutions, the courts could answer this question only by looking at precedents established by customary laws in the past. The consequence of this provision is that the Act is in effect making a division between traditional and new uses of TK, and mandating the involvement of the state in the latter.

These arguments may be better followed in the context of an example drawn from one of the very few court cases in the region that involves TK: the 'Nagol jump' dispute in Pentecost, one of the islands that comprise the country of Vanuatu. The facts of this case are set out in the Supreme Court's judgment,[55] but the essentials can be summarised as follows.

The Nagol jump is an important tradition in a number of villages on South Pentecost.[56] It involves men jumping from a specially constructed high tower to which they are tethered by vines tied to their ankles. Ideally, the vines are exactly the right length for the men neither to crash to their death nor be jerked back violently into the tower. In 1992 a group of men from South Pentecost (group X) decided that they were not adequately profiting from the tourism that has come from the Nagol jump, so proposed performing the jump on another island, Santo. They started negotiations with the relevant chiefly council,

---

54   *Model Law*, above n 5, s 4.
55   *In re the Nagol Jump, Assal & Vatu v the Council of Chiefs of Santo* [1992] VUSC 5 <http://www.paclii.org.vu>
56   See M Jolly, '*Kastom* as Commodity: The Land Dive as Indigenous Rite and Tourist Spectacle in Vanuatu' in L Lindstrom and G White (eds), *Culture, Kastom, Tradition: Developing Cultural Policy in Melanesia* (Institute of Pacific Studies, University of the South Pacific, 1994) 131, 141.

and the head of the council agreed that the jump could be done for the three following years, provided the National Council of Chiefs (NCC) agreed. The head of the council then went to the capital, Port Vila, to negotiate with the NCC. In his absence a number of the group decided to go ahead without waiting for his return. They were warned by customary leaders not to do so, but refused to listen. When they got to Santo they were met by the relevant chiefs there and told to pay a fine and to return to Pentecost to start discussions. Group X then applied to the Supreme Court for a declaration that their constitutional rights had been breached.[57]

So, is taking the jump to Santo customary use or not? According to the judgment, the Nagol had been performed outside Pentecost on two previous occasions for particular reasons. Arguably, therefore, taking it to Santo was not completely without precedent and could still be regarded as a customary use. On the other hand, it could be argued that it was a non-customary use, as the proper procedures for applying for it to be taken to Santo were not followed, and its historical association with Pentecost means its performance there is central to its very rationale.[58] This example demonstrates that there is not always a clear distinction between customary and non-customary use, and that customary institutions are able to deal in a fair and innovative way with new uses of TK. It also suggests the need to be careful before transferring jurisdiction over such disputes to the state or creating new avenues for 'appealing' and hence undermining decisions made by customary authorities (as occurred in the example case).

## (b) Determining Ownership

It can be assumed that ownership is likely to be controversial in many cases, especially if there is the real or imaginary prospect of a windfall gain. One has only to look at the bitter disputes that have accompanied the return of land to customary 'owners' when countries become independent and the distribution of royalties from resource developments across Melanesia to visualise the

---

57  They claimed that their rights under sections 5(1)(g), (h), (i) and (k) were breached. These are the rights to freedom of expression, freedom of assembly and association, freedom of movement, and equal treatment before the law. The court found there was no relevant law applicable and therefore it was necessary to follow section 47(1) of the Constitution, requiring the court to determine the matter according to 'substantial justice' and if at all possible in conformity with custom. His Honour then ordered that the Nagol jumping should return to Pentecost and that any future decision for it to leave Pentecost should only occur with the majority consent of the custom owners taken on a vote. This appears never to have occurred and the Nagol jump has remained in Pentecost. This case is in many ways a success, as the state legal system was able to reinforce the customary system. However, it was largely dependent upon the proclivities of the particular judge as there was no guiding law, and his Honour imposed a requirement on the movement of the Nagol (the requirement of a vote) that was uncalled for by the customary leaders and to an extent cut across their authority over the matter.

58  See Jolly, above n 34.

potential difficulties involved in determining rights to certain aspects of cultural heritage.[59] As with land, the problems of determining the limits of entitlement to TK claims are compounded by the movement of communities as a result of missionisation, plantation labour, epidemics and, more recently, urban drift.[60] The potential complexities of ownership can be illustrated by Lindstom's description of rights to kava in Vanuatu:

> [i]ndividuals (and their families and lineages) may claim overlapping rights to this or that kava variety, and would deny common cultural heritage. There are also (chiefly) titled versus untitled, and male versus female, claims to use and exchange kava. On the island of Tanna, for example, certain families have the right to consume specially grown and decorated *kava tapunga* at festivals celebrating boys' circumcisions. Overlapping claims to this sort of kava by scattered families across the island would be difficult to adjudicate. Any *sui generis* patent system that awarded general rights to kava to all ni-Vanuatu, or to the state, also could spark opposition from individuals, regions, kin-groups, and classes jealous of their particular kava claims.[61]

By introducing the concept of 'ownership' of TK by a finite group of people whose rights are backed by the state, the Model Law is therefore introducing a new and almost certainly troublesome concept into the regulation of TK in the region. The fact that it recognises that there may be communal or individual ownership does not avoid the difficulties that are likely to arise in determining the membership of the ownership group.

Under the Model Law, once a request to the cultural authority (CA) is made by a prospective user of TK, the CA is responsible for identifying the owners of the TK. This must be done by publishing a copy of the application in a newspaper and, if appropriate, on the radio or television.[62] The owners then have twenty-eight days to advise the CA of their claim. Then if the CA 'is satisfied that it has identified all the traditional owners' it must make a written determination.[63] There are no criteria to assist it in determining what standard of satisfaction is required. The only requirement is that the CA note down the parties who have advised they are the owners, and make a written decision and then publish

59  See, for example, C Filer, 'Grass Roots and Deep Holes: Community Responses to Mining in Melanesia' (2006) 18(2) *Contemporary Pacific* 215; N Haley and R May, *Conflict and Resource Development in the Southern Highlands of Papua New Guinea* (ANU E Press, 2007); J Bennett, 'Roots of Conflict in Solomon Islands — Though Much is Taken, Much Abides: Legacies of Tradition and Colonialism' (Discussion Paper, 2002/5 State, Society and Governance in Melanesia, 2002) <http://dspace.anu.edu.au/bitstream/1885/41835/2/bennett02-5. pdf> G Hassall, 'Conflict in the Pacific: Challenges for Governance' (2005) 20(1) *Pacific Economic Bulletin* 192.
60  See Jolly, above n 34, 141.
61  L Lindstrom, 'Kava Pirates in Vanuatu?' (2009) 16 *International Journal of Cultural Property* 291, 299-300.
62  *Model Law*, above n 5, s 16.
63  *Model Law*, above n 5, s 17.

it. This determination then provides a conclusive defence for any user of TK if the traditional owners specified in the determination have given their prior informed consent to the use.[64] This means that there is no effective way for contesting owners to appeal the CA's decision about ownership.

If the CA is not satisfied it has identified all the owners, or if there is a dispute, the CA 'must refer the matter to the persons concerned to be resolved according to customary law and practice or such other means as are agreed to by the parties'.[65] This is the closest the legislation comes to deep pluralism, and is clearly a step in the right direction. However, very clear thinking and development with the relevant customary institutions and leaders will be needed at the national implementation stage. It is not enough to create a new and controversial concept, and then to delegate responsibility for resolving claims to it to customary authorities without prior consultation. It is especially unfair to require customary authorities to deal with such claims within the presumably limited timeframe set down in the legislation. If the experiences of customary land tenure in the region are anything to go by, these are going to be particularly thorny issues that could generate a great deal of internal community conflict. Customary institutions must therefore be properly supported in preparation for such responsibility.

If the CA is satisfied that no owners can be identified or no agreement has been reached on ownership within the period set out in the legislation, it may take the somewhat draconian measure of making a determination that the CA is the traditional owner.[66] The only guidance given about whether or not the CA should make this decision is to consult with the relevant Minister. The CA is then free to enter into an agreement with the prospective user or not, with no guidance provided as to what should drive the decision-making (such as, for example, the views of the ownership contestants). The only limitation on the CA's power is that any benefits arising under the agreement must be used for traditional cultural development purposes. It is interesting that the possibility of holding them in trust until ownership is determined is not an option. This is the approach that has been taken in the Palau legislation, and seems preferable.[67] In other respects, however, the Palauan approach to ownership is far more unreasonable: the legislation provides that all the TK in Palau belongs to the state until ownership is proven otherwise.[68]

---

64   *Model Law*, above n 5, s 32.
65   *Model Law*, above n 5, s 18(1).
66   *Model Law*, above n 5, s 19.
67   Bill, above n 20, s 16.
68   Ibid.

## (c) Requirement of State Assent for Use of TK by a Pacific Islander

The Act is unclear about what rights a member of a community of traditional owners has with regard to TK. It appears that a member of the TK-holding community needs to get the prior informed consent of the other members of the community if he or she wants to use the TK in a way that is non-customary. Thus, the explanatory memorandum (EM) notes, 'if [a] person intends to perform [a dance from his/her community] in a non-customary way, for example performing the dance in non-customary costumes and with non-customary music, the person must obtain the prior and informed consent of the traditional owners as set out in Part 4'. This explanation also seems to suggest that 'customary use' is synonymous with 'traditional use' as discussed above.

To make matters more complicated, it is not enough to get the prior informed consent of all the owners. It is also necessary to involve the state — at the bare minimum, by advising the CA that the potential user has sought the prior informed consent of the other traditional owners, filling out a copy of the proposed user agreement, submitting it to the CA for advice, and providing a copy of the signed authorised user agreement to the CA no more than twenty-eight days after the agreement comes into force.[69] So if, for example, a group of school children wanted to perform a custom story from their village to a rap beat for their Christmas play, they would be required to go through this cumbersome process. Particularly in remote areas where the reach of the state is weak and communication difficult, this seems a ridiculously bureaucratic process, and one that is significantly disenfranchising of the local customary authorities whose decision is no longer sufficient.

## (d) Dispute Resolution

Although section 33 states that the parties can always use customary law and practice to resolve disputes, customary law is not mandated as a primary forum and the customary institutions are not given any state enforcement powers. It therefore appears highly unlikely that customary law and practice will be able to be used in hotly contested cases, as disputes about forum are likely to undermine its authority.[70] This is especially the case given the importance for the parties of meeting the statutory timeframe or else risking losing all to the CA.

The above discussion demonstrates that the approach adopted to date by the Model Law is not truly pluralistic, despite the many references to customary

---

69  *Model Law*, above n 5, s 25.
70  See Forsyth, above n 10, c 6.

law. At almost every turn, the state has been given a central role and customary institutions marginalised. Before discussing the problems that may arise from this, it is useful to reflect on why this approach has been adopted and to assess how much justification there is for it. The primary reason for its adoption is that customary institutions are perceived to be uncertain and difficult to access, whereas centralising control in the state has the apparent benefits of simplicity and efficiency. Thus a state-based system is seen to facilitate access to TK by outsiders.[71] A legislative reform whose only objective is the commercialisation of TK by outsiders may therefore prioritise a state-based approach, but it may be only a short-term solution because it may lead to the undermining of TK itself. The state is also seen as being more responsible and capable of making decisions to benefit the population as a whole. However, the example of the Tongan state entering into an agreement with a multinational company to collect samples of blood from its population for gene research,[72] and the high levels of government corruption in the region, show that the state is not necessarily to be implicitly trusted. Involvement of the state is also seen to be a safeguard against communities entering into unfair agreements with outsiders due to an imbalance in bargaining power. This is certainly a legitimate point, but safeguarding the communities against unfair contracts should be targeted with a great deal more precision than the current legislation does. Yet again this points to the necessity of clearly identifying the aims of the legislation, and perhaps separating competing aims into different pieces of legislation.

# 4. Potential Problems Arising from the Lack of a Deep Pluralist Approach

The preceding section demonstrated the lack of real engagement with customary institutions and law by the Model Law. This section discusses a range of problems that could arise if the legislation were implemented nationally in its present form. Drahos and Braithwaite remind us that this type of cost-benefit exercise is extremely important in the field of intellectual property, but that assessing the disadvantages of intellectual property protection is often overlooked while the advantages of greater levels of protection are emphasised.[73] As a general point, it may be said that the approach currently adopted by the Model Law shares many of the characteristics of traditional intellectual property legislation. However,

---

71  Lindstrom, above n 30, 298-99.

72  M Smith, 'Population-Based Genetic Studies: Informed Consent and Confidentiality' (2001-2002) 18 *Santa Clara Computer & High Technology Law Journal* 57, 70. See also Sister K A Kanongata'a, 'Autogen and Bio-Ethics in Tonga: An Ethical and Theological Reflection' in A Mead and S Ratuva (eds), *Pacific Genes and Life Patents* (Call of the Earth Llamado de la Tierra, United Nations University- Institute of Advanced Studies, 2007) 166.

73  Drahos with Braithwaite, above n 8, ix.

as Posey argues, such laws are 'inadequate and inappropriate for protection of traditional ecological knowledge and community resources' because, *inter alia*, 'they simplify ownership regimes, stimulate commercialisation, are difficult to monitor and enforce, and are expensive, complicated and time-consuming.'[74]

## (a) The New Framework Undermines Customary Institutions and Thus TK Itself

The inter-relationship between customary institutions, TK, and the social and economic basis of communities has been discussed above. The very intrusion of the state into this field threatens these important relationships, as it introduces a competing source of authority. One of the chief concerns with the Model Law is that it puts the evolution of TK into the state's hands, because it is the state that is deciding the threshold questions about what is customary and what is not. It thus usurps a very important role for customary institutions: that of finding a path through the challenges of modernity whilst maintaining those traditional values that continue to be of importance to the local community. It also undermines customary institutions by requiring the involvement of the state (through the CA) in every non-customary use of TK by the community, thus again cutting across the authority of the local institutions. As mentioned above, existing customary institutions are fragile in the region, and there is a real possibility that challenges to their authority by the state may cause them to break down altogether. As I demonstrated in another study in the context of criminal law, where there are two competing sources of authority (state and customary) there is a great temptation to avoid the authority of each by using one to criticise the legitimacy of the other.[75] The worst possible outcome would be for the new state structures to aid the disappearance of existing regulatory structures, but to be unable to provide an effective replacement due to the weakness of the state that characterises much of the region.

## (b) Fostering of Community Division

There is a very great risk that the Model Law and other initiatives in the Action Plan, such as the creation of databases, may become a catalyst for internal conflicts. Claims over ownership of particular traditional practices, particularly where there is a hope of economic benefit, have the potential to cause considerable community tension. Strathern argues:

---

74   D Posey, 'Commodification of the Sacred Through Intellectual Property Rights' (2002) 83 (1-2) *Journal of Ethnophramacology* 3, 9.

75   Forsyth, above n 11, c 6.

Intellectual property rights seem a poor social register and may even set people against one another. If the identification of individual authors or inventors becomes problematic in light of traditional authorship and collective inventions, then the identification of individual property holders becomes problematic in the light of multiple claims. Even if a group can be identified, who belongs to the group? Who is the representative to speak on its behalf? What about power inequalities between different interests within the group?[76]

The problem of disputes has already arisen in a database initiative in Fiji run by the Ministry of Indigenous Affairs. Reflecting on this programme, the Director of the Institute of Fijian Language and Culture notes that disputes by communities over ownership are an ongoing problem.[77] Such considerations make it essential that clear avenues for dealing with such disputes are firmly in place. Unfortunately, as discussed above, this is an area where the Model Law is extremely unclear.

The links between intellectual property and opportunistic behaviour recently outlined by Drahos also have application here.[78] Thus, the monopolistic approach set up in the legislation, whereby one group wins absolute access over TK (without even a limited time period, as in Western-style intellectual property legislation), is likely to promote rent-seeking behaviour by the particular 'owners' that will cause further divisions within society and restrict the traditional structures for the diffusion of TK. Moreover, by positivising TK by law and state bureaucracy, a number of well-known regulatory difficulties (for example, regulatory capture of patent offices) are potentially opened up, and these may be particularly problematic in developing countries because of weak and/or corrupt state institutions.

## (c) Unreasonably Raised Expectations

A related problem is that the push towards protecting TK may create unreal expectations of benefit amongst the local population. To an extent, this has already started. For example, the popular magazine *Island Business* stated: 'If one were to evaluate commercial potential beginning from the metaphysics to blood cells and going out to cultural expressions, flora and fauna, Pacific Islanders are sitting on a gold mine. They just don't fully comprehend it yet.'[79]

---

76  M Strathern, 'Multiple Perspectives on Intellectual Property' in K Whimp and M Busse (eds), above n 31, 47, 51-52.

77  M Qereqeretabua, above n 51.

78  P Drahos, above n 24, 30.

79  D Tabureguci, *The Pacific's Stolen Identity: How Intellectual Property Rights have Failed Pacific Cultures* (2007) <http://www.islandsbusiness.com/islands_business/index_dynamic/containerNameToReplace=Middl eMiddle/focusModuleID=18144/overideSkinName=issueArticle-full.tpl>

Strathern similarly comments: 'Intellectual property has suddenly become a topic of widespread international interest. Moreover, once articulated it rapidly catches the public imagination, and this is something to be taken into account in policy development.'[80]

There is a need to make sure there are realistic expectations about the probably modest amount of profit that TK commercialisation is likely to bring, following commentators such as Dutfield who have cautioned: 'it is important not to over-estimate the economic potential of TK'.[81] It is likely that envisaged gains will in no way be comparable to the cultural richness that could be lost by interfering with the current dynamic tradition of community-based exchange and use of TK.

## (d) The Problem of TK Already in the Public Domain

A question that has not been clearly addressed by the Model Law is how to deal with the problem of TK that has already spread from its ancestral location (if such can be located) and is being used in various places within a country or even outside the Pacific Island countries.[82] The people from the Fijian island of Beqa, for example, claim that the firewalking ceremony known as vilavilairevo belongs to them, and they have already started a campaign to get it back (that is, stop it being performed by other groups).[83] If it can be established that they are the 'owners' of the ceremony, the Model Law would require that no one else will be able to perform it without the consent of the Beqa people.[84] The effect of this (and similar situations) on the livelihood of countless tourist-based businesses throughout the Pacific, and the fierce disputes it would engender, are disturbing to contemplate. The only gain may be that preparing court cases will be a very good way of revitalising traditional knowledge, as exemplified by the 'Sawau Project', which was established to document the process and demonstrate its origin in Beqa.

---

80   Strathern, above n 76, 47.
81   G Dutfield, 'Developing and Implementing National Systems for Protecting Traditional Knowledge: Experiences in Selected Developing Countries' in S Twarog and P Kapoor (eds), *Protecting and Promoting Traditional Knowledge: Systems, National Experiences and International Dimensions* (United Nations Publication, 2004) 141, 144.
82   It could be argued that attempting to regulate this is like trying to shut the paddock gate after the horse has bolted, although the example of the recent success some European countries have had in re-gaining protection for commodities such as cheese and wine through the movement for GIs and appellations of origin may contradict this. However, to achieve such successes, significant economic bargaining power is required.
83   K Hennessy, 'A Ituvatuva Ni Vakadidike E Sawau: The Sawau Project DVD' (2009) 25(1) *Visual Anthropology Review* 90. The author of this article states, 'The Sawau project was conceived as a strategy for repatriating ownership of Sawau cultural heritage back to its place of origin on the island of Beqa, Fiji'. See also G Pigliasco, above n 48, 255.
84   Section 3 of the Model Law provides that it applies to TK that was in existence before the commencement of the Act.

In Palau this issue is dealt with in the TK Bill by requiring all pre-existing non-customary uses to be registered with the relevant Ministry within 180 days of the legislation taking effect. Then, commencing one year after the legislation has been in force, users of such TK are required to attach a label to objects that embody the TK, stating, 'This product includes elements of Palauan traditional knowledge or expressions of culture which have been used without the express guidance or approval of the traditional owner' or to make a speech at the start of a performance to the same effect.[85] It can be imagined how unpalatable this would be to the local tourist industry, and could be the reason the Bill has not as yet been promulgated.

## (e) Stifling of Internal Research, Use and Development of TK by TK Owners Themselves

One of the greatest dangers is that the legislation and associated initiatives could impede the current dynamic exchange and development of TK. There is a risk that such an initiative will foster a commercialisation mentality in which people seek to guard 'their' TK in order to profit from it in the cash economy. Dutfield observes that 'modern IPR [intellectual property rights] reflect, but also help to underpin (through the rewards they provide) a highly competitive winner-take-all business ethos',[86] and similar concerns arise in respect of the Model Law's determination of ownership by finite groups of people. Once again, the parallels with the social problems following the leasing of customary land and resources development in Melanesia are only too apparent. As mentioned above, if the free movement of TK between communities is impeded, this will diminish the cultural richness of the society as a whole and impede the evolution of TK. It is likely also to have negative impacts upon many aspects of people's livelihood which depend on the use of TK, such as primary health care and agriculture.[87]

The legislation could also have a curtailing effect on research that is currently being conducted by both indigenous researchers and foreign scholars. For example, the Vanuatu Fieldworkers, a network of indigenous researchers established by the Vanuatu Cultural Centre, conduct research on a different aspect of TK within their own communities each year.[88] If they are required to comply with the formalities of the legislation (and there is no reason why they should not, as conducting research is not a 'customary use'), then this is likely

---

85   Ibid, s 26(a).
86   Dutfield, above n 81, 145.
87   Ibid, 142-143. Dutfield notes that the WHO has stated that 80 per cent of the world's population depends on traditional medicine for its primary healthcare and that TK is indispensable for its survival.
88   See, for example, D Tryon and V K Senta (eds), *Woksop Blongol Filwoka Ples blong ol pig long kastom laef long Vanuatu: buk 1* [Customary pig pens in Vanuatu: Book 1, Vanuatu Cultural Centre's Fieldworkers Workshop] (Vanuatu KaljoralSenta, 1990).

to have a stifling effect on this important initiative. Surely the most important aim of any TK initiative is to keep TK alive, and so any procedures that make it more difficult for local people to use it should be avoided? How can communities share TK and learn and innovate if they are always up against a state authority? Although it may be argued that the law will be only selectively enforced, and so groups such as the Vanuatu Fieldworkers would not be in danger, this is not satisfactory for a variety of reasons, including the fact that criminal sanctions may possibly be involved.[89]

One of the particular problems in this regard is the enormously wide scope of the legislation: it aims to cover every conceivable type of TK and to provide rights over it in perpetuity. Whilst such an approach makes sense for certain types of TK, such as secret or sacred material, it appears unduly restrictive overall. A different approach is suggested by Dutfield, who states:

> Ideally the protectable subject matter should be defined in close consultation with the purported beneficiaries. Also, the broader the definition of TK, the more the rights provided should be limited in some way or another ... to treat all conceivable categories of TK as deserving strong and/or permanent protection is unreasonable and would almost certainly go beyond what customary law indicates anyway.[90]

In carrying out such a consultation, views of authors such as Boyle who demonstrate the importance of a wide public domain to generate new works should also be shared.[91] There is no reason why the careful balancing of rights of users and rights of the public that lies at the heart of Western-style intellectual property protection should not also be of relevance in the context of TK. One possible way of avoiding some of the identified dangers would be to extend the moral rights provisions to commercial and non-commercial use, but otherwise to tailor the provisions much more narrowly to meet specific objectives, such as preventing one person gaining a commercial advantage at the expense of others.

# 5. What Would a True Deep Pluralistic Approach Look Like?

A review of the international literature on TK protection does not currently provide a shining example of a national model of protection based on respect and support for customary norms and institutions. Much of the literature is contextualised within an indigenous rights narrative wherein the indigenous

---

89  The penalty provisions in sections 26-29 provide imprisonment as a possible penalty.
90  Dutfield, above n 81, 142.
91  Boyle, above n 7.

population is currently suppressed by a dominant other — but this is not the case in Pacific Island countries. Given this rare ability to exercise rights from a position of power,[92] the Pacific Island countries have a degree of liberty to shape a new approach to protection of TK that other indigenous groups may follow. Of course, this liberty is likely to be reduced as a result of multilateral and bilateral trade negotiations currently underway.[93] The aim of this section is to outline a particular path that may be followed to arrive at such a model of protection.

A true pluralist approach to the protection of TK would follow a bottom-up process, and would emerge following widespread consultations with community and customary leaders as a first step. This approach has the support of a recent global study into protecting and promoting TK, the editors of which state: 'There is general consensus that new approaches and measures (sui generis systems) that combine tools in an appropriate way need to be developed for the protection of TK at the national and international levels ... These systems should be developed in close consultation with indigenous and local communities.'[94] The benefits of such an approach appear self-evident, but to date this step has been neglected in most TK initiatives around the world. Thus Dutfield comments on 'how rare it is for indigenous peoples and local communities to be consulted about new [TK] legislation'.[95] This consultation would address a number of preliminary questions such as the desire and need for greater protection of TK, and the types of support existing customary institutions require to meet the needs identified.

As the substantive composition of the legal framework to emerge from such consultations cannot be known until those consultations have occurred, it is not possible to pre-empt it in any great detail. It is, however, possible to discuss and describe some of the principles that are likely to underpin any development emerging from such a process.

## (a) Customary Institutions Supported and Strengthened

The empowering of customary institutions and leaders to develop their processes and norms for regulating use of TK, both within and without their community, is likely to be central to any new protection system. Thus Solomon argues in the context of Māori laws: 'First priority needs to be given to strengthening and protecting customary law systems, because of the important values inherent in those systems, which are critical to the maintenance of the cultures concerned.'[96]

---

92   D Conway, 'Indigenizing Intellectual Property Law: Customary Law, Legal Pluralism, and the Protection of Indigenous Peoples' Rights, Identity and Resources' (2008-2009) 15 *Texas Wesleyan Law Review* 207, 208.
93   Such as the European Partnership Agreement and the 'PACER Plus' negotiations with Australia. See M Penjueli and W Morgan, 'Putting Development First: Concerns about a Pacific Free Trade Agreement' (2010) 25(1) *Pacific Economic Bulletin* 211.
94   Twarog and Kapoor, above n 45, xv.
95   Dutfield, above n 81, 150.
96   M Solomon, above n 45, 155, 164.

Such a model would involve a decentralised, locally based decision-making structure with responsibility for determining questions of access and equitable benefit sharing, rather than a state-centred one as envisaged in the Model Law. Swiderska, in her work with the International Institute for Development, argues:

> The best way for communities to protect their knowledge and resources is at local level. Community-based natural resource management, together with secure land-tenure, can strengthen community control of TK and natural resources, maintain traditional knowledge, conserve biodiversity and improve livelihoods.

She gives the example of the community-based Andean Potato Park that uses customary principles of reciprocity, equilibrium and duality to guide the management of the park at the local level.[97] Peter Ørebech similarly argues that customs that develop customary law systems 'play a critical role in achieving viable social systems'.[98]

As part of this process it will be necessary to create space for discussions with customary leaders about the competing aims of conservation and commercialisation, and developing processes that are able to mediate between these different demands while retaining key cultural principles. This is best done by creating a dialogue that seeks to facilitate an informed engagement with the issues, and avoids using the language of 'theft' and 'ownership'. Pacific Islanders are extremely inventive, and many of their customary leaders are very wise and informed by deep understandings of their communities and the forces at play within them. There is therefore every chance that, given the opportunity, they will come up with solutions unexpected to an outsider but which will work for their community. For example, Geismar has illustrated how, through a judicious use of traditional beliefs and practices, a group of men from North Ambrym ensured that the market in carved wooden gongs (tam-tams) for which they are famous has remained effectively in their hands.[99]

## (b) Minimal State Intervention

The state does have an important role to play in a truly pluralistic protection model, but it is as an advisor and facilitator, and not as a primary regulator. There are many useful functions the state can have, especially in regard to mediating between its citizens and outsiders who wish to use TK. The state may also need to develop processes by which it can assist local customary authorities in enforcing any decisions they have made concerning TK. In addition, it may

---

97   K Swiderska, 'Banishing the Biopirates: A New Approach to Protecting Traditional Knowledge' (2011) *International Institute for Development Gatekeeper Series* 129, 16-17.

98   P Ørebech et al (eds), *The Role of Customary Law in Sustainable Development* (Cambridge University Press, 2005) 9.

99   H Geismar, 'Copyright in Context: Carvings, Carvers and Commodities in Vanuatu' (2005) 32(3) *American Ethnologist* 437.

also work on initiatives such as developing systems of certification marks for different communities. It also has an important role in small island states as a gatekeeper, making sure that the activities of researchers and developers are monitored and opportunities for exploitation minimised — for example, through a system of research permits as currently operate in Vanuatu and Fiji. Finally, the state could ensure that its import rules forbid the importation of goods embodying the TK of the country, thus ensuring that only citizens of the country can profit from making such objects.[100]

## (c) Diffuse Benefit Sharing from Use of TK

A pluralist approach would encourage the benefits from TK being spread among as many communities and individuals as possible. This would be done by promoting the spirit of communal benefit that underlies TK in the Pacific Islands as a whole. For example, a land dispute in Vanuatu may traditionally have been resolved by allowing the 'losing' party to remain on a part of the land that was under contestation, whereas a court-adjudicated approach would require the winner to take all.[101] A similar approach is advocated by Swiderska, who argues that: 'Given that TK and genetic resources are often shared freely between communities, even across borders, collective rights, decision-making and benefit-sharing amongst neighbouring communities should be recognised.'[102]

## (d) Promoting the Use of TK by Local Communities

A central aim of a pluralist approach to protection is to facilitate access by local communities to their own TK, and to the TK of neighbouring communities, in accordance with reciprocal customary obligations. Any expensive or bureaucratic process that may work as an impediment to this should be avoided. The primary aim should be to use TK to improve the livelihoods of TK holders and communities through contributing to a rich cultural life, ecologically sound agricultural practices and primary health care. This approach is similar to that of the 'traditional economy' advocated by Vanuatu MP Regenvanu, who argues that it is constantly overlooked by policy-makers but has in fact been the major source of resilience for Melanesian populations for thousands of years.[103]

---

100  For example, if tam-tams were being made in Bali and shipped back to Vanuatu for sale in the tourist market, this would be prohibited by such restrictions.
101  Regenvanu states that in the traditional Melanesian economy 'everyone has access to land on which to make gardens for food and access resources, even people with no traditional claim over the land being used. However, the ill-considered alienation of land from the traditional economy in Vanuatu through leasehold titles, for example, is removing the means for ordinary people to be economically productive and enjoy food and social security.' Regenvanu, above n 26, 5.
102  Swiderska, above n 97, 17.
103  Regenvanu, above n 26.

# 6. Conclusion

The aim of this chapter has been to suggest that the current move to protect TK in the Pacific Island countries is taking a wrong direction in giving the state such a central role, and in prioritising the commercialisation of TK over use of TK by local communities. The brakes need to be applied and a deeper reflection made into the issues through a process of widespread community consultation. The current initiative is proceeding as if TK is *terra nullius*, whereas in fact each country in the region has a sophisticated customary legal system in which TK is deeply embedded. This chapter suggests that the first step in any move to protect TK should be to enquire into this system, and to see if and how it could be empowered to meet the new challenges posed to TK by globalisation. One significant advantage of doing this is that it will also support the underlying social and economic structures that produce TK. On the other hand, a failure to do so may very well risk undermining the customary structures that have led to the extraordinary wealth of TK in the region in the first place.

# Bibliography

## Books/Chapters/Journal Articles/Reports

I Abeyesekere, 'The Protection of Expressions of Folklore in Sri Lanka' in Christoph Antons (ed), *Traditional Knowledge, Traditional Cultural Expressions and Intellectual Property Law in the Asia-Pacific Region* (Kluwer Law International, 2009) 341

K Akerman and J Stanton, 'Riji and Jakoli: Kimberley Pearlshell in Aboriginal Australia' (Monograph Series 4, Northern Territory Museum of Arts and Sciences, 1994)

P Alford, *To Steal a Book is an Elegant Offense: Intellectual Property Law in Chinese Civilization* (Stanford University Press, 1995)

J C Altman, G J Buchanan and L Larsen, 'The Environmental Significance of the Indigenous Estate: Natural Resource Management as Economic Development in Remote Australia' (Discussion Paper No 286, Centre for Aboriginal Economic Policy Research, 2007)

J Anderson, 'The Politics of Indigenous Knowledge: Australia's Proposed Communal Moral Rights Bill' (2004) 27(3) *University of New South Wales Law Journal* 585

J Anderson, *The Production of Indigenous Knowledge in Intellectual Property* (PhD Thesis, University of New South Wales, 2003)

M Annas, 'The Label of Authenticity: A Certification Trade Mark for Goods and Services of Indigenous Origin' (1997) 3(90) *Aboriginal Law Bulletin* 4

C Antons, 'The International Debate about Traditional Knowledge and Approaches in the Asia-Pacific Region' in C Antons (ed), *Traditional Knowledge, Traditional Cultural Expressions and Intellectual Property Law in the Asia-Pacific Region* (Kluwer Law International, 2009) 39

C Antons (ed), *Traditional Knowledge, Traditional Cultural Expressions and Intellectual Property Law in the Asia-Pacific Region* (Kluwer Law International, 2009)

A E Appleton, *Environmental Labelling Programmes: International Trade Law Implications* (Kluwer Law International, 1997)

C Arup, 'Split entitlements? Intellectual property policy for clusters and networks' in C Arup and W Van Caenegem (eds), *Intellectual Property Policy Reform: Fostering Innovation and Development* (Edward Elgar, 2009) 285

M Asplet and M Cooper, 'Cultural Designs in New Zealand Souvenir Clothing: The Question of Authenticity' (2000) 21(3) *Tourism Management* 307

B Attwood and A Markus, *Thinking Black: William Cooper and the Australian Aborigines' League* (Aborigines Studies Press, 2004)

J Audier, *TRIPS Agreement Geographical Indications* (Office for Official Publications of the European Communities, 2000)

H Azaizeh, S Fulder, K Khalil and O Said, 'Ethnobotanical Knowledge of Local Arab Practitioners in the Middle Eastern Region' (2003) 74(1-2) *Fitoterapia* 99

K Basu, 'Marketing Developing Society Crafts: A Framework for Analysis and Change' in Janeen Arnold Costa and Gary J. Bamossy (eds), *Marketing in a Multicultural World: Ethnicity, Nationalism and Cultural Identity* (Sage Publications, 1995) 257

F Baum, C McDougall and D Smith 'Continuing Professional Education, Glossary: Participatory Action Research' (2006) 60 *Journal of Epidemiological CommunityHealth* 854

K Bavikatte and D F Robinson, 'Towards a People's History of the Law: Biocultural Jurisprudence and the Nagoya Protocol on Access and Benefit Sharing' (2011) 7(1) *Law, Environment and Development Journal* 35

K E Behrendt, 'Cancellation of the Washington Redskins' Federal Trademark Registrations: Should Sports Team Names, Mascots and Logos Contain Native American Symbolism?' (2000) 10 *Seton Hall Journal of Sport Law* 396

J Belson, *Certification Marks* (Sweet & Maxwell, 2002)

J Bennett, 'Roots of conflict in Solomon Islands - though much is taken, much abides: legacies of tradition and colonialism' (Discussion Paper 2002/5, State, Society and Governance in Melanesia, 2002)

F Berkes, 'Evolution of Co-Management: Role of Knowledge Generation, Bridging Organizations and Social Learning' (2009) 90 *Journal of Environmental Management* 1692

F Berkes, *Sacred Ecology* (Routledge, 2nd ed, 2008)

N Bernasconi-Osterwalder et al,*Environment and Trade: A Guide to WTO Jurisprudence* (Earthscan, 2006)

L Bernier, *Justice in Genetics. Intellectual Property and Human Rights from a Cosmopolitan Liberal Perspective* (Edward Elgar, 2010)

S Biber-Klemm and T Cottier, *Rights to Plant Genetic Resources and Traditional Knowledge: Basic Issues and Perspective* (CAB International Publishing, 2006)

D Bird, *Understanding Wine Technology: The Science of Wine Explained* (Wine Appreciation Guild, 2005)

R B Bird et al, 'The "Fire Stick" Hypothesis: Australian Aboriginal Foraging Strategies, Biodiversity, and Anthropogenic Fire Mosaics' (2008) 105(39) *Proceedings of the National Academy of Science* 14796

M Blakeney, 'Protection of Traditional Knowledge by Geographical Indications', in C Antons (ed), *Traditional Knowledge, Traditional Cultural Expressions and Intellectual Property Law in the Asia-Pacific Region* (Kluwer Law International, 2009) 87

M Blakeney, 'Protection of Traditional Knowledge by Geographical Indications' (2009) 3(4) *International Journal of Intellectual Property Management* 357

M Blakeney, 'Protecting Traditional Knowledge and Expressions of Culture in the Pacific' (2011) 1(1) *Queen Mary Journal of Intellectual Property* 80

Board of Studies NSW, *Protecting Aboriginal Indigenous Art: Ownership, Copyright and Marketing Issues for NSW Schools* (Board of Studies NSW, 2006)

R Boast, *Buying the Land, Selling the Land: Governments and Māori Land in the North Island 1865-1921* (Victoria University Press, 2008)

L Boroditsky and A Gaby, 'Remembrances of Times East: Absolute Representations of Time in an Australian Aboriginal community' (2010) 21(11) *Psychological Science* 1635

P W Bosland, 'Capsicums: Innovative Uses of an Ancient Crop' in J Janick (ed), *Progress in New Crops* (ASHS Press, 1996)

S Bowen, 'Development from Within? The Potential for Geographical Indications in the Global South' (2010) 13(2) *Journal of World Intellectual Property* 231

J Boyle, *The Public Domain* (Yale University Press, 2008)

K Bowery, 'Indigenous Culture, Knowledge and Intellectual Property: The Need for a New Category of Rights?' in K Bowery, M Handler and D Nicol (eds), *Emerging Challenges in Intellectual Property* (Oxford University Press, 2011) 46

J Braithwaite and P Drahos, *Global Business Regulation* (Cambridge University Press, 2000)

K Breu and C Hemingway, 'Researcher-Practitioner Partnering in Industry-Funded Participatory Action Research' (2005) 18(5) *Systemic Practice and Action Research* 437

S B Brush, 'Indigenous Knowledge of Biological Resources and Intellectual Property Rights: The Role of Anthropology' (1993) 95 *American Anthropologist* 653

M Cargo, T Delormier, L Levesque, K Horne-Miller, A McComber and A Macaulay, 'Can the democratic ideal of participatory research be achieved? An inside look at an academic-indigenous community partnership' (2008) 23(5) *Health EducationResearch* 904

W Carr and S Kemmis, *Becoming Critical: Knowing through action research* (Deakin University Press, 1983)

B Carson and T Dunbar et al (eds), *Social Determinants of Indigenous Health* (Allen & Unwin, 2007)

M Cassidy and J Langford, *Intellectual Property and Aboriginal People: A Working Paper* (Ministry of Indian Affairs and Northern Development, Ottawa, 1999) 22

C Charters 'A Self-Determination Approach to Justifying Indigenous Peoples' Participation in International Law and Policy Making' (2010) 17 *International Journal on Minority and Group Rights* 215

W Cherdshewasart, W Cheewasopit and P Picha, 'The Differential Anti-proliferation Effect of the White (*Pueraria mirifica*), Red (*Butea superba*) and Black (*Mucuna collettii*) Kwao Krua plants on the growth of MCF-7 Cells' (2004) 93 *Journal of Ethnopharmacology* 255

W Cherdshewasart and W Sutjit 'Correlation of antioxidant activity and major isoflavonoid contents of the phytoestrogen-rich *Pueraria mirifica* and *Pueraria lobata* tubers' (2008) 15(1-2) *Phytomedicine* 38

N Chomsky and M Foucault, *The Chomsky-Foucault Debate on Human Nature* (New Press, 2006)

M Chon, 'Marks of Rectitude' (2009) 77 *Fordham Law Review* 101

Chuulangun, 'Kaanju Ngaachi Wenlock and Pascoe Rivers IPA Management Plan 2011-2017' (Prepared by the Chuulangun Aboriginal Corporation with the assistance of funding from the Commonwealth IPA program, Chuulangun, Cape York Peninsula, Queensland, Australia, 2011)

Chuulangun Aboriginal Corporation, *Kaanju Homelands Wenlock and Pascoe Rivers Indigenous Protected Area Management Plan* (Chuula, Cape York Peninsula, Queensland, Australia, 2005)

D Claudie, 'We're tired from talking: The native title process from the perspective of Kaanju People living on homelands, Wenlock and Pascoe Rivers, Cape York Peninsula' (2007) in B Smith and F Morphy (eds), *The Social Effects of Native Title: Recognition, Translation, Coexistence* (Centre for Aboriginal Economic Policy Research, The Australian National University, 2007) 91

J Cleary, 'Business Exchanges in the Australian Desert: It's About More than the Money' (2012) 7(1) *Journal of Rural and Community Development* 1

J Cleary, R Grey-Gardiner and P Josif, 'Hands Across the Desert: Linking Desert Aboriginal Australians to Each Other and to the Bush Foods Industry' (Research Report, Desert Knowledge Cooperative Research Centre, Alice Springs, 2009)

D Conway, 'Indigenizing Intellectual Property Law: Customary Law, Legal Pluralism, and the Protection of Indigenous Peoples' Rights, Identity and Resources' (2008-2009) 15 *Texas Wesleyan Law Review* 207

C Correa, *Trade Related Aspects of Intellectual Property Rights: A Commentary on the TRIPS Agreement* (Oxford University Press, 2007)

T Cottier, 'The Agreement on Trade-Related Aspects of Intellectual Property Rights' in P F J Macrory et al (eds), *The World Trade Organization: Legal, Economic and Political Analysis*, vol 1 (Springer, 2005) 1041

C Cotton, *Ethnobotany Principles and Applications* (Wiley, 1996)

M Crisp and S Laffan et al, 'Endemism in the Australian flora' (2001) 28(2) *Journal of Biogeography* 183

T W Dagne, 'Harnessing the Development Potential of Geographical Indications for Traditional Knowledge-Based Agricultural Products' (2010) 5 *Journal of Intellectual Property Law & Practice* 441

C Dankers, *Environmental and Social Standards, Certification and Labelling for Cash Crops, Food and Agriculture Organization of the United Nations* (Kluwer Law International, 2003)

K Das, 'Prospects and Challenges of Geographical Indications in India' (2010) 13 *The Journal of World Intellectual Property* 148

N Dawson, *Certification Trade Marks, Law and Practice* (Intellectual Property Publishing Limited, 1988)

M Davies, 'The Ethos of Pluralism' (2005) 27(1) *Sydney Law Review* 87

C de Crespigney, I Kowanko, H Murray, W Wilson, J Ah Kit, & D Mills, 'A Nursing partnership for better outcomes in Aboriginal mental health, including substance use' (2006) 22(2) *Contemporary Nurse* 275

Desert Knowledge Cooperative Research Centre, *Aboriginal Research Engagement Protocol Template* (DKCRC, Alice Springs, 2006)

Desert Knowledge Cooperative Research Centre, 'Information = Power: Walking the Bush Tomato Value Chain' (Project Proposal to NT NRM Board, Alice Springs, 2008)

T Dob and C Chelghoum, 'Chemical Composition of the Essential Oil of *Artemisia judaica* L. from Algeria' (2006) 21(2) *Flavour and Fragrance Journal* 343

D R Downes and S A Laird, *Innovative Mechanisms for Sharing Benefits of Biodiversity and Related Knowledge Case Studies on Geographical Indications and Trademarks* (UNCTAD Biotrade Initiative, 1999)

P Drahos, 'A Networked Responsive Regulatory Approach to Protecting Traditional Knowledge' in D Gervais (ed) *Intellectual Property, Trade and Development: Strategies to Optimize Economic Development in a TRIPS-plus Era* (Oxford University Press, 2007) 385

P Drahos, *A Philosophy of Intellectual Property* (Dartmouth, 1996)

P Drahos et al, 'Pharmaceuticals, Intellectual Property and Free Trade: The Case of the US–Australia Free Trade Agreement' (2004) 22(3) *Prometheus* 243

P Drahos, 'Six Minutes to Midnight: Can Intellectual Property Save the World?' in K Bowery, M Handler and D Nicol (eds), *Emerging Challenges in Intellectual Property* (Oxford University Press, 2011) 30

P Drahos, 'Towards an International Framework for the Protection of Traditional Group Knowledge'(Report from UNCTAD-Commonwealth Secretariat Workshop on Elements of National *Sui Generis* Systems for the Preservation, Protection and Promotion of Traditional Knowledge, Innovations and Practices and Options for an International Framework, Geneva, 4-6 February 2004)

P Drahos and J Braithwaite, *Information Feudalism: Who Owns the Knowledge Economy?* (Earthscan, 2002)

R Du Plessis and Peggy Fairbairn-Dunlop, *The ethics of knowledge production – Pacific challenges* (UNESCO, 2009)

F Dussart, *The Politics of Ritual in an Aboriginal Settlement* (Smithsonian Institution Press, 2000)

G Dutfield, 'A Critical Analysis of the Debate on Traditional Knowledge, Drug Discovery and Patent-based Biopiracy' (2011) 33(4) *European Intellectual Property Review* 237

G Dutfield, 'Developing and Implementing National Systems for protecting Traditional Knowledge: Experiences in Selected Developing Countries' in S Twarog and P Kapoor (eds), *Protecting and Promoting Traditional Knowledge: Systems, National Experiences and International Dimensions* (UNCTAD/DITC/TED/10, 2004) 141

G Dutfield, 'Legal and Economic Aspects of Traditional Knowledge' in K E Maskus and J H Reichman (eds), *International Public Goods and Transfer of Technology Under a Globalized Intellectual Property Regime* (Cambridge University Press, 2005) 495

N Etkin and E Elisabetsky, 'Seeking a transdisciplinary and culturally germane science: the future of ethnopharmacology' (2005) 100 *Journal of Ethnopharmacology* 23

G Evans, 'The Comparative Advantages of Geographical Indications and Community Trademarks for the Marketing of Agricultural Products in the European Union' (2010) 41 *IIC-Int Rev Intell P* 645

P Everard and M Murika , T Tjampu, Kanytji, S Pumani, and Milatjari, *Punu: Yankunytjatjara Plant Use* (IAD Press, 2nd ed, 2002)

Expert Committee on Complementary Medicines in the Health System 'Complementary Medicines in the Australian Health System' (Report to the Parliamentary Secretary to the Minister for Health and Ageing, Canberra, Commonwealth of Australia, 2003)

D Fabricant and N Farnsworth, 'The value of plants used in traditional medicine for drug discovery' (2001) 109 *Environmental Health Perspectives* 69

O Fals-Borda, 'Participatory (Action) Research in Social Theory: Origins and Challenges' in P Reason and H Bradbury (eds), *Handbook of Action Research* (Sage, 2001) 27

Families, Housing, Community Services and Indigenous Affairs, *Closing the Gap on Indigenous Disadvantage: The Challenge for Australia* (AGPS, 2009)

C Filer, 'Grass roots and deep holes: community responses to mining in Melanesia' (2006) 18(2) *Contemporary Pacific* 215

C Fink and B Smarzynska, 'Trademarks, Geographical Indications and Developing Countries', in B Hoekman et al (eds), *Development, Trade, and the WTO: A Handbook* (World Bank, 2002) 403

M Forsyth, *A Bird that Flies with Two Wings: Kastom and State Justice Systems in Vanuatu* (ANU ePress, 2009)

M Forsyth, 'Cargo Cults and Intellectual Property in the South Pacific' (2003) 14 *Australian Intellectual Property Journal* 193

M Foucault, 'What is an Author?' in J Harari (ed), *Textual Strategies: Perspectives in Post-Structuralist Criticism* (Cornell University Press, 1979) 141

S Frankel, 'The Mismatch of Geographical Indications and Innovative Traditional Knowledge' (2011) 29 *Prometheus* 253

S Frankel, 'Third-Party Trade Marks as a Violation of indigenous Cultural Property' (2005) 8 *Journal of World Intellectual Property* 83

S Frankel, 'Trademarks and Traditional Knowledge and Cultural Intellectual Property' in G B Dinwoodie and M D Janis (eds) *Trademark Law and Theory, A Handbook of Contemporary Research* (Edward Elgar, 2008) 433

S Frankel and M Richardson, 'Cultural Property and 'the Public Domain': Case Studies from New Zealand and Australia' in C Antons (ed), *Traditional Knowledge, Traditional Cultural Expressions and Intellectual Property Law in the Asia-Pacific Region* (Kluwer Law International, 2009) 275

P Freire, *Pedagogy of the Oppressed* (Herder and Herder, 1970)

D S Gangjee, 'Geographical Indications Protection for Handicrafts under TRIPS' (MPhil Thesis, University of Oxford, 2002)

Hassall and Associates Pty Ltd, *Value Chain Workshop Notes for Desert Knowledge CRC* (Report no. AU1-517, Desert Knowledge Cooperative Research Centre, Alice Springs May 2007)

C Geiger, D Gervias, N Olszak and V Ruzek, 'L'Arrangement de Lisbonne, un véhicule pour l'internationalisation du droit des indications géographiques?' (2010) 35 *Propriétés Intellectuelles* 691

C Geiger, D Gervais, N Olszak and V Ruzek, 'Towards a Flexible International Framework for the Protection of Geographical Indications' (2010) 1(2) *WIPO Journal* 147

H Geismar, 'Copyright in Context: Carvings, Carvers and Commodities in Vanuatu' (2005) 32(3) *American Ethnologist* 437

D Gervais, 'Of Clusters and Assumptions: Innovation as Part of a Full TRIPS Implementation' (2009) 77(5) *Fordham Law Review* 2353

D Gervias, 'The Misunderstood Potential of the Lisbon Agreement' (2010) 1(1) *WIPO Journal* 87

D Gervais, 'Reinventing Lisbon: The Case for a Protocol to the Lisbon Agreement' (2010) 11(1) *Chicago Journal of International Law* 67

D Gervais, 'Spiritual but Not Intellectual? The Protection of Sacred Intangible Traditional Knowledge' (2003) 11 *Cardozo Journal of International and Comparative Law* 467

D Gervais, *The TRIPS Agreement, Drafting History and Analysis* (Sweet & Maxwell, 2nd ed, 2003)

D Gervais, *The TRIPS Agreement: Drafting History and Analysis* (Sweet & Maxwell, 3rd ed, 2008)

D Gervais, 'Traditional Knowledge & Intellectual Property: A TRIPS-Compatible Approach' (2005) *Michigan State Law Review* 137

G A Getty, 'The Journey Between Western and Indigenous Research Paradigms' (2010) 2(1) *Journal of Transcultural Nursing* 5

F Gevers, 'Geographical Names and Signs Used as Trade Marks' (1990) 8 *European International Property Review* 285

S Ghosh, 'Globalization, Patents, and Traditional Knowledge' (2003-2004) 17(1) *Columbia Journal of Asian Law* 101

D Giovannucci, E Barham and R Pirog, 'Defining and Marketing 'Local' Foods: Geographical Indications for US Products' (2009) 12 *Journal of World Intellectual Property* 6

G Giraud, 'Range and Limit of Geographical Indication Scheme: The Case of Basmati Rice from Punjab, Pakistan' (2008) 11 *International Food and Agribusiness Management Rev* 1

D Goodman, 'Rural Europe Redux? Reflections on Alternative Agro-Food Networks and Paradigm Change' (2004) 44(1) *Sociologica Ruralis* 3

J Gorman, D Pearson and P Whitehead, 'Assisting Australian Indigenous Resource Management and Sustainable Utilization of Species Through the Use of GIs and Environmental Modelling Techniques' (2008) 86 *Journal of Environmental Management* 104

C B Graber, 'Aboriginal Self-Determination vs. the Propertisation of Traditional Culture: The Case of Sacred Wanjina Sites' (2009) 13(2) *Australian Indigenous Law Review* 27

C B Graber 'Institutionalization of Creativity in Traditional Societies and in International Trade Law' in S Ghosh and R Malloy (eds), *Creativity, Law and Entrepreneurship* (Edward Elgar, 2011) 234

C B Graber, 'State Aid for Digital Games and Cultural Diversity: A Critical Reflection in the Light of EU and WTO Law' in C B Graber and M Burri-Nenova (eds), *Governance of Digital Game Environments and Cultural Diversity. Transdisciplinary Perspectives* (Edward Elgar, 2010) 170

L W Green, M A George, M Daniel, C J Frankish, C Herbert, W Bowie and M O'Neill, *'Study of participatory research in health promotion: Review and recommendations for the development of participatory research in health promotion in Canada* (University of British Columbia, Royal Society of Canada, 1995)

C Greenhalgh and M Rogers, *Innovation, Intellectual Property, and Economic Growth* (Princeton University Press, 2010)

A Griffiths, 'Customary Law in a Transnational World: Legal Pluralism Revisited' in R A Benton (ed), *Conversing with the Ancestors: Concepts and Institutions in Polynesian Customary Law* (Te Matahauariki Institute, University of Waikato, 2006) 9

J Griffiths, 'What is Legal Pluralism?' (1986) 24 *Journal of Legal Pluralism* 1

M Guerin-McManus and K Nnadozie et al, 'Sharing financial benefits: trust funds for biodiversity prospecting' in S Laird (ed), *Biodiversity and Traditional Knowledge:EquitablePartnerships in Practice,* (Earthscan, 2002)

N Haley and R May *Conflict and Resource Development in the Southern Highlands of Papua New Guinea* (ANU ePress, 2007)

P A Hall and D Soskice (eds), *Varieties of Capitalism: The Institutional Foundations of Comparative Advantage* (Oxford University Press, 2001)

D Harry and L Kanehe, 'The BS in Access and Benefit Sharing (ABS): Critical Questions for Indigenous Peoples' in B Burrows (ed), *The Catch: Perspectives on Benefit Sharing* (Edmonds Institute, 2005)

G Hassall 'Conflict in the Pacific: Challenges for Governance' (2005) 20(1) *Pacific Economic Bulletin* 192

P J Heald, 'Rhetoric of Biopiracy' (2003) 11 *Cardozo Journal of International and Comparative Law* 519

M Heinrich and S Gibbons, 'Ethnopharmacology in Drug Discovery: An Analysis of its Role and Potential Contribution' (2001) 53 *Journal of Pharmacy and Pharmacology* 425

K Hennessy, 'A Ituvatuva Ni Vakadidike E Sawau: The Sawau project DVD' (2009) 25(1) *Visual Anthropology Review* 90

E C Henson et al (eds), *The State of the Native Nations: Conditions under U.S. Policies of Self-determination* (Oxford University Press, 2008)

J Hughes, 'Champagne, Feta, and Bourbon: The Spirited Debate about Geographical Indications' (2006) 58 *Hastings Law Journal* 299

A Hutchens, *Changing Big Business: The Globalisation of the Fair Trade Movement* (Edward Elgar, 2009)

A Jäger, 'Is traditional medicine better off 25 years later?' (2005) 100 *Journal of Ethnopharmacology* 3

T Janke, *Minding Culture: Case Studies on Intellectual Property and Traditional Cultural Expressions* (WIPO, 2003)

T Janke, *Our Culture Our Future*: *Report on Australian Indigenous Cultural and Intellectual Property Rights* (Michael Frankel and Company Solicitors, 1998)

T Janke and R Quiggin, 'Indigenous Cultural and Intellectual Property and Customary Law' (Background Paper 12, Law Reform Commission of Western Australia, 2005)

M Jolly, '*Kastom* as Commodity: The Land Dive as Indigenous Rite and Tourist Spectacle in Vanuatu' in L Lindstrom and G White (eds), *Culture, Kastom, Tradition: Developing Cultural Policy in Melanesia* (Institute of Pacific Studies, University of the South Pacific, 1994) 131

M Jolly, 'Material and Immaterial Relations: Gender, Rank and Christianity in Vanuatu' in L Dousset and S Tcherkezoff (eds), *The Scope of Anthropology* (Berghahn Books, 2012) 110

S Kadidal 'United States Patent Prior Art Rules and the Neem Controversy: A Case of Subject-Matter Imperialism' (1998) 7(1) *Biodiversity and Conservation* 29

L Kalinoe, 'Ascertaining the Nature of Indigenous Intellectual and Cultural Property and Traditional Knowledge & the Search for Legal Options in Regulating Access in Papua New Guinea' (2000) 27 *Melanesian Law Journal* 1

S Kamene and K Sykes, 'The Work of the Zia Trust: a holistic extended case study from the Waria River Valley, Morobe' in K Sykes (ed), *Culture and Cultural Property in the New Guinea Islands Region: Seven Case Studies* (UBSPD, 2001)

Sister K A Kanongata'a 'Autogen and Bio-Ethics in Tonga: An Ethical and Theological Reflection' in A Mead and S Ratuva (eds), *Pacific Genes and Life Patents* (2007) 166

M Kartal, 'Intellectual property protection in the natural product drug discovery, traditional herbal medicine and herbal medicinal products' (2007) 21 *Phytotherapy Research* 113

I Keen, *Aboriginal Economy and Society: Australia at the Threshold of Colonisation* (Oxford University Press, 2004)

I Keen, *Knowledge and Secrecy in an Aboriginal Religion* (Clarendon Press, 1994)

J Kelsey, *Big Brothers Behaving Badly: The Implications for the Pacific Islands of the Pacific Agreement on Closer Economic Relations* (Pacific Network on Globalisation, 2004)

S Kidd and M Kral, 'Practicing Participatory Action Research' (2005) 52(2) *Journal of Counseling Psychology* 187

S King, T Carlson and K Moran, 'Biological diversity, indigenous knowledge, drug discovery and intellectual property rights: creating reciprocity and maintaining relationships' (1996) 51 *Journal of Ethnopharmacology* 45

I Kireeva and B O'Connor, 'Geographical Indications and the TRIPS Agreement: What Protection Is Provided to Geographical Indications in WTO Members?' (2009) *Journal of World Intellectual Property* 12

M Koebele and G LaFortune, 'Agreement on Technical Barriers to Trade. Article 4 and Annex 3 TBT' in R Wolfrum et al (eds), *WTO – Technical Barriers and SPS Measures* (Martinus Nijhoff Publishers, 2007) 196

Kommerskollegium National Board of Trade, 'Eco-Labelling and the WTO: Issues for Further Analysis and Clarification' (Report No. 119-007-2002, Global Trade Division, Sweden, 2002)

P Kruk, 'The Role of Customary Law Under Sui Generis Frameworks of Intellectual Property Rights in Traditional and Indigenous Knowledge' (2007) 17 *Indiana International and Comparative Law Review* 67

A Kur and P Knaak, 'Protection of Traditional Names and Designations' in S von Lewinski (ed), *Indigenous Heritage and Intellectual Property: Genetic Resources, Traditional Knowledge, and Folklore* (Kluwer Law International, 2004) 221

P Lamy, 'Stepping Stones or Stumbling Blocks? The EU's Approach Towards the Problem of Multilateralism vs Regionalism in Trade Policy' (2002) 25(10) *The World Economy* 1399

M Langton, '"The Fire at the Centre of Each Family": Aboriginal Traditional Fire Regimes and the Challenges for Reproducing Ancient Fire Management in the Protected Areas of Northern Australia' (National Academics Forum: Proceedings of the 1999 Seminar, *Fire! The Australian Experience* 2000) 3

P Latz, *Bushfires and Bushtucker: Aboriginal plant use in Central Australia* (IAD Press, 2005)

M Leiboff, 'Law's Empiricism of the Object: How Law Recreates Cultural Objects in Its Own Image' (2007) 27 *The Australian Feminist Law Journal* 23

M Lemley and M McKenna, 'Irrelevant Confusion' (2010) 62 *Stanford Law Review* 413

L G Liddy et al, *Wagiman Plants and Animals: Aboriginal Knowledge of Flora and Fauna from the Mid Daly River Area, Northern Australia* (Department of Natural Resources, Environment and the Arts, NT Government and the Diwurruwurru-jaru Aboriginal Corporation, 2006)

L Lindstrom, 'Big Men as Ancestors' (1990) 29 (4) *Ethnology* 313

L Lindstrom, 'Kava Pirates in Vanuatu?' (2009) 16 *International Journal of Cultural Property* 291

C Z Liu, S J Murch, M E L Demerdash and P K Saxena, 'Regeneration of the Egyptian Medicinal Plant Artemisia judaica L' (2003) 21(6) *Plant Cell Reports* 525

Q Liu et al, 'Bactericidal and cyclooxygenase inhibitory diterpenes from Eremophila sturtii' (2006) 67(12) *Phytochemistry* 1256

G Long, 'Plagium', in W Smith, *A Dictionary of Greek and Roman Antiquities* (John Murray, 1875)

J T McCarthy, *McCarthy on Trademarks and Unfair Competition* (4th ed, Clark Boardman Callaghan, 2002)

J McGown, *Out of Africa: Mysteries of Access and Benefit Sharing* (Edmonds Institute, Washington, and African Centre for Biosafety, 2006)

J McIntyre, 'Yeperenye Dreaming in Conceptual, Geographical and Cyberspace: A participatory action research approach to address local governance within an Australian Indigenous housing association' (2003) 16(5) *Systemic Practice and Action Research* 309

D McKnight, *People, Countries, and the Rainbow Serpent* (Oxford University Press, 1999)

M J McLeod et al, 'Early Evolution of Chili Peppers (Capsicum)' (1982) 36 *Economic Botany* 361

A H MacLennan, S P Myers and A W Taylor, 'The continuing use of complementary and alternative medicine in South Australia: costs and beliefs in 2004' (2006) 184(1) *Medical Journal of Australia* 27

L Malezer, C Charters and V Tauli-Corpuz (eds), *Indigenous Voices: The UN Declaration on the Rights of Indigenous Peoples* (Hart Publishing, forthcoming)

T Mandeville, *Understanding Novelty: Information, Technological Change, and the Patent System* (Ablex Publishing Corporation, 1996)

E Mansfield, 'Intellectual Property Protection, Foreign Direct Investment, and Technology Transfer' (Discussion Paper 19, International Finance Corporation, The World Bank, 1994)

D Marinova and M Raven, 'Indigenous knowledge and intellectual property: a sustainability agenda' (2006) 20 *Journal of Economic Surveys* 587

C Martinez and D Guellec, 'Overview of Recent Changes and Comparison of Patent Regimes in the United States, Japan and Europe' in OECD, *Patents, Innovation and Economic Performance: OECD Conference Proceedings* (OECD, 2004) 127

D Menival, 'The Greatest French AOCs: A Signal of Quality for the Best Wines' (Working paper 1, 2007)

G Miers, 'Cultivation and sustainable wild harvest of bushfoods by Aboriginal communities in central Australia' (Research Report No W03/124, Rural Industries Research & Development Corporation, Canberra, 2004)

G V Mohatt, K L Hazel, J Allen and M Stachelrodt, 'Unheard Alaska: Culturally anchored participatory action research on sobriety with Alaska Natives' (2004) 33(3-4) *American Journal of Community Psychology* 263

J Mokyr, *The Gifts of Athena: Historical Origins of the Knowledge Economy* (Princeton University Press, 2002)

P R Mooney, 'Why We Call It Biopiracy' in H Svarstad and S Dhillion (eds), *Bioprospecting: From Biodiversity in the South to Medicines in the North* (Spartacus Forlag, 2000) 37

H Morphy, *Ancestral Connections: Art and an Aboriginal System of Knowledge* (The University of Chicago Press, 1991)

R Muñoz, 'Agreement on Technical Barriers to Trade: Article 8 TBT' (2007) in R Wolfrum et al (eds), *WTO – Technical Barriers and SPS Measures* (Martinus Nijhoff Publishers, 2007) 300

National Health and Medical Research Council and Australian Vice Chancellors' Committee, 'Joint NHMRC/AVCC Statement and Guidelines on Research Practice' (Australian Government, Canberra, 1997)

National Health and Medical Research Council, 'Values and Ethics: Guidelines for Ethical Conduct in Aboriginal and Torres Strait Islander Health Research' (Commonwealth of Australia, Canberra, 2003)

R R Nelson, 'National Innovation Systems: A Retrospective on a Study' (1992) 1 *Industrial and Corporate Change* 347

N W Netanel (ed), *The Development Agenda. Global Intellectual Property and Developing Countries* (Oxford University Press, 2009)

R Niezan, 'Recognizing Indigenism: Canadian Unity and the International Movement of Indigenous Peoples' (2000) 42 *Comparative Studies in Society and History* 119

P Ørebech et al (eds) *The Role of Customary Law in Sustainable Development* (Cambridge University Press, 2005)

F Paisley, 'Australian Aboriginal Activism in Interwar Britain and Europe: Anthony Martin Fernando' (2009) 7 *History Compass* 701

L Palombi, *Gene Cartels: Biotech Patents in the Age of Free Trade* (Edward Elgar, 2009)

E A Palombo and S J Semple, 'Antibacterial Activity of Traditional Australian Medicinal Plants' (2001) 77(2-3) *Journal of Ethnopharmacology* 151

M Panizzon, *Traditional Knowledge and Geographical Indications: Foundations, Interests and Negotiating Positions*, (Working Paper No. 2005/01, 2006) 151

R K Paterson and D S Karjala, 'Looking Beyond Intellectual Property in Resolving Protection of the Intangible Cultural Heritage of Indigenous Peoples' (2003) 11 *Cardozo Journal of International and Comparative Law* 633

M Penjueli and W Morgan, 'Putting Development First: Concerns about a Pacific Free Trade Agreement' (2010) 25(1) *Pacific Economic Bulletin* 211

M Pennacchio and A Kemp et al, 'Interesting Biological Activities from Plants Traditionally used by Native Australians' (2005) 96 *Journal of Ethnopharmacology* 597

M Pennacchio and Y Syah, 'Cardioactive iridoid glycosides from Eremophila species' (1997) 4 *Phytomedicine* 325

G A Persoon, '"Being Indigenous" in Indonesia and the Philippines' in C Antons (ed), *Traditional Knowledge, Traditional Cultural Expressions and Intellectual Property Law in the Asia-Pacific Region* (Kluwer Law International, 2009) 195

G Phillips, *Addictions and Healing in Aboriginal Country* (Aboriginal Studies Press, 2003)

G Pigliasco, 'Intangible Cultural Property, Tangible Databases, Visible Debates: The Sawau Project' (2009) 16 *International Journal of Cultural Property* 255

B Pickersgill, 'Relationships Between Weedy and Cultivated Forms in Some Species of Chili Peppers (Genus Capsicum)' (1971) 25 *Evolution* 683

G Pigliasco, 'Visual Anthropology and Jurisprudence: The Sawau Project' (2007) *Anthropology News* 65

B Pink and P Allbon, *The Health and Welfare of Australia's Aboriginal and Torres Strait Islander Peoples 2008* (Australian Bureau of Statistics, Australian Institute of Health and Welfare, 2008)

M Polanyi, *Personal Knowledge: Towards a Post-Critical Philosophy* (Routledge and Kegan Paul, 1958)

J G Ponterotto, 'Qualitative Research in Counseling Psychology: A Primer on Research Paradigms and Philosophy of Science' (2005) 52(2) *Journal of Counseling Psychology* 126

P Poretti, 'Waiting for Godot: Subsidy Disciplines in Services Trade' in M Panizzon, N Pohl and P Sauvé (eds), *GATS and the Regulation of International Trade in Services* (Cambridge University Press, 2008) 466

D Posey, 'Commodification of the Sacred Through Intellectual Property Rights' (2002) 83 (1-2) *Journal of Ethnophramacology* 3

D Posey and G Dutfield, *Beyond Intellectual Property* (International Development Research Centre, 1996)

W Pretorius, 'TRIPS and Developing Countries: How Level Is the Playing Field?' in P Drahos and R Mayne (eds), *Global Intellectual Property Rights: Knowledge, Access and Development* (Palgrave Macmillan/Oxfam, 2002) 183

C D Quillen and O H Webster, 'Continuing Patent Applications and Performance of the United States Patent Office' (2001) 11(1) *Federal Circuit Bar Journal* 1

M Rai, 'Genetic Diversity in Rice Production: Past Contribution and the Potential of Utilization for Sustainable Rice Production' in D Van Tran et al (ed), *Sustainable Rice Production for Food Security: Proceedings of the 20th Session of the International Rice Commission, Bangkok, Thailand, 23-26 July 2002* (FAO, 2003) 89

D Rangnekar, 'Geographical Indications and Localisation: A Case Study of Feni' (Research Report, Economic and Social Research Council, The University of Warwick, 2009)

D Rangnekar, 'The Challenge of Intellectual Property Rights and Social Justice' (2011) 54 *Development* 212

Raukawa and the Raukawa Settlement Trust and the Sovereign in right of New Zealand 'Deed in Relation to a Co-Management Framework for the Waikato River' (17 December 2009)

P Reason, 'Human inquiry as discipline and practice' in P Reason (ed), *Participation in human inquiry* (Sage, 1994) 40

P Reason, 'Sitting Between Appreciation and Disappointment: A Critique of the Special Edition of *Human Relations* on action research' (1993) 46(10) *Human Relations* 1253

P Reason and H Bradbury, 'Inquiry and Participation in Search of a World Worthy of Human Aspiration' in P Reason and H Bradbury (eds), *Handbook of Action Research* (Sage, 2001) 1

R Regenvanu, 'The Traditional Economy as the Source of Resilience in Melanesia' (Paper presented at the Lowy Institute Conference 'The Pacific Islands and the World: The Global Economic Crisis', 2009)

N Resinek, 'Geographical Indications and Trade Marks: Coexistence or 'First in Time, First in Right' Principle' (2007) 29 *European Intellectual Property Review* 446

M Riley, *Māori Healing and Herbal* (Viking SevenSeas NZ, 1994)

M Rimmer, 'Australian Icons: Authenticity and Identity Politics' (2004) 3 *Indigenous Law Journal* 139

L Rivier and J Bruhn, 'Editorial' (1979) 1 *Journal of Ethnopharmacology* 1

D Robinson and J Kuanpoth, 'The Traditional Medicines Predicament: A Case Study of Thailand' (2009) 11(5-6) *Journal of World Intellectual Property* 375

D F Robinson, *Confronting Biopiracy: Challenges, Cases and International Debates* (Earthscan, 2010)

K Rogers and I Grice et al, 'Inhibition of platelet aggregation and 5-HT release by extracts of Australian plants used traditionally as headache treatments' (2000) 9 *European Journal ofPharmaceutical Sciences* 355

B Rose, 'No More Whining about Geographical Indications: Assessing the 2005 Agreement between the United States and the European Community on the Trade in Wine' (2007) 29 *Houston Journal of International Law* 731

D Rose, *Nourishing terrains. Australian Aboriginal Views of Landscape and Wilderness* (Australian Heritage Commission, 1996)

J Rostkowski, 'The Redman's Appeal for Justice: Deskaheh and the League of Nations' in C F Feest (ed), *Indians and Europe: An Interdisciplinary Collection of Essays* (University of Nebraska Press, 1989) 435

J Russell-Smith et al, 'Challenges and Opportunities for Fire Management in Fire-Prone Northern Australia' in J Russell-Smith, P Whitehead and P Cooke (eds), *Culture, Ecology and Economy of Fire Management in North Australian Savannas: Rekindling The Wurrk Tradition* (CSIRO Publishing, 2009) 1

J Russell-Smith et al, 'Contemporary Fire Regimes of Northern Australia, 1997-2001: Change Since Aboriginal Occupancy, Challenges for Sustainable Management' (2003) 12 *International Journal of Wildland Fire* 283

M Ryder, et al, 'Sustainable bush produce systems: Progress Report 2004–2006' (Working Paper No 31, Desert Knowledge Cooperative Research Centre, Alice Springs, 2009)

D Sanders, *The Formation of the World Council of Indigenous Peoples* (Fourth World Documentation Project, Center for World Indigenous Studies, 1980)

J Sanderson, 'Intellectual Property and Plants: Constitutive, Contingent and Complex' in K Bowrey, M Handler, and D Nicol (eds), *Emerging Challenges in Intellectual Property* (Oxford University Press, 2011)

P Sauvé, 'Completing the GATS Framework: Addressing Uruguay Round Leftovers' (2002) 57(3) *Aussenwirtschaft* 301

S Scotchmer, *Innovation and Incentives* (MIT Press, 2004)

S Scotchmer, 'Standing on the Shoulders of Giants: Cumulative Research and the Patent Law' (1991) 5 *Journal of Economic Perspectives* 29

S K Sell, *Power and Ideas: North-South Politics of Intellectual Property and Antitrust* (State University of New York, 1998)

S J Semple, G D Reynolds et al, 'Screening of Australian medicinal plants for antiviral activity' (1998) 60(2) *Journal of Ethnopharmacology* 163

K Serrano and M Stefanova, 'Between International Law, Kastom and Sustainable Development: Cultural heritage in Vanuatu' in D Niles and G Baldaccino (eds), *Futurability of Islands* (Springer, 2011) 19

K A Seton and J J Bradley '"When you have no law you are nothing": Cane toads, social consequences and management issue' (2004) 5(3) *The Asia Pacific Journal of Anthropology* 205

P Shand, 'Scenes from the Colonial Catwalk: Cultural Appropriation, Intellectual Property Rights, and Fashion' (2002) 3 *Cultural Analysis* 74

V Shiva, *Protect or Plunder: Understanding Intellectual Property Rights* (Zed Books, 2001)

P Sillitoe, 'The Development of Indigenous Knowledge: A New Applied Anthropology' (1998) 39 *Current Anthropology* 223

P Sillitoe, 'Trust in Development: Some Implications of Knowing in Indigenous Knowledge' (2010) 16 *Journal of the Royal Anthropological Institute* 12

A Simpson, C James and M Grow, 'The Relationship between Trademarks and Geographical Indications' (United States Group Report Q191/AIPPI Report 11, 2006)

V P Singh, 'The Basmati Rice of India' in R K Singh, U S Singh and G S Khush (eds) *Aromatic Rices* (Oxford and IBH Publishing, 2000) 135

B Smith, '"We got our own management": local knowledge, government and development in Cape York Peninsula' (2005) 2 *Australian Aboriginal Studies* 4

B Smith and D Claudie, 'Developing a land and resource management framework for Kaanju homelands, Central Cape York Peninsula' (Discussion Paper 256, Canberra, Centre for Aboriginal Economic Policy Research, The Australian National University, 2003)

J E Smith and D Tucker, et al 'Identification of antibacterial constituents from the indigenous Australian medicinal plant Eremophila duttonii F. Muell. (Myoporaceae)' (2007) 112(2) *Journal of Ethnopharmacology* 386

L T Smith, *Decolonizing Methodologies: Research and Indigenous Peoples* (Zed Books Ltd, 1999)

M Smith, 'Population-Based Genetic Studies: Informed Consent and Confidentiality' (2001-2002) 18 *Santa Clara Computer & High Technology Law Journal* 57

D D Soejarto and C Gyllenhaal et al, 'The UIC ICBG (University of Illinois at Chicago International Cooperative Biodiversity Group) Memorandum of Agreement: A Model of Benefit-Sharing Arrangement in Natural Products Drug Discovery and Development' (2004) 67 *Journal of Natural Products* 294

M Solomon, 'Strengthening Traditional Knowledge Systems and Customary Laws' in S Twarog and P Kapoor (eds), *Protecting and Promoting Traditional Knowledge: Systems, National Experiences and International Dimensions* (United Nations, 2004)

M Spencer and J Hardie, *Indigenous Fair Trade in Australia. Scoping Study*, (Australian Government Rural Industries Research and Development Corporation, 2010)

M Spencer and J Hardie, *Indigenous Fair Trade in Australia: Scoping Study* (Rural Industries Research and Development Corporation, Publication No 10/172, 2011)

W E H Stanner, *White Man Got No Dreaming 1938-1973* (Australian National University Press, 1979)

J Stein, 'The Legal Status of Eco-Labels and Product and Process Methods in the World Trade Organization' (2008) 1(4) *American Journal of Economics and Business Administration* 287

M Strathern, 'Multiple Perspectives on Intellectual Property' in K Whimp and M Busse (eds), *Protection of Intellectual, Biological and Cultural Property in Papua New Guinea* (Asia Pacific Press, 2000) 47

T Swain, *A Place for Strangers: Towards a History of Australian Aboriginal Being* (Cambridge University Press, 1993)

T Swanson and S Johnston, *Global Environmental Problems and International Environmental Agreements: The Economics of International Institution Building* (Edward Elgar, 1999)

K Swiderska, 'Banishing the Biopirates: A New Approach to Protecting Traditional Knowledge' (2006) 129 *International Institute for Development Gatekeeper Series* 16

A Tan and D Sze, 'Indigenous herbs and cancer' (2008) 7(1) *Journal of Complementary Medicine* 48

A Taubman, 'Saving the Village: Conserving Jurisprudential Diversity in the International Protection of Traditional Knowledge' in K E Maskus and J H Reichman (eds), *International Public Goods and Transfer of Technology Under a Globalized Intellectual Property Regime* (Cambridge University Press, 2005) 521

A Taubman, 'Thinking Locally, Acting Globally: How Trade Negotiations over Geographical Indications Improvise "Fair Trade" Rules' (2008) *Intellectual Property Quarterly* 3

A Taubman and M Leistner (2008) 'Analysis of Different Areas of Indigenous Resources, Traditional Knowledge' in S von Lewinski (ed), *Indigenous Heritage and Intellectual Property: Genetic Resources, Traditional Knowledge and Folklore* (2nd ed, Kluwer Law International, 2008) 127

J Taylor et al, 'The Station Community Mental Health Centre Inc; nurturing and empowering' (2010) 10 *Rural and Remote Health* 1411

S Thomas, 'Euphoria in the Pacific? Regional Economic Partnership Agreements – Implications for the Pacific' (Paper presented at the New Zealand Asia Pacific European Studies Association Conference, 'Outside Looking In', Christchurch, 9-11 September 2004)

M Torsen and J Anderson, *Intellectual Property and the Safeguarding of Traditional Cultures, Legal Issues and Practical Options for Museums, Libraries and Archives* (WIPO, 2010)

D Tryon and V K Senta (eds), *Woksop Blongol FilwokaPles blong ol pig long kastom laef long Vanuatu: buk 1* [Customary pig pens in Vanuatu: Book 1, Vanuatu Cultural Centre's Fieldworkers Workshop] (Vanuatu KaljoralSenta, 1990)

N and K Tsey et al, 'Indigenous Men Taking Their Rightful Place in Society? A preliminary analysis of a participatory action research process with Yarrabah Men's Health Group' (2002) 10(6) *Australian Journal of Rural Health* 278

E Tuck, 'Re-visioning Action: Participatory action research and Indigenous theories of change' (2009) 41 *Urban Review* 47

UKIPR Commission, *Integrating Intellectual Property Rights and Development Policy* (UKIPR, 2002)

UNCTAD – ICTSD, *'Resource Book on TRIPS and Development'* (Cambridge University Press, 2005)

W van Caenegem, *Intellectual Property Law and Innovation* (Cambridge University Press, 2007)

W van Caenegem, 'Pervasive Incentives, Disparate Innovation and Intellectual Property Law' in C Arup and W Van Caenegem (eds), *Intellectual Property Policy Reform: Fostering Innovation and Development* (Edward Elgar, 2009) 250

W van Caenegem, 'Registered Geographical Indications: Between Intellectual Property and Rural Policy – Part I' (2003) 6 *Journal of World Intellectual Property* 699

P van de Kop et al (eds), *Origin-Based Products: Lessons for Pro-Poor Market Development* (Royal Tropical Institute and French Research Centre for International Development, 2006)

G C J J Van Den Bergh, 'The Concept of Folk Law in Historical Context: A Brief Outline', in A D Renteln and A Dundes (eds), *Folk Law: Essays in the Theory and Practice of Lex Non Scripta* (University of Wisconsin Press, 1994)

P Van den Bossche, *The Law and Policy of the World Trade Organization*, (Cambridge University Press, 2nd ed, 2008)

H Verran, 'A Postcolonial Moment in Science Studies: Alternative Firing Regimes of Environmental Scientists and Aboriginal Landowners' (2002) 32(5-6) *Social Studies of Science* 729

C Visser, 'Culture, Traditional Knowledge, and Trademarks: A View from the South' in G B Dinwoodie and M D Janis (eds), *Trademark Law and Theory, A Handbook of Contemporary Research* (Edward Elgar, 2008) 468

S von Lewinski, 'An analysis of WIPO's latest proposal and the Model law 2002 of the Pacific Community for the Protection of Traditional Cultural Expressions' in C Antons (ed), *Traditional Knowledge, Traditional Cultural Expressions and Intellectual Property Law in the Asia-Pacific Region* (Kluwer Law International, 2009) 109

Waitangi Tribunal Report, *Ko Aotearoa Tēnei: A Report into Claims Concerning New Zealand Law and Policy Affecting Māori Culture and Identity* (2011)

B Wallerstein and B Duran, 'Using Community-based Participatory Research to Address Health Disparities' (2006) 7 *Health Promotion Practice* 312

N Watson, 'Implications of land rights reform for Indigenous health' (2007) 186 *Medical Journal of Australia* 534

K Whimp and M Busse (eds), *Protection of Intellectual, Biological and Cultural Property in Papua New Guinea* (Oceania Publication, 2002)

W F Whyte, *Participatory Action Research* (Sage Publications Inc, 1991)

P Wilner, 'The Madrid Protocol: A Voluntary Model for the Internationalization of Trademark Law' (2003) 13 *DePaul University Journal of Art and Entertainment Law* 17

WIPO, *Intellectual Property Handbook: Policy, Law and Use* (WIPO Publication 489, 2004)

L Wiseman, 'Regulating Authenticity' (2000) 9(2) *Griffith Law Review* 252

L Wiseman, 'The Protection of Indigenous Art and Culture in Australia: The Labels of Authenticity' (2001) 23(1) *European Intellectual Property Review* 14

R Wolfrum et al (eds), *WTO – Technical Barriers and SPS Measures* (Martinus Nijhoff Publishers, 2007)

D Yibarbuk et al, 'Fire Ecology and Aboriginal Land Management in Central Arnhem Land, Northern Australia: A Tradition of Ecosystem Management' (2001) 28 *Journal of Biogeography* 325

D Zografos, 'Geographical Indications & Socio-Economic Development' (Working Paper No 3, Iqsensato, 2008)

D Zografos, *Intellectual Property and Traditional Cultural Expressions* (Edward Elgar, 2010)

# Internet sources

18th Melanesian Spearhead Group Leaders' Summit, 'Communiqué' (2011) <http://www.msgsec.info/>

35th Cairns Group Ministerial Meeting, Punta del Este, Uruguay, *Communiqué* (2010) <http://www.cairnsgroup.org/Pages/100420_communique. aspx?noredirect=1>

A Bill for an Act to establish a *sui generis* system for the protection and promotion of Traditional Knowledge and Expressions of Culture for the people of the Republic of Palau (2005) s 16 <http://www.palauoek.net/senate/legislation/ sb/sb_7-3.pdf>

Alaska State Council on the Arts, *Silver Hand Program and Permit Application* <http://www.eed.state.ak.us/aksca/Forms/individuals/SH.pdf>

Arts Law Centre of Australia, *Certificates of Authenticity* (2004) <http://www.artslaw.com.au/images/uploads/AITB_CertificatesOfAuthenticity.pdf>

Australian Government Department of the Environment Water Heritage and the Arts, *Kaanju Ngaachi Wenlock and Pascoe Rivers Indigenous Protected Area* (2008) <http://www.environment.gov.au/indigenous/ipa/declared/kaanju.html>

Australian Government Department of Foreign Affairs and Trade, *Pacific Island Forum* <http://www.dfat.gov.au/geo/spacific/regional_orgs/spf.html>

Cairns Group, *Agricultural Trade and the Cairns Group* <http://cairnsgroup.org>

Chuulangun Aboriginal Corporation website <www.kaanjungaachi.com.au>

Commonwealth, *Parliamentary Debates: United Nations Declaration on the Rights of Indigenous Peoples* (2007) Senate (Speech by Sen Marise Payne) <http://parlinfo.aph.gov.au/parlInfo/genpdf/chamber/hansards/2007-09-10/0075/hansard_frag.pdf fileType=application%2Fpdf>

Creative New Zealand, *Statement on toi ihoTM*(2001) <http://www.creativenz.govt.nz/en/news/creative-new-zealand-statement-on-toi-iho>

Department of Sustainability and Environment, *Landscape Mosaic Burns: Land and Fire Management Information Sheet* (2010) <http://www.land.vic.gov.au/CA256F310024B628/0/58AF2C45BEF36828CA257749000BE0D2/$File/landscape+mosaic+burning_factsheet_JUN10.pdf>

Desert Knowledge CRC, *Legacy Website* <www.desertknowledgecrc.com.au>

European Commission, *Negotiations and Agreements* (2012) <http://ec.europa.eu/trade/wider-agenda/development/economic-partnerships/negotiations-and-agreements/#pacific/>

European Commission, *Trade, Africa, Carribean, Pacific* <http://ec.europa.eu/trade/creating-opportunities/bilateral-relations/regions/africa-caribbean-pacific/>

FLO, *About the Mark* (2011) <www.fairtrade.net>

FLO, *Aims of Fairtrade Standards* (2011) <www.fairtrade.net>

FLO, *Benefits of Fairtrade* (2011) <www.fairtrade.net>

FLO, *Certifying Fairtrade* (2011) <www.fairtrade.net>

FLO, *Facts and Figures* (2011) <www.fairtrade.net>

FLO, *Fair Trade at a Glance* (2010) <http://www.fairtrade.com.au/files/FTF10/Glance.pdf>

FLO, *Fairtrade is Unique* (2009) <http://www.fairtrade.net/fileadmin/user_upload/content/2009/resources/Fairtrade_is_Unique.pdf> 2

FLO, *Frequently Asked Questions* (2011) <www.fairtrade.net>

FLO, *Geographical Scope of Producer Certification for Fairtrade Labelling* (2009) <http://www.fairtrade.net/uploads/media/Aug09_Geographical_scope.pdf>

FLO, *Growing Stronger Together. Annual Report 2009-10* (2010) <http://www.fairtrade.net/fileadmin/user_upload/content/2009/resources/FLO_Annual-Report-2009_komplett_double_web.pdf> 24-25

FLO, *History of Fairtrade* (2011) <www.fairtrade.net>

FLO, *Making the Difference: The Global Strategy for Fairtrade* (2009) <http://www.fairtrade.se/obj/docpart/c/c6ad566a479f10986c87188d237057d1.pdf>

FLO, *Products* (2011) <http://www.fairtrade.net/products.html>

FLO, *Standards for Small-scale Producer* (2011) < www.fairtrade.net>

FLO, *Using the FAIRTRADE MARK* (2011) <www.fairtrade.net>

FLO, *What is Fairtrade* (2011) <www.fairtrade.net>

FLO, *Why Fairtrade is Unique* (2011) <www.fairtrade.net>

FLO-CERT, *Certification for Development* (2010) <www. flo-cert.net>

Grupo de Investigación sobre, 'Politicas Públicas de Propriedad Intelectual' (Universidad de Los Andes, Mérida, Venezuela) <http://www.cjp.ula.ve/gpi/documentos/fieb_content_def1.pdf>

K Hoyumpa and L Schmiere, *Europe lifts kava ban and south Pacific hopeful for resumed kava trade* (2009) <http://www.nakamalathome.com/blog/europe-lifts-kava-ban-and-south-pacific-hopeful-for-resumed-kava-trade.html>

J Kelsey, 'Acceding Countries as Pawns in a Power Play: A Case Study of the Pacific Islands' (2007) <http://uriohau.blogspot.com/2007/08/acceding-countries-as-pawns-in-power.html>

INTA, *Resolution on Protection of GIs and Trademarks* (24 September 1997) <www.inta.org>

Intellectual Property Office of New Zealand, *Practice Guidelines 16 – Māori Advisory Committee & Māori Trade Marks* (2012) <http://www.iponz.govt.nz/cms/trade-marks/practice-guidelines-index/practice-guidelines/16-maori-advisory-committee-maori-trade-marks>

International Institute for the Environment and Development, *Protecting Community Rights over Traditional Knowledge Project* (2005-2009) <http://www.iied.org/natural-resources/key-issues/biodiversity-and-conservation/protecting-community-rights-over-tradition>

Melanesian Spearhead Group, *MSG Framework Treaty on Traditional Knowledge and Expressions of Culture* (2012) <http://www.msgsec.info/index.php?option=com_content&view=article&id=103:msg-framework-treaty-on-traditional-knowledge-and-expressions-of-culture&catid=39:msg-culture&Itemid=162>

*Model Law on Traditional Biological Knowledge, Innovations and Practices* <http://www.sprep.org/legal/documents/MLv11.doc4Apr_000.pdf>

Neue Zürcher Zeitung *Fair Trade hält auch in der Reisebranche Einzug* (2010) <http://epaper.nzz.ch/nzz/forms/page.html>

New Zealand's National Business Review, *Māori Tobacco Branding Lights up Furore* (2005) <http://www.nbr.co.nz/article/maori-tobacco-branding-lights-furore-updated>

NIAAA, *Policy and Objectives* (2011) <http://www.culture.com.au/exhibition/niaaa/about.htm>

Northern Territory Government, *Central Australian Human Research Ethics Committee, Policy and Procedures Manual* <http://www.health.nt.gov.au/library/scripts/objectifyMedia.aspx?file=pdf/12/26.pdf&siteID=1&str_title=CA HREC Policies and Procedures.pdf>

Office of Treaty Settlement, *Involving Iwi in Natural Resource Management through Historical Treaty of Waitangi Settlements* (2010) <http://www.lgnz.co.nz/library/files/store_024/Cabinet_decisions_treaty_settlements_and_local_government_october_2010.pdf>

Pacific Islands Forum Secretariat, *Traditional Knowledge Implementation Action Plan* (2009) <http://www.forumsec.org.fj/resources/uploads/attachments/documents/Traditional%20Knowledge%20Action%20Plan%202009.pdf>

M Qereqeretabua, 'The Safeguarding of Intangible Cultural Heritage in Fiji' (Paper presented at the International Seminar on the Safeguarding of

Intangible Cultural Heritage: Current Situations and Challenges on the Safeguarding measures in the Asia-Pacific Region, 14 January 2010) 3 <http://www.tobunken.go.jp/~geino/e/ISSICH/IS2010.html>

Senator L Rhiannon, *Adjournment Speech: Pacific trade negotiations* (2011) <http://lee-rhiannon.greensmps.org.au/content/parliament/speech/lees-speech-on-pacific-trade-negotiations>

D F Robinson and E Defrenne, *Argan: A Case Study on ABS?* (2011) <http://www.ethicalbiotrade.org/dl/UEBT_D_ROBINSON_AND_E_DEFRENNE_final.pdf>

Small Grants Programme, 'Replacement of Chemical fertilizer and pesticide by organic farming for sustainable production of vegetable crops' (IND/SGP/OP4/Y2/RAF/2009/34/BHR 05) <http://sgp.undp.org/web/projects/14100/replacement_of_chemical_fertilizer_and_pesticide_by_organic_farming_for_sustainable_production_of_ve.html>

Alex Steenstra, *The Waikato River Settlement and Natural Resource Management in New Zealand* (2008) <http://www.nzares.org.nz/pdf/The%20Waikato%20River%20Settlement.pdf>

Dionysia Tabureguci, *The Pacific's Stolen Identity: How Intellectual Property Rights have Failed Pacific Cultures* (2007) <http://www.islandsbusiness.com/islands_business/index_dynamic/containerNameToReplace=MiddleMiddle/focusModuleID=18144/overideSkinName=issueArticle-full.tpl>

*The complete Feb 10, 2011 text of the US proposal for the TPP IPR chapter* <http://keionline.org/node/1091>

*Trans-Pacific Strategic Economic Partnership Agreement* <http://www.mfat.govt.nz/downloads/trade-agreement/transpacific/main-agreement.pdf>

UN *Development Programme—What are the Millennium Development Goals?* (2011) < http://www.undp.org/mdg/basics.shtml>

UNDP *Consultation on Indigenous Peoples' Knowledge and Intellectual Property Rights* appendix 11 <http://www.idrc.ca/cp/ev-30152-201-1-DO_TOPIC.html>

US Green Building Council, *What LEED Is* (2012) <http://www.usgbc.org/DisplayPage.aspx?CMSPageID=1988>

F Walsh and J Douglas, *Angka Akatyerr akert: A desert raisin report* (Desert Knowledge Cooperative Research Centre, Alice Springs, Australia, 2009) <http://www.desertknowledgecrc.com.au/researchimpact/downloads/DKCRC_Angk-Akatyerr-akert_A-Desert-raisin-report.pdf>

WTO, *Agricultural Negotiations: Geographical Indications* <http://www.wto. org/english/tratop_e/agric_e/negs_bkgrnd21_ph2geog_e.htm>

WTO, *Environment: Issues Labelling* (2011) <http://www.wto.org/english/ tratop_e/envir_e/labelling_e.htm>

WTO, *Harnessing Agriculture for Development through Trade* (2011) <http:// www.wto.org/english/news_e/sppl_e/sppl188_e.htm>

WIPO, *Intergovernmental Committee* <http://www.wipo.int/tk/en/igc/index. html>

WIPO, *Lisbon Bulletin No 37* <http://www.wipo.int/lisbon/en/bulletin/archive. html>

WIPO, *Lisbon Express Database* < http://www.wipo.int/ipdl/en/lisbon/>

WIPO, *Members of the Madrid Union* <http://www.wipo.int/madrid/en/ members/>

WIPO, *Report on Fact-finding Missions on Intellectual Property and Traditional Knowledge* (1998-1999) <www.wipo.int/tk/en/tk/ffm/report/final/Cached, 9 March 2012>

WIPO, *Search Appellations of Origin (Lisbon Express)* <http://www.wipo.int/ ipdl/en/search/lisbon/search-struct.jsp>

WIPO IGC Secretariat, *Decisions of the Seventeenth Session of the IGC* (2010) <http://www.wipo.int/meetings/en/details.jsp?meeting_id=20207>

# Newspaper Articles

R Callick, 'Fiji Casts Shadow on Pacific Forum', *The Australian* (online), 5 September 2011 <http://www.theaustralian.com.au/news/features/fiji-casts-shadow-on-pacific-forum/story-e6frg6z6-1226129262121>

J H Dobrzynski, 'Honoring Art, Honoring Artists', *New York Times* (New York), 6 February 2011 <http://query.nytimes.com/gst/fullpage.html?res=9C06E4 DF1E39F935A35751C0A9679D8B63&pagewanted=all>

D Downie, 'Let Them Eat Big Macs', *Salon* (online), 7 July 2000, <http://www. salon.com/business/feature/2000/07/06/frenchfood/index.htm>

'Experts Hail Australia's Backing of UN Declaration of Indigenous People's Rights', *UN News Center* (online), 3 April 2009 <http://www.un.org/apps/ news/story.asp?NewsID=30382>

D Flitton, 'Pacific Islands Accuse Australia's Aid Agency of Coercion', *The Age* (online), 29 August 2011 <http://www.theage.com.au/national/pacific-islands-accuse-australias-aid-agency-of-coercion-20110828-1jgnv.html>

International Society for Ethnopharmacology, 'Editorial' (2006) 6(1) *ISE Newsletter* 1

D Jopson, 'Aboriginal Seal of Approval Loses its Seal of Approval', *Sydney Morning Herald* (online), 14 December 2002 <http://www.smh.com.au/articles/2002/12/13/1039656221205.html>

New Zealand Government, 'Press Release: Māori Party's Head in the Clouds' (Press Release, 14 September 2007) <http://www.scoop.co.nz/stories/PA0709/S00272.htm>

'New Zealand Indigenous Rights Stance "Shameful" — Māori Party', *Stuff* (online), 14 September 2007 <http://www.stuff.co.nz/archived-stuff-sections/archived-national-sections/korero/45362>

A Osborn, 'Māoris Win Lego Battle', *Guardian Unlimited*, 31 October 2001

Pacific Islands Forum Secretariat 'TK Implementation Action Plan Progressing Well' (Press Release, 27 September 2010)

'Raids on Haka to Continue as Cultures Can't Copyright', *The Dominion Post* (Wellington), 15 July 2006

R Santa Ana III, 'Texas Plant Breeder Develops Mild Habanero Pepper' *AgNews – News and Public Affairs. Texas A&M University System Agriculture Program* (Texas), 12 August 2004

Craig Simcox, 'Māori Russian Dolls Made in China, Sold in NZ', *The Dominion Post* (online), 11 April 2008 <http://www.stuff.co.nz/dominion-post/361204>

T Watkins, 'New Zealand does U-turn on Rights Charter', *Stuff* (online), 20 April 2010 <http://www.stuff.co.nz/national/politics/3599153/NZ-does-U-turn-on-rights-charter>

# Legislation

*Actes Du Congres De Dresde 1895*

*Council Regulation (EC) No 1493/1999 of 17 May 1999 on the Common Organisation of the Market in Wine* [1999] OJ L 179

*Council Regulation (EEC) No 2081/92 of 14 July 1992 on the Protection of Geographical Indications and Designations of Origin for Agricultural Products and Foodstuffs* [1992] OJ L 208

*Council Regulation (EC) No 510/2006of 20 March 2006 on the Protection of Geographical Indications and Designations of Origin for Agricultural Products and Foodstuffs* [2006] OJ L 93

*Lanham Act 1946* (USC)

*Native Title Act 1993* (Cth)

*Plant Breeder's Rights Act 1994* (ACT)

*Plant Variety Protection Act 1970* (USC)

*Trade Marks Act 1995* (Cth)

*Trade Marks Act 2002* (NZ)

## Judicial Decisions

*Budĕjovický Budvar v Office for Harmonisation in the Internal Market (Trade Marks and Designs)* (2008), Joined Cases T 225/06, T 255/06, T 257/06 and T 309/06

*Federal Republic of Germany and Kingdom of Denmark v Commission of the European Communities* (2005) European Court of Justice, Joined Cases C-465/02 and C-466/02

*Fejo v Northern Territory of Australia* (1998) 195 CLR 96

*In re the Nagol Jump, Assal & Vatu v the Council of Chiefs of Santo* [1992] VUSC 5 <http://www.paclii.org.vu>

*Mabo v Queensland* [No 2] (1992) 175 CLR 1

*Milpurrurru & Ors v Indofurn Pty & Ors* (1994-1995) 30 IPR 214

*Western Australia v Ward* (2002) 213 CLR 1

*Yanner v Eaton* (1999) 201 CLR 351

# International Materials

*Actes Du Congres De Dresde* (1895)

*Actes De La Conférence Réunie À Lisbonne Du 6 Au 31 Octobre 1958* (BIRPI, 1963) 813

*Agreement on Subsidies and Countervailing Measures (SCM Agreement)*, 1867 UNTS 14 (signed 15 April 1994, Annex 1A of the Marrakesh Agreement Establishing the World Trade Organization)

*Agreement on Technical Barriers to Trade (TBT Agreement)* 1868 UNTS 120 (signed 15 April 1994, Annex 1A of the Marrakesh Agreement Establishing the World Trade Organization)

*Agreement on Trade-Related Aspects of Intellectual Property Rights* (*TRIPS Agreement*), 1869 UNTS 299 (signed 15 April 1994, Annex 1C of the Marrakesh Agreement Establishing the World Trade Organization)

AIPPI, 'Resolution on Q62' (Yearbook 1998/VIII) 389-392

AIPPI, 'Working Guidelines Q191: Relationship Between Trademarks and Geographical Indications' (Yearbook 2006/II) 18

*Amendment to the TRIPS Agreement*, WTO Doc WT/L/641 (2005)

*Argentina, Australia, Canada, Chile, Costa Rica, Dominican Republic, Ecuador, El Salvador, Guatemala, Honduras, Japan, Korea, Mexico, New Zealand, Nicaragua, Paraguay, the Separate Customs Territory of Taiwan, Penghu, Kinmen and Matsu, South Africa and the United States*, WTO Doc TN/IP/W/10/Rev.2 (2008)

*Berne Convention for the Protection of Literary and Artistic Works* (Paris Act), 1161 UNTS 18388 (24 July 1971)

*Communication by the EC and its Member States to the TRIPs Council on the review of Article 27.3 (b) of the TRIPs Agreement, and the relationship between the TRIPs Agreement and the Convention on Biological Diversity and the protection of traditional knowledge and folklore*, WTO Doc IP/C/W/383 (2002)

*Communication from Albania, Brazil, China, Colombia, Ecuador, the European Communities, Iceland, India, Indonesia, the Kyrgyz Republic, Liechtenstein, the Former Yugoslav Republic of Macedonia, Pakistan, Peru, Sri Lanka, Switzerland, Thailand, Turkey, the ACP Group and the African Group*, WTO Doc TN/C/W/52 (2008)

*Communication from Argentina, Australia, Canada, Chile, Guatemala, New Zealand, Paraguay and The United States* , WTO Doc IP/C/W/289 (2001)

*Communication from Argentina, Australia, Canada, Chile, Ecuador, El Salvador, New Zealand and the United States*, WTO Doc TN/IP/W/9 (2004)

*Communication from Bulgaria, the Czech Republic, Egypt, Iceland, India, Kenya, Liechtenstein, Pakistan, Slovenia, Sri Lanka, Switzerland and Turkey*, WTO Doc IP/C/W/204/Rev.1 (2000)

*Communication from Bulgaria, Cuba, Cyprus, The Czech Republic, The European Communities and their member states, Georgia, Hungary, Iceland, India, Kenya Liechtenstein, Malta, Mauritius, Pakistan, Romania, The Slovak Republic, Slovenia, Sri Lanka, Switzerland, Thailand and Turkey*, WTO Doc IP/C/W/353 (2002)

*Communication from the European Communities*, WTO Docs WT/GC/W/547, TN/C/W/26, TN/IP/W/11 (2005)

*Communication from Turkey*, WTO Doc IP/C/W/107/Rev.1 (2000)

*Convention on Biological Diversity*, 1760 UNTS 79 (entered into force 29 December 1993)

*Convention on the Protection and Promotion of the Diversity of Cultural Expressions* (UNESCO, 2005)

*Convention Establishing the World Intellectual Property Organization*, 848 UNTS 3 (signed and entered into force 14 July 1967)

European Commission, *Agricultural Product Quality Policy: Impact Assessment, Part B, Geographical Indications* (2009)

European Commission, *Communication from the Commission to the Council, the European Parliament and the European Economic and Social Committee, 'Contributing to Sustainable Development: The Role of Fair Trade and Non-governmental Trade-Related Sustainability Assurance Schemes'*, EU Com Doc COM (2009)

European Commission, *Green Paper on Agricultural Product Quality: Product Standards, Farming Requirements and Quality Schemes* (Brussels, 2008)

European Commission, *Proposal for a Council Regulation on the Protection of Geographical Indications and Designations of Origin for Agricultural Products and Foodstuffs* (Brussels, 2006)

M Ficsor, *Challenges to the Lisbon System*, WIPO Doc WIPO/GEO/LIS/08/4 (2008)

GATT Panel Report, *United States — Restrictions on Imports of Tuna I (Mexico)*, GATT Doc BISD 39S/155 (1991, unadopted)

General Assembly of the International Vine and Wine Office Resolution O.I.V./ECO 3/94

M Geuze, *Let's Have another Look at the Lisbon Agreement: − Its Terms in Their Context and in the Light of Its Object and Purpose*, WIPO Doc WIPO/GEO/BEI/07/10 (2007)

IIED, *Protecting Community Rights Over Traditional Knowledge: Implications of Customary Laws and Practices: Key Findings and Recommendations* (2005-2009)

IRAN − Declaration of Refusal of Protection, Appellation 001 and 002 (10 December 2007)

ITC and WIPO, *Marketing Crafts and Visual Arts: The Role of Intellectual Property. A Practical Guide* (ITC and WIPO: Geneva, 2003)

Julayabinul Statement (1993)

Kari-Oca Declaration (1992)

*Lisbon Agreement for the Protection of Appellations of Origin and their International Registration,* 923 UNTS 205 (signed 31 October 1958, revised at Stockholm on 14 July 1967, and amended on 28 September 1979)

*Madrid Agreement Concerning the International Registration of Trademarks*, 828 UNTS 389 (14 April 1891)

Mataatua Declaration (1993)

*Multilateral System of Notification and Registration of Geographical Indications under article 23.4 of the TRIPS Agreement*, WTO Doc TN/IP/W/8 (2003)

*Nagoya Protocol on Access to Genetic Resources and the Fair and Equitable Sharing of Benefits Arising from their Utilization to the Convention on Biological Diversity* (2010)

*Paris Convention for the Protection of Industrial Property*, 828 UNTS 305 (signed March 20 1883, last revised at the Stockholm Revision Conference, 14 July 1967)

*Preparations for the 1999 Ministerial Conference the TRIPS Agreement Communication from Kenya on Behalf of the African Group*, WTO Doc WT/GC/W/302 (1999)

*Preparations for the 1999 Ministerial Conference Agreement on TRIPS Extension of the Additional Protection for Geographical Indications to Other Products,* WTO Doc WT/GC/W/249 (1999)

*A Proposal For Modalities In The WTO Agriculture Negotiations, Specific Drafting Input by the EC,* WTO Doc JOB(03)/12 (2003)

*Protocol Relating to the Madrid Agreement Concerning the International Registration of Marks* (June 28, 1989) 28 *Industrial Property Law* and Treaties 3-007, 001 (July-August 1989)

*Regulations under the Lisbon Agreement for the Protection of Appellations of Origin and Their International Registration* (latest version entered in force on 1 April 2002)

*Request for Establishment of a Panel by Australia, European Communities - Protection of Trademarks and Geographical Indications for Agricultural Products and Foodstuffs,* WTO Doc WT/DS290/18 (2003)

*Request for Establishment of a Panel by United States, European Communities – Protection of trademarks and Geographical Indications for Agricultural Products and Foodstuffs,* WTO Doc WT/DS174/20 (2004)

*Swalopmund Protocol on the Protection of Traditional Knowledge and Expressions of Folklore within the Framework of the African Regional Intellectual Property Organization (ARIPO)* (9 August 2010)

UN Creative Economy Report, *The Challenge of Assessing the Creative Economy: Towards Informed Policy-making,* UN Doc UNCTAD/DITC/2008/2 (2008)

*United NationsDeclaration on the Rights of Indigenous Peoples,* A/RES/61/295 (adopted by the General Assembly 2 October 2007)

UN Permanent Forum on Indigenous Issues, *Recommendations Specifically Pertaining to Indigenous Women and the Girl Child, adopted by the Permanent Forum on Indigenous Issues, Report of the Second Session,* UN Doc E/C.19/2003/22 (2003)

UNCTAD, *Analysis of Options for Implementing Disclosure of Origin Requirements in Intellectual Property Applications. A contribution to UNCTAD's response to the invitation of the Seventh Conference of the Parties of the Convention on Biological Diversity,* UNCTAD Doc UNCTAD/DITC/TED/2004/14 (2006)

UNESCO Executive Office Sector for Culture, *The United Nations Recognizes the Role of Culture for Development* (2010)

UNESCO, *Symposium on the protection of traditional knowledge and expressions of indigenous cultures in the Pacific Islands* (Final Declaration, Noumea, 1999)

UNESCO/ITC, *International Symposium on Crafts and the International Market: Trade and Customs Codification*, (Final Report, Manila, 1997)

United Nations Development Group, *Guidelines on Indigenous Peoples' Issues* (2009)

*Vienna Convention on the Law of Treaties*, 1155 UNTS 331 (entered into force 27 January 1980)

WIPO, *Draft Paper on Customary Law & the Intellectual Property System in the Protection of Traditional Cultural Expressions and Traditional Knowledge* (December 2006)

WIPO Assemblies of Member States of, *Matters Concerning the Intergovernmental Committee on Intellectual Property and Genetic Resources, Traditional Knowledge and Folklore* (Agenda Item 31, Decision, Fortieth, 20th Ordinary Session, 26 September to 5 October 2011)

*WIPOCopyright Treaty*, 2186 UNTS 121 (adopted 20 December 1996)

WIPO Doc, *Disclosure of Origin or Source of Genetic Resources and Associated Traditional Knowledge in Patent Applications*, WIPO Doc WIPO/GRTKF/IC/8/11 (2005)

WIPO Doc, *Draft Objectives and Principles Relating to Intellectual Property and Genetic Resources Prepared at IWG 3*, WIPO Doc WIPO/GRTKF/IC/18/9 (2011)

WIPO Doc, *Possible Improvements by the Procedures Under the Libson Agreement*, WIPO Doc LI/WG/DEV/1/2 Rev (2010)

WIPO Doc, *Possible Solutions for Conflicts Between Trademarks and Geographical Indications and for Conflicts Between Homonymous Geographical Indications*, WIPO Doc SCT/5/3 (2000)

WIPO Doc, *Proposed Amendments to the Regulations Under the Lisbon Agreement*, LI Doc LI/A/25/1 (2009)

WIPO Doc, *Traditional Knowledge and the Need to Give it Adequate Intellectual Property Protection*, WIPO Doc WO/GA/26/9 (2000)

WIPO Doc, *Working Group on the Development of the Lisbon System (Appellations of Origin)*, WIPO Doc LI/WG/DEV/1/2 (2009)

WIPO Doc, *Working Group on the Development of the Lisbon System (Appellations of Origin), Summary by the Chair*, WIPO Doc LI/WG/DEV/1/3 (2009)

WIPO General Assembly, *Report of the Thirty-Fourth (18th Ordinary) Session*, Geneva, 24 September to 3 October 2007, WIPO Doc WO/GA/34/16 (2007)

WIPO General Assembly, *Report of the Thirty-Eighth (19th Ordinary) Session*, Geneva, 22 September to 1 October 2009, WIPO Doc WO/GA/38/20 (2009)

WIPO IGC, *Draft Articles of the Open-Ended Informal Drafting Group of IGC 17* (9 December 2010)

WIPO IGC, *Draft Articles on the Protection of Traditional Knowledge*, Prepared at IWG 2, WIPO Doc WIPO/GRTKF/IWG/2/3 (2011)

WIPO IGC, *Draft Objectives and Principles Relating to Intellectual Property and Genetic Resources*, Prepared at IWG 3, WIPO Doc WIPO/GRTKF/IWG/3/17 (2011)

WIPO IGC Secretariat, *Compilation of Comments on WIPO/GRTKF/IC/16/7 'Submission by Australia, Canada, New Zealand, Norway and the United States of America*, WIPO Doc WIPO/GRTKF/IC/17/INF/10 (2010)

WIPO IGC Secretariat, *Consolidated Analysis of the Legal Protection of Traditional Cultural Expressions*, WIPO Doc WIPO/GRTKF/IC/5/3, 52 (2003)

WIPO IGC Secretariat, *Draft Articles on the Protection of Traditional Cultural Expressions/Expression of Folklore Prepared at IWG 1*, WIPO Doc WIPO/GRTKF/IC/17/9 (2010)

WIPO IGC Secretariat, *Draft Articles on the Protection of Traditional Knowledge Prepared at IWG 2*, WIPO Doc WIPO/GRTKF/IC/18/7 (2011)

WIPO IGC Secretariat, *Draft Provisions on Certain Matters Addressed by the Working Group in the Context of the Review of the Lisbon System*, WIPO Doc LI/WG/DEV/3/2 (2011)

WIPO IGC Secretariat, *Genetic Resources: List of Options*, WIPO Doc WIPO/GRTKF/IC/11/8 (a) (2007)

WIPO IGC Secretariat, *Geographical Indications*, WIPO Doc SCT/10/4 (2003)

WIPO IGC Secretariat, *Operational Principles for Intellectual Property Clauses of Contractual Agreements Concerning Access to Genetic Resources and Benefit-Sharing*, WIPO Doc WIPO/GRTKF/IC/2/3 (2001)

WIPO IGC Secretariat, *Proposal of the African Group on Genetic Resources and Future Work*, WIPO Doc WIPO/GRTKF/IC/17/10 (2010)

WIPO IGC Secretariat, *Protection of Traditional Knowledge: Overview of Policy Objectives and Core Principles*, WIPO Doc WIPO/TKGRF/IC/7/5 (2004)

WIPO IGC Secretariat, *Protection of Traditional Cultural Expressions/Cultural expressions of Folklore. Revised Objectives and Principles*, WIPO Doc WIPO/GRTKF/IC/17/4Prov (2010)

WIPO IGC Secretariat, *Report on the Review of Existing Intellectual Property Protection of Traditional Knowledge*, WIPO Doc WIPO/GRTKF/IC/4/7 (2002)

WIPO IGC Secretariat, *Review of Existing Intellectual Property Protection of Traditional Knowledge*, WIPO Doc WIPO/GRTKF/IC/3/7 (2002)

WIPO IGC Secretariat, *Submission by Australia, Canada, New Zealand, Norway and the United States of America*, WIPO Doc WIPO/GRTKF/IC/16/7 (2010)

WIPO IGC Secretariat, *The Protection of Traditional Cultural Expressions: Draft Articles*, WIPO Doc WIPO/GRTKF/IC/19/4 (2011)

WIPO IGC Secretariat, *The Protection of Traditional Cultural Expressions/ Expressions of Folklore: Revised Objectives and Principles*, WIPO Doc WIPO/GRTKF/IC/8/4 (2005)

WIPO IGC Secretariat, *The Protection of Traditional Cultural Expressions/ Expressions of Folklore: Revised Objectives and Principles*, WIPO Doc WIPO/GRTKF/IC/9/4 (2006)

WIPO IGC Secretariat, *The Protection of Traditional Cultural Expressions/ Expressions of Folklore: Revised Objectives and Principles*, WIPO Doc WIPO/GRTKF/IC/17/4 (2010)

WIPO IGC Secretariat, *The Protection of Traditional Knowledge: Revised Objectives and Principles,* WIPO Doc WIPO/GRTKF/IC/9/5 (2006)

WIPO IGC Secretariat, *The Protection of Traditional Knowledge: Revised Objectives and Principles*, WIPO Doc WIPO/GRTKF/IC/18/4 (2011)

WIPO IGC Secretariat, *The Protection of Traditional Knowledge: Revised Objectives and Principles*, WIPO Doc WIPO/GRTKF/IC/18/5 (2011)

*WIPO Performances and Phonograms Treaty*, 36 ILM 76 (signed 20 December 1996, entered into force 1997)

WTO Appellate Body Report, *Canada – Measures Affecting the Export of Civilian Aircraft*, WTO Doc WT/DS70/AB/R (1999)

WTO Ministerial, *Doha Declaration*, WTO Doc WT/MIN(01)/DEC/1 (2001)

WTO Panel Report, *Australia – Subsidies Provided to Producers and Exporters of Automotive Leather*, WTO Doc WT/DS126/R (1999)

WTO Panel Report, *European Communities — Protection of Trademarks and Geographical Indications for Agricultural Products and Foodstuffs*, WTO Doc WT/DS174/R (2005)

WTO Panel Report, *European Communities — Protection of Trademarks and Geographical Indications for Agricultural Products and Foodstuffs'*, WTO Doc WT/DS290/R (2005)

WTO Panel Report, *United States – Measures Treating Exports Restraints as Subsidies*, WTO Doc WT/DS194/R (2001)

WTO Report of Chairman, *Multilateral System of Notification and Registration of Geographical Indications for Wines and Spirits*, Report by the Chairman, Ambassador C. Trevor Clarke (Barbados) TN/IP/19 (2009)

WTO Report of Chairman, *Multilateral System of Notification and Registration of Geographical Indications for Wines and Spirits*, Report by Chairman Ambassador Darlington Mwape (Zambia) TN/IP/20 (2010)

WTO Report of Chairman, *Multilateral System of Notifications and Registration of Geographical Indications for Wines and Spirits*, WTO Doc TN/IP/21 (2011)

WTO Secretariat, *The Relationship between the TRIPS Agreement and the Convention on Biological Diversity: Summary of Issues Raised and Points Made* WTO Doc IP/C/W/368/Rev.1 (2006)

www.ingramcontent.com/pod-product-compliance
Lightning Source LLC
Chambersburg PA
CBHW061227270326
41928CB00025B/3397

www.ingramcontent.com/pod-product-compliance
Lightning Source LLC
Chambersburg PA
CBHW061227270326
41928CB00025B/3397